Understanding
Social Enterprise

Understanding
Social Enterprise
Theory & Practice

Rory Ridley-Duff | Mike Bull

Los Angeles | London | New Delhi
Singapore | Washington DC

First published 2011
Reprinted 2011

SAGE Publications Ltd
1 Oliver's Yard
55 City Road
London EC1Y ISP

SAGE Publications Inc
2455 Teller Road
Thousand Oaks, California 91320

SAGE Publications India Pvt Ltd
B1/I 1 Mohan Cooperative Industrial Area
Mathura Road
New Delhi 110 044

SAGE Publications Asia-Pacific Pte Ltd
33 Pekin Street #02-01
Far East Square
Singapore 048763

Library of Congress Control Number: 2010930011

British Library Cataloguing in Publication data

A catalogue record for this book is available from the British Library

ISBN 978-1-84860-198-7
ISBN 978-1-84860-199-4 (pbk)

Typeset by C&M Digitals (P) Ltd, Chennai, India
Printed in the UK by the MPG Books Group
Printed on paper from sustainable resources

Social enterprises are 'stakeholder owned' rather than 'shareholder owned'. With the champion of the 'shareholder value' movement, Jack Welch, describing it as 'the dumbest idea in the world' following the credit crunch, the time for stakeholder value has arrived and this book sets out exactly what that will mean in practice.

Professor Jonathan Michie, President, Kellogg College, University of Oxford

This book represents an important contribution to social enterprise scholarship that will also be of considerable interest to practitioners and policy makers. Its integration of management frameworks, social theory and public policy approaches provides a fresh set of perspectives and insights on this increasingly influential sector.

Dr Alex Nicholls, Lecturer in Social Entrepreneurship, The Saïd Business School, University of Oxford

The authors have raised the bar. This book is well written, necessary, comprehensive, intellectually stimulating and informed by practical experience. This will aid student understanding of the key debates and issues relating to social enterprises, explores the likely challenges facing social enterprises and offers insights into the evolution of the sector. Packed with examples, case studies and student revision tasks, this is a fine addition to the existing literature and is sure to be a core text.

Declan Jones, Head of Student Enterprise, Caledonian Business School, Glasgow Caledonian University

Combining a thorough study of the current state of literature and a deep understanding of working with social enterprise, the authors present an excellent overview of the state of thinking that will be of use to those studying and those working with social enterprises. It presents the key challenges and different views found within the practice, research and policy community and sets out the debates for future years. This is a valuable contribution to our understanding of this rapidly changing sector.

Professor Fergus Lyon, Director of ESRC/OCS Social Enterprise Research Cluster, Middlesex University

A good thorough analysis of social enterprise and its context, drawing on a range of relevant theory and evidence. It should become an essential text on the field.

Roger Spear, Senior Lecturer and Chair of the Co-Operatives Research Unit, The Open University

This is a well written, well researched, and above all, critical investigation into the notion of social entrepreneurship. It is essential reading to any student or practitioner who wishes to understand how social entrepreneurship has developed, its intellectual antecedents, and why it is so important to contemporary society.

Tim Curtis, Senior Lecturer, Unltd and HEFCE Ambassador for Social Entrepreneurship in Higher Education, University of Northampton

A valuable and timely book which is relevant to academics and practitioners alike. There is a welcome emphasis on providing practical learning activities grounded in a discussion of both historical and contemporary concepts of social enterprise.

Dr Linda Shaw, Head of Research, The Co-operative College

This book is important reading for students of social enterprise, both inside and outside the academy. It illuminates the social and political impulses underpinning current trends in this field, and provides nuanced comparative insights into how practice has developed in different world regions. The book is a rare combination; theoretically informed and practically applicable to the establishment and management of businesses that trade for a social purpose.

Dr Jo Barraket, Associate Professor of Social Enterprise and Entrepreneurship, Queensland University of Technology

Summary of Contents

Contents

Author Biographies

Dr Rory Ridley-Duff
After 12 years as a director of a worker cooperative creating ICT systems for third and public sector organisations, Rory wrote one of the early texts on social enterprise (Ridley-Duff, 2002). This led – indirectly – to him winning a Hallam PhD Studentship, during which he undertook an ethnographic study in one of the UK's fastest-growing companies during its conversion from a private to a social enterprise. He joined the teaching staff at Sheffield Business School in 2003, securing a permanent appointment in 2007, and recently founded its MSc Co-operative and Social Enterprise Management course. He is now one of UnLtd's Ambassadors for Social Entrepreneurship in Higher Education, a member of the editorial board of the *Social Enterprise Journal*, and a non-executive director of the award-winning social firm Viewpoint Research CIC.

Mike Bull
Having spent 16 years in the printing industry for private, public and third sector organisations, Mike moved into academia looking for a new challenge. Between 2004 and 2007 he undertook two research projects funded by the European Social Fund (ESF) into the management practices in social enterprises. The result was Balance, an online diagnostic tool that creates the space for reflection on strategic management issues and performance (see www.socialenterprisebalance.org). Employed within the Centre for Enterprise, Manchester Metropolitan University (MMU), he pursues his interest in critical reflection diagnostics, having subsequently been commissioned for a number of other projects. Mike also leads social enterprise teaching on the university's undergraduate courses, is a Director of Social Enterprise North West and Together Works (the social enterprise network for Greater Manchester), and is an editorial board member of the *Social Enterprise Journal*.

Acknowledgements

Every book is a collaborative effort. This is our chance to thank the great many people who have helped us over the last two and a half years to undertake research and support the writing of the text. We would like to acknowledge the following people and organisations for their generous help with various aspects of the book.

Firstly, we would like to thank Pam Seanor and Tracey Chadwick-Coule whose knowledge and experience, not to mention time and effort, in co-authoring Chapters 4, 9, 10 and 12 (and related teaching materials) have been invaluable.

Secondly, a great many people have helped us to write, or prepare, teaching cases based on their work as practitioners and researchers. Others have provided support and feedback by proofreading chapters and teaching materials. In no particular order, they include: Deborah Munt, Jon Griffith, Ralph Spence, David Laughton, Siobhan Newton, Tim Curtis, Doug Foster, Linda Banks, Liz Doherty, Chelle Davey, Connie Thorpe, Mark Powell, Alistair Ponton, Geof Cox, Morgan Killick, Anna Whitty, Jim Chandler, Mikel Lezamiz, Fred Freundlich, Pam Seanor, Adrian Ashton, Martin Halton, Gerry Stone, Lorna Leaston, Chris Dabbs, Tracey Chadwick-Coule and Graham Duncan. Our enduring thanks to you all.

Thirdly, the support of colleagues at conferences and academic institutions has been invaluable. Our thanks to Sheffield Hallam University and Manchester Metropolitan University for creating an environment in which we can pursue our interest in social enterprise teaching and research. Also, we would like to thank the organisers and participants of the Social Entrepreneurship Research Conference (2006, 2007, 2008), the Institute of Small Business and Entrepreneurship Conference (2008, 2009, 2010) and the International Social Innovation Research Conference (2009) who have peer reviewed both our (and others') work, talked with us about a wide variety of authors' work late into the night, and contributed so much to our understanding of the concepts and issues raised by this book.

Fourthly, every author needs good back-up and support for the publication process. Special thanks to Linda Purdy from the Adsetts Library, Sheffield Hallam University, for work on obtaining permissions to reproduce materials, and to Clare Wells and Natalie Aguilera at Sage Publications for their faith in our work, as well as practical support throughout the publication process.

Last, and certainly not least, we would like to thank our families. For every evening and weekend outing that was delayed or cancelled, our deep apologies. For every cup of tea and coffee you brought to keep us going, and for help and support that only families can provide, our lifelong love and thanks.

For Caroline, Natasha and Bethany, and for Katie, Esme, Freddie and Miles with love.

Guided Tour

Welcome to the guided tour of *Understanding Social Enterprise: Theory and Practice*. This tour will take you through the main sections and special features of the text.

Learning objectives: A clear set of learning objectives are provided for each chapter.
Introduction: The introduction provides you with an overview of the topics covered in each chapter.

Case studies: Short cases provide you with real life examples of topics covered and discussion questions, aiding learning and understanding.

Class Exercises: Individual and class exercises have been designed to enhance learning and engagement with the text.

Boxed definitions: Key concepts and ideas are explained in order to aid understanding and to help you to explore topics in greater depth.

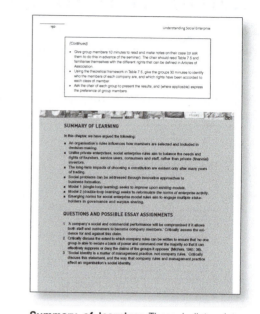

Conclusions: This section reviews the main concepts and issues covered in the chapter in order to be sure that you are clear on what was covered and why.

Summary of learning: These bullet points summarize the key points in the chapter.
Questions: Sample essay questions are provided to aid revision and encourage you to explore what you have learnt.

Further reading: A selection of relevant articles and book chapters that enhance and compliment your understanding of the chapter. Many of these articles can be found on the companion website www.sagepub.co.uk/ridleyduff.
Useful resources: A list of useful web-based resources that allow you to further explore topics in the book.

Glossary: At the end of the book you will find a detailed glossary of all the key concepts covered in the book.

Companion Website

Be sure to visit the companion website at http://www.sagepub.co.uk/ridleyduff to find a range of teaching and learning materials for both lecturers and students, including the following:

For instructors:

- **Instructors' manual**: A comprehensive instructors' manual containing learning outcomes, key arguments, chapter summaries, useful resources, further reading and a number of sample essay questions for each chapter.
- **PowerPoint slides**: Detailed PowerPoint slides provided for each chapter. These slides can be edited by instructors to suit teaching styles and needs.
- **Additional case studies**: Additional case studies and accompanying questions provide tutors with helpful resources for use in seminars and tutorials.

For students:

- **Full-text journal articles**: Full access to selected journal articles provides students with a deeper understanding of the topics covered in each chapter.
- **Links to relevant websites**: Direct links to online information about social enterprise projects.

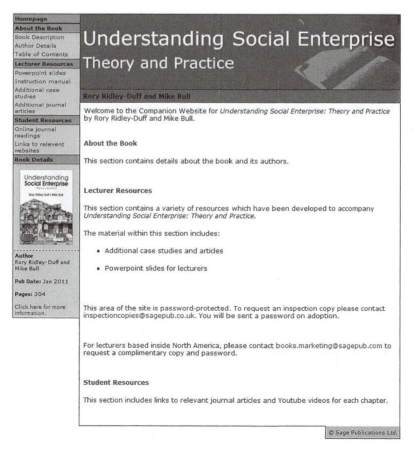

Introduction

This book invites students, academics and practitioners to develop a critical understanding of *social enterprise* through an exploration of the relationship between theory and practice. Over the last decade, this new term – and the related concept of *social entrepreneurship* – has reached an increasing audience. Social enterprise is being used by growing numbers of activists, entrepreneurs, organisations and government officials as an umbrella term for any form of organisation that innovates or trades for a social purpose. In some cases, the results have been so spectacular and on such a scale that politicians of all shades, from all corners of the world, are taking an interest in how social enterprise might offer new trajectories for engaging 'more-than-profit' and 'non-profit' organisations in their own aspirations for social change.

This growing popularity, paradoxically, also presents a significant challenge. As authors, we will argue that the concept evolved in the EU within a fairly close-knit community of 'activist' businesses and regional support networks, while in the US it evolved out of concern that philanthropic ventures should be sustainable over the longer term. Whilst adopting a range of approaches, these early initiatives shared a commitment to developing trading relationships that promoted social democracy and financial equity across society. With the formation of support agencies around the globe, the seductive appeal of the term 'social enterprise' became a way for many more people (governments, charities, voluntary groups, environmental organisations and 'social businesses') to articulate an alternative to profit-maximising private enterprise. As a result, many groups now use the term to describe themselves and others, with an equal number feeling unsettled by a perceived attack on their identity. A significant part of this book, therefore, is devoted to navigating through the confusion that has arisen as social activists, umbrella organisations and governments advance the concept while others resist changes they associate with a 'business' agenda.

Our motivations to collaborate on this book are also paradoxically straightforward and complex. In 2006, we each presented papers at the 3rd Social Entrepreneurship Research Conference (SERC) held at London South Bank University. The straightforward motive for the book lies in the friendships that developed and the enjoyment we continue to take in comparing and contrasting our experiences and research findings. These friendships were strengthened when Mike Bull organised an event at Manchester Metropolitan University titled Critical Perspectives on Social Enterprise. The authors were joined by Jon Griffith (University of East London), Pam Seanor (Huddersfield University), Doug Foster (Surrey University) and Tim Curtis (then at Oxford Saïd Business School, now at

Northampton University). The energy generated by this event prompted the speakers to dub themselves the Manchester Critical Group. The event became a catalyst for the development of an informal network that continues to this day. While the text has been credited to two members of this network, it can be viewed as a product of the critical thinking that emerged within this group, as well as their ongoing debates at academic conferences.

Like Paton (2003), we bring a social constructionist perspective to issues of theory and practice in social enterprise. Our assumption, therefore, is that people are – and have to be studied as – sentient beings who use their existing knowledge and experience to interpret the situations they face. As a result, prescriptions for entrepreneurial or management practice – based on the assumption that people will react or adapt in consistent ways – are not viewed as a helpful approach to social enterprise education. We assume that people are selective in the way they notice the world. The theories most useful to them are the ones that are carefully worked out in response to challenges in their cultural, social and physical environment. The concepts and learning opportunities we present, therefore, are not aimed at teaching the 'truth' about the 'real' world. They are research-informed theories, and experiential learning activities, that have been sufficiently useful to us, our students and research participants that they are worth committing to paper and disseminating more widely.

As authors, we have connections both inside and outside the world of social enterprise practice. Our 'insider' status is expressed through previous and current experience working in the sector, and also contributions to knowledge that we have individually and jointly contributed as members of academic institutions. Some of these theories are now embedded in 'tools' that support the development of new practices in strategic management and enterprise governance (www.socialenterprisebalance.org). Our 'outsider' status, however, is expressed in critical analyses of the way these theories (including our own) are not only limited and partial representations of what is 'out there', but also the latest additions to a long-running critique of the role of private property in economic development. When we started writing, the heartlands of capitalism were imploding as some of its most revered institutions collapsed, shrunk and were taken (back) into state ownership. As we finish writing, a new crisis (rooted in the 2008 crisis) is threatening to spread unrest from Greece across Europe and destabilise the eurozone. Some fresh social and economic thinking, therefore, is timely.

No book can provide an exhaustive examination of a subject. We have been selective by drawing attention to theories that have helped our research participants and students contribute to practice in social enterprises. Those in other cultures and parts of the world, we are sure, would select differently. While drawing on international examples, the text inevitably reflects our work with diverse communities of practice in the UK, and the Anglo-American and European contexts in which we disseminate our work.

One or other author took the lead in producing a first draft of each chapter with support and critique from the other: in this sense the writing is a co-production. Chapters 4, 10 and 12 were drafted with the assistance of Pam Seanor, while Chapter 9 was co-authored with Dr Tracey Chadwick-Coule. Rory took an editorial lead in the final period of writing, linking the arguments across chapters, and making difficult choices about what to keep and what to cut. He ensures there is a consistent editorial and educational perspective throughout the text. Importantly, he is there to take the blame for our individual and collective mistakes, while all the authors can share the credit for the book's enduring insights.

We are sensitive to the argument that academic writers have the power to define what is taken to be 'true' or 'real' social enterprise, potentially affecting allocation of resources in the sector, and the development of legal and regulatory frameworks. We mitigate this 'danger' by adopting a social constructionist approach that prioritises the exploration of discourses that are emerging, tracing their historical and political trajectory, and the influence they wield in shaping (and perhaps fragmenting and limiting) social enterprise development. Our goal is to make them sufficiently accessible that students can critique and debate them effectively. If this text significantly increases the number of people who can understand, engage with and contribute to the theory and practice of social entrepreneurship, then we will be happy.

The Structure of the Book

This textbook provides readers with a critical companion as they engage with social enterprise theory and practice. As well as providing a rich source of existing knowledge and learning, the book aims to question and explore assumptions, highlighting critical perspectives and insights. The first part of the book focuses squarely on the developments in different sectors that have created the conditions for social enterprise to emerge. In the early chapters, consideration is given to social issues and political trends, and the ways these have contributed to the emergence of social enterprise theory and practice.

We are careful to look at historical issues in order to appreciate how and why competing definitions and theories have surfaced to serve different interest groups. As a result, Part I is designed to have broad cross-disciplinary appeal to students, academics and practitioners internationally whose primary interest is to deepen their understanding of the phenomenon that is social enterprise. We expect the following groups will get the most from Part I:

- students and lecturers in disciplines such as management, public administration, politics, sociology and economics, who want to integrate social enterprise into their educational programmes
- students who are also policy makers, consultants, politicians and representatives of local communities and other statutory bodies (especially commissioners) who need a better understanding of social enterprise to develop strategies for local and regional development.

The second part of the book examines the phenomenon of social enterprise from the perspective of those attempting to bring about change by creating, supporting and running social enterprises. Part II will be of greater interest to:

- business school students and lecturers who need to develop presentations, projects, lectures and modules on social enterprise as part of their degree programmes
- students in any discipline who self-identify as social entrepreneurs and/ or social activists, and want to integrate social enterprise into their study programmes
- students who are also legislators and regulators in the public sector being asked to develop, fund, support or commission work from social enterprises
- students who are trustees, executives and professionals in the voluntary and community sector working out whether they should engage with or resist the rise of social enterprises
- students who are executives and professionals in the private sector wondering how they might democratise or alter management practices to achieve double or triple bottom line goals.

Taking Parts I and II together, the book provides a curriculum for professional bodies and universities in the United Kingdom developing courses at QAA levels 6 and 7, or seeking to develop executive education programmes for medium to large organisations wishing to support social enterprise.

Part I: Theoretical Perspectives on Social Enterprise

Chapter 1, 'The Third Sector and the Social Economy', sets out the history of social movements that are now grouped into a 'third sector' that is distinct from the private and public sectors. It discusses the boundaries of the sector by comparing the concepts of *civil society*, *third sector* and *social economy*. By comparing and contrasting charitable, voluntary and cooperative approaches to organisation, we examine the contribution of each to social enterprise theory.

In Chapter 2, 'New Public Management and the Private Sector', we argue that it is necessary to consider the impact of social economy development on the public and private sectors, as well as the way that business thinking has increased its influence across society. The tension between *new public management* (private sector management techniques and markets in the delivery of public services), and *cooperative*, *employee-owned* and *fair trade* approaches to market trading, offers another perspective on how enterprise can be 'socialised' rather than 'privatised'.

Following this overview of historical currents, Chapter 3, 'Defining Social Enterprise', explores how different definitions and perspectives are linked to ideology and economic interests. Firstly, we explore views that have emerged in Europe, the UK, the USA and the international cooperative movement. Having considered practitioner descriptions, we discuss theories of social enterprise that locate it on a 'spectrum' of entrepreneurial possibilities, or as a hybrid 'cross-sector' form of organisation. The chapter concludes with a discussion of social enterprise as an activity rather than a form of organisation.

The presentation of social enterprise as a 'cross-sector' form of entrepreneurship raises the question of its contribution to community cohesion and development.

Chapter 4, 'Social and Ethical Capital', explores the theoretical underpinnings of social capital, as well as the emergent concept of ethical capital. We explore how social networks and relationship dynamics contribute to (social) enterprise creation and regional development, and also the different attitudes that theorists have adopted towards different forms (and uses of) social capital. In the final part of the chapter, we view the range of choices on enterprise activity through the lens of ethical theory.

In Chapter 5, 'Globalisation and International Perspectives', we start by critiquing the concept of globalisation, and explore its effects on both national and international power relations. Fair trade is introduced as an example of social enterprise that is both a product of and a response to globalisation. In the second half of the chapter, we consider US-inspired examples of global social enterprise, and also reactions to globalisation in the development of the Grameen Bank in Asia and the 'reclaimed company movement' of South America.

Part II: The Practice of Social Enterprise

The second half of the book switches from the interests of historians, political theorists, sociologists, economists and philosophers to the issues that face management practitioners and academics. While continuing to use teaching cases from different parts of the world, Part II focuses on the challenges facing social entrepreneurs as they attempt to create, support and develop their social enterprises. Despite the national focus, we expect that the questions we raise, and the debates that surface, will have relevance for those living and working elsewhere.

Chapter 6, 'Management Debates', is based on a series of exchanges between social enterprise researchers and educators to clarify the following:

Debate 1: Should social entrepreneurs accept private and public sector management theory?

Debate 2: How far should social entrepreneurs embrace democratic management theory?

Debate 3: What is 'social' about social enterprise?

Debate 4: Is social enterprise a form of organisation or an entrepreneurial process?

Debate 5: How is power understood, developed and deployed in social enterprises?

Debate 6: What approaches to learning are most helpful to social enterprise managers?

Debate 7: What are the key challenges in social enterprise management?

The way practitioners and advisers navigate their way through these debates has a lasting impact on their style of management, as well as the management systems that are considered appropriate by regional support organisations. In concluding the chapter, we consider which management issues have surfaced in key texts, and the various strategies that can be adopted to advance management education.

Chapter 7, 'Identities and Legalities', examines the first strategic choice facing an enterprise. What identity should be projected, and how can its legal form support this? Particular attention is paid to tensions between the founders' aspirations, statutory requirements and the need to attract funding from different sources. Examples are used to illustrate how choices made during enterprise formation have long-term and significant impacts. Using four case studies, the chapter finishes with a consideration of multi-stakeholder approaches, and the rationales that underpin their legal models.

Chapter 8, 'Strategic Management and Planning', explores the purpose and practice of strategic planning. The traditional rationalist approach to business planning is contrasted with reflexive and critical approaches. Using three contrasting cases, we illustrate the range of approaches that can be adopted, and how these influence the management culture of an enterprise. Towards the end of the chapter, we consider Mike's work on analysing strategic management performance.

We continue this debate in Chapter 9, 'Governance, HRM and Employee Relations', in which we give explicit consideration to theoretical perspectives that compete to shape our understanding of the way people are managed at work. We make the case for an inter-disciplinary approach, drawing on concepts from corporate governance (to provide an owner perspective), human resource management (to provide a managerial perspective) and employee relations (to provide a workforce perspective). In the second part of the chapter, we use four cases to explore recruitment, induction and conflict management practice. In doing so, we outline how written and psychological contracts are formed, and can be influenced, in a social enterprise context.

Chapter 10, 'Leadership and Social Entrepreneurship', considers the way in which theories of leadership influence approaches to social entrepreneurship. Leader-centred and follower-centred perspectives on leadership are outlined and explored using case studies. In the second half of the chapter we discuss collective forms of entrepreneurship (cooperative entrepreneurship and associative entrepreneurship) and the way leadership both shapes and is shaped by cultural assumptions.

In Chapter 11, 'Income Streams and Social Investment', we examine how income generation and financial investment strategies support social enterprises. We start with a consideration of trading activity and the use of charitable funds, then consider the issues that influence access to debt finance (loans) and equity (shares). Towards the end of the chapter, we consider new sources of funding aimed directly at the social enterprise sector, and critically examine the role of social investment funds and community banking.

To conclude Part II, in Chapter 12, 'Measuring Social Outcomes and Impacts', we examine the multifaceted nature of 'performance' and the rise of social accounting to address perceived shortcomings in financial accounting. We consider two approaches that have attracted support: social accounting and audit (SAA) aimed at assessing stakeholder perceptions of an organisation's social and economic performance; and social return on investment (SROI) and its potential role in public commissioning and social investment.

To close the book, a Postscript, 'Social Enterprise in 2050', allows each of the authors to set out their personal views on the way social enterprise will develop. Drawing on some of their own research, as well as the debates outlined in the book, each provides their view on what may happen in the decades ahead.

Theoretical Perspectives on Social Enterprise

PART I

The Third Sector and the Social Economy

1

Learning Objectives

In this chapter, we outline the concepts of third sector and social economy and we compare and contrast the types of organisations within them. By the end of this chapter you will be able to:

- explain third sector and social economy concepts and terms

- critically evaluate the size and scope of the third sector in different countries

- articulate ideological and historical differences in third sector organisations

- discuss the third sector contexts in which social enterprises are emerging.

The key arguments that will be developed in this chapter are:

- Third sector organisations vary in their organisational forms, values and beliefs.
- The third sector develops alternative cultures outside the state- and market-led economy.
- The 'social economy' is an emergent concept adopted to help define the third sector.
- The public and private sectors compete and collaborate with the third sector.

Introduction

In the short history of the social enterprise movement, writers have – not surprisingly – been keen to ask the question, 'What is a social enterprise?' Normally, by the end of the first chapter, whether through historical analysis, advocating alternative values and practices, or painting a vivid picture of community life, the reader encounters a definition, or gains a sense of social enterprise as a concept. In this book, we resist the attempt to set out a definition of social enterprise too early in order to consider the historical developments that have led to its emergence.

In the last decade, *third sector organisations* (TSOs) have been increasingly drawn into government agendas and had considerable sums invested to increase their capacity to deliver services. In the UK, the establishment of an Office of the Third Sector (OTS) in May 2006 and a Centre for Third Sector Research in 2008 marks the political acceptance (and social construction) of the third sector as a distinct grouping with its own rationale and outlook. It is sensible, therefore, to examine the terms used to describe the third sector, and to focus on the characteristics of the organisations that define its size and scope. Outside the UK, 'third sector' is more commonly referred to as 'non-profit sector', 'social economy' or sector comprising 'non-governmental organisations' (NGOs) (Mertens, 1999; Monzon and Chaves, 2008). These terms have a bearing on how both the third sector and social enterprise are understood, so some discussion prepares the ground for later chapters.

Our research experiences suggest that there is good rationale for caution. Social enterprise is used in an increasing number of contexts, cultures and national settings. Social enterprise may be characterised as a subgroup of organisations in the 'social economy' (Pearce, 2003) or a new economic engine (Harding and Cowling, 2004). Disarmingly simple and inclusive definitions include organisations 'where people have to be business-like, but are not in it for the money' (Paton, 2003: Preface). If social enterprise means different things to different people, it is necessary to engage in socio-historical analysis to understand why this is the case.

Stone et al. (2007) suggest that although the third sector has existed for some time, there is insufficient empirical research or theory to fully understand it. As Kuhn (1970) has argued, research programmes proceed on the basis of accepted theoretical frameworks (that constitute a scientific paradigm). This legitimises the identification of research questions and suggests practical courses of action. Where no accepted frameworks exist, the field is regarded as pre-paradigmatic. The task of the research community – and in part the task of this book – is to piece frameworks together from widely scattered data and concepts.

In this chapter, we progress this goal by identifying propositions about the relationship of the third sector to social enterprise development. We start by linking the concept of *civil society* to Pearce's (2003) model of a *third system*. Taken together, these two bodies of theory provide a starting point for appreciating the different cultural identities and social contexts of the third sector. Based on our research experience, we are aware that the motive for defining a third sector is contentious; the definition process itself is invested with political dimensions and sectional interests. There is a narrow, perhaps misleading, definition that the third sector is 'non-profit' in its outlook. This obscures both the notion of 'not for private profit' and a century of history and knowledge about the effectiveness of cooperatives and mutual societies.[1] In exploring the notion of the third sector, therefore, we give regard to academic research and government commissioned reports that seek to define and classify the 'social economy' (Monzon and Chaves, 2008). This can be helpful as it opens up debate about the breadth of organisations that make up the third sector, and also prompts questions about the motives of the public sector in seeking to label and classify its organisations. At EU level, the social economy is believed to include trading organisations as well as non-market providers of goods and services. By considering the history of the sector, we can trace debates back several centuries that clarify the rationale for their inclusion. As Coule points out:

> Voluntary action preceded the development of both state and market welfare provision in the UK, surviving the emergence of a statutory 'welfare state' and continuing to function alongside providers from a number of different service sectors (Alcock, 1996). Indeed, in the late 1800s, the majority of welfare services were provided through private charity or through mutual aid organisations, with state support limited to filling gaps in this provision (Brenton, 1985) ... By the time of the Wolfenden Committee Report ... published in 1978

there had been a dramatic turnaround, with the report suggesting it is the voluntary sector that exists to fill gaps in state provision. The perception now was of the voluntary sector as more of a 'junior partner in the welfare firm' (Owen, 1964, p. 527). (2008: 1)

An argument can be made that public and private organisations have advanced economic efficiency. More recent analyses question whether they are *socially* efficient due to increasing rates of suicide, a widening gap between rich and poor, community breakdown and endemic health issues, even in the most 'developed' nations (Gates, 1998). So, instead of simply asking how the third sector has emerged from debates about the limitations of the public and private sectors, we will also ask whether the public and private sectors have proactively marginalised, and developed a discourse that hides from view, third sector approaches to economics, trading and welfare provision (Kalmi, 2007).

Civil Society and a Third System

The UK's National Council for Voluntary Organisations (NCVO) recently decided to adopt the term *civil society* to describe the organisations in its flagship publication on the voluntary sector.[2] This reflects its CEO's interest in three strands of the debate on civil society (Edwards, 2004; Etherington, 2008). Firstly, 'civil society' describes informal and formal associations that people establish outside the public and private sectors. In this sense, civil society is the coming together of people independently, free from state or commercial intervention, and has roots in the democratic right to 'freedom of association'. Secondly, it captures the concern of these voluntary associations to advance the quality of public debate. Here, civil society is about creating arenas where people can debate social and economic issues, discover their common interests, and negotiate their differences. An integral part of the 'quality of public debate' strand is how to provide a check on the power of the state and large-scale corporations. The third strand engages a moral question: what would it be like to live in a 'good society'? In this case, the concern is how society *should be*, rather than how it is, and whether the norms propagated by different institutional and societal processes should be sanctioned or opposed. The *Civil Society Almanac*, therefore, advances these perspectives through acknowledgement of the contribution of voluntary organisations, charities and cooperatives as well as universities, trade unions and housing associations to civil society. This perspective theorises the third sector as a group of non-state, non-capitalist organisations committed to advancing one or more aspects of civil society.

This framework raises some provocative questions. Firstly, it moves well beyond the views expressed in a paper presented by Murdock at the Social Entrepreneurship Research Conference in 2007 in which 'civil society' is limited to the informal interactions between families, friends and citizens. Paton (2003) also describes civil society as a combination of informal and self-help groups, and leisure networks, that contribute to the development of *social capital* (see Chapter 4). In contrast, Schwabenland (2006) adopts a critical tone, regarding civil society as a new rhetoric emanating from the *state*, part of a modernisation agenda to restore civic responsibility through involvement in organisations that rebuild community life. She draws a boundary between organisations supporting the state's narrative on civic responsibility (which, presumably, includes NCVO) and other third sector organisations (TSOs) that continue to challenge it. One aspect of the resurgence of the third sector, therefore, is an increasingly vibrant dialogue about the role of the state and radical organisations in developing alternatives to private enterprise (Westall, 2001) and NGOs.

For the purposes of this chapter, we need to be aware that civil society – while its meaning is not agreed – captures a perspective that is motivated neither by the pursuit of political power using the apparatus of the state, nor by the goal of capital accumulation through trading in a market (Mertens, 1999; Lindsay and Hems, 2004). In its place is a discourse that combines social democratic language with values of mutual support and civic responsibility (Giddens, 1998). As Haugh and Kitson comment:

> The Third Way was a political philosophy that sought to resolve the ideological differences between liberalism and socialism; it combined neoliberalism with the renewal of civil society and viewed the state as an enabler, promoted civic activism and endorsed engagement with the voluntary and community sector to address society's needs. (2007: 983)

While Edwards (2004) is somewhat dismissive of this view, it represents an alternative that rejects both Weber's ideal of bureaucracy (based on logic and rationality) and a market capitalism that is concerned only with higher standards of living (Rothschild and Allen-Whitt, 1986; Gates, 1998). If there is a 'third way', it follows there must be a 'third system' that not only compensates for the shortcomings of the state and market, but offers the potential to go beyond it (Pearce, 2003; Ransom, 2004). An early attempt to theorise this appears in Pearce (2003), shown in Figure 1.1.

The appeal of Pearce's diagram lies in features that are omitted from other economic models. Firstly, it recognises entities at neighbourhood, district, national/regional and international levels (compare Paton, 1991). It differentiates between a 'community economy' that may be formally organised and a 'self-help' economy that is grounded in family life. Pearce's model locates informal and formal voluntary groups with non-trading **charities**, and differentiates these from trading charities, community enterprises and **social firms**. He adds into the model social businesses (that engage in **philanthropic** trading activities), mutual societies (that use reciprocity as an underlying trading principle), **fair trade** companies (that pay a *social premium* to producers), and cooperatives (designed to promote social and economic participation in production and consumption).

The *quality* of life that is generated by the third system is captured in the film *It's a Wonderful Life* (Case 1.1). The political dimension of the film is strongest in the final scenes where the viewers have a chance to consider what life would have been like if George Bailey had never been born.

Case 1.1   It's a Wonderful Life (Frank Capra)

In developing an appreciation of differences between the first, second and third systems, popular culture is helpful. In the film *It's a Wonderful Life* (1948), George Bailey runs a credit union called the Bailey Building and Loan that provides a refuge from the profit-maximising activities of Henry Potter. The Bailey Building and Loan is portrayed as having few cash reserves while the Potter business empire is awash with money. A stark contrast is drawn between the economically wealthy Henry Potter and the relatively poor

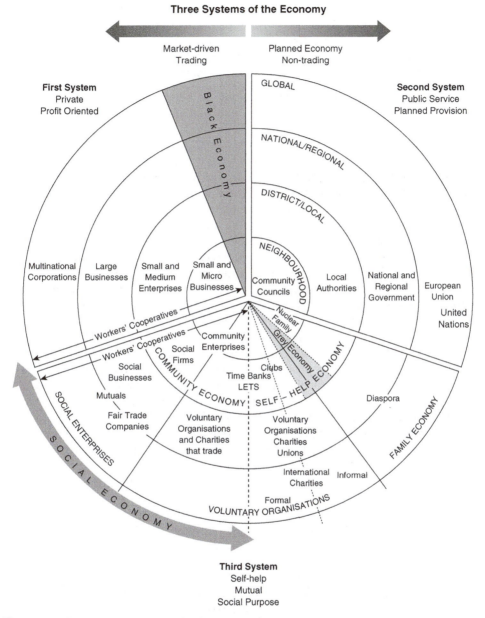

Three Systems of the Economy

Market-driven
Trading

Planned Economy
Non-trading

First System
Private
Profit Oriented

Second System
Public Service
Planned Provision

GLOBAL

NATIONAL/REGIONAL

DISTRICT/LOCAL

NEIGHBOURHOOD

Black Economy

Multinational Corporations

Large Businesses

Small and Medium Enterprises

Small and Micro Businesses

Community Councils

Local Authorities

National and Regional Government

European Union

United Nations

Workers' Cooperatives

Workers' Cooperatives

Community Enterprises

Social Firms

Nuclear Family

Grey Economy

Social Businesses

Time Banks
LETS

Clubs

COMMUNITY ECONOMY

SELF – HELP ECONOMY

Mutuals

Diaspora

Fair Trade Companies

Voluntary Organisations and Charities that trade

Voluntary Organisations Charities Unions

SOCIAL ENTERPRISES

FAMILY ECONOMY

SOCIAL ECONOMY

International Charities

Informal

Formal

VOLUNTARY ORGANISATIONS

Third System
Self-help
Mutual
Social Purpose

Figure 1.1 The first, second and third systems of an economy

By permission of Calouste Gulbenkian Foundation. Pearce, J. (2003), *Social Enterprise in Anytown*, London: Calouste Gulbenkian Foundation.

George Bailey. After mislaying $6000, and facing bankruptcy, George Bailey contemplates suicide. An angel is sent from heaven to dissuade George from killing himself. When George says he 'wished he had never been born', the angel shows George Bailey what the town would have been like if he had not existed. The town is a desolate place, with casinos and bars transforming its landscape and character. The houses and communities built by the Bailey Building and Loan (a credit union established by George Bailey's father) no longer exist because George was not alive to oppose a takeover by Potter. While the town has plenty of *economic capital*, it has little *social capital*. These final scenes offer a proxy for what life would be like without a third sector.

A longer teaching case with student questions can be found at www.sagepub.co.uk/ridleyduff.

It's a Wonderful Life is a useful example for introducing the third sector concept of *mutuality* as an organising principle, and the way mutuality is linked to the development of *social capital* (see Chapter 4). The Bailey Building and Loan is cash poor (its capital is invested in house building). During a financial crisis, therefore, it depends on social capital, rather than economic capital, to survive.

Mertens (1999) notes that the term 'third sector' is linked to the idea of a third estate – neither the aristocracy nor the clergy, neither capitalist nor socialist, but a collection of organisations that fill the gap between state and market. She portrays a sector that grows and shrinks as the fortunes of the private and public sectors change, with boundaries drawn not so much in terms of what the third sector is but more in terms of what the public and private sectors are not.

There are problems with this view. Historically, as Coule (2008) points out, TSOs predate both capitalist production and state welfare provision. As Prochaska (1990: 358) writes, at the turn of the twentieth century 'the average middle class family was spending more on **charity** than on any other single item except food' and the income of London charities alone was 'greater than that of several nation states'. Weinbren (2008) provides some insights into this by revealing the amounts paid in Bristol (South West England) for sickness and death benefit in 1870: friendly societies and charities (third sector) paid out 73 per cent of all welfare benefits, with the Bristol Corporation (public sector) meeting only 27 per cent of the total.

Another consideration is the role that TSOs played in developing institutions that later transferred to the public and private sectors. Hudson (2002: 4) lists well-known hospitals established in the twelfth and thirteenth centuries (St Bartholomew's and St Thomas') that are now part of the NHS. Other trusts and associations now shape modern approaches to welfare and legal rights (e.g. Red Cross and Barnardo's) and are largely state funded (Murdock, 2007). To this, we can add the friendly societies that built a membership of 9.5 million by 1910, an achievement that demonstrated the viability of social insurance covering the whole population (Weinbren and James, 2005). Indeed, 'approved' friendly societies managed the state system until 1942 when services were finally taken over by state employees. Lastly, cooperative stores dominated grocery retailing before World War II and pioneered the concept of a retail supermarket. While price deregulation affected the UK market after the war, there has been a recovery over the last 10 years that coincides with expanding cooperative retail businesses in Italy and Spain (Kalmi, 2007). As Chandler (2008) has successfully argued, many public and private enterprises start life as municipal or third sector initiatives. When their viability is demonstrated, larger organisations use their

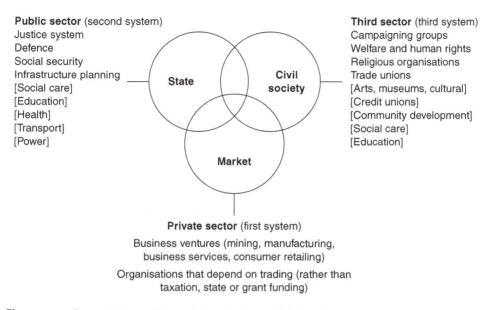

Public sector (second system)
Justice system
Defence
Social security
Infrastructure planning
[Social care]
[Education]
[Health]
[Transport]
[Power]

State

Civil
society

Third sector (third system)
Campaigning groups
Welfare and human rights
Religious organisations
Trade unions
[Arts, museums, cultural]
[Credit unions]
[Community development]
[Social care]
[Education]

Market

Private sector (first system)
Business ventures (mining, manufacturing,
business services, consumer retailing)

Organisations that depend on trading (rather than
taxation, state or grant funding)

Figure 1.2   Organisations of the public, private and third sectors

political or economic muscle to acquire them, not because this is necessarily more efficient, but because they operate on a scale that can be used to advance the interests of the state or private capital.

A useful way to define the third sector (and social economy) is that it comprises organisations where 'shares' (of social wealth) are allocated to people in proportion to their needs and activities rather than property (private) or political (public) rights. Takeovers by state or private sector organisations, therefore, may have motives other than the delivery of greater 'efficiency'. In some cases, takeovers may be motivated by a desire to replace the social economy's approach to resource allocation with an alternative that is less threatening to state or corporate interests; thus power is a factor in the relationship between the sectors.

Organisations of the Third Sector

Figure 1.2 presents examples of organisations that make up each sector (those in square brackets may shift from one sector to another). Typically, TSOs deliver goods and services that are not available through the state or market; offer an alternative to the private sector; and extend or replace services offered through the state. Other TSOs campaign for change, or seek to strengthen civil society at local, regional and national level. TSOs can be characterised as social purpose organisations operating in a range of contexts (see Table 1.1), and which use capital but do not work *for* capital.

In the UK, examples of TSO legal forms include: **company limited by shares (CLS); company limited by guarantee (CLG); community interest company (CIC); charitable incorporated organisation (CIO); industrial and provident society (IPS);** and mutual and

Table 1.1 Subsectors of the third sector

• Arts	• Health	• Education
• Religion	• Politics	• Culture
• Leisure	• Environment	• Sport
• History	• Heritage	• Human rights
• Food and drink	• Retail	• Transport
• Animal welfare		

community benefit society (BENCOM). Unincorporated forms that might fall under the radar include charitable trusts or informal associations (Cabinet Office, 2007). Business formats range from social firm, **workers cooperative, consumer cooperative, intermediate labour market (ILM),** voluntary and community organisation (VCO), **employee-owned company** and **development trust.**

CLASS EXERCISE   Identifying the third sector

Materials to support this exercise can be found at www.sagepub.co.uk/ridleyduff.

On your own, sort the following organisations into three groups:

- group 1: first system, private sector
- group 2: second system, public sector
- group 3: third system, third sector.

Advisory Conciliation and Arbitration Service (ACAS)   Oxfam
National Society for the Prevention of Cruelty to Children British Telecom (BT)
E.ON   The Crown Prosecution Service
The Co-operative Group   Body Shop
Shell   St Thomas' Hospital
Comic Relief   London University

Pair up with another person. Are your groupings the same? If any organisations are placed in different groups, discuss the differences of opinion.

Suggestion: why not include organisations from your own area, region or country? You can include well-known regional services, companies, associations, charities and cooperatives.

Assessing Size, Scope and Contribution

There are a number of ways to assess the contribution of TSOs. Below, we consider three traditional perspectives (the employment provided; the number of organisations; the financial value of their trading activities) to illustrate how the frame of reference can radically alter perceptions of the size of the sector. The US and EU both have legal definitions for TSOs. In the US, non-profit organisations fall under Section 501 of the Internal Revenue Code, and include more than two dozen categories of organisation that are tax exempt. These are permitted to provide employment, but cannot pay **dividends** to shareholders. In the EU, the concept of the social economy embraces a similar, but slightly different, range of organisations. In the mid 1990s it was recognised that classification into investor-led (private) enterprises and intervention-led (public) organisations was inadequate. The EU's national accounting system now includes Sections 11 and 12 (social economy 'business subsector') and 14 and 15 (social economy 'non-market producers'). This makes TSOs more visible (as a sector) and more amenable to government support and intervention (Monzon and Chaves, 2008).

The business subsector comprises cooperatives, mutual organisations and social firms that satisfy **democratic** criteria set out in the CEP-CMAR *Charter of Principles of the Social Economy*. Unlike the US, dividends are payable to members but must reflect 'activities or transactions with the organisation' rather than capital contributions (2008: 558). In addition, there is a 'non-market-producer subsector' that includes associations and foundations producing (or funding) non-market goods and services for household consumption. Whereas the US definition is broadly defined to include philanthropic and political organisations, the EU definition leans strongly toward democratic criteria and the production of goods and services; 'non-democratic' voluntary organisations are only included if they 'conduct an activity with the main purpose of meeting the needs of persons rather than remunerating capitalist investors' (2008: 558).

Table 1.2 shows data from a recent report commissioned by the European Commission on employment in the social economy. As can be seen from the table, the social economy in some EU countries is dominated by associations (Belgium, Netherlands and the United Kingdom) and in others by cooperatives and mutuals (Italy, Spain and Poland). Across the EU as a whole, 36 per cent of social economy employment is provided by cooperatives and mutuals, while the remaining 64 per cent is provided by voluntary associations (and charities). Moreover, the social economy is growing faster than the private and public sectors, at 5–10 per cent per year (Avila and Campos, 2006: 109), although is it still a relatively small part of the whole economy, providing under 10 per cent of employment.

Table 1.2 Paid employment in the European Union, 2002–3

Country	Cooperatives	Mutual societies	Associations	Total
Belgium	17,047	12,864	249,700	279,611
France	439,720	110,100	1,435,330	1,985,150
Ireland	35,992	650	118,664	155,306
Italy	837,024	–[a]	499,389	1,336,413
Portugal	51,000	–[a]	159,950	210,950
Spain	488,606	3,548	380,060	872,214
Sweden	99,500	11,000	95,197	205,697
Austria	62,145	8,000	190,000	260,145

(Continued)

Table 1.2   *(Continued)*

Country	Cooperatives	Mutual societies	Associations	Total
Denmark	39,107	1,000	120,657	160,764
Finland	95,000	5,405	74,992	175,397
Germany	466,900	150,000	1,414,937	2,031,837
Greece	12,345	489	57,000	69,834
Luxembourg	748	n/a	6,500	7,248
Netherlands	110,710	n/a	661,400	772,110
United Kingdom	190,458	47,818	1,473,000	1,711,276
Cyprus	4,491	n/a	n/a	4,491
Czech Republic	90,874	147	74,200	165,221
Estonia	15,250	n/a	8,000	23,250
Hungary	42,787	n/a	32,882	75,669
Latvia	300	n/a	n/a	300
Lithuania	7,700	0	n/a	7,700
Malta	238	n/a	n/a	238
Poland	469,179	n/a	60,000	529,179
Slovakia	82,012	n/a	16,200	98,212
Slovenia	4,401	270	n/a	4,671
Total	3,663,534	351,291	7,128,058	11,142,883

[a]The data on mutual societies are integrated into those of cooperatives for Italy and those of associations for Portugal.

Source: Avila, R.C. and Campos, R.J.M. (2006) The Social Economy of the European Union, CIRIEC, No. CESE/COMM/05/2005 (The European and Social Committee) p. 45, Table 6.1 © European Communities, 1995–2006.

Case 1.2   The Scott Bader Group and the Scott Bader Commonwealth

Scott Bader Group provides an example of ambiguity in the definition of TSOs. Scott Bader, established in 1921, is a chemicals company that makes and exports polymers around the world. In 1951 the company established an employee trust, and then transferred ownership to a charitable trust in 1963. Employees, upon completing their probation, become members of the trust. In 2007 there were 630 employees, of whom 77 per cent were members of the Scott Bader Commonwealth. Six of the nine board members of the Commonwealth are elected from the workforce. Four of the 10 Scott Bader Group board are elected from the workforce. Each year, any profit sharing payment must be matched by a payment to the charitable trust. Trust members nominate and vote each year on which two charities will receive £25,000 (see www.employeeownership. co.uk, 'Case studies').

Scott Bader is claimed by different authors as belonging to different parts of the third sector. As it is a company limited by guarantee, owned by a charitable trust whose members and trustees are elected from amongst its employees, Paton (2003) discusses it both as a charity and as an employee-owned company. At the same time, Oakeshott (1990) discusses it as a cooperative enterprise.

The Scott Bader Commonwealth is a registered charity and has been structured so that the Scott Bader Group and Commonwealth assets would pass to the UK **Charity Commission** upon dissolution.

The UK situation is complicated by the existence of charity law. Whilst other national classification systems – such as the US or France – include types of associations and non-profits that receive recognition for charity-like activities, UK organisations can apply for charity status where the bulk of their activities or services meet a specified public interest (Morgan, 2008). As charities are approved on the basis of their activities, and not their legal form, it can be hard to draw distinctions between different parts of the third sector in the UK. Nevertheless, a number of mapping exercises have been conducted.

The Office of the Third Sector (OTS) estimates that the third sector includes more than 164,000 charities, 200,000–500,000 voluntary and community groups and 55,000 social enterprises (Lincoln, 2006). Cooperatives UK (2007) states that there are 4370 cooperatives in the UK. NCVO (2008) estimates that the broader civil society is made up of approximately 865,000 organisations (inclusive of trade unions and universities, with a total income in excess of £100 billion annually). Table 1.3 summarises data for the third sector in the UK.

Table 1.3 Approximate number and proportions of UK third sector organisations, 2007

Voluntary/community organisations (Stone et al., 2007)	200,000–500,000	40–60 per cent
Charities (NCVO, 2008)	160,000	30 per cent
Social enterprises (Lincoln, 2006)	55,000	10 per cent
Cooperatives and mutuals (Cooperatives UK, 2007)	4,370	2 per cent

The problems with the figures in the table are: firstly, the unmappable micro providers that fall under the radar at one end (estimated to involve 2 to 5 million people in the UK by MacGillivray et al., 2001); and secondly, the separation of cooperatives and social enterprises, with the result that larger cooperatives and mutuals get excluded from social enterprise surveys (Woodin, 2007). As we will discuss in Chapter 3, the cooperative movement's involvement in establishing key social enterprise institutions justifies a claim that they are *de facto* social enterprises. Perhaps more significantly, the figures do not reflect the level of activity. In the UK, the largest three cooperatives (Cooperatives UK, 2007: Table 2) generate more trading activity (£16.4 billion) than all voluntary, community and charity organisations combined (£15.6 billion) (NCVO, 2008).[3] Moreover, the 'co-ownership sector', which excludes consumer cooperatives but includes wholly or partially owned employee-controlled organisations, is 'prudently' estimated to contribute £20–25 billion to the UK economy (Knell, 2008), while the broader mutual sector is estimated to contribute £98 billion (Mutuo, 2009: 5). This is more than three times the total income generated by the charity sector from all sources (estimated at £31 billion by NCVO, 2008). *The boundaries chosen, and the lens adopted, dramatically alter perceptions of the size, contribution and potential of the third sector.*

Having set out the scope and size of the sector, we now consider it from a socio-historical perspective to better understand the diversity of values and beliefs. We start by examining trusts and charities to understand the role of trustees and beneficiaries. We then examine the early development of democratic associations through an exploration of cooperative and mutual society history. Lastly, we examine the link between voluntary associations, secular society and the membership principle. In doing so, some of the differences between TSOs become more apparent (Case 1.2).

A word of caution is necessary before embarking on the discussion that follows. While charities have a largely religious heritage and cooperatives became associated with secular traditions, successive generations have been attracted to their legal forms without appreciating their social heritage. Many organisations choose their legal form for pragmatic reasons, and may not conform to the norms depicted in the next section.

The Development of Trusts and Charities

In tracing the roots of 'non-profit' organisations, Hudson (2002: 1) points to charitable and philanthropic acts in Egyptian times, using the example of the Pharaoh himself who provided clothing, shelter and bread to the poor. Indeed, Hudson claims the word 'charity' originates from the Greek word *charis*, meaning favour, kindness or goodwill, and gives a few examples:

- In *c*.274 – 232 BC Emperor Asoka (India) ordered wells to be dug and trees planted for the benefit of society.
- Jewish prophets campaigned for social, economic and political justice.
- In Roman times, the right to free corn was a benefit of citizenship.
- Christian churches have a long tradition of supporting the sick and protecting disadvantaged groups.
- Philanthropy in Islam has a long history of 'hardship funds' and hospital building.

Morgan (2008: 3) traces the concept of charity not to the Greeks but to early Christian writings on 'love' in the sense of an 'absolute willingness to give everything for the sake of another'. He distinguishes between charity as a mode of human behaviour and the institutional forms that started to develop from around AD 600.[4] As an institutional form, charity involves the organisation of financial giving (donations) to a group of people who are regarded as sufficiently responsible to administer funds and ensure they are used for charitable purposes (trustees).

For well over a millennium, charitable giving was organised under the auspices of the church. As Luxton (2001) notes, elaborate relationships developed between wealthy people and church authorities as people started to believe that their charitable donations would guarantee them entry into heaven. As charities grew, however, it became harder to ensure that the funds donated were used for the purposes intended. Although many adopted the form of a charitable trust, trust law came to be seen as inadequate. In 1597, a precursor of the Statute of Charitable Uses Act was passed by the UK Parliament, but it was in 1601 that two far-reaching welfare reforms took place. Firstly, there was a revision of the Charitable Uses Act, regulating the use of trust funds by the churches in the provision of education and welfare. Secondly, the Poor Law was introduced to enable local councils to raise money from ratepayers to provide welfare benefits to those in need. As Morgan comments:

> From the outset, one of the key planks of charity law has been the principle of voluntary trusteeship – that is, that those who are entrusted with charitable funds should apply them to advance the charity's objects without seeking personal benefit … charity trustees can only be paid in exceptional circumstances. (2008: 5)

Even though much of the 1601 Act was later repealed, two principles have remained to this day: there must be a *charitable purpose* (as defined in the original and subsequent Acts), and this must be in the *public interest* (Morgan, 2008). Both of these concepts have been subject to evolution and refinement. For example, the early statutes specified that charities were for the advancement of religion, education, the relief of poverty or anything else that provided a clear community benefit. In the Charities Act 2006 (UK), there was concurrently a broadening of activities that were recognised as charitable (for example amateur sports) and a tightening of the public interest principle (see box).

Charities Act 2006, Section 1, Clause 2(2)

Definition of 'Charitable Purposes':

(a) the prevention or relief of poverty;
(b) the advancement of education;
(c) the advancement of religion;
(d) the advancement of health or the saving of lives;
(e) the advancement of citizenship or community development;
(f) the advancement of the arts, culture, heritage or science;
(g) the advancement of amateur sport;
(h) the advancement of human rights, conflict resolution or reconciliation or the promotion of religious or racial harmony or equality and diversity;
(i) the advancement of environmental protection or improvement;
(j) the relief of those in need by reason of youth, age, ill-health, disability, financial hardship or other disadvantage;
(k) the advancement of animal welfare;
(l) the promotion of the efficiency of the armed forces of the Crown, or of the efficiency of the police, fire and rescue services or ambulance services.

In tracing the influence of charities, a notable date in the UK was 1834 when the Poor Law Amendment Act was passed to save the state money (Harrison, 1969). The Act encouraged a cultural separation between two types of poor – the 'deserving' and the 'undeserving'. The deserving poor could qualify for charity or philanthropic help; the undeserving were sent to the workhouse. The government's aim to halve the welfare budget, and the increasingly hostile attitude of both state and charity organisations to the 'undeserving poor', led to the growth of new societies that discouraged working people from relying on charity (MacDonald, 2008). Between the amendment of the Poor Law (1834) and the introduction of National Insurance (1910), membership of friendly societies in the UK rose from under 1 million to 9.5 million. This uptake was not confined to the UK and spread throughout the British Empire. In Australia, for example, it is estimated that over 80 per cent of working age men eventually joined a friendly society (Weinbren and James, 2005). Even so, charities continued to grow in influence (Coule, 2008) until states introduced social insurance.

As third sector organisations, there are a number of value propositions in charities that potentially match or clash with the values advocated by other TSOs. Firstly, the act of giving and self-sacrifice (either financially or in the form of labour) is a *core value* built into culture and the legislative framework. In charities, this is expressed both through the requirements that trustees act in a voluntary capacity (unpaid) and through a more positive attitude to developing a volunteer labour force than is the case with cooperatives. The requirement to act as a voluntary trustee, however, means that positions of power – generally – are taken up by people with the wealth to devote leisure time to charitable work. This tradition survives today in the form of a reliance on celebrities to give credibility to fundraising initiatives, and the inclusion of the 'great and good' on boards, irrespective of their professional or specialist skills. There is also an inevitable bias in favour of those who come forward with mission-driven interests and educated people with social standing, given the need to manage and account for the use of the charitable funds.

As charities have grown and adapted to operating in cultures with employment laws, so the treatment of *employees, volunteers* and **trustees** has become more complex. Firstly, by accepting payment for their labour, employees are automatically deemed to have a conflict of interest that prevents them from acting as trustees (Frail and Pedwell, 2003). Secondly, there is a both a legal and a cultural divide between 'responsible persons' who act as *trustees* and those who are *beneficiaries* (i.e. in receipt of the benefits defined in an organisation's charitable objectives). Culturally, this separation of beneficiaries and trustees traditionally demarcated a class and a religious divide (MacDonald, 2008). It took until the 1990s for the Charity Commission to clarify that there was no legal barrier to members of the beneficiary group becoming trustees, providing they avoided a conflict of interest.

Case 1.3   The Ragged Trousered Philanthropists by Robert Tressell

The Ragged Trousered Philanthropists was published posthumously in 1914, and was based on the author's own experiences after emigrating from South Africa to England. It describes, in fictional form, Tressell's desire for a cooperative commonwealth to end his poverty and exploitation at work, and provide for his daughter Kathleen whom he feared would be sent to the workhouse should he become ill (Hunt, 2004). The book is a powerful analysis of the influence of the impact of ideology amongst working people who view their own employment as the '**philanthropy**' of their 'betters'. Tressell highlighted how, and why, people defend an economic system that exploits them when they lack the education to consider any alternative. In one passage, he describes the experiences of those applying for charity:

Another specious fraud was the 'Distress Committee'. This body, or corpse, for there was not much vitality in it, was supposed to exist for the purposes of providing employment for 'deserving cases'. One might be excused for thinking that any man, no matter what his past may have been, who is willing to work for his living, is a 'deserving case': but this was evidently not the opinion of the persons who devised the regulations for the working of this committee. Every applicant for work was immediately given a long job, and presented with a double sheet of foolscap paper ... it was called a 'Record Paper', three pages of which were covered with insulting, inquisitive, irrelevant questions concerning the private affairs and past life of the 'case' who wished to be permitted to work for his living, and which had to be answered to the satisfaction of ... the members of the committee before the case stood any chance of getting employment.

However, not withstanding the offensive nature of the questions on the application form, during the five months that this precious committee was in session, no fewer than 1237 broken spirited and humbled 'lion's whelps' filled up the forms and answered the questions as meekly as if they had been sheep. (Tressell, 2004: 435)

The extract in Case 1.3 is not a historically factual account, but it is indicative of the discourse that developed amongst both liberals and socialists regarding the poverty brought about by capital intensive industry.[5] It fuelled arguments for a national system of social insurance and legal rights for workers to protect employment. Those arguments rested on the need not simply to provide welfare payments to the unemployed, but also to end gaps in welfare provision created by friendly societies which viewed people as 'too risky' to insure, or which failed to cover members' relatives (Weinbren, 2008). Increasingly, a debate developed regarding the role of 'charity' (as institutionalised in law and economic thought) in reproducing dependency and *preventing* relief of poverty. While cooperative thinkers grew hostile to institutional forms of charity (see Ellerman, 2005), others robustly defended the record of charities as institutions relieving poverty and contributing to community development (Glasby, 1999).

Prior to the welfare states that developed in the twentieth century, concerned liberals and trade unionists started experimenting with new ways of organising business activity. In Tressell's novel, the seemingly impossible task of persuading low-skilled workers to organise work in a different way is articulated through a character called Owen. This was a tribute to Robert Owen, a philanthropist whose name became synonymous with cooperative communities at New Lanark in the UK and at Harmony in the USA. Owen – both the fictional and the historical versions – believed that relief from poverty would not occur until cooperative principles became dominant in society.

This brings us back to the distinction between charity as form of a human behaviour and charity as a particular institutional form (Fulda, 1999). While one interpretation of 'charity' (now embedded in charity law) led to the development of a trustee–beneficiary model that reproduces and reinforces class differences, 'charity' as a commitment to mutual care and reciprocity followed a different path. In the mid nineteenth century a new body of law permitted the establishment of fully self-governing institutions called friendly societies. In the next section, we consider their development.

The Development of Cooperatives and Mutual Societies

Robert Owen is often incorrectly credited as the founder of the cooperative movement. Cooperative storekeepers who pioneered new trading relationships were found in Scotland from 1769 onward (Harrison, 1969), while Rothschild and Allen-Whitt (1986) report that cooperatives appeared in the United States from 1790. Every 20 years or so, a new wave of cooperatives formed as social movements influenced the pace of political change.

Robert Owen is rightly credited, however, with one of the first convincing critiques of capitalist production. He presented a report to the House of Commons in 1817, and subsequently expressed his abhorrence at the 'atomisation' that developed in his factories as well as the system of church-led education that reproduced inequality (Owen, 1849; Harrison, 1969). He was also a critic of changes to the family brought about by industrialisation that separated women and men in daily life. Owen argued for a cooperative ethic based on community ownership of property. The inherent ambiguity in this statement created disagreement amongst Owen's followers over the boundary of the 'community'. These debates are still played out today between advocates of 'common ownership' and 'collective ownership' (Ridley-Duff, 2009a).

Although his experiments did not work as expected, Owen continued as a social reformer, writing and lecturing for the rest of his life. In 1824, the London Cooperative Society was founded and established a journal. By 1844 the Rochdale Pioneers had established a set of principles that have survived to the present day (see Case 1.4). Today, most cooperative movements pay tribute to the Rochdale principles rather than Owen's vision. Nevertheless, the success of cooperative networks in Italy and Spain shows that Owen's dream was not unrealisable, only premature. As people have discovered more effective ways of embedding cooperative principles, national and international movements have developed, coordinated through the International Cooperative Alliance (founded in 1895).

Two aspects of cooperative thinking stand in sharp contrast to the trustee–beneficiary model of charity. Firstly, the 'member economic participation' statement by the ICA in 1995 embeds the idea that members should contribute to, and then share in the economic **surpluses** generated by, their enterprise. This is operationalised through the distribution of benefits in proportion to a member's transactions with their cooperative. In cooperative stores, members receive a dividend (akin to the loyalty schemes that many modern supermarket chains have now introduced). In producer cooperatives (manufacturing goods or delivering services) fair payment for work and a share of profits are the norm (Ridley-Duff, 2007). Volunteering – in the sense of working for the organisation without pay – is discouraged by international agreements (ICA, 2005).

Case 1.4   The Rochdale Pioneers

The Rochdale Pioneers were a group of weavers and artisans who were inspired by the attempts of Robert Owen. They opened cooperative stores and pooled their resources to buy and sell items they could not afford individually. They set out principles that have been adapted over the last 150 years, but which are still recognisable today as an aspirational form of organisation that combines economic and social responsibility. These principles are now embedded in codes of governance that inform the development of modern-day cooperative practices (see Cooperatives UK, 2008).

The 1844 Rochdale Principles

1   Open membership.
2   Democratic control (one person, one vote).
3   Distribution of surplus in proportion to trade.
4   Payment of limited interest on capital.
5   Political and religious neutrality.
6   Cash trading (no credit extended).
7   Promotion of education.

The Revisions of the International Cooperative Alliance (ICA) in 1966

1   Open, voluntary membership.
2   Democratic **governance**.
3   Limited return on equity.
4   Surplus belongs to members.
5   Education of members and public in cooperative principles.
6   Cooperation between cooperatives.

1995 ICA Statement of Co-operative Identity

1   Voluntary and open membership.
2   Democratic member control.
3   Member economic participation.
4   Autonomy and independence.
5   Education, training and information.
6   Cooperation amongst cooperatives.
7   Concern for community.

For further details see: http://www.ica.coop/coop/principles.html

The second principle that stands in contrast is the commitment to democratic member control, which is incompatible with the charity system based on *trustees* and *beneficiaries*. While a cooperative may elect some of their members to govern their affairs, the legal form is intended to prevent elites appointing themselves to positions of power and holding these without the consent of the communities they serve (i.e. their staff, customers or beneficiaries). For example, those taking out an account at a mutual building society acquire the right to attend annual general meetings and elect members of the society's board. Staff in worker cooperatives acquire rights to govern themselves and elect or dismiss their executives (Cornforth et al., 1988; Ridley-Duff, 2009a). These rights are not granted to staff in private sector corporations, or to account holders in private banks. Staff in charities cannot directly remove their board of trustees, unless the charity is constituted as an association that allows staff members; they are reliant on 'whistleblower' legislation (e.g. Public Interest Disclosure Act 1998) or approaches to government regulators. The democratic principles advocated for (and in) social economy businesses, therefore, represent a challenge to political and business systems that seek to divide people into social classes (based on one group's automatic and unquestioned 'right' to govern or take management decisions). In cooperatives, the goal is the democratic control of the organisation's capital by its consumer and/or worker members (see Chapter 7). Since the 1930s, an **'employee ownership'** movement has also spread from the US to other parts of the world (Gates, 1998). Where employee-owners directly or indirectly control more than 50 per cent of voting shares, support agencies tend to recognise them as worker cooperatives. The Employee Ownership Association (in the UK) also recognises *co-owned* companies where the workforce owns a 'substantial' minority holding under 50 per cent (Reeves, 2007).

Secular Associations and a Voluntary Sector

The religious roots of charities and the secular origins of cooperatives have been substantially eroded as successive generations have been attracted to their legal forms without appreciating their social history. Today, **secular organisations** may adopt charitable status for pragmatic rather than religious reasons. Successful networks of cooperatives have been established in faith communities, particularly where Catholic liberation theology has taken root. In the celebrated case of **Mondragón** (Whyte and Whyte, 1991), it was a Catholic priest who helped to found both the cooperative schools and the engineering enterprises.

Nevertheless, a distinction can also be made between secular and religious organisations in the *non-profit* (non-market) sector of the social economy. Nowhere is this more acute than in France where *associations* were founded on explicit secular values. As Lindsay and Hems comment:

> The French non-profit sector ... did not emerge from a desire to address problems of social need. Neither was it created as a consequence of a number of private organizations addressing social problems, nor as a hinterland between public and private sectors ... delivering social welfare provision ... Rather, the French non-profit sector emerged as a result of the ideological struggle between republicanism and the Catholic Church over the rights of the individual. Until 1901, the legal right of individuals to associate in groups was heavily restricted and only allowed by specific permission of the government. The creation of associations ... was therefore seen as the final victory of the Republic over the Catholic Church in France. (2004: 266)

While other countries did not adopt such extreme solutions, the issues were still present elsewhere. Fox (1974) notes that in the UK, only a strong political culture of **liberalism** made it difficult for the propertied classes to remove 'freedom of association' from members of friendly societies. The working class used the same laws to defend freedom of association in societies as the wealthy used to protect their commercial interests. Nevertheless, with the shift in moral values brought about by the Victorian era, there were attempts to shut down friendly societies on the basis that meetings took place in public houses, and therefore breached the societies' own commitments to religious norms of temperance (Harrison, 1969). This was, however, a rhetorical strategy that masked the growing fear of ruling elites that trade unionism – spread through friendly societies – would result in a revolution (as in France in 1789) and remove them from power (Weinbren and James, 2005). In the USA, similar issues arose 100 years later during the early McCarthy era when right-wing (and religious) concern was expressed at the possibility of communism spreading via the cooperative societies. This triggered congressional hearings in 1948 to curb their increasing popularity (Dahlgren, 2007).

The success of secular associations in developing organisations that can maintain autonomy from churches, states and private companies has given rise to the concept of a **voluntary sector**. This term broadens the scope of the 'non-market' social economy beyond charity (or charity-like) organisations to include many sports and social clubs and performing arts organisations. It also provides a natural home for civil society organisations that, on account of their political lobbying, cannot register as charities.

As Bridge et al. (2009) comment, the association form has also spread into trade unions, independent schools, housing associations, employer and staff associations, and even political parties. Lindsay and Hems (2004) draw out the restrictions that often apply to associations (particularly in France) where income must be derived primarily from membership fees to prevent competition with private sector companies operating in open markets. In the UK, while trading restrictions are not as tight as in other countries, a theoretical distinction between associations (who generate income from and act for members), charities (who generate income from donors and charitable trading, and act for beneficiaries) and cooperatives (who act for members through the way they organise market trading) is helpful to appreciate differences in third sector organisations (see Figure 1.5).

The Modern Third Sector and Social Economy

In the last decade, the third sector gained recognition after Anthony Giddens (1998) adopted the phrase 'the third way' to describe Tony Blair's political philosophy. The collapse of the European communist states led to a new wave of thinking in Europe, the Americas and other Anglo-American cultures. While the third way is not synonymous with the third sector, it implied a major shift in the attitude of the public sector towards it. In the UK, the term 'third sector' predates 'third way' by nearly a decade (evidenced by the emergence of a trade magazine). Nevertheless, the acceptance of the term in the UK has been rapid since the election of a Labour government in 1997 (Haugh and Kitson, 2007). Commenting on Tony Blair's approach, Dickson (1999 [online]) argues that:

there is no ideological commitment to public sector provision – there is a willingness to contemplate private and not for profit alternatives, something manifestly different from more traditional Labour policy which at times was indifferent to the voluntary sector and often hostile to private involvement in welfare ... Indeed it is the social services white paper that is the most explicit on this, stating quite clearly that 'who provides' is not important.

Even though the sociological roots have become blurred, the *thinking* associated with a top-down hierarchy of control and organisation – rooted in the propagation of God's will, organised and disseminated through *trustees* who select *beneficiaries* – remains embedded in charity law. This still concretely impacts on the cultures that develop in TSOs applying for charity status (Hudson, 2002). Similarly, the egalitarian *thinking* that derives from principles of voluntary association, combined with the ideology of democratic control over capital and labour, has progressively become embedded in those countries that have bodies of law covering the formation of societies and cooperatives.

What *unites* members of both subsectors, however, is their ability to mobilise collective responses to social issues, engage moral and social reasoning in their business activities, and use their capacity to generate surpluses to advance a social purpose. Moreover, they share hostility to decision-making power based on capital ownership, preferring instead to decide membership on the basis of a person's commitment to the organisation's social objectives or willingness to contribute labour. Monzon and Chaves (2008) set out the definition that now informs thinking on the social economy within the EU. It integrates social democratic traditions with social purpose goals to create a social economy comprising

private, formally organized enterprises, with autonomy of decision and freedom of membership, created to meet their members' needs through the market by producing goods and services, insurance and finance, where decision-making and any distribution of profits or surpluses among the members are not directly linked to the capital or fees contributed by each member, each of whom has one vote. The Social Economy also includes private, formally organized organizations with autonomy of decision-making and freedom of membership that produce non-market services for households and whose surplus, if any, cannot be appropriated by the economic agents that create, control or finance them. (2008: 557)

Implications for Social Enterprise

There are two clear views of social enterprise in relation to the third sector. Firstly, there is the argument of Defourny (2001) that social enterprises are embedded *within* the third sector at the boundary area between cooperatives and non-profits (see Figure 1.3).

A similar argument is found in Pearce's (2003) *third system,* where social enterprise is depicted as a subsector sitting *between* voluntary and charity organisations and the private sector (which cooperatives also border). In contrast to both these

Figure 1.3 Social enterprise at the 'crossroads' of non-profit and cooperative economies

Reprinted with permission from the Taylor & Francis Group. Defourny, J. (2001) 'Introduction: from third sector to social enterprise' in Borzaga, C. and Defourney, J. (eds) *The Emergence of Social Enterprise*, p. 22, Figure 1.

views, however, comes a perspective influenced by US thinking on social entrepreneurship (see Leadbeater, 1997; Westall, 2001). In this case, the areas *between* the third and the public sectors, and *between* the public and the private sectors, are the environments for social entrepreneurship. In this body of theory, the institutional forms created by social entrepreneurs are *de facto* social enterprises (Spear, 2006). *This view, however, places social enterprise at the margins of the third sector rather than embedded in its heart.* The implications of this are set out in Figure 1.4, showing organisations that do not fit neatly into one or other sector.

In Chapter 3 we will examine this perspective more closely. For now, it is worth problematising Defourny's view that social enterprise lies *within* the third sector (civil society). Each of the examples in Figure 1.4 represents an organisation that formed, or operates, by drawing together thinking and organisational practices from more than one economic sector. For example, Peattie and Morley (2008) point out how the UK **National Lottery** is an initiative with a clear social purpose, organised through collaborations between the state and private businesses, delivering funds to TSOs. Another example of ambiguity is offered by Jones (2000). Traidcraft (see Case 1.5) achieves its social mission through altering the trading relationships between producers in disadvantaged communities and advanced market economies. Notwithstanding commitments to social activism in the Christian tradition, and a sustainability agenda drawn from environmental awareness, Traidcraft adopted the form of a public limited company (plc), more readily associated with private sector companies.

Third sector expertise running public services, or securing public sector
partnerships to achieve social outcomes
Royal National Institute for Deaf People
Citizens Advice Bureaux (CAB Service)
International Red Cross/Red Crescent Movement

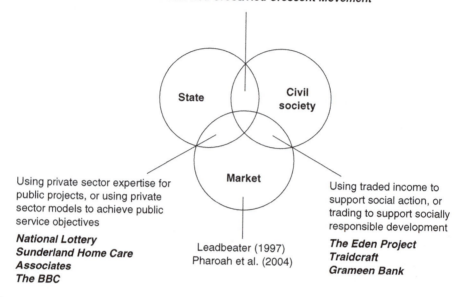

Using private sector expertise for
public projects, or using private
sector models to achieve public
service objectives

National Lottery
Sunderland Home Care
Associates
The BBC

Leadbeater (1997)
Pharoah et al. (2004)

Using traded income to
support social action, or
trading to support socially
responsible development

The Eden Project
Traidcraft
Grameen Bank

Figure 1.4   Hybrid organisations

Case 1.5   Traidcraft

Traidcraft, founded in 1979, established trading links and market opportunities for hand-
icrafts, cards, books, tea, coffee, paper products and food from overseas cooperative and community businesses. Its business ethics are based on Christian values. It
products are sourced from 26 different countries sold through a volunteer network of
5000 sellers. In 1983 the company took the decision to float on the stock market, to
deliberately increase participation, but offered no dividend on the £1 share. Despite
this, the offer of 300,000 shares was over-subscribed by 60 per cent. In 1993 Traidcraft
plc became the first plc to publish a social audit (undertaken by the New Economics
Foundation) and sent it to the stock exchange's top 100 chief executives as part of
the campaign to promote social accounting. Traidcraft also established the Traidcraft
Exchange, a charity which organises educational projects around the globe.

As a *fair trade network*, Traidcraft plc brings together cooperative and community
businesses, then sells their products through a public limited company, albeit with a
third sector ethic and a social ownership ethos. The addition of a charity to the group
broadens its capacity to undertake educational and social projects.

Traidcraft provides an example of an organisation that is hard to locate in any existing
sector.

Source: with permission from Traidcraft PLC.

So, as we consider theoretical perspectives on social enterprise itself, we need to be mindful that there is disagreement over its relationship to existing sectors of the economy. In one case (Defourny, 2001), social enterprises form *within* the third sector at the point where the non-profit and cooperative sectors influence each other. In the other cases, social enterprises are believed to form at the *boundaries* of the third sector where it is influenced by interactions with the private and public sectors (i.e. in employee-owned organisations, or voluntary organisations contracting to deliver public services).

Different theorisations of the relationship between the third sector and social enterprise lead to different understandings of social enterprise itself. Nevertheless, the third sector has become an important concept in understanding the fabric of society outside the private and public sectors (Stone et al., 2007). Crucially, TSOs differ from mainstream business in that they aim to follow a mission that typically serves a community or public good, with activities not constrained or prioritised on the basis of their profit potential. Financial surpluses are still desirable, but these are used to support limited profit distribution or reinvestment using criteria that are different from private sector norms. This is now being challenged by the creation of markets in health and social care, and a proactive move from grants to contracts.

Defourny and Nyssens (2006: 7), in discussing social enterprise, shed light on two key tensions. Firstly, there are differences in the ideologies that underpin the three categories of TSO (associations, mutuals and cooperatives). At one end of the continuum is the 'non-profit school' comprising charitable and voluntary organisations. At the other end is a 'more-than-profit' school comprising cooperative and mutual organisations. Whilst the 'non-profit school' ideology has been based on a *non-market* mindset, the cooperative school accepts a form of *market trading* within an altered set of assumptions regarding financial management. The non-profit mindset is grounded in philanthropy and giving. The cooperative mindset is grounded in trading activity in a market or with members.

The second tension is the organisation's democratic commitments. The cooperative school is committed to democratic member control, placing control of the organisation's mission into the hands of its wider membership, and (in the case of worker cooperatives) seeking to replace 'employment' with 'member ownership' (ICA, 2005). As a result, they typically have an *internal orientation*, seeking to benefit members. In non-profit associations, the mission is based on and for the good of society, or a particular segment of society. While opposed to the employment of trustees, many charities are comfortable employing staff to professionalise their operations. In this case, there is an *external orientation* with regard to beneficiaries. These, in turn, have impacts on the organisation of labour; human resource practices, attitude to management control and ownership. Theorising these differences helps to understand the variability of TSOs. Figure 1.5 provides a framework to further clarify this diversity.

Conclusions

There are a few points worth summarising that relate to forthcoming discussions about the definition of social enterprise. Firstly, many third sector organisations (voluntary associations, charities and cooperatives) have a claim on the term 'social

	External	Beneficiary orientation	Internal
	Aim to benefit general public or external group	← Mixed orientation →	Aim to benefit members of the organisation
Pro-market (trading)	Charities and voluntary organisations that trade to fund or subsidise public services	Multi-stakeholder organisations trading to support more than one stakeholder	Co-ops that trade to fund members' and workers' welfare and secure a sustainable income
Market and fundraising orientation	Charities and voluntary organisatons that use mixed income strategies to fund a public or community service	Multi-stakeholder organisations using mixed income strategies to support more than one stakeholder	'Social' coops and friendly societies using mixed income strategies for the benefit of members

Figure 1.5   Theorising the orientations of third sector organisations

enterprise' depending on their beneficiary and market orientation. The more market oriented they are, and the more they are oriented toward public and community benefit, the more they are accepted as part of the social enterprise mainstream (Lyon and Sepulveda, 2009). Secondly, the social economy and third sector are not the same thing. At **EU** level, third sector organisations that do not produce any goods or services for household or business use are excluded from the definition of the social economy. Moreover, definitions of social economy are more explicit about the 'social' aspects of organisation. While third sector organisations may have a social purpose, social economy organisations value 'social' rather than 'private' ownership and control (e.g. democratic member control and/or decision-making power not based on capital ownership). This being the case, the relationship between the social economy and social enterprise appears to be more direct than the link between the third sector and social enterprise. As will become clear in Chapter 2, it is not possible to draw a direct line between the third sector and social enterprise. It is, however, possible to draw a direct link between the social economy and social enterprises. This being the case, *social economy* is perhaps a more useful term (and concept) in the forthcoming debate.

SEMINAR EXERCISE   Theorising third sector organisations

Materials to support this exercise can be found at www.sagepub.co.uk/ridleyduff.

The purpose of this exercise is to critically review the market and membership orientations of third sector organisations and decide which are part of the social economy.

(Continued)

(Continued)

1 Obtain descriptions of the charity status, social aims and ownership structure of some third sector organisations.
2 Form students into groups of three.
3 Give three descriptions to each student.
4 Give the students 10 minutes to read and reflect on the examples.
5 Ask each student to summarise their organisations for the other members of their group.
6 Ask the group members to locate all the organisations on the 'theoretical map' of the third sector shown in Figure 1.5.
7 Ask the students to discuss which of these organisations are part of the 'social economy'.

Why not get students to research the websites of local third sector and social economy organisations and use these instead of the materials provided with the book?

SUMMARY OF LEARNING

In this chapter we raise a number of issues that impact understanding of the third sector.

- Civil society organisations attempt to promote voluntary (rather than coercive) forms of association outside the state and private sectors, to advance democratic debate, and to pursue moral and social goals.
- A three sector model of the economy (private, public, third) recognises three competing ideologies: (1) market supply and demand; (2) public interest; (3) social purpose.
- Third sector language ('non-profit sector', 'charity sector', 'voluntary sector' and 'social economy') impact on perceptions of the 'third sector'.
- The organisations of the social economy include cooperatives, mutual societies and charitable and/or voluntary associations that produce goods and services.
- Different perspectives on the third sector's size and scope can be derived from assessing the number of organisations of each type, the number of people employed and the scope and scale of trading activity.
- Understanding the history of charities, trusts, cooperatives, mutuals and voluntary associations helps us to appreciate their (potentially) different value commitments and orientation toward members and beneficiaries.
- The diversity of TSOs can be accounted for by considering their orientation towards beneficiaries (internal and/or external) and orientation toward income generation (market and/or grants and fundraising).
- There are different views about the relationship of social enterprises to the third sector: the first locates social enterprises within the third sector; the second locates social enterprises at the margins of all sectors.
- The definition of a 'social economy' may be a more useful concept to understand social enterprise than 'third sector'.

QUESTIONS AND POSSIBLE ESSAY ASSIGNMENTS

1 'The third sector is part of the private sector.' Critically discuss the accuracy and implications of this statement.
2 'The "non-profit sector", the "social economy" and the "voluntary/community sector" are three ways of describing the same thing – the third sector.' Critically discuss the meaning of these terms and, using case examples, assess the extent to which the claim can be substantiated.
3 Can a cooperative be a charity? Using theory and examples, explore the tensions between charities and cooperatives. Consider possible solutions to the question.

FURTHER READING

Amin's (2009b) paper on the social economy is a good starting point for understanding the motives of those who work in the sector. A useful introductory textbook *Understanding the Social Economy and the Third Sector* is available from Palgrave (Bridge et al., 2009). *The Emergence of Social Enterprise* (Borzaga and Defourny, 2001) contains a useful history of both cooperative and non-profit traditions (Chapter 1) as well as Defourny's (2001) construction of social enterprise at the overlap of both. More information on Pearce's (2003) three-sector model can be found in Chapter 2 of *Social Enterprise in Anytown*.

Scholarly discussions on the classification of third sector and social economy organisations can be found in Mertens' (1999) paper 'Nonprofit organisations and social economy: two ways of understanding the third sector'. More recent coverage, including consideration of the way the social economy is being operationalised within EU institutions, is in an excellent paper by Monzon and Chaves (2008) titled 'The European social economy: concept and dimensions of the third sector' and in Lyon and Sepulveda's (2009) review of social enterprise mapping. Arguments on alternative motives for entrepreneurship can be found in Williams' (2007) paper

on the public policy implications of social entrepreneurship.

An accessible history of charities and voluntary action can be found in Chapter 1 of Hudson's (2002) book *Managing Without Profit,* and in 'The spirit of charity' on the companion website. The history of cooperativism, including its theoretical underpinnings, is well covered in *The Cooperative Workplace* by Rothschild and Allen-Whitt (1986). Critical coverage of Giddens' views in his *Third Way* can be found in Haugh and Kitson's (2007) paper titled 'The third way and the third sector: New Labour's economic policy and the social economy'.

Further reading material is available on the companion website at www.sagepub.co.uk/ridleyduff.

USEFUL RESOURCES

Center on Philanthropy and Civil Society, http://www.philanthropy.org/
Charity Commission, http://www.charity-commission.gov.uk/
Cooperatives UK, http://www.cooperatives-uk.coop/
EMES European Research Network, http://www.emes.net/index.php?id=235
International Society for Third Sector Research, http://www.istr.org/

National Council for Voluntary Organisations (NCVO), http://www.ncvo-vol.org.uk/

Office of the Third Sector, http://www.cabinetoffice.gov.uk/third_sector.aspx

The European Civil Society Corner, http://www. civilsociety.se/

The Social Economy Network, http://www. socialeconomynetwork.org

The Social Economy Student Network, http://socialeconomy.info/en/english

Third Sector European Network, http://www.tsen.org.uk/

Third Sector Magazine, http://thirdsector.co.uk/

NOTES

1 The *Annals of Public and Cooperative Economics* celebrated its 100th anniversary in 2008.

2 *The Voluntary Sector Almanac* was renamed the *Civil Society Almanac* in 2008.

3 The three largest UK cooperatives are: Co-operative Group (CWS) Ltd, John Lewis Partnership and United Co-operatives Limited.

4 The oldest active charity on the UK Charity Commission register was established in 597.

5 This is not, however, meant to imply that it is historically inaccurate.

New Public Management and the Private Sector

2

Learning Objectives

In this chapter we critically evaluate the impact of new public management (NPM) and the rise of community economic development as a *response* to NPM. By the end of this chapter you will be able to:

- explain the concept of new public management (NPM)

- describe the impacts of NPM on public–private sector relationships

- critically evaluate local government and community business responses to NPM

- outline US and EU movements to democratise ownership and control of business

- articulate public and private sector influences on the emergence of social enterprise.

The key arguments that will be developed in this chapter are:

- The move to NPM in the 1980s was a formative influence on social enterprise development.
- NPM sought to legitimise business methods and markets in the pursuit of social objectives.
- Community and cooperative businesses reacted against the liberalism implicit in NPM.
- US and EU institutional support for employee ownership advanced democracy at work.
- Social enterprise cannot be fully understood without an appreciation of NPM and attempts to transform the private sector through democratic ownership and participation at work.

Introduction

In this chapter, we adopt a perspective that is rare in the study of social enterprise. Existing texts locate social enterprise either as a product of third sector development where cooperative and non-profit trading practices are blurred (Defourny,

2001), or as the advance of private sector practices into the third sector (Dart, 2004). In this chapter, we consider an alternative view that social enterprise is a product of the tension between attempts to reform the *public* sector through the introduction of private sector management rhetoric, and radical responses to those attempts by local politicians and community entrepreneurs with socialist sympathies.

The link to contemporary social enterprise is not immediately obvious, so initially we review the way economic thinking changed in the 1970s and was popularised by governments around the world (including those of Margaret Thatcher and John Major in the UK), and its subsequent impact on entrepreneurship, the rise of small firms, and new ideas on leadership in the social economy. In outline, the argument runs as follows:

1 A breakdown in the post-war political consensus regarding macro-economic management and full employment coincided with the rise of the 'new right' in politics.
2 The 'new right' advanced a set of principles that led to *new public management* (NPM) as a way of legitimising private sector thinking in public administration.
3 The 'new left' (a loose alliance of people holding anarchist, socialist and social democratic beliefs) responded through community regeneration using cooperative and employee-owned enterprises.
4 New Labour (in the UK) and social democratic parties across the EU adopted *supply-side* economics combined with commitments to social justice, equality and employment protection as a *third way.*
5 The social enterprise movement (and its thinking) emerged out of the tension between *liberal capitalist* ideas embedded in NPM and the *market socialism* that responded to it.
6 By the late 1990s, the embryonic social enterprise movement entered the political domain by establishing its own institutions and by questioning public, private and third sector thinking.

To appreciate this perspective, it is first necessary to consider the breakdown of the post-war consensus regarding economic thought and policies on employment (between 1945 and 1976). This is followed by an outline of the central tenets of *new public management* (see Hood, 1995) and then consideration of reactions to NPM by progressive liberal and socialist politicians (Chandler, 2008). The final section of the chapter provides some examples of the way social enterprises are actively transforming parts of the public and private sector.

The End of the Post-War Consensus

Macro-economics in **OECD**[1] nations in the latter part of the twentieth century was dominated by two schools of thought. From World War II onwards, economic planning was increasingly dominated by the views of John Maynard Keynes. Keynes developed his analysis in the 1920s through an alternative explanation of the stock market crash in 1929 and the subsequent depression. He challenged the view that a 'free market' would quickly self-correct by arguing that group psychology impacts on economic decision-making. In times of boom people tend to grow over-confident, whereas in times of economic depression people become over-cautious. These habits of thought become culturally embedded, leading to over-long periods of boom and bust. He argued that governments could counter the 'natural' tendency of people to be over-confident and over-cautious and stabilise the economy by spending and taxing to regulate *demand*.

Keynesian economics is associated with an expansionary policy by the state that supports interventions into the economy. The main critique comes from the **Chicago School** of economists who argued that government intervention is the *source* of the boom and bust cycle, and contributes to inflationary policies that make recessions worse (see Sloman and Sutcliffe, 2001: 598). They argued that government should limit itself to regulating the supply of money. These views, associated strongly with Milton Friedman (1968), came to be seen as *supply-side* economics, which sought to regulate inflation and employment by matching the supply of money (monetarism) to the productive capacity of the economy.

Up to the 1970s, Keynesian economics increased its influence worldwide. However, after an oil crisis led to sharp rises in prices, a situation occurred that ran counter to Keynesian arguments (rising prices *and* rising unemployment) and this created more opportunities for Friedman's arguments to undermine Keynesian thought. Supply-side economics was accompanied by a new rhetoric on freedom, liberty and enterprise (Friedman, 1962) that tapped dissatisfaction amongst wealthier voters, as well as those hostile to trade unions and the public sector. In the UK, as elsewhere, public sector policy shifted and this eventually fed arguments for entrepreneurial approaches to social problems based on new approaches to market trading (Hood, 1995; Cook et al., 2001).

EXERCISE   Milton Friedman: freedom and capitalism

In the YouTube video at the link below, Milton Friedman debates the rights and wrongs of Ford failing to install a $13 safety device that would have saved 1000 lives over the course of several years. The debate centres on the question of freedom of choice amongst consumers, and the role of the justice system in regulating the market. Watch the video and consider the following questions:

1   To what extent should decisions regarding human welfare depend on financial considerations?
2   To what extent are you convinced by Friedman's argument that freedom of choice in the marketplace should not be heavily regulated through government intervention?

Video: http://www.youtube.com/watch?v=iPqdRqacpFk

The advance of supply-side economics undermined the idea that public sector accountability was progressive (McNulty and Ferlie, 2004). Hood (1995) outlines a deep shift in both accounting and management practices that reflected the supply-side arguments of monetarism, leading to a diminishing role for the state as a manager of public enterprises, and the employer of choice in public services and utilities. Gradually, politicians accepted arguments to withdraw from direct provision and either use taxes to commission services from third parties, or privatise service delivery. Hood argues that this spread gradually, but not completely, across OECD countries. It took root quickly in the UK, Canada, New Zealand, Australia and Sweden, partially in France, Austria, Norway, Ireland and Finland, but not in countries like Japan, Greece, Spain and Turkey.

Klein (2007), however, argues that Friedman's advocacy of monetarism was advanced by capitalising on disasters – both accidental and manufactured – rather than its intrinsic merits. She argues that private sector control of the media permitted the spread of **new right** thinking through media empires that were not controlled by the state. It was not until the internet age that counter-arguments could be spread rapidly through new democratised forms of communication and publishing.

EXERCISE   Naomi Klein: disaster capitalism

In her YouTube video (link below), Naomi Klein, a key critic of Milton Friedman's economic thinking, tracks how both accidental and deliberately manufactured crises of the 1980s and 1990s were seized upon by well-prepared thinkers to advance liberal capitalism around the world. In contrast to popular opinion, she argues that the 'battle of ideas' between socialist and capitalist ideology was never lost at the grassroots level. It was, however, lost in media and political circles. The emergence of social enterprise, therefore, is arguably the political expression of grassroots organising that has taken time to establish its voice. Watch the video and answer the following questions:

1   During the fall of the communist countries in the late 1980s and early 1990s, what kind of economic and political reforms did people at grassroots level actually want?
2   What kind of economic and political reforms did they actually get, and why did these occur?

Video: http://www.youtube.com/watch?v=JG9CM_J00bw&feature=fvw

The Effects of New Public Management

Chandler (2008) views NPM as an ideological shift towards new right thinking in the management of public services. In the short term, this is manifest in UK programmes to privatise utility companies (**British Gas, British Telecom** etc.). In the longer term, and perhaps more significantly, NPM manifests itself in a number of 'doctrines' that replace collaborative approaches based on professional judgement with target-driven approaches based on managerial control. Hood (1995) sets out the ideological shifts as well as the accompanying operational and accounting implications (Table 2.1).

Table 2.1 The seven doctrines of new public management

Public sector distinctiveness

No.	Doctrine	Justification	Replaces	Operational implications	Accounting implications
1	Transformation of public sector bodies into corporatised units organised to deliver discrete products and services	Makes units manageable; focuses blame for failure; splits commissioning and production to reduce waste	Belief in uniform, inclusive public sector; belief in collaborative approaches to public service provision	Erosion of single service employment; arm's-length management to separate commissioning and provision of services; devolved budgeting	More cost centres; move to activity-based costing (ABC)
2	More contract based, competitive tendering; internal markets and fixed-term contracts	Competition will lower costs and improve standards; contracts enabling setting of performance standards	Unspecified employment contracts, open-ended provision agreements; linking purchase, provision and production to achieve efficiencies throughout the supply chain	Distinction of primary and secondary public sector labour force (through separation of commissioners and providers)	Stress on identification of costs and cost structures; providers treat cost data as commercially confidential; cooperative behaviour discouraged
3	Emphasis on private sector styles of management	Private sector management tools are 'proven' to be efficient and need application in the public sector	Stress on public service ethics, fixed pay and hiring rules, acting as a model employer, centrally determined personnel structure; job for life	Move away from public sector pay, career service, non-monetary rewards, and 'due process' in employee entitlements	Private sector accounting norms
4	More stress on discipline and frugality in use of resources	Need to cut direct costs, raise labour discipline, do more with less	Stable base budgets and financial norms; minimum standards; union voice/veto	Less primary employment; less job security; less producer-friendly working practices	More stress on bottom line and cost benefits

(Continued)

Table 2.1 *(Continued)*

No.	Doctrine	Justification	Replaces	Operational implications	Accounting implications
Rules versus discretion					
5	More emphasis on visible hands-on top management	Accountability requires clear assignment of responsibility, not diffusion of power	Paramount stress on policy skills and rules, not active management	More freedom to manage by discretionary power	Fewer constraints on handling cash, contracts and staff; more financial data for management accountability
6	Formal standards and measures of performance and success	Accountability to include clearly stated aims; efficiency based on 'hard' outcome goals	Qualitative standards and implicit norms	Erosion of self-management by professionals	Performance indicators and audit culture
7	Emphasis on output controls	Greater stress on results	Collaborative procedures and control processes	Resources and pay based on performance	Move to broad cost centre accounting and blurring of staff and activity costs

Source: this article was published in *Accounting, Organisation and Society*, vol 20, Hood, C., 'The "New Public Management" in the 1980s: Variations on a Theme', p. 93–109, Table 1 © Elsevier (1995).

Case 2.1 illustrates how the practices associated with NPM influenced public sector reform, and can be linked to social enterprise. The National Health Service in the UK has been divided into **commissioning** and provider bodies to create a quasi-market. This is now encouraged through a 'right to request' policy that allows staff to externalise existing services into discrete social enterprises separate from the public sector (NHS, 2008).

Case 2.1   The 'right to request' in the UK National Health Service

The contemporary expression of NPM in the form of social enterprise can be found in the National Health Service of the UK (NHS). In November 2008, the NHS published *Social Enterprise – Making a Difference: A Guide to the Right to Request*. The 'right to request' allows any health professional to put a 'business case' to its primary care trust board to set up a social enterprise. The presentation of social enterprise to health professionals states that it is 'fundamentally about business approaches to achieving public benefit' (2008: 6). The focus on innovation, reorganisation into business units providing discrete services, and outcome-driven management is evident in the Chief Health Professions Officer's statement:

Social enterprise will not be the answer for everyone, but allied health professionals have a long history of providing innovative services in a variety of sectors, settings and throughout care pathways and patient journeys. Consequently, allied health professionals are in an excellent position to take advantage of the 'right to request'. This may be for a particular profession, such as podiatry or physiotherapy, a specialism such as musculoskeletal physiotherapy, a particular care group, or a combination of these. What is most important though is that this is about developing a service that will meet local need and maximise your potential to innovate and ultimately improve outcomes for patients, clients and families, whilst remaining part of the NHS family. (2008: 3)

Interestingly, Hood finds it difficult to distinguish between a privatisation agenda and a social democratic reaction to NPM that uses social enterprise to *limit* the influence of the private sector:

it might be argued that NPM has been adopted in some contexts to ward off the New Right agenda for privatisation ... and in other countries as the first step towards realizing that agenda. Much of NPM is built on the idea (or ideology) of homeostatic control; that is, the clarification of goals and missions in advance, and then building the accountability systems in relation to those preset goals. (1995: 107)

Concern that non-profits and social enterprises are being sucked into a 'contracting culture' (Dart, 2004) is based on analyses of the deep shift in management thought.

Contracts typically embed new forms of management control and governance that are considerably less 'empowering' than the rhetoric accompanying them (Curtis, 2008). The increased formalisation (visioning, mission statements, audit), and the outcome-driven character of measurement (targets, service-level agreements and competition), represent a cultural shift in the direction of a legal-rational society based on knowledge derived from a **positivist** philosophical outlook. Hebson et al. (2003) found that the replacement of bureaucracy with contracting 'partners' decreases the opportunity for collaborative decision-making. Transparency decreases and the use of legal remedies increases as service commissioners adapt to their monitoring function, and use their power to adjust rewards (i.e. pay) in line with service-level agreements.

Positivist research is generally associated with attempts to strengthen political and social control through the advancement of 'objective' knowledge that presents management as a politically neutral activity (Grey and Mitev, 1995). Critical research, on the other hand, is associated with attempts to democratise organisations and secure emancipatory change by exposing the political agendas implicit in scientific and managerial rhetoric (see Burrell and Morgan, 1979; Alvesson and Willmott, 2003). It is, therefore, appropriate to question whether the assumptions encouraged by NPM are an appropriate basis for management education in *social* enterprises (see Grey, 2005). Are social enterprises pursuing innovative social change better served by knowledge derived from positivist or critical research agendas?

Whatever motive may apply in each case, the practices characteristic of NPM advance the interests of entrepreneurial and management classes, and erode the influence of professionals seeking to maintain collaborative management practices driven by social need (Hebson et al., 2003). NPM invites a new breed of entrepreneurial professional or, failing this, a new layer of managers to supervise professional practice, equipped with a range of hard and soft HRM techniques (see Chapter 9) to instil 'discipline' that 'drives up standards'. Its advocates portray it as progressive because:

> the state is recast in the role of enabler rather than provider [where] government is moving away from those standardized, mass production, models of service delivery which arose in the 1900–1940 period towards a new form of entrepreneurial government which is more concerned to use public resources in new ways to maximize productivity and effectiveness. This echoes many of the arguments for greater organizational flexibility, adaptability, and customer orientation to be found in the private sector 'excellence' literature. (Ferlie et al., 1996: 18)

Arguably, this is a continuation of a long-established trend to import US entrepreneurial thinking into the UK (and other OECD countries). Kalmi (2007), for example, tracks how European approaches to economic development and analysis (institutional, firm based and cooperative) have been 'hidden' by the dominance of US textbooks in the educational marketplace. This has occurred despite grassroots economic development in the social economy that runs counter to the doctrines of NPM. Kalmi found that the number of pages given over to cooperative economics in textbooks fell in the post-war period even though the size and scale of cooperative business activity have continued to increase (see also Holmstrom, 1993; Jensen, 2006).

Local socialism

Chandler (2008) highlights the dichotomous reaction of local and central government politicians to NPM doctrines. While NPM became embedded in the political agendas of both Margaret Thatcher (Conservative Party) and Neil Kinnock (Labour Party), the 1980s also bore witness to socialist politicians winning control of large urban councils and establishing economic development units to challenge the philosophical orientation of central government. As Chandler argues:

> Local socialist authorities had ... the common characteristic that they were prepared to challenge the decline of their services and the Government that had created the malaise. Although politically a passing phase, **local socialism** has left a valuable legacy. Economic development was put on the menu of central local authority functions ... Sheffield established the first council sub-committee dedicated to economic redevelopment, while the GLC under Livingstone created a Greater London Enterprise Board to preferentially fund cooperative business start-ups. (2008: 249)

Where these initiatives and policies garnered popular support (particularly within London and Liverpool), they were marginalised by the elites of both mainstream parties. Margaret Thatcher abolished the **Greater London Council** precisely because it became so popular under the leadership of Ken Livingstone (Livingstone, 1988). In Liverpool, the Labour leadership used allegations that the Militant group had created a 'party within a party' to exclude young university educated politicians who followed Marxian rather than Fabian socialist principles (Cliff and Gluckstein, 1988).

In hindsight, it is not surprising that well-established social enterprise networks (in London, Liverpool and Manchester) surfaced where there were strong community development networks during the 1980s. Although their radicalism moderated when **New Labour** came to power, Chandler (2008) argues that local agencies were an important influence on political commitments to decentralise and devolve government to national parliaments, and establish regional development agencies throughout England, Wales, Scotland and Northern Ireland. A further shift towards social enterprise rhetoric appears in the form of a 'triple bottom line':

> in contrast to the ideas of the preceding Conservative administrations, the enabling role [of the state] was not to be simply a residual activity distributing contracts to private sector services but would involve strategic leadership for the locality, and to that end local governments were given in the Local Government Act, 2000, the duty to promote the economic, social and environmental well-being of their communities. (2008: 289)

Advances in Employee and Community Ownership

Friedman's (1962) advocacy of freedom and choice stimulated a new attitude to entrepreneurship generally, but his views were oriented towards a consumer-led, not producer-led, economy. Despite making some persuasive arguments that a vibrant market economy punishes producers who adopt discriminatory practices (see Chapter 4), Friedman's rhetoric changes dramatically when talking of the relationship between the workforce, senior managers and shareholders. In this matter, he continued to advocate that the workforce (at all levels) should be subservient to the goal of maximising profit for shareholders. While some concessions might be made to workers to align their sympathies with investors (through share ownership), Friedman (2003) argued against corporate social responsibility to any group other than shareholders.

Forms of organisation that allocated capital to worker-investors gained support after World War I. Amongst American and Australian thinkers, democratisation of the workplace was put forward as a coherent and necessary approach to limit the influence of institutional shareholders (see Ellerman, 1990; 1997; 2005; Gates, 1998; Turnbull, 1995; 2002). Gates (1998) describes a period during the 1920s and 1930s when US conceptions of business ownership came under sustained attack from the state governor Huey Long. In the early 1930s Long was elected to the Senate and gave radio speeches that proposed limits on personal wealth together with a redistribution of wealth and ownership. With the US in the grip of depression, Long received the mass support required to organise a presidential challenge to Roosevelt. In 1935 he was assassinated. His legacy, however, continued through his son Russell who entered the Senate and worked on influential finance committees with Louis Kelso to establish the legality of employee share ownership plans (ESOPs).

By the late 1980s the ESOP was introduced to the UK and, by 2000, 80 per cent of the top 100 **FTSE** companies had established them. Tens of millions of employees in the UK/US now hold shares in their own company (**ESOC**, 2000). However, as Melman (2001) discusses, despite Thatcherite rhetoric that share ownership would increase individuals' control over their own destiny, these changes made little impact on the lives of workers or corporate practice in the majority of cases. Shares did not confer any control rights; they made little difference to the pattern of worker layoffs, profitability or organisation except in cases of majority employee ownership.

Meanwhile, in Europe, cooperative companies networked successfully and started to outperform their private sector counterparts. In parts of northern Spain and Italy, local economies became dominated by cooperative networks of industrial companies, retailers, schools and universities. These have been linked to positive health outcomes and increased life expectancy (Erdal, 2000). The **MCC** in Spain (see Case 2.3) provides an example of sustained economic and social development based on cooperative principles. Notable innovations are the rejection of the employer/employee relationship (Ellerman, 1990) and the distribution of power to separate governing bodies representing staff, manager and owner interests (see Whyte and Whyte, 1991; Turnbull, 1995; 2002).

The significance of these developments is twofold. Firstly, US ESOPs established pluralist models of ownership where the legitimacy of worker ownership (either individually, collectively or a mix) is accepted alongside arrangements for external investors. Secondly, the cooperative movement shifted towards ownership models that recognise suppliers, consumers and workers as 'strategic stakeholders' (Turnbull, 2002) coordinated through pluralist forms of corporate control.

Expanding a theme propounded by Ellerman (1990), Major (1996) argued that ownership and control are not inextricably linked. They can be separated through different classes of share: voting shares and value added shares. This approach, however, has proved less enduring than one promoted by the Baxi Partnership (see Erdal, 2008: Chapter 17). Based on US-style leveraged employee buyouts (Rodrick, 2005), private sector companies or common ownership cooperatives are converted to majority employee-owned companies.

Major (1996; 1998) has researched the problems faced by coops and ESOPs in the USA and contends that most suffer from 'equity degeneration' – a situation where one or more stakeholders is unable to realise the full value of their past efforts, risk taking, investments and decisions. To overcome this, organisations typically have to sell equity on the open market to obtain full value for employee shareholders. For example, Eaga plc, a public sector spinout that seeks to end fuel poverty (see Case 2.2), changed itself from a company wholly owned by an employee trust to a plc that permits external investors to buy a minority stake, and managers to buy their own shares. The perceived danger of this approach is that 'social ownership' is eroded and replaced by private ownership, as happened to the UK building societies that demutualised in the 1980s and 1990s (see Cook et al., 2002).

Case 2.2   Eaga plc: a new model for public service delivery

Eaga plc was formed from a public sector spinoff involving five members of staff who wanted to create an information and advice service for fuel poverty. Initially the company was structured as a company limited by guarantee (CLG), but in 2000 it decided to switch to the model of ownership and control used by the John Lewis Partnership (based on an employee benefit trust). During this period, the company secured public sector contracts and grew to 4000 staff. In 2006 the organisation decided that it needed to diversify to reduce dependence on public sector contracts. By floating on the stock exchange, with 51 per cent of shares remaining in the hands of the employee trust and its managers, it secured the finance to establish new operations in India and Canada.

In addition to its original public service goal – to reduce environmental mismanagement and address issues of fuel poverty – the company uses a Partners' Council to discuss personnel issues, company performance and communication with the executive board. In 1993 it also set up the Eaga Partnership Charitable Trust which draws income from the trading organisation and has invested £3million in projects and research to develop knowledge about fuel poverty.

Source: http://www.employeeownership.co.uk/case-studies.htm#EagaPartnership

Baxi's approach is to use a profitable track record and growing asset base to secure loans that establish a charitable or employee benefit trust (EBT) which can acquire the business (see Spear, 1999). In such an arrangement, most (or all) of the shares are initially held in trust. Subsequent annual surpluses are used to buy the shares and distribute them to individual share accounts. In some cases (e.g. Scott Bader: see Case 1.2), a charitable rather than employee trust owns the company, and staff bonuses are matched by contributions to charitable projects (Paton, 2003). Providing 50 per cent (+1) of shares with control rights remain in trust, and there is an embedded mechanism issuing new shares to individual member accounts, a profitable company cannot be acquired by outside investors against the wishes of the workforce. However, the protection of 'social ownership' as the dominant model depends on **Mondragón**-type democratic controls (see Case 2.3) that prevent a management group takeover (see Ridley-Duff, 2010).

Cooperative Transformation of the Private Sector

The growth of worker cooperatives and employee-owned businesses highlights a new phenomenon. The social enterprise movement has developed an approach to acquiring private companies and transforming them into enterprises that bear the characteristics of social economy organisations, rather than private companies or public authorities. The journal extract in Case 2.3 is based on previously unpublished findings from a study involving a field trip to Spain (Ridley-Duff, 2005). This describes a meeting with Mikel Lezamiz, the director of the Mondragón Management School, in which he talks about the process of acquiring private companies:

Case 2.3   The Mondragón Cooperative Corporation (MCC)

A longer teaching case and exercise can be found at the accompanying website at www.sagepub.co.uk/ridleyduff.

The Mondragón Cooperative Corporation (MCC) was established in the late 1950s by a priest and five engineers after they were denied the opportunity to invest in the company that employed them. In 2003 the United Nations celebrated the social and economic achievements of the corporation they created. By 2009 this had grown to over 100,000 staff, with over 80 per cent of ownership by staff on the basis of one person, one vote. During a field trip, Mikel Lezamiz – the director of the Management School in Mondragón – described how staff in the MCC work with staff in a newly acquired company to transform it into a cooperative. He discusses this as a gradual transition:

1   a move from private to employee ownership
2   a shift from employee ownership to participative management etc.
3   the introduction of cooperative management (elected councils)
4   a vote to transfer the business into cooperative ownership

Employee ownership is seen only as the start of a much longer process. The main goal is cooperative management and ownership (which can take many years to achieve). As an example, he talked about eDesa, a company the local council asked MCC to buy (to save 1000 jobs). It took from 1989 to 1994 to educate and prepare the workforce to take a vote on their own future. In 1994, the workforce voted by 87 per cent to 13 per cent to convert to a coop (via a vote in a General Assembly). At eDesa, the reaction of trade unions was interesting. Two were supportive; two were sceptical but eventually came around. With the backing of all four unions, the company eventually converted to a cooperative. Even now the unions still have an 'ambiguous' attitude to the MCC. Nevertheless, many union members (about 100 people) are active in disseminating information on the values and principles of the cooperative.

Source: Journal transcript, 6 March 2003, Mondragón Cooperative Corporation

Mikel Lezamiz contended that it can take between five and 10 years before a workforce develops the readiness to completely take over both ownership and control of their enterprise (i.e. embed cooperative management into an organisation, and then convert to a cooperative legal form). Interestingly, he distinguished the progression process as: *employee ownership* (financial participation); *participative management* (the introduction of soft **HRM** practices); *cooperative management* (putting in place elected governing and social councils to take decisions outside the executive management group); and *cooperative ownership* (transferring assets and membership to a cooperative legal entity). At Mondragón, development involves a close relationship with the Caja Laboral Popular (Bank of the People's Labour). A *contract of association* setting out the governance arrangements for the cooperative is needed before the bank provides financial support and ongoing business advice (Turnbull, 2002).

Erdal (2008) confirms the gradual nature of change during transfers to employee ownership. Staff at Loch Fyne Oysters developed their knowledge incrementally as they saw others benefit from the workings of an employee trust. Once they realised they could acquire and trade shares *within* the trust (not publicly), they began to appreciate their value in providing for retirement. One issue (with the potential to corrupt the process) is the speed at which managers grasp the potential advantages of the new arrangements and exploit them for their own advantage. It is for this reason that an external party (in Loch Fyne Oysters' case the Baxi Investment Trust) is advisable to ensure that employees' interests are not subverted by the kind of opportunism noted by Williamson (1989).

These examples raise substantive issues for social enterprise theory. The linking of a charity to a company form does not necessarily involve a fundamental shift in authority relations; both rest on social norms and bodies of law that institute a **unitary** board, top-down authority, and rhetorical injunctions to exclude or limit the involvement of employees in both ownership and governance. The transition to employee ownership and control is a more radical change as it has the potential to restructure authority relations at the level of *class* (Kalmi, 2007). Traditional notions of investor ownership, management control and 'employment' are so deeply embedded in the consciousness of investors, managers and employees that it should not be a surprise that it takes *years* to relinquish and replace them with new ways of thinking. Often, new attitudes cannot be developed without the experience of active participation (or observation) of enterprises that have embedded member ownership and control (Knell, 2008).[2]

It is not only the workforce that takes years to relinquish modes of thought associated with investor-led and hierarchically controlled enterprise. The educational implications for business support staff, academics, accountants, trade unionists, bankers, funders and lawyers are equally substantive. Current course curricula and assessment strategies for professions reinforce dominant approaches to accounting, management, learning and dispute resolution (Johnson, 2003). To support worker (and community) ownership, these ways of thinking may need to be relinquished completely, or substantially modified, to provide effective support (Paton, 2003; Knell, 2008; Ridley-Duff and Bennett, 2009).

Moreover, the expectations that spring from worker ownership, as set out by Ellerman (1990), involve the workforce (as a whole) accepting responsibility for both the assets and the liabilities that accompany ownership and control. While acquiring responsibility for assets (cash, investments, property, equipment etc.) is a psychological barrier relatively easy to overcome, developing the confidence to accept responsibility for *liabilities* is harder (i.e. paying staff, suppliers and creditors, and assuming legal responsibility for the well-being of fellow workers).

The key contribution of Ellerman (1982; 1984; 1990) to the question of *social* enterprise, however, comes from his argument that it is a socialised form of entrepreneurship fostered by personal non-transferable member ownership rights, rather than transferable property rights. It raises the question of whether democratically owned and controlled enterprises are *de facto* social enterprises. This argument is supported by repeated transformations of public *and* private organisations into social enterprises based on personal membership rights (with elected leaders) rather than property rights (with appointed leaders). Examples include Greenwich Leisure (Bibby, undated), Sunderland Home Care Associates (SEC, undated) and School Trends Ltd (Ridley-Duff, 2010), each of which integrated cooperative management and ownership during periods of transformation.

As Ellerman argues:

> The old public/private distinction is supported by both capitalists and state-socialists. The former use it to argue that the idea of democracy is inapplicable to private industry, and the latter use it to argue that democracy can only come to industry by nationalizing it. But both arguments are incorrect, and the public/private distinction itself must be recast. The word 'private' is used in two senses: (1) 'private' in the sense of being non-governmental, and (2) 'private' in the sense of being based on private property. Let us drop the first meaning and retain the second. Similarly 'public' is used in two senses: (1) 'public' in the sense of being governmental, and (2) 'public' in the sense of being based on personal rights. Let us use the second meaning and take it as the definition of 'social' (instead of 'public'). Thus we have the suggested redefinitions:
>
> Social institution   =   based on personal rights
> Private organisation =   based on property rights
>
> By these redefinitions, a democratic firm is a social institution (while still being 'private' in the other sense of being not of the government), while a capitalist corporation is a private firm (not because it is also non-governmental but because it is based on property rights) (1997: 38).

For Ellerman, an enterprise becomes *social* when it rejects private property rights as the sole rationale for participation rights in management and governance.[3] This is aligned with the definition of the social economy (see Chapter 1). Whether an organisation is not-for-profit, non-profit, more-than-profit or for-profit does not enter into the debate. What matters is the *basis on which participation rights are granted*: in a private (economy) enterprise, membership is acquired when investors purchase private property rights; in a social (economy) enterprise, membership is acquired when people are recognised for their labour and trading (consumer) contributions to the sustainability of the enterprise.

Conclusions

In this chapter, we have considered the context in which the public sector has itself become an agent for social entrepreneurship (through enacting the doctrines of NPM) and social enterprise (through the devolution of public service delivery to organisations owned by former public servants). We have also considered the response of 'local socialism' to NPM as a community-based business movement advancing democratic governance and participation rights. Both developments support moves to develop a *social economy*, but are not necessarily or automatically supportive of voluntary and charitable models of service delivery in other parts of the third sector (see Chapter 1).

While the emerging literature on social enterprise is well populated with discussions about the impact of 'business practices' on the voluntary and charity sector (Goerke, 2003; Seanor et al., 2007), another aspect is a long-established argument that 'social enterprise' comprises commercial activity where ownership and control rights are allocated (primarily) to productive labour (Pateman, 1970; Dholakia and Dholakia, 1975; Ellerman, 1982; 1984; 1990). The danger, particularly in an Anglo-American context, is that this older tradition of social enterprise is supplanted by government slogans that reduce it to 'business with a social purpose' (Dart, 2004; Peattie and Morley, 2008). While the ambiguity may broaden its appeal, it risks introducing greater competition over the underlying premises and assumptions that drive social enterprise development.

The debate about the impact of 'business' practices is a salient issue for voluntary and charity organisations converting to social enterprise, but it is less of an issue for cooperatives and employee-owned organisations that have established their market presence and exhibit mature (albeit somewhat different) 'business' practices. The latter are more interested in the nature and quality of the business practices that develop, whether they effectively combat staff alienation, and whether *distributive* mechanisms for social and economic democracy improve the overall quality of life of affected stakeholders (Ridley-Duff, 2008a).

Consequently, advocates of social enterprise to transform the public and private economy (rather than the third sector) focus less on 'social purpose' and more on 'socialisation' of entrepreneurship, ownership, management and trading (Ellerman, 1982; Gates, 1998; Allan, 2005). We considered how this is achieved by the Mondragón Cooperative Corporation, through ending the employment relationship and replacing it with member ownership underpinning participation rights in management and governance (Ellerman, 1990; Turnbull, 1995; Ridley-Duff, 2010).

Taken together, Chapters 1 and 2 review the full range of social, political and economic changes that are contributing to the emergence of social enterprise as both a concept and a form of organisation. Firstly, voluntary organisations and charities are increasing their market orientation and increasing trading activity to generate income for public and community services. Secondly, social economy organisations (particularly cooperatives and mutuals) are finding ways to advance their argument for democratic models of ownership and control. In the public sector, spinouts of services encouraged by NPM are adopting social economy models to deliver public services in a quasi-market. Lastly, well-capitalised social economy organisations are finding ways to buy and transform private enterprises, or bid for public services, through cooperative and charitable models. In the next chapter, we draw together these strands and wrestle with the inevitable difficulty of reaching a consensus on the definition of social enterprise.

 CLASS EXERCISE   The work and writings of David Ellerman

Materials to support this exercise can be found at www.sagepub.co.uk/ridleyduff.

Read the following statement by David Ellerman and discuss the questions that follow:

A capitalist economy within a political democracy can evolve to an economy of economic democracy by extending the principle of democratic self-determination to the workplace. It would be viewed by many as the perfection of capitalism since it replaces the demeaning employer–employee relationship with ownership and co-entrepreneurship for all the workers.

A state socialist economy can evolve into an economic democracy by restructuring itself along the lines of the self-management socialist tradition. It would be viewed by many as the perfection of socialism since the workers would finally become masters of their own destiny in firms organized as free associations of producers. (1997: 108)

1   To what extent is the USA extending the principle of 'democratic self-determination to the workplace' through the widespread use of employee share ownership plans (ESOPs)?
2   To what extent can 'self-management in the socialist tradition' support new forms of community enterprise, self-employment and cooperatives?
3   What factors in the US political and economic system inhibit the development of 'firms organized as free associations of producers' as envisaged by Ellerman?

SUMMARY OF LEARNING

In this chapter, we have argued that:

- The rise of new public management as a supply-side economic policy replaced Keynesianism. This accelerated the trend from public sector to private sector accounting and management practices in some countries.

- The application of NPM in public sector reform resulted in arguments for social entrepreneurship in the development of social services commissioned by public bodies.

- The concept of 'local socialism' arose to resist NPM by stimulating community economic development through local enterprise, fair trade, cooperatives and employee ownership.

- A movement for 'economic democracy' is developing. This was illustrated through discussions of private and public sector transformations to social enterprise in the UK and Spain.

- Restructuring authority relations at the level of class can take 5–10 years because it takes a long time to replace investor-led, hierarchically organised governance with worker-led democratic governance.

- *Social* enterprise extends to a system based on personal (public) rights to participate in enterprise governance based on forming an active relationship (worker and consumer).

QUESTIONS AND POSSIBLE ESSAY ASSIGNMENTS

1 Using examples to illustrate your argument, explain the basis of Ellerman's contention that all democratically controlled businesses are social, rather than private, organisations.
2 'The switch to new public management (NPM) was the principal catalyst for social entrepreneurship in the public sector.' Using examples, discuss the extent to which you agree with this statement.
3 'Social enterprise is primarily about democratising public and private organisations, not transforming charities and voluntary groups into businesses with a social purpose.' Using examples, critically assess this statement.
4 What is the legacy of 'local socialism' to the social enterprise movement?

FURTHER READING

Ellerman's (1997) book *The Democratic Corporation* is now freely downloadable from the internet. This book outlines a clear moral, economic and intellectual justification for worker ownership as the basis of social enterprise. His later text, *Helping People Help Themselves* (2005), captures his work for the World Bank on the importance of self-determination in economic development. For technical discussions (useful to accountants and solicitors) see Rodrick's (2005) book *Leveraged ESOPs and Employee Buyouts,* available from the The National Center for Employee Ownership (in the USA).

A key text to understand how 'economic democracy' is being exported from the US to other parts of the world is Gates' *The*

Ownership Solution (1998). Both Gates' work on legal forms, and Shann Turnbull's work on governance practice, have been an influence on the members of the Employee Ownership Association (EOA) in the UK. The EOA's website contains a series of helpful publications, parliamentary reports and case studies on how to implement 'economic democracy' in the UK (see www. employeeownership.co.uk).

Hood's (1995) paper 'New public management' is a well-argued distillation of the doctrines of NPM as well as its spread amongst OECD countries, while Hebson et al. (2003) consider the issues this created in the public sector. In the UK, the DTI consultation document *Social Enterprise: A Strategy for Success* (2002) and the more recent NHS publication *Social Enterprise – Making a Difference: A Guide to the Right to Request* (2008) provide insights into the link between social enterprise, NPM and public sector reform.

A compelling overview of the business trajectory implied by the themes in this chapter is found in the final chapter of Alec Nove's (1983) book *The Economics of Feasible Socialism*. Despite its age, Nove's discussion about the potentialities and limitations of a society in which worker participation and ownership are the dominant ideology, but where local private enterprise also takes place, resonates well with contemporary debates. For a present-day critical debate about the intersection between 'for-profit' and 'non-profit' views on social enterprise, see 'Social Enterprise as a Socially Rational Business' (Rory Ridley-Duff, 2008a).

We recommend three further articles on the companion website: Curtis' (2008) paper on resistance to new public management, Fawcett and Hanlon's (2009) paper on the 'return to community' and Simmons (2008) account of leisure trusts delivering public services.

Further reading material is available on the companion website at www.sagepub.co.uk/ridleyduff.

USEFUL RESOURCES

The Employee Ownership Association, www.employeeownership.co.uk

David Ellerman, http://www.ellerman.org

Shann Turnbull, http://papers.ssrn.com/sol3/cf_dev/AbsByAuth.cfm?per_id=26239

Baxi Partnership, http://www.baxipartnership. co.uk/

Eaga plc, http://www.eaga.com/

The Mondragón Experiment (BBC Horizon Documentary, 1980), http://video. google.com/videoplay?docid=756558 4850785786404&hl=en

The Mondragón Cooperatives as a Model of Collaborative Business (US speaker returning from Mondragón), http://video.google. com/videoplay?docid=-63485984 61397509798&hl=en

New Public Management, http://en.wikipedia. org/wiki/New_Public_Management

NOTES

1   Organisation for Economic Cooperation and Development.

2   See Chapters 6–9 for teaching cases and discussion on the practical aspects of these debates.

3   In Chapter 7 we discuss in further detail the (legal) property rights defined in the Articles of Association of a company. They can be summarised as rights to: liquidate the company; acquire capital gains; transfer property; derive an income; vote on key decisions; access information; grant public access to information.

Defining Social Enterprise 3

Learning Objectives

In this chapter we debate the concept of social enterprise, drawing on tensions and perspectives from a number of sources. By the end of this chapter you will be able to:

- explain the practical relevance of debates about social enterprise definition

- compare and contrast linear and cross-sector theories of social enterprise

- Identify popular definitions of social enterprise and understand their value commitments

- clarify the potential of social enterprise in different sectors of society.

The key arguments that will be developed in this chapter are:

- There are different ways of understanding social enterprise.
- Social enterprise can be defined in terms of:

  a) balancing economic and social goals
  b) developing social capital
  c) hybrid forms of organisation
  d) the purpose of a project or activity.

- Social enterprise has the potential to develop in all sectors of the economy.
- Social enterprise can develop concurrently in different contexts.

Introduction

Every organisation that self-defines (or is defined by others) as a social enterprise continually engages in a debate about definition that feeds into policies and practices (both internally and externally). Social enterprise advisers in consultancies and infra-structure bodies will be faced regularly with questions as to whether an individual or organisation will qualify for social enterprise support. Every law to regulate social enterprise, every **kitemark** developed to promote it, every strategy devised to support it, also requires engagement with criteria that will influence the legitimacy accorded to individuals and organisations. The definition of a social enterprise, therefore, is not an abstract intellectual exercise: it is a dynamic process engaged with on a daily basis by people deciding how to develop the identity of their enterprise, what the rules for economic support are and how far 'those rules can be bent'.

In Chapters 1 and 2 we explored the third, public and private sector contexts that have influenced the emergence of social enterprise. These historical analyses make explicit the political interests and power struggles that shape their emergence. Internationally, the meaning of social enterprise can differ (Kerlin, 2006). This can give rise to differences not only in regional development, but also in the bodies of knowledge that receive recognition and institutional legitimacy (Dart, 2004). Peattie and Morley (2008) warn that the nature, role and traditions informing the development of social enterprise are different between the United States and UK.

Initially, we use well-publicised descriptions of social enterprise to illustrate different approaches. These are critiqued on the basis that social enterprise can be better understood as a spectrum of options that give varying emphasis to social mission and enterprise activity. The idea of a spectrum, however, is also limited as it obscures public sector involvement and wider environmental issues. To address this, cross-sector models have emerged to conceptualise social enterprises as capacity building organisations that assist economic regeneration, and which enable the state to devolve the delivery of public services. In this case, the ability to build social capital and bridge differences between the public, private and third sectors is perceived to give them a unique character. Lastly, social enterprise is discussed from the perspective that it is an activity rather than an organisation. In this guise, social enterprises are reconceptualised as products of social entrepreneurship. The chapter closes by contextualising these different perspectives and examining whether there are any defining characteristics.

The Origins of the Language of Social Enterprise

The terms *social enterprise* and social entrepreneurship have various historical points of reference. Banks (1972) applied the term 'social entrepreneur' to Robert Owen, widely credited as the philanthropist who pioneered cooperative communities in the 1820s. In the US, Etzioni (1973) described the space for social entrepreneurship as a 'third alternative' between state and marketplace with the power to reform society. We found the term 'social enterprise' first used in Dholakia and Dholakia (1975) to distinguish marketing activities in state and cooperative enterprises from private sector approaches. Westall (2001) claims that another influence was the community business movement who established a magazine called *New Sector* in 1979 to advance social democracy as an alternative to the neoliberalism of Margaret Thatcher (in the UK) and Ronald Reagan (in the USA).

The two terms gained salience in the UK via different international routes. *Social entrepreneurship* was popularised at **ARNOVA** in the USA by Bill Drayton. Throughout the 1980s and 1990s it became associated with international development and fair trade (Grenier, 2006) before appearing, in a 1995 article published by *The Independent*, to describe individuals who founded the UK social entrepreneurial movement (Mawson, 2008). In 1997 the School for Social Entrepreneurs was established, followed quickly by the Community Action Network in 1998 and UnLtd in 2000. UK scholarship received a boost in 2004 when the Skoll Foundation invested in the Skoll Centre for Social Entrepreneurship at Oxford University.

The term *social enterprise*, on the other hand, entered the UK mostly via initiatives in Europe. Ellerman (1982) wrote an article on the 'socialisation' of entrepreneurship in Spanish cooperatives. By 1991, Italy had passed legislation for 'social cooperatives' that combined commercial capability with active promotion of physical, social and mental health. The earliest article discussing 'cooperatives as a social enterprise' appeared two years later (Savio and Righetti, 1993). According to Spear (2008), the experience of the Italian Social Cooperatives was one of the inspirations behind the founding of EMES, the European research network on social enterprise and third sector issues. In 1996 researchers from 13 countries established this network and, with CECOP (a European federation of 'worker cooperatives, and social and participative enterprises') as a partner in their first research project, investigated 'the emergence of social enterprise' in Europe (Borzaga and Defourny, 2001). Although Harvard University in the USA had also used the term during 1993 (for its Social Enterprise Initiative), its approach followed the philanthropic model of commerce rather than the democratic orientation of cooperatives and non-profits highlighted in the EMES study (see Defourny, 2001).

Within the UK, the term 'social enterprise' gained institutional support within the cooperative movement and community regeneration sector (see Cases 3.1 and 3.2). Social Enterprise Europe was founded in 1994 (in the north of England) by consultants developing social audit tools for cooperatives. By late 1997, a coalition of cooperatives and cooperative development agencies had formed Social Enterprise London (see Case 3.1). As regional links developed, a national body – the Social Enterprise Coalition – was created to lobby for cooperatives, social firms, trading charities, community and employee-owned enterprises.

Case 3.1   Social Enterprise London: a founder's story

In 1997, discussions started amongst London cooperatives and their development agencies (CDAs) on creating a new London-wide support agency. We had several discussions in general meetings at Computercraft Ltd, then Phil Cole and I attended the meetings that established the new agency in early 1998. All but one of the founding subscribers had direct links to the cooperative movement. My recollection was that we discussed this as a rebranding exercise. It was by no means clear that we would use the term 'social enterprise' and we discussed various alternatives. I recollect Malcolm Corbett (from the worker cooperative Poptel) acting as chair. He was aware of developments in Europe through his discussions with Pauline Green, an MEP involved in international cooperative development. Malcolm had sway, so we were persuaded. In 2002, the Social Enterprise Coalition (SEC) was formed by Helen Barber (of Cooperatives UK) and John Goodman (a consultant with links to Employee Ownership Solutions Ltd).

The registered office was the Cooperative Union in Manchester. Jonathan Bland, CEO at Social Enterprise London, moved to the **Social Enterprise Coalition,** but not before establishing a degree programme at the University of East London, and securing funding for an academic journal.

Source: based on correspondence with Rory Ridley-Duff

At the end of the 1990s, the Social Exclusion Unit was formed by Tony Blair's 'New Labour' government. This body produced a strategy for 'neighbourhood renewal' in which 'social enterprise' was used to describe community businesses and trading charities oriented toward the needs of socially excluded groups (published 1999, cited in Westall, 2001).

Case 3.2   Coin Street Community Builders (CSCB): from voluntary action to social enterprise

In 1977, the Coin Street Action Group started campaigning to prevent the development of a luxury hotel and office complex on the south side of the River Thames (London). In its place, they drew up plans for mixed use of local land, including housing, a river park, shops, leisure facilities and a walkway. After seven years, and two public inquiries, the developers decided to sell the land to the Greater London Council (GLC), who in turn sold the land to a newly formed company limited by guarantee called Coin Street Community Builders. The case provides an example of a voluntary group making the transition from campaigners into social entrepreneurs, evolving into an incorporated company, diversifying its income generating activities through social purpose commercial activities using a variety of social enterprise forms.

> *The ethos of the CSCB is to create affordable housing, recreational space, workspaces, shopping and leisure facilities, for use by the whole community. Revenue streams are varied. Commercial lets, for example to Harvey Nichols, help to subsidise rents to artists and designers in Oxo Tower Wharf, and for social housing provision. The Wharf itself was refurbished through a mix of bank loans, Housing Corporation and English Partnership grants and CSCB equity. CSCB also established Coin Street Secondary Housing Co-operative as a registered housing association which is creating six housing developments that are being set up as primary tenant-owned housing co-operatives. (Westall, 2001: 5)*

Source: additional material from http://www.coinstreet.org/history_background.aspx

The origins of the language, and the meanings assigned by its advocates, are influenced by experiences in different parts of the third sector as well as public and private initiatives drawn to social enterprise models of ownership and control. One

Table 3.1   Framing the boundaries of the social enterprise debate

EU-style social enterprise	US-style social entrepreneurship
• Collective action	• Individual action
• Labour movement or government responses to social issues	• Entrepreneurial (market) responses to social issues
• Incremental building of **social capital** and assets	• Fast effective achievement of social outcomes
• **Solidarity** and mutuality	• Champions and change agents
• Accommodation of stakeholders	• Adherence to a 'vision'
• Democracy (bottom-up governance)	• Philanthropy (top-down governance)
• Social economy	• Any sector

way of drawing boundaries around the definitional debate is to outline the foci of EU and US traditions. Whilst cautioning against stereotypes, Table 3.1 summarises the dominant narratives at the boundaries of the definitional debate.

US-style 'social entrepreneurship' has strong links with philanthropy, whereby money raised from wealthy individuals and government grants supports 'non-profit' organisations that act in the *public interest* (Dees, 1998). Its individual and philanthropic character is evident in definitional work at Stanford Institute:

> the social entrepreneur's value proposition targets an underserved, neglected, or highly disadvantaged population that lacks the financial means or political clout to achieve the transformative benefit on its own. (Martin and Osberg, 2007: 35)

The emphasis is on solutions *brought to* the poor by a visionary individual, whereas EU-style 'social enterprise' draws more on voluntary action, self-help and cooperative principles derived from secular and Christian socialist traditions (Amin et al., 2002). Communitarian sentiments embedded in Islamic banking and business practices (Gates, 1998) and the kibbutz movement amongst Jewish communities (Melman, 2001) represent significant non-Christian traditions. In all these cases there is a challenge to the authority-driven model based on individual entrepreneurship – a challenge rooted in a stronger voice for collective models of management and ownership.

Westall captures the two dominant approaches in the UK when she comments:

> This history of the 'third sector' organisations in the UK is in some ways the history of two alternative strands – that of self-help (mutuals and cooperatives) and of charities where the paradigm, at least historically, is more related to helping others unable to help themselves. (2001: 24)

This dual history persists to this day (see Case 3.3) but we will argue that a simple dualism is no longer adequate as a theoretical framework for social enterprise. Westall (2001: 24) proceeds to argue that social entrepreneurs seek to 'break free of historical baggage', so a distinction based on third sector traditions is 'no longer tenable'. As practices change, so legal frameworks and social institutions have come under increasing pressure to adapt to a new multi-stakeholder perspective (see Chapter 7).

Case 3.3   The Grameen Foundation

In 1976, Muhammad Yunus returned from abroad to teach economics in Bangladesh. Deeply affected by the poverty he could see from his classroom window, he went out into the streets and talked to women struggling to escape loan sharks. Using the money in his pocket, community networks rather than material assets to provide security ('mutual guarantee groups'), and interpersonal trust rather than property-based collateral, he established a micro-finance organisation that now serves 6 million people.

Muhammad Yunus received the Nobel Laureate in January 2008 and in doing so introduced the term *social business* into the business world. In his book *Creating a World without Poverty* (2007), he sets out two perspectives and urges their use in tackling poverty around the world. The first model is a social business that is social-objective driven: in this case, the company's mission is to create a 'non-loss' business that reinvests all profits back into the company. The second model is profit driven, but owned and operated entirely by a disadvantaged group who receive company profits.

Source: http://www.grameenfoundation.org/what_we_do/, accessed 8 October 2008

Now that we have set out where boundaries have been drawn, in the following sections we explore different definitions of social enterprise. We start with descriptions that have attracted attention in policy debates in order to make explicit the perspectives that compete for influence.

Descriptions of Social Enterprise

The four examples in this section have been selected to illustrate different perspectives. In all cases, social enterprises are seen as socially driven organisations with social and/or environmental objectives combined with a strategy for economic sustainability. By comparing the four definitions, different emphases become apparent. We discuss definitions that have appeared in:

1 a Social Audit Toolkit for worker and community cooperatives
2 the EMES European Research Network
3 a consultation by the UK government on the 'community interest company'
4 a report for the Inter-American Development Bank.

The first definition appears in the 1979 edition of Spreckley's Social Audit Toolkit. It is interesting for its adoption of language characteristic of the cooperative movement (Definition 1). Spreckley's definition embraces a **triple bottom line** (personal, environmental and social benefits). These are organised through a worker or community cooperative that subverts the dominant power relationship between capital and labour. The practical issue here is whether the representatives of capital (investors and funders) or those working and benefiting from the enterprise (labour and beneficiaries) have the final say in running the organisation and deciding what to do with financial surpluses and losses. This arrangement is unproblematic if individual members have committed their own money. Issues arise as soon as members go outside the organisation to raise money. In Spreckley's definition, there is a preference that capital, rather than labour, is paid a fixed return. This is, theoretically speaking, the reverse of 'the employer' paying fixed wages to 'employees' then acquiring all residual profits. Instead, capital is 'hired' at a fixed rate of interest (or fixed dividend) and any residual profits go to the workforce or community.

Definition 1

Social enterprise as a cooperative (published 1979)

An enterprise that is owned by those who work in it and/or reside in a given locality, is governed by registered social as well as commercial aims and objectives and run cooperatively may be termed a social enterprise. Traditionally, 'capital hires labour' with the overriding emphasis on making a 'profit' over and above any benefit either to the business itself or the workforce. Contrasted to this is the social enterprise where 'labour hires capital' with the emphasis on personal, environmental and social benefit.

Source: Spreckley, 2008: 4

This definition gives no recognition to social enterprises that are registered as charities and follow the trustee–beneficiary model, nor does it reflect the situation in membership associations that use a mix of paid and unpaid labour to pursue social goals. The definition also takes 'community' to mean people in a local area as opposed to a community of interest: while local focus can be a characteristic of social enterprise, social enterprise does not have to be locally based or small in scale. Lastly, Spreckley's definition gives no recognition to partnerships and multi-stakeholder enterprises involving state and private organisations.

In 1996, a study by the EMES European Research Network set out a series of social and economic characteristics used to select organisations for a pan-European study of social enterprise (Definition 2). The EMES definition has some of the hallmarks of Spreckley's definition, but is less prescriptive about employee ownership and control. Autonomy and entrepreneurial risk taking, combined with social and economic participation, are hallmarks of the EMES definition, but the door is left open for different stakeholders (users, customers, funders, suppliers and employees) to participate in the enterprise. Compared to Definitions 3 and 4, more emphasis is placed on democratic control over production and delivery of goods and services. There is no intrinsic assumption that the organisations be 'businesses' or that they should adopt 'business practices'. As a definition, the researchers and participants found that it was useful, but also that it represented an *ideal*. In practice, organisations fulfilled some or most of these criteria, but rarely all.

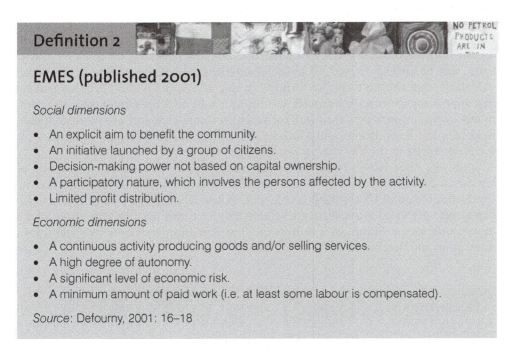

Definition 2

EMES (published 2001)

Social dimensions

- An explicit aim to benefit the community.
- An initiative launched by a group of citizens.
- Decision-making power not based on capital ownership.
- A participatory nature, which involves the persons affected by the activity.
- Limited profit distribution.

Economic dimensions

- A continuous activity producing goods and/or selling services.
- A high degree of autonomy.
- A significant level of economic risk.
- A minimum amount of paid work (i.e. at least some labour is compensated).

Source: Defourny, 2001: 16–18

In 2002, the **Department of Trade and Industry** in the UK published its definition (Definition 3). This definition appears in a strategy document that announced there would be a consultation on a **'community interest company' (CIC)**, a new company form intended as a brand for social enterprise in the UK. Some of the EMES criteria are accepted (benefit to the community, decision-making power not based on capital ownership, limited profit distribution, continuous activity). Others were either explicitly rejected as statutory requirements (participatory nature), left vague (economic risk, autonomy, citizen involvement, minimum amount of paid work), or left unaccounted (such as innovative ways of working).

Definition 3

Department of Trade and Industry (published 2002)

A social enterprise is a business with primarily social objectives whose surpluses are principally reinvested for that purpose in the business or in the community, rather than being driven by the need to maximise profit for shareholders and owners.

Source: DTI, 2002: 7

The UK consultation (DTI, 2002; 2003) set out the thinking that informed CIC legislation. On the one hand, the UK government accepted the merits of leaving social entrepreneurs free to determine organisation structures and levels of participation. On the other hand, it is evident that the government intended its regulator, rather than the organisation's own stakeholders, to have the strongest powers of intervention. In practice, the UK government's loose definition has drawn a great many people and organisations into the debate. Social entrepreneurs, perhaps operating on a self-employed basis, may be viewed as engaged in social enterprise. Similarly, trading charities and voluntary organisations (whether formally democratic or not in their decision-making and appointment processes) as well as a broad range of cooperatives (whether commonly owned or owned by their staff) can all be recognised as part of a national framework. On this basis, Peattie and Morley (2008) draw out two core characteristics for social enterprise in the UK: *trading organisations* that prioritise *social aims*.

In the US, Alter (2007) reviewed a wide range of definitions in the preparation of her *Social Enterprise Typology*. While her definition (Definition 4) is not necessarily representative of all US thinking (see http://www.se-alliance.org), it does reflect two key aspects of the US focus. Firstly, it reflects the more business-like aspirations of the 'non-profit' sector. Secondly, it reflects the desire to adopt private sector 'discipline, innovation and determination'.

Definition 4

Virtue ventures (first published 2003)

A social enterprise is any business venture created for a social purpose – mitigating/reducing a social problem or a market failure – and to generate social value while operating with the financial discipline, innovation and determination of a private sector business.

Source: Alter, 2007

In common with the DTI's definition in the UK, there is no reference to ownership or democratic control as defining characteristics. As a result, there is scope for the inclusion of US-style entrepreneurial solutions as well as EU and ICA (2005) preferences for collective solutions. However, as Rothschild (2009) comments, in the US workers' cooperatives are a 'forgotten' route to social enterprise. One aspect of this definition, absent from all others, is the *direct* focus on solving or mitigating a social problem or a market failure (although this is often taken to be implicit). Alter's definition reflects the focus of 'non-profits' in the USA that run hospitals, schools, colleges, universities and social services more than their UK and EU counterparts. Secondly, in developing economies (where the state is weak) this definition serves to cover those organisations that act as a proxy for the state by providing services that would attract public funding in EU states (Somers, 2007). Nevertheless, Alter's definition remains less sympathetic to employee-owned businesses and cooperatives whose social purpose may be limited to the transformation of trading and workplace relationships, rather than immediately pressing problems of social exclusion, or failure by the market and the state. Lastly, Alter's definition is the only one that explicitly mentions *innovation*. As Perrini argues:

Social enterprise entails innovations designed to explicitly improve societal well-being, housed within entrepreneurial organizations, which initiate, guide or combine change in society. (2006: 24)

The focus on innovation is strongest in the US literature where the value propositions of social entrepreneurs are taken as the driver of social change (Alter, 2007; Martin and Osberg, 2007).

This kind of definitional debate is by no means over. These examples illustrate the democratic and cooperative heritage of European definitions and the entrepreneurial, business-like emphasis of Anglo-American approaches.

CLASS EXERCISE   Defining social enterprise

Materials to support this exercise can be found at www.sagepub.co.uk/ridleyduff.

Divide the class into groups of four and give one social enterprise definition to each person in each group. Members should not show their definitions to other group members.

Scenario

You are attending a directors' development meeting on the topic of social enterprise. Next week, you will brief senior company managers on social enterprise as a way to develop and deliver services. A consultant has researched four definitions but has not been invited to the meeting. Following the consultant's advice, each director has been given one definition to present at this meeting.

In groups (no more than four people per group):

1   Take 5–10 minutes to read the definition and prepare for a 30 minute meeting.
2   Each group member has up to 5 minutes to read their definition and outline the critique.
3   After hearing all four definitions, the group agrees a definition for the briefing of their senior managers (10 minutes).

As a class:

4   Ask each group to read out its final definition.
5   Critically debate issues that may arise if you propose this form of social enterprise to:

   (a) a panel of venture philanthropists (investing in charities and non-profit organisations)
   (b) a panel of business angels (e.g. similar to 'Dragon's Den') wishing to make ethical investments.

Suggestion: you might adapt this exercise by using definitions from local social enterprise support agencies, or national or international bodies that support local development in your area.

Each of the four definitions draws out a different aspect of 'social' and 'enterprise'. As Bull (2006) found, social enterprises position themselves at all points along a continuum (see Figure 3.1). They adopt a variety of arguments to justify their emphasis, and they show varying levels of conviction to particular positions (the larger crosses and the smiley faces indicate greater conviction regarding their position on the spectrum).

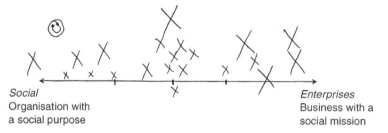

Figure 3.1   Participants positioning themselves on a continuum

'Social purpose' can be *external* (in terms of the products and services offered) or *internal* (transforming social relationships to distribute power and wealth more equitably). 'Economic purpose' is similarly complex, spanning debates about competitiveness in markets, social inclusion, individual empowerment and modernisation of the state (Westall, 2001). In the next section, we explore how theorists have identified points along this continuum.

Social Enterprise as a Spectrum of Options

Social enterprises are often described as *double bottom line* organisations that practise both altruism and commercial discipline. Nyssens (2006) describes this as a process of *hybridisation* that challenges traditional models of organising and produces a cross-fertilisation of ideas. A model by Dees (1998: 60) has been influential in promoting understanding of social enterprise in the 'non-profit' sectors of the USA and the UK where organisations were experiencing falls in charitable giving and government grants. Useful as this theory is for stimulating new conversations in charity, voluntary and community organisations, it does not capture the essence of cooperative and fair trade networks. For example, organisations like Divine Chocolate, Traidcraft, the Mondragón Cooperative Corporation (Spain) and Cooperative Group (UK) have operated in commercial markets from the outset, and also talk of a *triple* bottom line (inclusive of the environment).

Kim Alter (2007) builds on Dees' model to propose a *sustainability spectrum* that describes six gradations between 'traditional non-profit' and 'traditional for-profit' enterprises. She places social enterprise on the 'social sustainability' side, more aligned with traditional 'non-profit' than 'for-profit' enterprises. Given the cooperative and fair trade examples earlier in this chapter (and also Chapters 1 and 2), it is more useful to adapt Alter's model (see Figure 3.2).

Non-profit forms of social enterprise as well as common ownership cooperatives typically take the form of a CLG (company limited by guarantee) that does

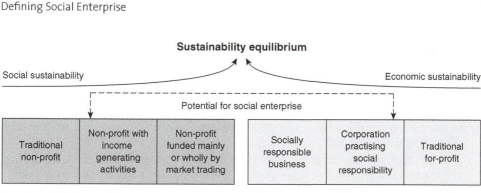

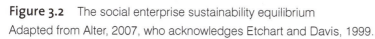

Figure 3.2 The social enterprise sustainability equilibrium
Adapted from Alter, 2007, who acknowledges Etchart and Davis, 1999.

not issue share capital. The assumption is that this will help to retain surpluses for reinvestment and be attractive to philanthropic capital (see Case 3.4). 'More-than-profit' forms of social enterprise (Ridley-Duff, 2008a) tend to be constituted as a CLS (company limited by shares) or an IPS (industrial and provident society). This is the preference of cooperatives and employee-owned enterprises that issue share capital to members of staff and consumers (see Case 3.5). In fair trade companies, such as Divine Chocolate, the form is adapted to distribute surpluses and control rights to stakeholders in the **supply chain** (see Doherty et al., 2009a).

In practice, it is counter-productive to debate whether 'non-profit organisations with trading activities' or 'socially responsible businesses' have greater claim to be social enterprises (see Cases 3.4 and 3.5). Both make significant contributions in different ways. Nevertheless, the granularity of Alter's model makes explicit some of the tension points between advocates of different models. For example, UK policy papers and academic studies sometimes use a minimum of 50 per cent income from *trading* as a benchmark for distinguishing between charities that use trading to supplement income and social enterprises that use trade to pursue their social purpose (Smallbone and Lyon, 2005; RISE, 2008).

Case 3.4   Charity or social enterprise?

Furniture Resource Centre Group is made up of three organisations. The Furniture Resource Centre (FRC) was founded in 1988 as a CLG to enable people on low income to buy furniture. They 'design, manufacture, recycle, refurbish, sell and deliver furniture to people in need and so create work for the jobless and offer long term unemployed people salaried training' (FRC, 2000). In six years, the FRC switched from being a small local charity (£300,000 turnover with 15 staff) to a company generating

£5 million with over 120 employees. Ninety per cent of income is generated through sales of products and services. Grants are only used for particular pieces of work such as building refurbishment. Liam Black, then CEO, stated that 'our financial independence from statutory and charitable trust funding has liberated us. We are masters of our own destiny and we choose where we go and how we do it. Free of funders' handcuffs and the risk averse conservatism of regeneration quangos, we are free to experiment and innovate.'

Liam Black won the 'Social Entrepreneur of the Year' award in 2003. He left FRC in 2004 to manage Fifteen, Jamie Oliver's chain of restaurants. In 2008, after successfully establishing franchises in Holland and Australia, he left to pursue new projects.

This case illustrates the drive within certain types of charitable organisations to make the transition into fully fledged social enterprises.

Source: based on Westall, 2001, and subsequent press reports

Smallbone and Lyon (2005) have criticised restrictive definitions. They argue that early stage social enterprises, or charities increasing their trading activities, often have less than 50 per cent traded income. Should this be used to exclude them from being defined as social enterprises in sector surveys? Should they be refused sector-specific support? However, such an argument ignores that *trading* activity alone does not define a social enterprise (as many community and voluntary organisations are trading organisations, yet fail to exhibit other social enterprise characteristics). Liam Black (see Case 3.4) underlines the *mindset* that trading is a *means* of achieving autonomy, so that an organisation can choose its own destiny, become more entrepreneurial, and increase its social innovation and impact. This constitutes a counter-argument to Smallbone and Lyon (2005) on the basis that social enterprises use trading relationships to transform (social) power and change the pattern of (economic) wealth distribution. If an organisation trades in such a way that it reproduces dependency, or reinforces existing (market) power relations, it has a tenuous claim to being a social enterprise.

Case 3.5   Socially responsible business or social enterprise?

Sunderland Care Home Associates (SCHA) was formed as a successor to the Little Women cooperative in 1994 and was initially constituted as a CLG (common ownership rules) with a £1 share for each of its 20 members. In 1998, 'for both tax and philosophical reasons', the organisation voted to change to an employee-owned model based on a CLS. Initially, just over 50 per cent of shares were held in trust, with the remainder held by the original cooperative. After six share allocations, reflecting business performance and the availability of shares through an internal market, the employee trust held 56.7 per cent of the shares, 16.8 per cent were in employees' own names, and 26.5 per cent remained in the founding cooperative. By 2007, the organisation had a turnover in excess of £2 million and employed 223 staff, of which 85 per cent were women.

Margaret Elliot, the founder, felt that this arrangement would give employees a real, growing stake rather than just a £1 share and that this would 'increase their commitment and help to raise staff retention and the quality of the service we provide'. Staff turnover has been reduced to 3.5 per cent, a full 10 per cent below the industry average. The board consists of five elected employees, the founder and a tax/legal expert. General meetings are held bimonthly, and working parties are created to consider specific issues.

SCHA was rated 'Top Social Enterprise' at the 2006 Enterprising Solutions Awards and has now established Care and Share Associates (CASA) to oversee the replication of its business model to other regions. Margaret Elliot was awarded an OBE in the 2008 UK New Year Honours List.

Sources: Companies House; Fame company database; case study published by the Employee Ownership Association (www.employeeownership.co.uk); press reports

Both Alter (2007) and Dees (1998) locate social enterprise as a hybrid between cooperatives and the voluntary/community sector (compare Defourny, 2001). As such, little attention is given to public sector involvement. This omission can be explained in part by Kerlin's (2006) analysis of the United States and Europe. She notes that the term 'social enterprise' means different things stemming from the national context and the influences driving development. She points out that *social economy* has been slow to gain recognition in the US, nor is there a strong public sector tradition in welfare provision and market intervention. The effect is to understate the influence of local and central government in economic regeneration, a point picked up by Somers (2007) in her theory of public sector social entrepreneurship. She argues that people in the public sector use social entrepreneurship to act as a *modernising agent* (see also Chapter 2). They are creating an environment in which welfare services can be delivered through quasi-markets in social and health care (see Figure 3.3 and Case 3.6). This is a shift away from the *command and control model* of public service delivery towards a *network model* involving a range of public and third sector organisations, including infrastructure bodies stimulating regional development. Ironically, she argues that this constitutes an expansion, not a contraction, of the state, and constitutes a route to 'third way' socialism.

Curtis (2008) has characterised this as *state-sponsored social enterprise* likely to undermine the entrepreneurial spirit and know-how needed to ensure the sustainability of the social economy. Nevertheless, both Somers and Curtis recognise that social enterprise cannot be fully theorised without including state and public sector activity. Under the influence of new public management (see Chapter 2), public servants in developed economies are proactive in creating alternatives to traditional state-run public services.

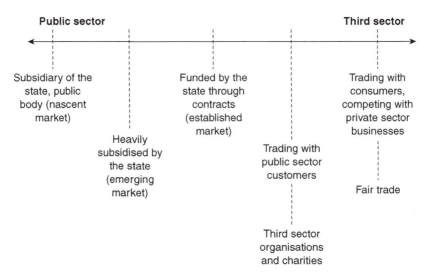

Figure 3.3   The public sector and social entrepreneurial activity

With permission from the author Alter, K. (2007) *Social Enterprise Typology*, www.virtueventures. com/typology (version 1.5, published 27th November 2007).

Case 3.6   Entreprenurses CIC

Established by David Dawes, a former CEO and commissioner in the NHS, and public servant at the Department of Health, Entreprenurses uses the new community interest company (CIC) legislation in the United Kingdom as a vehicle for the 'right to request' a social enterprise.

Entreprenurses is a Community Interest Company which is a type of social enterprise. What that means is we want to change the world and we want to do it in a business-like and entrepreneurial way. Specifically we:

- *Support the growth and development of entrepreneurs (particularly social entrepreneurs and nurse entrepreneurs)*
- *Develop the art and science of nurse entrepreneurship*
- *Encourage the development of social enterprises in health and social care*
- *Improve the delivery of healthcare*

What we want to do is help make the world a better place by improving some of it ourselves but mainly by helping other people improve their bit of the world themselves.

Source: based on http://www.entreprenurses.com/about/about_us.php, accessed 16 October 2008

Finally, what about activity taking place at the boundary of the public and private sectors? As Defourny (2001: 23) acknowledges, 'the [non-profit] literature is not able to embrace the whole reality of the social enterprise'. The realisation that some social enterprises are not ideologically hostile to declaring profits or sharing surpluses has prompted high-profile figures to challenge the sector to adopt a 'more-than-profit' orientation. This is reflected in one of the early definitions used by the Social Enterprise Coalition (SEC):

> A social enterprise is not defined by its legal status but by its nature: its social aims and outcomes; the basis on which its social mission is embedded in its structure and governance; and the way it uses the profits it generates through trading activities. (NEF/ SAS, 2004: 8)

Two parts of this definition open up the concept of social enterprise considerably. Firstly, a social mission can be 'embedded' in structure and **governance**. This recognises the role that organisation structures and culture play in distributing power and wealth and influencing engagement in decision-making (see Grey, 2005). Secondly, there is the issue of how profits are used. The SEC definition recognises that the way profits are distributed, and the practice of making *social* investments (see Chapter 11), differentiates social from private enterprise.

Based on this definition, cooperative enterprises – both majority employee-owned and consumer or multi-stakeholder enterprises that transform patterns of ownership, power and wealth – gain legitimacy as social enterprises. Their products and services may be indistinguishable from those produced by others, and may be sold at market rates. This is, however, to miss the point. Trading is the *means* by which a different social mission is achieved (see Gates, 1998; Allan, 2005; Brown, 2006). As Gates argues, a combination of investor, worker and consumer ownership can alter management practices:

> 'Inside' ownership improves performance both directly (by encouraging insider challenges to poorly conceived management decisions) and indirectly – by influencing managers who know that the firm's owners are now working amongst them. Similarly, by including a component of consumer ownership, the utility's managers (and their families) would live among shareholders who are also neighbors, schoolmates and teammates. Such a community-focused ownership stake could change the quality of business relationships. (1998: 13)

Large mainstream businesses, and not just those currently identified as part of the social enterprise sector, can lay some claim to effective stakeholder involvement, commitment to diversity, and practices that address social exclusion (see Case 3.7). How then should we theorise their contribution to social enterprise? Does this further compromise the concept of 'social enterprise'? Our view is that it does not. Rather, it invites a fuller consideration of a third axis that spans the public and private sector. As we discussed in Case 3.5 (Sunderland Care Home Associates), social enterprises can switch away from (rather than embrace) common ownership to pursue a social purpose and increase their social impact. For this reason, a third axis is needed that theorises how public and private sector support creates further opportunities for social enterprise (see Figure 3.4).

Case 3.7 Corporate social responsibility or social enterprise? Merck and the Mectizan drug project

Merck elected to develop and give away Mectizan, a drug to cure 'river blindness', a disease that infected over a million people in the Third World with parasitic worms that swarmed through body tissue and eventually into the eyes, causing painful blindness. A million customers is a good-sized market, except that these were customers who could not afford the product. Knowing that the project would not produce a large return on investment – if it produced one at all – the company nonetheless went forward with the hope that some government agencies or other third parties would purchase and distribute the product once available. No such luck, so Merck elected to establish a trust to give the drug away free to all who needed it ... at its own expense. When asked why the company had pursued the project despite the possibility of making a financial loss, senior executives said that they saw it as important to maintain the morale of their scientists.

Source: adapted from Collins and Porras, 2000

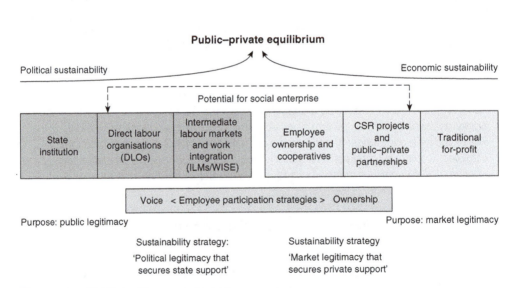

Figure 3.4   Public legitimacy and private support

A three-dimensional, rather than two-dimensional, theory of social enterprise leads us now into a consideration of social enterprise as a cross-sector phenomenon.

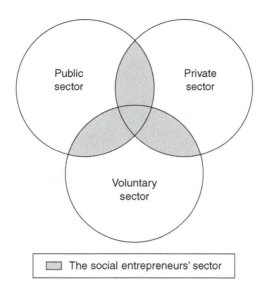

Figure 3.5   Cross-sector social entrepreneurship that creates social capital

Reproduced with permission of Demos (www.demos.co.uk). Leadbeater, C. (1997) *The Rise of the Social Entrepreneur*, London: Demos.

Cross-Sector Models of Social Enterprise and Social Capital

In 1997, Leadbeater used a cross-sectoral model to theorise how social entrepreneurs acquire their skills and outlook (see Figure 3.5). Initially, when social enterprise theory was focused on a continuum between the voluntary and the private sector, Leadbeater's view of social entrepreneurship stood in contradiction to social enterprise theory. By acknowledging the potential for social enterprise in the public and private sectors, cross-sector models offer a way to reconcile social entrepreneurship and social enterprise theory. In cross-sector models, social enterprise is seen as a way of bridging sectors by integrating the skills and abilities of statutory providers, private businesses and voluntary organisations. In short, social enterprise creates bridging *social capital* between economic sectors (see Chapter 4).

As Birch and Whittam argue, social entrepreneurship is a process that catalyses cooperation between parties who would normally avoid each other:

> Thus, in relation to social capital, the activity of social enterprise has two major functions in regional development. First is the binding of different groups together in a network, both within specific places such as local communities and, more broadly, at the regional and national scale. Second is the linking of diverse and often disparate normative frameworks (e.g. mutualism and profit-seeking) and structures (e.g. social firms and private companies), which produces new insights and resources through inter-group learning. (2008: 443)

Billis (1993) argued that the three worlds each have their own culture and rules for workplace organisation: they accommodate and establish different governance systems, employment practices and value systems. Seanor and Meaton (2008) argue

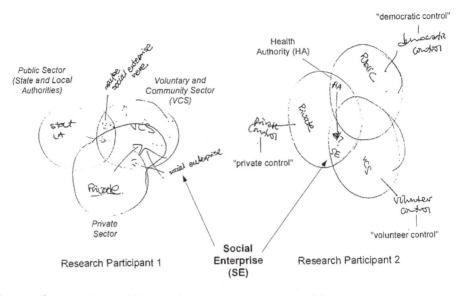

Figure 3.6   Locating social enterprise on a cross-sector model

that social enterprises can benefit from this ambiguity by managing their uncertain identity and tapping into several streams of support and funding. Moreover, they can develop hybrid organisations that serve multiple interests. Seanor, in presenting research findings to a seminar (Seanor and Meaton, 2006), suggested that social enterprises are located at the crossover points between the three worlds. At the suggestion of one of her participants, Seanor independently took Billis' model into a period of fieldwork and allowed participants to locate their organisation on the diagram.

Two examples are shown in Figure 3.6. On the left side, the research participant locates social enterprise between the state and the 'voluntary and community sector' (VCS) as well as between the private and voluntary sectors. Interestingly, they also regarded social enterprise as having a negative and invasive effect (as a form of private enterprise moving into the voluntary sector): hence the expanded boundary area between the two. On the right side of the figure, the participant sees a link between activity in health authorities (HA) between the public and private sectors and a shift in the delivery of health services to social enterprises located between the private and voluntary sectors. In other cases – not shown here, but reported in Seanor et al. (2007) – participants drew arrows *across* the boundaries of the sectors to illustrate the advance of public and private sectors into the voluntary sector, or from the voluntary sector into the private sector.

Cross-sector theories take a different position from Defourny (2001) and Pearce (2003). Instead of social enterprises occupying a space in the social economy between non-profit and for-profit businesses, they are regarded as a type developing in all sectors and which may take many forms: charity trading, social firms, social responsibility projects, public–private partnerships, cooperatives, mutual societies and employee-owned businesses. Figure 3.7 combines the three social enterprise spectra of Figures 3.2, 3.3 and 3.4 to clarify a triangle of activity within which social enterprises may operate.

The advantage of placing social enterprise within a 'lumpy' landscape (Aitken, 2006) is that cross-sector models promote an understanding of the ambiguity, origins and ethos of social enterprise activity (Spear et al., 2007). They provide a

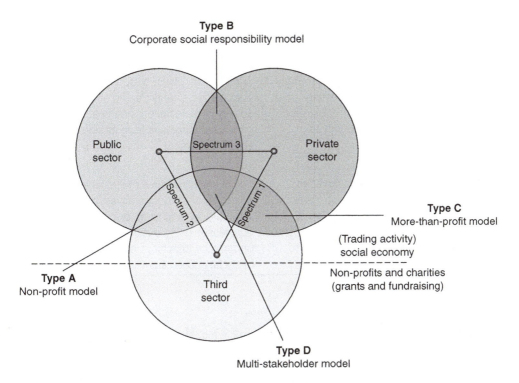

Figure 3.7   A composite theory: the triangle of social enterprise

mechanism for understanding diversity based on alliances and hybrid organisations that vary in the extent they embrace the values of other sectors. This theoretical perspective was used by Ridley-Duff (2008a) to account for the different approaches to social enterprise and the variety of legal forms and governance practices that are adopted (Table 3.2).

Table 3.2   A social enterprise typology

Type A: Non-profit model	
In the boundary areas of the public and third sectors. Shares a 'public interest' outlook and hostility to private sector ownership and equity finance	Social enterprise as a 'non-profit' organisation: obtains grants and/or contracts from public sector bodies and other third sector organisations; structured to prevent profit and asset transfers except to other non-profit organisations
Type B: Corporate social responsibility model	
In the boundary areas of the public and private sectors. Suspicious of the third sector as a viable partner in public service delivery and economic development	Social enterprise as a corporate social responsibility project: environmental, ethical or fair trade business; 'for-profit' employee-owned business; public/private joint venture or partnership with social aims

(Continued)

Table 3.2   *(Continued)*

Type C: More-than-profit model	
In the boundary areas of the private and third sectors. Antipathy to the state (central government) as a vehicle for meeting the needs of disadvantaged groups, and realistic about the state's capacity to oppress minorities	Social enterprise as a 'more-than-profit' organisation: single or dual stakeholder cooperative, charity trading arm, membership society or association, or a trust that generates surpluses from trading to increase social investment
Type D: Multi-stakeholder model (ideal type)	
At the overlap of all sectors. It replaces public, private and third sector competition with a democratic multi-stakeholder model. All interests in a supply chain are acknowledged to break down barriers to social change	Social enterprise as a multi-stakeholder enterprise: new cooperatives, charities, voluntary organisations or co-owned businesses using direct and representative democracy to achieve equitable distribution of social and economic benefits

Source: adapted from Ridley-Duff, 2008a

Nyssens captures the essence of this outlook when she comments:

> we argue that social enterprises mix the economic principles of market, redistribution and reciprocity, and hybridize their three types of economic exchange so that they work together rather than in isolation from each other. (2006: 318)

Even though cross-sector models address the theoretical weaknesses of two-dimensional spectra, they do not, on their own, provide the same level of detail or insight into practice. Both spectra and cross-sector models are needed to capture the micro and macro aspects of social enterprise theory.

SEMINAR EXERCISE   Analysing the nature of social enterprise

Materials to support this exercise can be found at www.sagepub.co.uk/ridleyduff.

On your own, choose five organisations that you believe 'break the mould' in terms of contributing to environmental, social or economic sustainability. Using a cross-sectoral model of the economy, write the names of the organisations you have listed onto the appropriate part of the diagram. Add notes to explain your choices.

Pair up with another person. Compare your diagrams. If any organisations are unknown to the other person, explain why you selected them and how they 'break the mould'. Debate with each other your reasons for selecting these organisations, and discuss whether they are, or are not, social enterprises.

Find another partner, compare diagrams, and have another discussion.

In the next section, we consider the view that social enterprise is an activity, rather than an organisational form or embryonic socio-economic system. As such, it is to be found in different sectors, but will not be a sector of its own. This perspective links to the idea that social enterprise is a process rather than an outcome, a way of organising the supply of goods and services rather than an account or a description of new organisational forms.

Social Enterprise as an Activity

So far, social enterprise has been represented as a business movement rooted in the concept of *social rationality*. This emphasises economic activity as a means of sustaining and developing relationships, rather than for the sake of completing tasks and missions (Ridley-Duff, 2008a). This view, however, is now being questioned by those who want to use the relationship building capabilities of the social enterprise instrumentally, and frame it as an activity rather than an organisational form. Their argument is closer to US conceptions of social entrepreneurship, in which 'business practices' improve the efficiency and effectiveness of mission-driven 'projects'.

> This conceptualization makes social enterprise distinct from the common definition used by the Department of Trade and Industry (DTI), which covers an array of different organizations with distinct and sometimes disparate objectives (e.g. charity and workers cooperative) ... Therefore, it is more useful to argue that social enterprise concerns the pursuit of particular activities rather than representing certain social forms (e.g. cooperatives, democratically run organizations) with the aim of producing collective benefits (Laville and Nyssens, 2001). Birch and Whittam (2008: 439–44)

More 'useful' to whom? The switch to 'activities' is useful for the purposes of public administration: social enterprises can be started to meet public sector goals (and shut down if they do not). There is evidence of a similar view in the charity sector. As Morgan argues:

> Social enterprise is *not*, in my view, a type of organisation, it is a type of *activity*, where a trading venture is undertaken primarily with a social aim: such as running a community bus, or providing employment for people with special needs. Social enterprise activities can be undertaken in *any* of the three sectors. (2008: 2)

A possible reason for framing social enterprise *as an activity* is that it suits those who want to use social enterprises for 'project management'. This *instrumental* view (that social enterprise trading entities can be set up to achieve public, charitable and CSR objectives) requires an *anti*-democratic argument regarding ownership and control. If social enterprises are constituted as democratic enterprises, their 'parent' organisations will not be able to dissolve them if they achieve social and economic viability and (democratically) change their social or economic priorities. To be controllable, social enterprises must *not* be democratically constituted or able to make decisions autonomously. This brings back into focus how the 'social' is theorised in definitions of social enterprise. Regarding social enterprise as an activity is based on a different perspective on what it is to be 'social', and a different political argument to the creation of a sustainable cooperative economy (Woodin, 2007; Ridley-Duff, 2008a), vibrant civil society (Edwards, 2004) or financially independent voluntary sector (Coule, 2008).

There are, however, some practical advantages to viewing social enterprise as an activity. It would, for example, be liberating to fund social enterprise 'activities' without having to insist that the recipient incorporates as an organisation, or adopts a specific legal form.[1] Moreover, there may be political advantage to the public and private sectors in reframing their own social entrepreneurial activities as worthy of receiving funding earmarked for social enterprises.

A danger, however, lurks in uncritically accepting the reframing of social enterprise as a way of 'healing' an *existing* system, and not promoting an alternative economic system. From a critical perspective (Alvesson and Deetz, 2000), the 'activity' debate sounds like a rhetorical ploy aimed at obfuscating and neutralising the threat of social enterprise by characterising it as a helpful, even benign addition, rather than a pattern-breaking process that acts as a catalyst for social change (dare we suggest *radical* social change!).

The fatal flaw in the 'activity' argument comes from the frequency with which 'activities' evolve into institutional forms. Whenever they do, questions arise regarding governance, liability, power, ownership, control and managerial authority that have to be resolved both on paper and in practice (see Table 3.3). Social enterprise, therefore, may be an activity and a process, but it also has to decide upon form (Spear, 2006; Bull, 2008). As Spear argues, this issue is resolved by accepting that social enterprises (forms) are the product of social entrepreneurship (process) and that social entrepreneurship is more than a product of trading (or raising funds to support charitable giving in support of public sector priorities).

Table 3.3   Laws passed in Europe to support social enterprise development

1991	Italy	Social Co-operatives Law
1993	Spain	Social Initiative Co-operatives (regional laws start to be introduced in 12 regions)
1995	Belgium	Social Finality Enterprise Law
1996	Portugal	Social Solidarity Co-operative Code
1998	Portugal	Social Solidarity Co-operative (legislative decree)
1999	Spain	Social Initiative Co-operative (national law)
2001	France	Collective Interest Cooperative Society (SCIC)
2004	Finland	Social Enterprise Law
2004	United Kingdom	Community Interest Company (CIC)
2005	Italy	Social Enterprise Law
2006	Italy	Social Enterprise Law Decree
2006	Poland	Social Cooperative Law

Source: CECOP, 2006

Conclusions

Dees (1998) suggests that because of the complex structure of social enterprises, and variance in their definition, any generalisations are problematic. There is no single, agreed set of words that clearly defines social enterprise. Such debate is inevitable, not only because many parties are competing to influence the definitions that are used on the ground, but also because it takes time for a social movement to learn which forms and activities work sufficiently well in practice to warrant institutional support.

Private enterprise is expressed through many forms of activity – self-employment, partnerships, limited liability partnerships, unincorporated companies, limited liability companies, public limited companies – some of which may in turn be owned by other companies, trusts, charities, cooperatives or governments. Although the limited liability company has become the most popular form of private enterprise, it took 150 years for joint-stock companies (originally established for groups of 20 or more people) to replace partnerships, chartered corporations and trusts as the dominant institution of the private sector (Davies, 2002). It may take another 150 years before generations of social entrepreneurs express their preferences consistently and the definitional debate will undoubtedly continue to evolve.

While some perceive the lack of a single (simple) definition as problematic for the development of the sector (see Pearce, 2003), we view the 'blurred' nature of the concept as accurately reflecting the political battles over control of a new business concept (Light, 2006). The question, therefore, is how 'wide' or 'narrow' the definition should be for the purposes of promotion and support. Paton (2003), for example, claims that 'social enterprise' is a more meaningful and accessible term than 'third sector' and 'voluntary sector' that provides a way to talk about any enterprise where people 'are not in it for the money'. Pearce, however, does not like the 'vagueness' of existing definitions, and calls for 'a clear and unambiguous understanding of what social enterprises are' (2003: 31). He gives two reasons: firstly, there is a need to differentiate social enterprise from other systems by establishing their unique selling point (USP); secondly, there is a need to establish what is *not* a social enterprise.

We find the cross-sector analysis and conception of social enterprise the most useful for future debates. We believe there is a nascent ideology – distinct and different – at the centre of the three-sector model that bodes the arrival of a broad social movement (see Social Enterprise Alliance, http://www.se-alliance.org/). *Here the 'defining characteristic' is a combination of characteristics: value-driven entrepreneurship combined with social democratic awareness that actively manages tensions between private, environmental and social interests at both enterprise and institutional levels.* This locates social enterprise in the social economy rather than in the 'third' sector (which presumably lags behind the 'first' and 'second' sectors even through predating them both historically).

Over the longer term, social enterprise will be determined not by theorists but by social practices and institutions that are associated with, and labelled as, social enterprises. The role of the theorist is to provide frameworks that are adequate for the purposes of making practices and organisational forms intelligible and accessible for discussion. While this chapter provides a number of lenses through which to understand social enterprise, the choices that matter will be made by those who self-consciously pursue sustainable ways of creating social, environmental and economic value.

SUMMARY OF LEARNING

■ Different meanings are attached to social enterprise in the American non-profit sector, UK third sector, European social economy and international cooperative movement.

■ Social enterprises transcend traditional sector boundaries and have the potential to form a *social economy*
with distinct characteristics and language.

■ Models and diagrams can help to describe and explain the boundaries of the social economy, and its link to other economic sectors.

■ Social enterprise is a useful umbrella terms for any (democratic) organisational form or activity where 'people are not in it for the money' but still generate a financial surplus.

■ Social enterprise can be seen as a 'fix' for the ills and addictions of a capitalist system, or as a social democratic movement intent on transforming economic and social relationships.

QUESTIONS AND POSSIBLE ESSAY ASSIGNMENTS

1   'Social enterprise concerns the pursuit of particular activities rather than ... the democratic transformation of trading organisations'. Critically discuss the limitation of this perspective.

2   Compare and contrast Pearce's three-system model, and the position of social enterprises within it, with other theoretical perspectives on social enterprise. To what extent is social enterprise a cross-sector phenomenon?

3   Critically assess the DTI definition of social enterprise in relation to US and European perspectives on social entrepreneurship.

FURTHER READING

There are some good texts at introductory, intermediate and advanced level. Pearce's *Social Enterprise in Anytown* (2003) has established a good reputation as an entry-level text, and this has recently been joined by Price's *Social Enterprise: What It Is and Why It Matters* (2008). A broad and swift journey through the literature up to 2007 can be found in Peattie and Morley's (2008) monograph for the ESRC. Kim

Alter's *Social Enterprise Typology* (2007) remains a good source for the definitional debates in the US, while the contexts affecting European debate are well covered in Chapter 1 of *The Emergence of Social Enterprise* (Borzaga and Defourny, 2001), with updated coverage in the introduction to Nyssens' *Social Enterprise at the Crossroads of Market, Public and Civil Society* (2006). International perspectives and the potential of employee ownership can be gauged by reading *Reluctant*

Entrepreneurs (Paton, 1989) and *The Ownership Solution* (Gates, 1998).

Scholarly debate can be found in articles submitted to the *Social Enterprise Journal*, particularly Nicholls' (2006b) introduction to the second volume, plus Reid and Griffith's (2006) discussion of 'Social enterprise mythology'. There are articles from a critical perspective in a special edition of the *International Journal of Entrepreneurial Behaviour and Research* (edited by Bull, 2008). Further clarifications on the merits of 'narrow' and 'broad' views of social enterprise can be found by comparing Pearce (2003) and Haugh (2005) with the opening chapters of Paton (2003) and Light (2006). Lastly, no consideration of social enterprise could be complete without reviewing the achievements of the Mondragón cooperative. The most comprehensive and critical coverage of its history, structures, issues and potential is still *Making Mondragón* (Whyte and Whyte, 1991).

We also recommend three articles on the companion website. Lyon and Sepulveda's (2009) article on mapping the sector clarifies why there will be ongoing difficulties in the definitional debate. Seanor et al. (2007) provide some visual insights into the way practitioners construct their world views. Lastly, Domenico et al. (2009) provide a theoretical and empirical analysis of cross-sector collaboration.

Further reading material is available on the companion website at www.sagepub.co.uk/ridleyduff.

USEFUL RESOURCES

Harvard Business School, http://www.hbs.edu/socialenterprise/about/history.html

Social Enterprise Alliance, http://www.sealliance.org

The Social Enterprise Coalition, http://www.socialenterprise.org.uk/

Social Ventures Australia, http://www.socialventures.com.au/

Community Interest Company Regulator, http://www.cicregulator.gov.uk/

Social Enterprise Ambassadors, http://socialenterpriseambassadors.org.uk/

EMES European Research Network, http://www.emes.net

Cooperatives UK, http://www.cooperativesuk.coop/

Social Enterprise Mark, http://www.socialenterprisemark.co.uk/

Social Enterprise Magazine, http://www.socialenterprisemag.co.uk/

The Social Enterprise Institute, http://www.sml.hw.ac.uk/socialenterprise/

Office of the Third Sector, http://www.cabinetoffice.gov.uk/third_sector/social_enterprise.aspx

NOTES

1 UnLtd remains one of very few funders supporting social enterprise in the UK that insists on supporting individuals rather than incorporated organisations.

Social and Ethical Capital 4

Rory Ridley-Duff, Pam Seanor and Mike Bull

Learning Objectives

In this chapter you are encouraged to consider the implications of social and ethical challenges in social enterprise. By the end of this chapter you will be able to:

- explain and compare theories of social capital and their role in community development

- describe the ways in which people analyse social capital

- critique the roles of social networks in developing social capital and social enterprises

- articulate the role of ethical values in forms of enterprise development

- apply ethical theories to understand differences between private and social enterprise values.

The key arguments that will be developed in this chapter are:

- Social and ethical issues are of central importance to members of social enterprise.
- Social capital encompasses numerous ideas including trust, civic spirit, goodwill, reciprocity, mutuality, shared commitment, solidarity and cooperation.
- Perceived power affects the development of social capital.
- Social capital offers a useful theoretical framework for conceptualising the value of social enterprises in community development and public policy debates.
- Ethical capital offers a useful theoretical framework for conceptualising the motivations and orientation of social entrepreneurs, as well as members of social enterprises.

Introduction

In this chapter, we discuss different theories of social capital and ethics. Laville and Nyssens (2001) argue that social enterprises generate greater amounts of social capital than public or private sector organisations. Not only does this provide them with a competitive edge in the market, it becomes a public policy argument for supporting them (Birch and Whittam, 2008).

In the previous three chapters, we have examined in detail the role of social enterprises in creating a more equitable and just society. While some writers focus on social and environmental contributions (Preuss, 2004; Krueger et al., 2009), others examine how social entrepreneurs can gain a competitive edge from their 'entrepreneurial virtues' (Mort et al., 2003), their 'ethical fibre' (Drayton, 2005) and the 'ethical capital' they are able to create (Bull et al., 2008).

A recent survey by the Social Enterprise Coalition (SEC, 2009a) attempted to quantify social motives in social enterprises. The majority of respondents had a social, community or environmental motivation, with the top responses being 'putting something back into the community' (45%) and 'a better way to achieve social or environmental goals' (24%). The most frequent responses on 'core values' were 'helping the community' (32%) and being 'socially motivated' (31%). Based on this, the study concluded that social and community benefit is the key motivator for those working for social enterprises (compare Amin, 2009a).

If social capital is viewed as a public benefit of creating and supporting social enterprises, we need to appreciate what people mean when they talk about social capital, and understand the role of ethical values in its creation. One of the unstated questions is: what do people mean when they talk of creating social value? Is 'social value' the ability to find new ways of doing things? If social enterprises are more flexible and robust, and offer new ways to address complex problems, then they create social value. Is it the ability to act collectively? Della Porta and Diani (2006) argue that deliberating together deepens understanding of our experiences and contributes to the creation of social value. Lastly, we might ask: what is the relative importance of creating social and economic value? The ability to ask and debate this question is of value (rather than automatically subordinating every decision to the calculus of 'cost-effectiveness' or 'profit'). Exploring these issues provides an introduction to social capital and ethical values.

Understanding Views on Social Capital

The 'social' component of social enterprise is often interpreted as an organisation's social purpose or mission. According to Mort et al. (2003), a social enterprise's primary purpose is to create social value for its clients. While this is one interpretation, another way to interpret their social value is to consider the ways in which they have been organised to distribute power and wealth more equitably throughout their communities (Ellerman, 1990; Ridley-Duff, 2008a).

The concept of *social capital* is a metaphor found across numerous fields of study. Similar to the term 'social enterprise', it welds together two disparate concepts. Tan et al. (2005) define 'social' in terms of *altruistic* motives, while Smith and Kulynych (2002) discuss how the term 'capital' was originally used to discuss a *reserve* and a *provision for the future*. The question posed by Chell (2007) is whether combining these terms creates a contradiction. Is it possible to develop a 'reserve' of 'altruism'?

While we need to consider these issues, there is agreement amongst writers that social capital implies the development of *trust, civic spirit, goodwill,* **reciprocity,** *mutuality, shared commitment, solidarity* and *cooperation*. It offers a way to recognise resources that are difficult to quantify in economic theory, but which are recognised as important (Coleman, 1988; Putnam, 2001; White, 2002). Adler and Kwon (2002) frame these aspects, despite their ambiguous and elastic meanings, as things that make it easier to achieve a common goal or action.

Hanifan is credited as being the first to use the term in 1916 while writing about 'goodwill, fellowship, mutual sympathy, and social intercourse among a group of individuals and families' to enhance education (Smith and Kulynych, 2002: 154). Social capital also evolved as a concept in discussions of Coleman's *social exchange theory* to argue that communities benefit when children and young people grow up in similar school networks, supported by parent and teacher associations.

Fukuyama (2001) discusses how social capital may also be viewed as the 'cohesiveness' of relationships at the inter-organisational level, especially at stressful times. In this respect his theorising differs from Coleman who emphasised relationship stability as a condition for social capital to develop. These differences have prompted authors to seek explanations for divergent conceptualisations of social capital. For example, Law and Mooney (2006) argue that those on the political left use the term to describe solidarity and collectives, whilst those on the political right use it to denote specific ethical, community and family values (see Figure 4.1).

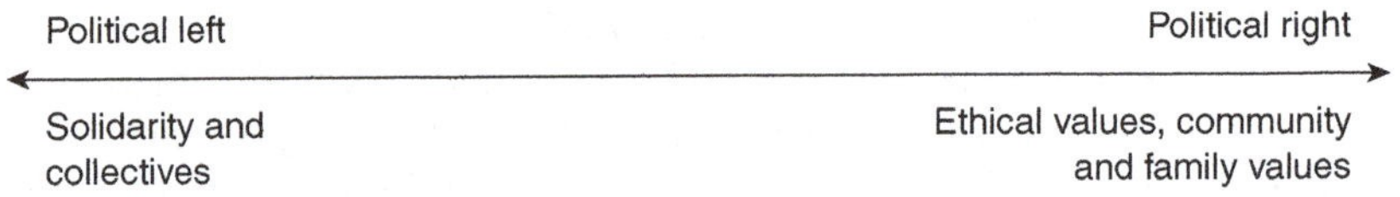

Political left   Political right

◄───►

Solidarity and   Ethical values, community
collectives   and family values

Figure 4.1   Political spectrum and social capital (Law and Mooney, 2006)

Putnam popularised the concept by exploring the importance of relationships, especially membership of voluntary associations, in Italy and the USA. Putnam is critical of Coleman's approach as focusing upon the family restricts the usefulness of the concept to explain access to wider social networks. As Preuss comments:

> the most common function of social capital … lies in its ability to provide network-mediated benefits beyond the immediate family. (2004: 157)

Bourdieu (1986) uses the term to discuss class relations. He argued that social capital can empower members of a group to take social action that brings about political change. However, when Putnam discusses Bourdieu, he emphasises how social capital can benefit all members of society without reference to political power (see Edwards, 2004). White (2002), therefore, theorises that Bourdieu's approach to social capital is a polar opposite to Putnam and Coleman. Figure 4.2 summarises White's contention that Bourdieu uses the term to describe the pursuit of social justice and empowerment through voluntary social action, while Putnam and Coleman view social capital as a way to strengthen traditional family and community organisations.

Critically questioning dominant assumptions highlights that interpretations of 'social capital' perpetuate different understandings about 'good society'. Critics of

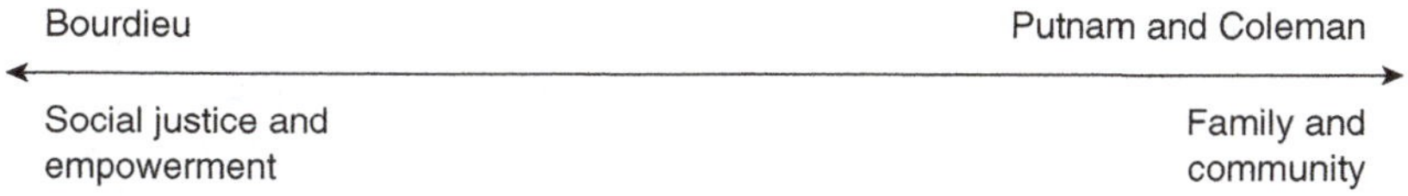

Bourdieu   Putnam and Coleman

←——→

Social justice and   Family and
empowerment   community

Figure 4.2   White's view of Bourdieu's approach to social capital

Putnam's approach point out that he does not consider power dynamics in relationships, or issues of advocacy and resistance to the state and market (Smith and Kulynych, 2002). Nor does Putnam consider the civil rights movement, the women's movement, gay rights and anti-war protests as products of social capital. Edwards (2004) critiques Putnam's approach as an attempt to recreate 1950s nostalgia, a 'Rockwell perspective', depicting the 'good old days' and not the civil rights campaigns that challenged inequality throughout American society. For Putnam, the 1960s and 1970s are periods during which social capital was *lost* rather than developed.

Cope et al. (2007: 215) comment that research has an 'almost evangelical faith in the gains from social interaction'. They draw attention to findings that 'collaborators may cheat or free-ride on goodwill leading to a breach of trust and a breakdown in relations'. Interestingly, Portes (1998) claims that 'success stories' can *undermine* group cohesion and that 'exception stories' (i.e. cautionary tales) are used to control group members. In the case of social enterprise, 'success stories' may be divisive, selectively granting legitimacy and contributing to power asymmetries that undermine the creation of a tolerant and diverse business culture (compare Kotter and Heskett, 1992). Other negative effects that have been noted include an over-reliance on others, an over-embeddedness that constrains actions and leads to missed opportunities, and a lack of innovation. Birch and Whittam (2008) extend this to the 'contracting culture' that over-emphasises the size of supplier organisations, creating opportunities for some but severely limiting opportunities for smaller organisations.

A critical edge is apparent in the comments of Law and Mooney:

> Social capital is one of those elusive terms that provide think tanks, academics, journalists, politicians and policy-makers with a way to speak as if something meaningful is under discussion. Talk of social is permitted so long as it is accompanied by an orthodox emphasis on capital. (2006: 127)

Despite this, Putnam's views are gaining prominence in UK government policy, and are now actively driving debate. In a recent Cabinet Office report, it was claimed that:

> social capital consists of the networks, norms, relationships, values and informal sanctions that shape the quantity and co-operative quality of society's social interactions. (2002: 5)

'Third way thinkers' use social capital as a concept in social policy and regeneration programmes to promote stakeholder involvement and partnership approaches

(White, 2002). The government's *Social Enterprise: A Strategy for Success* (DTI, 2002), *Third Sector* review (HM Treasury, 2006; Cabinet Office, 2007) and empowerment White Paper (CLG, 2009) advocate developing social capital to stimulate the third sector and social enterprises. The White Paper recommends giving ownership and control to local people, while local authorities are encouraged to ensure social enterprises are able to compete fairly for public sector contracts. Though not specifically aimed at social enterprise, *Communities in Control: Real People, Real Power* (CLG, 2009) declares government is 'changing the terms of the debate' to influence, control and power. Despite this, a detailed examination reveals a focus on volunteering, suggesting more alignment with Putnam's 'communities' than Bourdieu's social justice and community empowerment.

EXERCISE   Social capital and community empowerment

Social capital is believed to promote political and social reform through civil engagement and cooperative working. Governments see social enterprise as a way to unlock 'hard to reach' communities so that social capital can be rebuilt. This discourse emphasises being 'civil', with an implicit expectation that third sector organisations and social enterprises will be 'good citizens' (i.e. non-disruptive). Yet, conversely, social entrepreneurs are described as disruptive change agents and mavericks.

In light of Bourdieu's views on social capital, what are the implications for social enterprises when they work with disadvantaged groups? Consider:

- How social capital affects the 'voice' of groups in society (will they be heard?).
- How charity law – requiring the board of trustees to be unpaid – might affect the development of social capital amongst individuals on low incomes (will they participate?).
- How Bourdieu's views on social capital might underpin a strategy for community action.

Additional questions:

1 How might social entrepreneurs play a role in building (different types of) social capital?
2 How might this affect their ability to secure contracts to deliver local services?
3 How might a social entrepreneur's motives and actions be interpreted using social capital theory?

In this section, debates in the social capital literature have been summarised and linked to recent developments in public policy. In the next section, we consider how people have sought to analyse levels of social capital.

Structural approaches

The study of social capital, and attempts to measure its strength, are approached through either *structural* or *contextual* analysis. Writers utilising the structural approach concentrate on connections and ties between people. The cliché for this approach is that 'it is who you know, not what you know', reflecting a view that network structures and the connections between people enable network members to get ahead. Another useful metaphor is that social capital acts as the 'glue' that holds people together (see Granovetter's 1983 study on weak and strong ties in securing employment). The dominant metaphors of a structural approach are 'ties', 'bridges' and 'bonds' (see Bridge et al., 2009; Doherty et al., 2009b). Borch et al. (2007) propose that social entrepreneurs rely heavily upon the structural context of the environment to create situations for cooperative action. Network interactions are based upon 'strategic alliances' giving improved access to ideas and information. These interactions are often portrayed as networking spaces facilitated at workshops, conferences and events. Based on empirical work, Cope et al. comment that:

> since economic activity is embedded in society, the innovative entrepreneur develops social capital through building networks which provide external sources of information, support, finance and expertise allowing mutual learning and boundary crossing. (2007: 214)

The 'boundary crossing' of entrepreneurs represents 'bridging capital' where people can use their social capital to work with people in different groups to gain access to resources and ideas. In contrast to this is the concept of 'bonding capital' that 'glues' people together in a group, often by establishing shared norms and social rituals. Hosking and Morley (1991) talk of the number and position of connections and ties to explain levels of access to network resources.

Latour (2005) criticises the structural approach for metaphorically representing a network as a series of connections through which information 'flows' like water. He argues that information does not flow in this fashion amongst a group of people, and that the number of connections cannot explain how information is communicated. The *quality* of relationships at interpersonal and inter/intra-group level, as well as the number of dimensions on which relationships operate, all affect the amount and quality of the information communicated between network members (see Ridley-Duff, 2005: Chapters 4 and 5). For this reason, we need to consider the *contextual* approach that focuses on the way that social norms and values develop, and their impact on interpersonal trust.

Contextual approaches

The alternative view is that network structures do not adequately capture the extent to which social capital depends on the *quality* of the relationships in a network. Table 4.1 summarises Adler and Kwon's (2002) analysis of the two approaches to analysing social capital.

Table 4.1   Structural and contextual approaches to social capital

Structural	Contextual
Networks	Trust
Connections	Norms
Weak and strong ties	Values
Bridges or bonds	Attitudes
Actions	Reciprocity
Responsibilities	
Accountable decision-making	
Processes	

In social enterprise development, Amin et al. (2002) argue that local context is a crucial factor. The context and content of communications, and the relationships themselves, affect how information is understood and acted upon. A contextual approach focuses upon the development of trust, the process by which organisational norms are established, and the role of ethical values. As Smith and Kulynych comment, Putnam does not:

> distinguish among different kinds of trust – interpersonal, organizational, governmental – or adequately specify the relations among them. (2002: 159)

Various authors have focused attention on civic commitment, mutual trust, the promotion of collective action and social equity. As Evers states:

> Taking social capital building as a term of reference offers the advantage of making it possible to take account not only of the social and economic goals of the organisations, but also the other dimensions and effects of activities, which are specific to social enterprises. This may also help to sensitise us to the organisational challenges linked with the aim of balancing multiple goals and commitments that have an economic, a social and a civic dimension. (2001: 303)

Contextual approaches to social capital theory, therefore, help us to understand how communities develop competencies beyond contracted outputs, through the nurturing and valuing of social networks as ends in themselves (Westall, 2001).

Fenton et al. (1999) warn of the potential damage to trust, confidence and an altruistic culture from becoming more business-like. The public still prefer to support charities precisely because they do not generate profits, and perceive them as being more trustworthy than 'for-profit' businesses. This is supported by a report from the Home Office (2008) that suggests there is greater distrust of businesses and public sector bodies than of third sector organisations. Trust in the UK government is particularly low (at 24 per cent) – the lowest for a European government in the EU25 (Parker and Parker, 2007).

Social networking

In considering the issue of relationships between sectors, the role of intermediate agencies is important. Cohen and Prusak (2001) stress the need for organisations to place trust in support agencies. Attempts to develop social capital are often supported by government action to create social networks. Table 4.2 outlines two sets of views offered by recent UK government documents on the value of networking to social enterprise.

The reports, however, omit mention of trust, or the role of networks in understanding complex situations, and the opportunities that networks offer to alter power and influence. In short, their view is limited to a structural view of social capital. Doherty et al. state that the advantages for social enterprises from networking derive from the fact that:

> Relationships are established with existing and potential customers and a level of familiarity, trust and recognition of professional competency may lead to commissioned or negotiated contracts and invitations to tender. (2009b: 159)

Table 4.2 UK government views of the benefits of social enterprise networks

View	Benefits
Office of the Third Sector	Opportunities to share knowledge and experience
	Shared approach to accessing external funding
	Mutual support and encouragement
	Opportunities to share good practice
	Easier access to structured support
	Reduction in costs allows general networking
Department of Trade and Industry	Useful in building contacts
	Widening access to support
	Building broader understanding and knowledge

They report that networks are used to influence opportunities and actions and that this is a 'reciprocal process' where **actors** gain an understanding of complex situations by sharing ideas about what is important and what it is necessary to do. This contextual approach emphasises mutual learning, creating reputations and learning about the trustworthiness of others to develop partnerships. Murdock speculates that this trust comes from 'a shared set of values or beliefs':

> So far the literature offers some evidence that trust is founded in values and beliefs and it is important because it facilitates collaboration, but trust depends on reciprocity and engagement. (2005: 3)

The last part of this comment raises the question of whether or not reciprocity and engagement are found in practice. Murdock comments that social enterprise network characteristics:

> embrace the idea of a group identifying a number of individuals sharing common values, where knowing and relating are important elements, where reciprocity is an important function and where peer pressure may shape processes and rules. (2005: 9)

In doing so, Murdock implies there is an expectation that motivations are based upon more than the utilitarian purposes (e.g. mobilisation of resources) associated with networking and there are underlying expectations and motivations that influence actions. Like other writers he suggests that social enterprise networks are held together by common values combined with peer pressure (Pearce, 2003; Pharoah, 2007).

There is surprisingly little research examining trust, or perceived trust, between social enterprises. While Sydow (1998) has asserted that the frequency and openness of inter-organisational communication increases the possibility of trust, an empirical study of local support networks found that interactions are coloured by mistrust between organisations, community users and agencies within the networks (Seanor and Meaton, 2008).

Sydow (1998) noted that actors might perceive competition as a threat to their organisation and that members of smaller organisations might feel too vulnerable to share ideas with members of other organisations. Hence, size might be an important factor in social enterprise networks. Social enterprises and support agencies competing with other organisations and agencies in a 'contracting culture' might find that trust is fragile, prone to a 'calculative trust' mentality. More problematic is the question of whether competitive markets deplete social capital *even where organisations are in the same sector undertaking much the same work, and operating within social networks with many 'connections'*. In Seanor and Meaton's (2008) study, the poor quality of social capital, irrespective of 'connections', resulted in a fear of collaboration even with the agencies established to help the social enterprise sector. Even if trust is a vital mechanism to absorb the complexity of interactions between organisations (Sydow, 1998), distrust serves the same function. Unfortunately, distrust depletes the *quality* of social capital throughout the community.

In concluding this section, it is worth raising whether the ability to generate trust and social capital is contingent on the political and economic environment. In light of Hebson et al. (2003), who found that a 'contracting culture' with large commissioners is not conducive to the development of trusting relationships (and therefore the development of social capital), we need to consider how the competitive environment influences the development of trust relations. While social capital may be a useful concept to describe a cooperative culture that develops under a regime of decentralised governance and wealth sharing (Bourdieu, 1986; Turnbull, 2002), it is more problematic in economies where there are huge wealth inequalities or large numbers of suppliers competing for large contracts. The policy implication is that 'economies of scale' carry the risk of reducing economic efficiency if they destroy social capital.

Values, Ethics and Sustainability

Pearce (2003) argues that people in social enterprises are motivated by ethical values of cooperation, doing good work and trust. This imagery was reflected in the first version of the Social Enterprise Quality Mark (*c.* 2009) showing a halo above the words 'social enterprise'. To evaluate ethical standards, it is first necessary to problematise ethics itself. Granitz and Loewy (2007) identify six ethical theories that influence human action (see Table 4.3). This framework enables the debate to move beyond simplistic discussions of whether social enterprises (or social entrepreneurs) are 'more' ethical, to a consideration of *how their ethics differ* from those developed in other contexts.

The theories in Table 4.3 cover a range of perspectives. The first two are associated primarily with the negative and positive aspects of self-interest (liberal philosophy). The third and fourth theories focus on normative positions that aim to advance collective interests (**communitarian** philosophy). The final two are rooted in ethical strategies geared towards the management of complex social situations and cultural diversity (**constructivist** philosophy). In the discussion that follows, these theories are used to clarify different ethical values and their likely impacts.

Pharoah found in a study that:

> *[voluntary] organisations defined their own development needs in terms of their ability to defend their values and promote the interest of their clients. This is a significant affirmation of the values-driven nature of voluntary organisations and of their important role as advocates of client need. (2007: 14)*

Table 4.3   The implications of different theories of ethics

Ethical theory	Implications
1 Machiavellianism	Emphasis on the effectiveness of any proposed action, irrespective of alternative moral or political considerations. It has come to be associated, perhaps unkindly, with selfishness and unfettered self-interest. An action is 'ethical' if it achieves its objective, irrespective of process. In its corrupted form, it has been linked with the use of deceit and lying for personal or political gain.
2 Rational self-interest (rationalism)	Emphasis on pursuing self-interest through a series of 'fair exchanges', and assessing whether particular 'trades' are fair to both parties (a fair exchange of 'benefits'). Proposed actions will be evaluated in terms of procedural justice (that the process will be fair and equitable for all parties).
3 Deontology	Emphasis on understanding belief systems, developing agreement on what is 'right' and 'wrong', and cultivating moral sensitivities through reinforcement of the 'right' behaviours. Proposed actions are influenced by the 'rightness' and 'wrongness' of the proposed behaviour.
4 Utilitarianism	Emphasis on achieving the best outcome for the greatest number of people, and calculating the balance of costs and benefits in order to achieve the 'best' overall outcome. Proposed actions will be influenced by evaluations of whether more people will benefit from (not) taking a proposed action.
5 Situational ethics (consequentialism)	Emphasis on the level of opportunism and opportunity costs, with consideration of the situation or circumstance that prompts different behaviour. Proposed actions will be evaluated in terms of the benefits/costs of taking action, and whether any action is 'reasonable' given the specifics of the situation.
6 Cultural relativism	Emphasis on *cultural* norms of 'right' and 'wrong', and the different cultural settings that impact on beliefs. Proposed actions are evaluated in terms of sensitivity to others' cultural awareness: will they have the ability to participate fully, or will the action enhance cultural understanding and awareness? Is the proposed action culturally appropriate?

While this statement might be taken to imply that other organisations have *no* values, the question we need to answer is *which* values are being defended. Is this a cultural relativist position (i.e. meeting 'client need')? What values come into play when short-term outputs are prioritised over longer-term social outcomes? Is this a utilitarian argument (that more people will benefit if action is guided by long-term, rather than short-term, interests)?

Ethics are not easily objectified, so the challenge of assessing them is one of evaluating statements of ethical or social values. For example, Mook et al. argue that:

An ethical accounting statement provides measures of how well an organization lives up to the shared values to which it has committed itself. [It] is not objective. It does not prove anything, but draws a rich and informative picture of how stakeholders perceive their relationships with the organization. (2007a: 55)

Mook et al. argue that ethical values characteristic of 'business' are changing management practice in parts of the social economy. They cite Campbell (1998: 28) that:

Once upon a time [voluntary organisations] were called non-profit organizations to emphasise that the provision of service took precedence over the permanent amassing of funds. The breakeven philosophy was the dominant management ethic and adherence to that ethic demanded honest and diligent management ... if management is entirely relieved of the public obligation inherent in the breakeven philosophy [from changes experienced over time], what alternative ethic will emerge to prevent undue hoarding of resources? With tacit approval for an 'ok-to-profit' ethic, is the final and irrevocable 'must-profit' phase far behind? (2007a: 6)

The assumption in this extract is that *profiting* from a social or economic exchange is unethical, based on utilitarian reasoning that 'profit-seeking' harms more people than it benefits because it leads to the 'hoarding of resources'. Leadbeater (1997), on the other hand, describes the ethical qualities of the individuals in social enterprises as a key difference between them and people in other organisations. Mort et al. (2003) supports this view by arguing that virtue (e.g. integrity, love, empathy, honesty) is the key difference between members of social and other enterprises. These are mostly deontological positions based on an assumption that people have fixed character traits that determine their level of 'virtue'.

By way of example, Bill Drayton of **Ashoka** speaks of 'ethical fibre', qualities such as honesty, trust and commitment to serve others, which are deemed essential characteristics in the selection of social entrepreneurs. To test for such qualities Ashoka uses an 'intuitive test' that asks an interviewer to imagine themselves in danger, and to assess how comfortable they would be in getting out of their situation if an applicant was with them. They are asked to give a high mark (10) if they feel secure and a low mark (1) if the new applicant leaves them feeling insecure. This is their test for 'ethical fibre'.

Ashoka's approach requires all senses and human faculties to be used in evaluating potential social entrepreneurs. While this suggests a deviation from a 'rational' approach to recruitment, it can be challenged on the basis that intuition is an insufficient way to evaluate 'ethical fibre'. How can you, for example, counter the effects of stereotyping and prejudice (see Aronson, 2003)?

A case in point is described in Ridley-Duff (2010) who found that, between 1999 and 2003, the values-driven strategy applied to induction at School Trends Ltd was linked to staff turnover that was four times higher than expected (given their industry and their qualified human resource management officers). This suggests that the application of deontological ethics in the screening and evaluating of human character traits in HRM can dramatically *increase* social exclusion.

Bull et al. (2008) explore the utilitarian link to happiness in a critical appraisal of ethical systems that influence social enterprise development, and note that only some social enterprises have overt goals and actions that promote the utilitarian concept of 'the common good'. A 'common good' perspective, however, is a useful way to evaluate notions of 'public interest' (required for charities) and 'community interest' (required for community interest companies). Utilitarian ethics influences the evaluation of social enterprises that seek to adopt these legal forms. Evers highlights that support may not be forthcoming if:

> the special purpose of a singular association is not necessarily in line with the notion that the broader public or policy-makers have of the public good. (2001: 300)

Lastly, Sen (2000) argues for a pragmatic approach that is not based upon a theory of happiness, well-being or love. In doing so, he steers debate towards *situational ethics* that take account of *cultural relativism*. Sen, like Edwards, emphasises how meaning is interpreted and negotiated. He argues that pluralism and critical reflection contribute to a 'good society' (Edwards, 2004). As Pearce (2003: 34) adds: 'the purpose of social enterprises is to contribute to the common good, to benefit society and, more widely, the planet'.

In short, ethical values are used to both justify and appraise approaches to social enterprise. In seeking to understand and theorise social enterprise (and social entrepreneurship), we cannot ignore the ethical frameworks that underpin different approaches as these encourage particular management practices and cultures and have different social impacts. This consideration of *critical ethics* (a useful umbrella term for all ethical reasoning that considers situational, historical and cultural factors) goes back to Kant's (1998 [1781]) argument about the difference between noumena ('things in themselves', separate from human perception) and phenomena ('things that have meaning for us', only knowable to us through our perception). Kant's categorical imperative is that ethical actions should be grounded in the premise of *treating others as you wish them to treat you*. While this has been erroneously presented as a 'universal' code of good conduct (on the basis that it postulates a universal ethical law), Kant leaves open the possibility that ethical values may change as we develop new perceptions and understandings about the way to treat each other. Kant was clear that human beings should not be treated in an instrumental way (as a means), and should be regarded as 'ends' (i.e. that social life should be organised to develop human sensibilities and capabilities).

On this basis, Edwards (2004) argues that an important aspect of ethics is *the willingness to discuss the meaning and value of difference*. He argues that it is not diversity *per se* that constitutes a significant difference between the third sector and other sectors, but that organisational norms develop based on human rights, peaceful negotiations, tolerance, trust, cooperation and freedom from want. These norms are difficult to negotiate with large public agencies who want political control and corporations that want to control markets. As a result, members of smaller organisations will not implicitly trust larger and more powerful organisations because they cannot negotiate with them on an equitable basis.

EXERCISE   Ethics as the capacity for critical reflection

Critical theorists have evaluated the 'social' aspect of enterprise by drawing upon the works of:

- Karl Marx, who advocated social and communal ownership and control of the means of production.
- Anthony Giddens, who argues that human agency can modify entrenched social structures.
- Jurgen Habermas, who argues that asymmetries in social power distort decision-making.

Habermas (1984; 1987) is credited with reviving interest in democratic forums to create 'ideal speech' situations as a way of improving decision-making. These perspectives argue that asymmetries in power need to be addressed before meaningful empowerment at both individual and organisational levels can take place. All three authors consider historical contexts and cultural influences. This being the case, they draw on situational and cultural ethics to expose the fallacy that individual reflection on rational self-interest can ever be 'fair' and 'equitable'. Habermas argues that all 'rationality' is a social product of 'communicative action'. Without democratic control, those who control resources (a 'ruling class') organise communication to their own advantage and determine which thoughts, ideas and concepts will be taught. Democratic forums are seen as the fairest (and most rational) way to debate and make social and economic decisions.

1 To what extent do members of social enterprises follow their own, or their community of users', concerns in making strategic decisions?
2 To what extent is the notion of consensus used to guide social action?
3 What are the ethical challenges in deciding a course of action if there are numerous and complex views of a particular problem?

Ethical Capital as a Framework for Understanding Social Enterprise

Gupta et al. (2003: 979) set out a view that *ethical capital* is created when particular ethical values are used to guide the creation of social capital. In particular, this occurs in the context of:

> *investments and institutional arrangements that may be governed by ethical norms of accountability, transparency, reciprocity and fairness to both human and non-human sentient beings.*

They suggest that in working relationships, cultural norms to nurture cooperation and social networking are not well established. Ethical capital arises when a *contextual* approach to social capital development takes priority. For Preuss (2004), this means that ethical capital is not so much a subset of social capital, but a phenomenon in its own right. Table 4.4 summarises Wagner-Tsukamoto's (2007) view that levels of ethical capital in commercial practice can be analysed.

Wagner-Tsukamoto stops short of considering the ethical values of the social economy, so Bull et al. (2008) extend the debate. They suggest a fourth level of

Table 4.4 Levels of ethical capital

Level 1:
Passive unintended moral agency – accumulated through Adam Smith's 'invisible hand' of the free market – where the accumulation of wealth and distribution achieves some level of ethical capital, such as through rising living standards. However, the core belief and responsibility is managing an organisation to maximise financial profit.
Machiavellian ethics moderated by rational self-interest
Level 2:
Passive, intended moral agency – accumulated through following the rules of the game, obeying the codes of conduct in the norms and customs of society, operating without deception or fraud (for example, regulations set by governments and local authorities). This rule-following behaviour achieves the lowest intended moral code. Bull et al. (2008) describe this level as the bottom end of corporate social responsibility: 'Good must be done for reason of profit' (Friedman, 1970/2003). Hence, it could include more consideration of the environment so long as it is profitable to do so.
Rational self-interest evolves into deontological ethical standards
Level 3:
Active, intended moral agency and the creation of ethical capital. Bull et al. (2008) describe this as organisations at the top end of the corporate social responsibility spectrum – Café Direct, Divine Chocolate – and organisations that go beyond the minimum rules of market morality. Hence, profit is an outcome of ethical thinking linked to market opportunities.
Deontological norms subjected to utilitarian ethical reasoning

Source: based on Wagner-Tsukamoto, 2007; Bull et al., 2008

active, intentional **'blended value'** where social and economic factors are combined to develop ethical capital. Creating blended value involves a consideration of *situational* and *cultural* factors, moving beyond a universal notion of 'utility' or 'common good' to one that is socially and historically embedded.

While the first three levels of ethical behaviour (Table 4.4) focus on 'profitability' in terms of economic capital, at level 4 (see Table 4.5) it is reconceptualised as a way of building social capital (compare Ridley-Duff, 2008a). At level 4, business ethics are reframed so that explicit consideration is given to the development of social *and* economic capital: double bottom line accounting. Where the environment is also considered, triple bottom line accounting occurs. Level 5 embraces the concept of 'charity', where economics is subordinated to social and ethical reasoning, and financial management is guided wholly by social and charitable objectives.

A useful way to visualise this involves adaptation of Alter's (2007) sustainability equilibrium (Figure 4.3). Levels 1, 2 and 3 represent the ethics of traditional private businesses that are primarily based on economic value creation. Level 1 represents the traditional 'for-profit' business aligned with passive unintended moral agency. Level 2 represents corporations passively practising social responsibility, while level 3 involves active, intended moral agency and the conscious creation of ethical capital. At level 4, enterprises are not created solely for reasons of profit. While level 5 might

Table 4.5   Levels 4 and 5 of ethical capital

Level 4:
Active, intended moral agency that moves beyond corporate social responsibility to actively create social capital through ethical trading and management practices. Examples include the Mondragón Cooperative Corporation (see Chapter 2) and Grameen Bank (see Chapter 5). Profitability is an important but secondary goal, a by-product of ethically informed action that accelerates the conversion of social capital into economic capital that is distributed to advance equity and solidarity.

Utilitarian goals contextualised and localised using situational ethical reasoning

Level 5:
Active, intended moral agency that subordinates entrepreneurship and business activity to the creation of social and ethical capital using the highest level of ethical reasoning. Business practices are culturally sensitive and grounded in situational reasoning. Profitability is acceptable only for a social purpose, and both social and economic capital are placed at the disposal of a democratically accountable polity that considers community benefit. Capital is used to foster a tolerant, culturally diverse and socially cohesive economy that is responsive to civil society.

Utilitarian goals contextualised and localised using both situational and cultural reasoning

Source: based on Bull et al., 2008

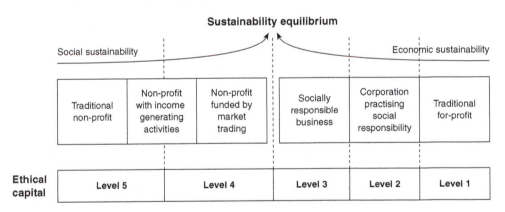

Figure 4.3   Ethical capital and Alter's sustainability framework

way to organise. Hence, these levels act primarily to provoke debate about the relative importance of ethics in organisational decision-making, and the compromises that might be made to ensure organisational sustainability.

The implication of the theoretical perspective in Figure 4.3 is that a socially sustainable society requires charitable and social economy organisations that balance (and limit) the effects of 'for-profit' entrepreneurship. This could be achieved either internally (within the organisation) under the agency of a democratically organised business, or in the marketplace (external to the organisation) through the creation of charitable and social economy businesses that offer alternatives to private and public sector provision.

Conclusions

The purpose of this chapter has been to explore social and ethical capital, in order to offer another perspective on the contribution of social enterprises to a modern economy. The contribution of social capital theory is to provide a (socially constructed) language for discussing the intangible aspects of enterprise development. The experience of people involved in regional and economic development confirms that the number of connections in a social network does not wholly explain long-term social and economic outcomes. The quality of the connections, and the ethical values that guide them, also affects rates of development. Social capital provides an imperfect, but useful, framework for discussing the efficacy of social networks and the relationships that develop within them. As Westall and Chalkley argue:

> In order to fully grasp the implications of these visions and realise the potential of social enterprise, we need to break out of our usual ways of looking at the world, particularly about the 'natural' business model or the narrow but hugely powerful concepts and implications of mainstream economics. (2007: 17)

One of the ways we can do this is to deploy the concepts in this chapter on the role and purpose of 'business'. If, as various studies suggest, creating and sustaining social capital and expressing ethical values enhance business success (see Collins, 2001), why is so much attention still focused upon getting the sector to adopt conventional business models? Should collaborative rather than competitive market models be informing the development of social enterprise networks?

This chapter has not offered a normative approach to the creation of social and ethical capital. Instead, it has sought to clarify different perspectives so that readers can re-evaluate notions of trust, accountability, transparency, reciprocity and fairness. In doing so, it is possible to evaluate the practical usefulness of attempting to create and measure social and ethical capital.

SUMMARY OF LEARNING

In this chapter, we have argued that:

- Social, community, ethical and environmental issues are considered important to those creating and working in social enterprises.
- UK policy is framed by Putnam's approach to social capital, while Bourdieu's notion of power has been neglected.
- Writers mean different things when they discuss *social value* and *social capital*.
- There are two approaches to conceiving and analysing social capital: *structural* (based on 'ties', 'bonding' and 'bridging') and *contextual* (based on trust, values, reciprocity and mutuality).
- A contextual approach to social capital requires detailed consideration of ethical values.

- There are different theories of ethics that can be linked to different approaches to organisational development and management practice.
- The ethical values that sustain social enterprise are grounded in utilitarian goals that are culturally sensitive and situationally appropriate.

QUESTIONS AND POSSIBLE ESSAY ASSIGNMENTS

1 'A "structural approach" to social capital is an inadequate way to understand the development of community enterprise networks.' Using examples, critically assess this statement.
2 'We just want to deliver a service; we don't want to change the way the system works.' Drawing on theories of ethics, critically assess the social value of an enterprise that 'just delivers a service'.
3 Critically assess the potential contribution of the Social Enterprise Mark to the development of ethical, social and economic capital.

FURTHER READING

For background on social networks, see Granovetter's work in the 1970s and 1980s on the strength of weak ties (e.g. 1983). A good starting point for social enterprise is Chapter 6 in Pearce's *Social Enterprise in Anytown* (2003). For clarifications of the concept see Evans and Syrett's (2007) paper on social capital in economic regeneration. In the last decade there have been a number of detailed discussions on the contribution of social capital to social enterprise (and vice versa). See two chapters in *The Emergence of Social Enterprise* by Evers (2001) and Laville and Nyssens (2001) that focus squarely on perspectives within the social enterprise research community. For a public sector perspective, see the paper in the journal *Regional Studies* by Birch and Whittam (2008). New textbooks on the social economy (Bridge et al., 2009) and social enterprise (Doherty et al., 2009b) have useful introductions to business ethics and social capital in the context of social enterprise. For more radical coverage, and the conversions between forms of capital, see Bourdieu's (1986) 'The forms of capital', and for a discussion of mistrust see Seanor and Meaton's

(2008) paper on the companion website. For a perspective that connects relationship dynamics (social rationality), social capital and social enterprise see 'Social enterprise as a socially rational business' by Ridley-Duff (2008a).

For further coverage on ethics see Wagner-Tsukamoto (2007) and Bull et al.'s (2008) paper on 'ethical capital' (downloadable from http://shura.shu.ac.uk/758/).

Further reading material is available on the companion website at www.sagepub.co.uk/ridleyduff.

USEFUL RESOURCES

Office of National Statistics (Social Capital Project), http://www.ons.gov.uk/about-statistics/user-guidance/sc-guide/index.html

The Concise Project, http://www.concise.mdx. ac.uk

The Social Capital Gateway, http://www.socialcapitalgateway.org/index.htm

The Improvement and Development Agency, http://www.idea.gov.uk/idk/core/page.do?pageId=1347434

The World Bank, http://web.worldbank.org/

Globalisation and International Perspectives

5

Learning Objectives

In this chapter, we further develop consideration of international perspectives on social enterprise development, and the concept and impact of globalisation. By the end of this chapter you will be able to:

- critically evaluate globalisation as a historical and contemporary phenomenon

- apply the theories of Polanyi to critique liberal markets and Marxian socialism

- critically discuss the contribution of social enterprises from outside Europe and America

- critically appraise how social enterprises respond to the opportunities and threats presented by 'free markets'.

The key arguments that will be developed in this chapter are:

- Attempts to create global markets in goods and services are a recurrent cycle in economic history.
- Globalisation enables new forms of social enterprise to develop.
- Globalisation triggers forms of social enterprise that seek to limit or resist the effects of globalisation.
- Social enterprises challenge the assumptions of globalisation by reframing attitudes to land, money and people.

Introduction

In the previous chapters, we have considered social enterprise mainly from Anglo-American and European perspectives. In this chapter, we tie this analysis to developments in global economics and international political institutions. In the first half of the chapter, we explore the concept of globalisation and how this can facilitate new forms of social enterprise. In doing so, we consider the use of new global communications technologies to facilitate international trading activities. In the second half of the chapter, we switch the focus of analysis to enterprise networks in Asia and South America that seek to counter or mitigate the impact of globalisation on local economies. Due to space limitations, and a focus on discussing the theoretical implications of social enterprise in developing countries, only a limited number of cases have been selected to illustrate international developments. Further reading is suggested at the end of the chapter.

Two key arguments will be developed. Firstly, social enterprises offer either a partial or a complete rejection of established 'rules' of international capitalism. Specifically, they draw their intellectual heritage from historical forms that adopt different policies towards the deployment and hiring of labour, the use of land and the role and character of money. In some cases, these attitudes are consciously developed and cultivated to avoid treating people, land and money as if they were commodities in a market (Polanyi, 2001). Secondly, we will argue that outside the EU, social enterprises play a much larger role in providing welfare and community services that would otherwise be unavailable.

The Rise of Global Capital and International Markets

Before we consider the impact of globalisation on social enterprise, it is worth discussing the dynamics of the world economy and globalisation. Gray (1998) argues that globalisation as a concept is not new: it can be traced back to the rise of merchant capitalism, exemplified by the East India Company. In this venture, investors shared the risks of international trade by jointly funding the establishment of trading routes and shipping operations around the globe. Their joint action diversified the risks of trading by sharing the necessary investment and establishing multiple shipping routes to insulate individual ships and crews from local disputes. Today, the concept of globalisation has taken on many shades of meaning, all linked to the technological, business and social institutions that make it possible to trade with people anywhere in the world as if they were part of a single global market. As Gray states:

> globalisation is shorthand for the cultural changes that follow when societies become linked with, and in varying measures dependent on, world markets ... Behind all these 'meanings' of globalization is a single underlying idea, which can be called de-localization: the uprooting of activities and relationships from local origins and cultures. It means the displacement of activities that until recently were local into networks of relationships whose reach is distant or worldwide. (1998: 57)

As the scale of ventures increased, so a banking system developed to support them. In the mid nineteenth century, a group of nations adopted the 'gold standard' to facilitate international trade. The idea behind the gold standard was surprisingly simple. National governments backed their currencies with reserves of gold and agreed an exchange rate between their own local currency and international gold reserves. This was expected to make it easier to trade internationally as national governments committed not only to using their gold reserves to settle international debts but also to securing the value of their local currencies with something of tangible value.

As Polanyi (2001) describes, an international banking system under the control of the Rothschild family started to function as an international agency. It achieved a level of independence from even the most powerful governments and central banks, but remained closely connected to them through tacit involvement in diplomacy and long-range financial planning. Whether planning for peace or war, national governments and the international financiers began to take account of each other's interests. Giddens (1982) argues that, in practice, this hastened a transition from merchant capitalism to colonial rule. Weaker nations sought to protect themselves from the effects of deflation brought about by adherence to the gold standard, while richer nations sponsored attempts to secure new markets through the expansion of their empires. Their goal was not necessarily to develop indigenous economies and industries, but often to secure cheap and plentiful materials for manufacturing operations in industrialising economies. At the end of the nineteenth century, there was a rush to secure direct rule rather than trading relationships.

Gray (1998) regards this period (from 1871 to 1914) as the first of two in recent history when international trade was dominated by institutions that used the rhetoric of free markets to secure advantage for the economies that were industrialising. The first period came to an abrupt end when World War I broke out. As Block writes:

> The gold standard was intended to create an integrated global marketplace that reduced the role of national units and national governments, but its consequences were exactly the opposite. Polanyi shows that when it was widely adopted in the 1870s, it had the ironic effect of intensifying the importance of the nation as a unified entity. Although market liberals dreamed of a pacified world in which the only international struggles would be those of individuals and firms to outperform their competitors, their efforts to realize these dreams through the gold standard produced two horrific world wars. (2001: xxxi)

Polanyi (2001) tracks the disintegration of the institutions of free trade between the world wars, as currency crises ripped through successive economies and eventually 'engulfed' the USA in 1929. After World War II (and the defeat of fascism's main advocates) economic theory shifted to popular governments regulating a *political economy* based on Keynesian ideals (see Chapter 2). This period is characterised by an increased role for the state in regulating a mixed economy, or a more explicit **Marxian** doctrine of using the state to transfer wealth from the private to the public sector. Important for an understanding of current social enterprise movements, however, is a second period during which international institutions again sought to create a global economy, this time based on fluctuating currencies.

According to Gray (2009), the second period occurred from the late 1970s (after the election of Margaret Thatcher in the UK, and Ronald Reagan in the US) and ended with the collapse of confidence in the institutions of global capitalism in 2007–8. In 2008, governments again had to provide financial and social security by taking over major parts of the banking system and reasserting local control. As a result, Polanyi's (2001) analysis of the relationship between international and national institutions has increased in relevance, and provides a compelling critique of the assumptions behind globalisation. He argued that during periods when control over national governments by international institutions is weak, conflict erupts *between* states in the form of war. During periods when international institutions dominate national governments, conflict erupts *within* nation states as governments quell labour and civil unrest. Local disputes escalate as global financial policies disrupt regional and local economies (for a contemporary analysis, see Klein, 2007), eventually leading to a change of government (policy) to prioritise national interests. Polanyi's words, first published in 1944, are as extraordinarily prescient today given the situation that developed in 2008:

> The true nature of the international system under which we were living was not realized until it failed. Hardly anyone understood the political function of the international monetary system; the awful suddenness of the transformation took the world completely by surprise … Not even when the cataclysm was already upon them did their leaders see that behind the collapse of the international system there stood a long development within the most advanced countries that made that system anachronistic; in other words, the failure of market economy itself still escaped them. (2001: 21)

Importantly, for contemporary debates on social enterprise, Polanyi argued that liberal economic theory fails to distinguish between 'real' and 'fictitious' commodities. Three items, in particular, are singled out for discussion: labour, money and land (i.e. the environment). Polanyi regarded these as 'fictitious' commodities. The assumptions of globalisation extend beyond the trade of tangible goods and services to the commodification of money (through currency speculation), labour (by removing collective bargaining rights and minimum wage protection) and land (through attaching prices to natural resources, such as water, land, carbon and airspace). Polanyi argues, in sharp contrast to Fukuyama's (1995) advocacy of high-trust liberalism, that during historical periods in which money, labour and land are treated as commodities, commerce destroys social capital and the natural environment. However, he stops short of condemning the market mechanism itself (so long as it trades in 'real' goods), marking a clear departure in his thinking from the Marxian tradition. He regarded the market as a useful information system, providing its operations were subordinated to democratic control at the level of both governmental institutions and the workplace.

Gray explains why speculative investment leads to banking crises:

> transactions in foreign exchange markets have now reached the astonishing sum of … over 50 times the level of world trade. Around 95 per cent of these transactions are speculative in nature, many using complex new derivative financial instruments based on futures and options. (1998: 62)

Put simply, nearly all transactions in global financial markets produce nothing of tangible value (i.e. a product or a service that has direct utility value outside the financial sector). Vast quantities of labour (and money) are engaged in 'casino capitalism', producing 'fictitious' rather than 'real' goods and services. As currency values bear no relation to the trading of 'real' goods, they eventually destabilise markets and increase economic volatility.

These critiques, therefore, have salience today as they converge in their rejection of some fundamental market principles, primarily in respect of labour, money and environmental resources. They concur that throughout human history, markets are responsive to the rules created by people, and are always determined by political factors. According to Klein (2007) 'free markets' do not exist without state repression (to remove or marginalise competing economic systems). Free markets (and economic theory to support them) are not separate from human beliefs; they are as utopian as the assumptions of altruism under communism (Gray, 1998).

This background is useful for understanding the spread of social enterprise as a concept, and the way its practitioners are selective in accepting and rejecting tenets of capitalism and communism. Moreover, social enterprises – particularly in the way they are founded and develop – reflect the full range of attitudes to globalisation. They may use enabling technologies that transform participation in global information and trading systems. Alternatively, they may seek to subvert the logic of the free market, and change relationships between money, land and people and 'real' goods and services. We will consider these points by firstly exploring two examples (eBay and Wikipedia) that accept globalisation and use it to advance social entrepreneurial enterprises in the US tradition (Martin and Osberg, 2007). Secondly, we use three further examples (fair trade, micro-finance and cooperative factory takeovers) to illustrate how social enterprises can act to limit the effects of globalisation, and *relocalise* political and economic control.

Social Enterprise as a Global Enterprise

Social enterprises that take advantage of globalisation are typically grounded in an Anglo-American approach to economics and a liberal philosophy based on individualism. A well-known example of this is eBay, and its accompanying financial management system PayPal (Robinson and Halle, 2002). eBay works *with* the assumptions of globalisation by creating a technocratic, rule-based system for global trading activity. The *Official eBay Guide* (Kaiser and Kaiser, 1999, cited in Robinson and Halle, 2002: 363) states the assumptions made by eBay's founders about people:

- *We believe people are basically good.*
- *We believe that everyone has something to contribute.*
- *We believe that an honest, open environment can bring out the best in people.*
- *We recognize and respect everyone as a unique individual.*
- *We encourage you to treat others the way that you want to be treated.*

A key innovation in eBay's approach is the use of a peer rating system allowing customers to rate suppliers. The PayPal system for electronic transfers, while backed by traditional bank accounts, allows buyers and sellers in any participating country to transfer funds directly to each other. As an expression of US social entrepreneurial values based on individualised trading in a global market, it is groundbreaking (Robinson and Halle, 2002).

Another global venture that uses internet technologies is Wikipedia. Although financed wholly through fundraising rather than trading activities, it can be viewed as a social enterprise for its innovative approach to knowledge production and dissemination. The editorial guidelines echo enlightenment thinking based on the rationality assumed to underpin liberal democracy. Knowledge is viewed as a product of rational debate, so editorial contributions are expected to be objective, neutral and balanced, and based on evidence from credible and authoritative sources.

Both eBay and Wikipedia are breathtaking in their ambition to provide global trading and information systems that are both multilingual and widely accessible. They satisfy the US-based theoretical perspective on social entrepreneurship by emphasising social innovation (Martin and Osberg, 2007). Using new technology to enfranchise people and individualise power, they meet a market-based view of participative democracy. Disparities in access come not *directly* from membership criteria (which are open): instead they are *indirectly* related to socio-economic disparities in power and wealth that affect whether people have access to the internet and banking.

Both projects, however, raise substantive questions as well. eBay has been dubbed 'feeBay' (Ruzicho, 2006: 14) because you get 'fee'd to death' not only for listing products, but also when taking payments via PayPal. Further questions have been raised by eBay shareholders after they launched legal actions against Goldman Sachs for bribing eBay 'insiders' to manipulate investment opportunities for private benefit (Chandler, 2004). Wikipedia, on the other hand, has attracted praise for the openness and transparency of its editorial process (Besiki et al., 2008), but is criticised for the variable accuracy and reliability of its content. There is, from a critical perspective, a naïvety in the assumptions behind the editorial arrangements characteristic of a liberal philosophy that ignores group process, the formation of elites, and the consequent effects on the ability to collaborate as social equals in productive activity (Luyt et al., 2008). Wikipedia, it can be argued, fails to deal adequately with the implications of its own editorial assumptions: that it is possible to adjudicate knowledge through the application of neutral, rational and objective criteria (Johnson and Duberley, 2000).

Social Enterprise as Opposition to Globalisation

From a non-US perspective it is questionable whether eBay or Wikipedia would be regarded as social enterprises. eBay is owned by individual and institutional shareholders who invest for private benefit. This falls well short of the capital ownership requirements specified in the social enterprise definition developed by the EMES research network (see Chapter 3). The business model is geared to maximising profits, even if there is a palpable public benefit. Wikipedia, on the other hand, is a classic philanthropic charitable venture, dependent on donations of around $6 million a year to employ staff and maintain its infrastructure. It bars advertisers (and the use of advertising revenues) and, while it deploys a radical democratic model in information production, there is no trading income or market activity. Therefore, it falls short on the 'enterprise' criteria set out in many UK models (see the UK's Social Enterprise Mark as an example).

In the remainder of this chapter, we consider three international examples that meet established definitions of social enterprise on both sides of the Atlantic, but which also reject the assumptions that underpin globalisation. The first of these examples involves fair trade.

Fair trade organisations offer an established international solution to mixing social and economic aspects of enterprise that is supportive of both community and cooperative development (Lacey, 2009). While they operate globally, they modify market operations and subordinate them to human needs by altering the norms embedded in trading relationships (Nicholls and Opal, 2004). As Jones' (2000) study of Traidcraft reveals, the motive to initiate a fair trade enterprise is grounded in political and religious ethics. These incline entrepreneurs to actively limit the influence of the market in economic planning, not only with regard to the supply and distribution of goods, but also sometimes in the sphere of labour relations. Fair trade enterprises depend on ethical capital (see Chapter 4) by not permitting prices to fall so low that producers cannot develop their communities. Unlike past colonial ventures based on the acquisition of land, and master–servant relations developed during the industrial era (Melman, 2001), fair trade typically involves the creation of cooperatives and community enterprises that combine their produce to meet demand in established market economies. Distribution companies and retailers pay an agreed minimum price for goods (limiting the effects of the global market), and use profits to pay a *social premium* to fund investment in the producer's community (Nicholls and Opal, 2004).

Doherty et al. (2009a) discuss the advantages that this ethical form of business accorded Divine Chocolate and Café Direct. Ownership of the supply chain is shared with producers (who are mostly based in Africa). Doing so not only redistributes financial capital but also creates social capital. Sustainability is achieved through the cultivation of social networks, particularly in public and third sector procurement and retailing activities. Through these approaches, Polanyi's (2001) 'fictitious goods' of land, money and people acquire a changed status, while 'real' goods continue to use (regulated) market mechanisms to provide information on supply and demand. Land is less frequently treated as a commodity: it remains a productive asset under the control of community institutions or producer cooperatives. Working relationships are oriented towards stakeholder engagement and returns from social enterprise, rather than wage-labour as within a private corporation. Lastly, market prices (money) are subordinated to political and social imperatives if they become unsustainable for producers.

In the rest of this chapter, we consider two further examples: the Grameen Bank in Bangladesh and the *empresas recuperadas* (reclaimed companies) in Argentina. These have been selected for different reasons. The Grameen Bank has been particularly effective in transforming the lives of the rural poor (Bornstein, 1996). Academic studies are helpful in problematising and assessing the socio-economic contribution of the Grameen Bank, not just to the situation in Bangladesh, but also to the rethinking of financial institutions around the world (Jain, 1996; Dowla, 2006). Its underlying model not only calls into question the assumptions that underpin lending based on property ownership, but also illustrates how a bank can build social capital by organising its operations in a particular way (Dowla, 2006).

The reclaimed company movement in Argentina has been selected for a different reason. It contrasts initiatives to help poor communities in rural areas and illustrates how industrial working classes can respond to globalisation (Lewis and Klein, 2004; Klein, 2007). In this case, the concept of *expropriation* underpins a new social arrangement that permits the occupation of an abandoned or idle factory in order to continue or restart production (Howarth, 2007). The theoretical significance is that this challenges business norms regarding the primacy of property rights, and creates an embryonic legal system that permits the protection of jobs and communities against the effects of globalisation (Ranis, 2005). Let us start with the Grameen Bank.

The Grameen Bank was established by Muhammad Yunus as an action research project in 1976. It constituted itself as a bank working exclusively with the 'rural poor' in 1983.[1] There are two key aspects of the Grameen Bank's expansion that are highly significant. Firstly, after 20 years of operation, the bank claimed that it achieved a default rate on loans of only 2 per cent with the poorest sections of the community (Jain, 1996). Such a default rate for credit is extremely low, even in an 'advanced' economy, so this finding alone created strong interest in the Grameen Bank's approach. It also confounded assumptions that property is needed as collateral (assets that can be turned into cash if a borrower defaults on repayments) when lending to 'high-risk' customers. Secondly, the Grameen Bank's approach to banking has contributed to the creation of social capital and a culture of community-based welfare. In doing so, there have been notable impacts on the social status of women, due to the level of successful lending to them (Dowla, 2006).

CLASS EXERCISE   The Grameen Bank: a first look

Watch the following video clip about the Grameen Bank in Bangladesh:

http://www.youtube.com/watch?v=MrUQKuvsmvw&feature=fvw

Based on this clip, consider the following issues:

1 What are the key challenges faced by the Grameen Bank in Bangladesh?
2 Critically assess the way that 'social collateral' is used to guarantee loan repayments.
3 Critically assess the goal of Muhammad Yunus of a poverty-free Bangladesh.

Jain (1996) explores the institutional arrangements that produce low default rates amongst borrowers. The bank has been lauded for its use of 'social collateral' (group guarantees to repay a loan if one group member misses a repayment). Jain argues, however, that the low default rate cannot be attributed to this policy alone. In practice, it was found that Grameen Bank workers and managers do not enforce the group guarantee scheme. The lending policies, he argues, are similar to cooperative banking institutions that have much higher default rates; an explanation has to be found in the internal working arrangements of the bank, rather than its lending policies.

Borrowers are organised into groups of five people. Each group elects a 'chief'. The members of each group cannot come from the same family. They undergo seven days of training on bank policy and the role played by members. Once a group forms, they have to establish a track record of saving before being granted any credit. In the first instance, two members of each group receive credit; the creditworthiness of the other group members depends on the first two borrowers' repayment record.

A bank centre comprises 10 groups. Each week a bank worker visits the group to collect repayments and consider new applications for credit. Studies reveal that the weekly meeting is vitally important, as it establishes social norms and rituals to reinforce a culture of regular saving and prompt repayment (Dowla, 2006). New applications for credit and regular repayments take place with all members of the centre present (50 people): they are not conducted in private (as is the norm in westernised banking institutions). Jain (1996) reports that these arrangements influence both borrowers *and* bank workers. Financial and procedural discipline comes both from the bottom-up control of members (who will challenge deviations from bank policy) and top-down checks that are routinely carried out by branch and area managers.

The training regime for bank workers, branch and area managers is demanding (Jain, 1996). The first six months involves writing case studies on the impact of poverty. Hours are long, regular travel to remote villages is required, and workers have to embrace not only banking responsibilities, but also the welfare of members. Woolcock (1998: 120, cited in Dowla, 2006) found that bank managers are 'likely to find [themselves] assuming the roles of marriage counsellor, conflict negotiator, training officer, civic leader, and bank manager ... at times ... more demanding and intense than that of an emergency room doctor'.

Dowla (2006) considers key challenges that were overcome during the growth of the Grameen Bank. Muhammad Yunus, then an economist in Chittagong, encountered resistance from other bankers, as well as political interference from religious groups and politicians:

> When a supportive finance minister proposed a separate bank to expand the Grameen experiment, the commercial bankers put up all possible hurdles (Yunus, 1999, p. 118, 119) ... When the bank first attempted to introduce housing loans, the Central Bank resisted, arguing that the bank can provide credit only for productive purposes ... Grameen Bank countered by suggesting that a house is like a factory building where all household-based production occurs and as such owning a house is an important input of production in addition to being consumption. On one occasion the bank received a terse letter asking it to justify why the majority of the borrowers of the bank were women. Professor Yunus retorted that the central bank itself ought to justify why the majority of [its] borrowers ... were men. (2006: 105)

Culturally, the struggle was not only to convince political institutions and commercial bankers that the scheme was viable. It also involved convincing the poor:

> the poor could not believe that a government sponsored bank could be seriously interested in their welfare ... [Yunus] had to struggle to convince the eligible women to accept credit ... they would not go in [front] of him because of the purdah norm, so he ended up talking with them with a screen ... Moreover, they were reluctant to accept credit because ... they had been taught that money is something that should be handled by men only. (2006: 106)

Further local obstacles came from the spread of rumours about Christian missionaries, socialist plots and jail sentences for defaulters, while mainstream institutions sought to question the business model and accounting practices of the Grameen Bank, claiming that they hid the true level of defaults (Pearl and Phillips, 2001, cited in Tesfatsion, 2007).

The progress of the Grameen Bank, however, has been transformative on a number of levels. Firstly, it used share ownership by members to build trust that the bank would not be taken over by governmental or private interests. From registration in 1983, over the course of 20 years, members' share of capital has increased from 40 per cent to 93 per cent. Dowla (2006: 112) describes this as 'an absolutely new norm of corporate governance for Bangladesh'. Secondly, through successful lending, subsidiary companies (e.g. Grameen Telecom) have contributed to changes in the status and role of women in the community. Bangladesh and Islamic laws enabling women to own property had been limited by social custom (Subramanian, 1998). The Grameen Bank's lending activities have increased not only the property holdings of women, but also the educational opportunities for both their sons and their daughters. A practice of addressing members by name at meetings means that many women are now known by other members of their community as individuals, no longer merely as someone's sister, wife or daughter.

In terms of 'fictitious goods' (Polanyi, 2001), the Grameen Bank rewrites the textbook on risk management by demonstrating that lending against assets and property is a political and ideological choice (to privilege those who possess property), and not one based on intrinsic economic and social benefit or improved commercial performance (Ellerman, 2005). Banking practices using social collateral, backed by processes that deliberately build social capital through participatory economics (Albert, 2003), are effective in reducing defaults on loan repayments even when compared to commercial banks who lend to much wealthier clients (McIndoe, 2007).

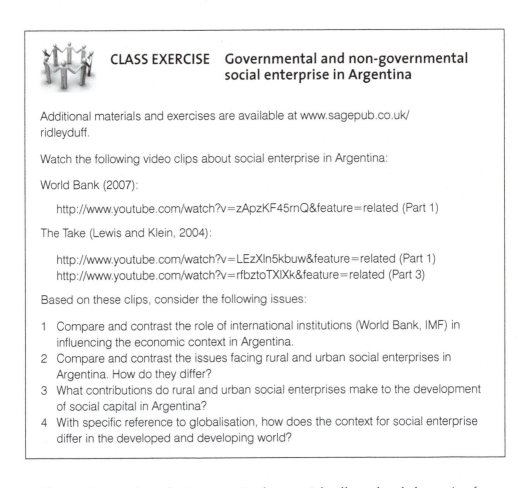

CLASS EXERCISE   Governmental and non-governmental social enterprise in Argentina

Additional materials and exercises are available at www.sagepub.co.uk/ridleyduff.

Watch the following video clips about social enterprise in Argentina:

World Bank (2007):

> http://www.youtube.com/watch?v=zApzKF45rnQ&feature=related (Part 1)

The Take (Lewis and Klein, 2004):

> http://www.youtube.com/watch?v=LEzXIn5kbuw&feature=related (Part 1)
> http://www.youtube.com/watch?v=rfbztoTXIXk&feature=related (Part 3)

Based on these clips, consider the following issues:

1 Compare and contrast the role of international institutions (World Bank, IMF) in influencing the economic context in Argentina.
2 Compare and contrast the issues facing rural and urban social enterprises in Argentina. How do they differ?
3 What contributions do rural and urban social enterprises make to the development of social capital in Argentina?
4 With specific reference to globalisation, how does the context for social enterprise differ in the developed and developing world?

The conclusions from the Grameen Bank on social collateral and alternative forms of organisation provide a useful starting point for our second discussion: the development of social enterprise in Argentina. Unlike Bangladesh, which is one of the poorest countries in the world, Argentina has twice been on the verge of joining the 'first' world. Firstly, in 1910, its GDP per capita was ahead of France and Germany, and second only to the industrial economies in the British Empire (Della Paolera and Taylor, 2004). By the 1970s, it was again the strongest economy in South America, this time interrupted by a military coup (Klein, 2007). Following the 1970s coup, economic advisers, schooled in neoliberal economic theory, visited Argentina to help establish regimes committed to a policy of 'free' markets. As became the norm during this period, foreign investment (loans from the **IMF** or **World Bank**) was often conditional on making public assets available for private acquisition.

The effects of the privatisation and the 'liberalisation' programme have been well documented (Klein, 2007; Howarth, 2007). By 2001, many millions of jobs had been lost and the number of jobless poor had risen from 18 per cent (in 1994) to over 50 per cent (in 2001). In response, both rural and industrialised regions of Argentina have started to establish initiatives that promote self-management. In rural areas, social enterprise is based on micro-finance movements similar to the Grameen model (World Bank, 2007). In the cities, however, a more radical approach based on 'recovered companies' is spreading outwards from Buenos Aires to other parts of South America (Trigona, 2006; Klein, 2007). As Lewis and Klein (2004) recall, the movement began when people organised themselves to take over factories abandoned during a financial crisis in 2001. Wilson (2004, cited in Howarth, 2007: 5) comments that:

> The workers' response was instinctive – to work together to safeguard jobs, and the skills and competencies on which their livelihoods and those of their communities depended. They did not know of, did not work with, and did not draw upon the vast collective memory and experience of the global co-operative movement. They simply organised collectively to take over and keep the businesses running ... As in the early nineteenth century, it is virtually impossible to distinguish between what we would consider today to be the realm of trade union activities and those of a co-operative.

Howarth's (2007) study is useful for understanding how and why small groups of industrialised workers reacted to the effects of globalisation. It supports Polanyi's (2001) argument that whenever 'free' (i.e. international) markets start to dominate, the effect on local economies is highly variable. Industrialised economies (or regions) benefit from a transfer of wealth, while job losses and political repression occur in weaker economies (or regions). In Argentina, this took the form of political action to break up organised labour and protest movements during a second wave of 'liberalisation' in 1994. The effects, however, devastated employment amongst both skilled and unskilled workers, leading to the formation of a new cooperative movement.

Spontaneously, initially without government or international support, workforces started taking over abandoned factories to resume production. They were able to do this under laws that allow a cooperative to secure court permission to use idle equipment for a two-year period. Howarth (2007) reports that local courts upheld by-laws that require former owners to negotiate with cooperative members over the rental and purchase of abandoned equipment. In other cases, local government authorities bought the assets and leased them back to the cooperatives.

One high-profile case is Zanon, a ceramics factory that has grown to 300 staff and achieved international recognition. Due to high levels of community support, it has survived six attempts to restore ownership to its previous (private) owners (Lewis and Klein, 2004), and in 2009 it was granted its wish of permanent cooperative ownership by the provincial legislature (Trigona, 2009). As Ranis points out:

> There are multiple examples of recuperated factories lending their facilities to the surrounding communities for health clinics, art exhibits, theatre evenings, and adult learning centres with university faculty providing courses for credit (the author visited several such factory culture programmes in the city of Buenos Aires). These neighbourhood and community contacts stood them in good stead when threatened with police interventions on behalf of the previous owners. (2005: 106)

Howarth (2007) explains the use of *expropriation,* the legal basis for occupying and claiming the assets of an abandoned factory. In liberal economies, the rights of property dominate: if there is a conflict between defending a person's right to dispose of their property or defending the jobs of a workforce, the rights of the property owner are given priority. In Argentina, the law now recognises – in the case of reclaimed companies in Buenos Aires – that there are circumstances where the rights of a person to support their family and community may take precedence over the owners' property rights. As Ranis (2005) argues, Argentine and regional governments have constitutional provisions that allow cooperatives (and only cooperatives) to expropriate properties for reasons of 'public utility', or in defence of the 'common good'. This is different both from liberal economies (such as the US and UK) and also from expropriation by the state to nationalise whole industries (as happened in many countries dominated by Marxian economic thinking).

In summarising the cases of the Grameen Bank and Argentine cooperatives, it is easy to highlight their different development paths and contexts. However, there are also some interesting similarities that draw on the material of the previous chapter. Firstly, both approaches were dependent on the development of community-based social capital that emphasised solidarity (see Chapter 4). Furthermore, the strength of this social capital empowered the social enterprises to defend their institutional arrangements from interference by powerful commercial and state interests. Secondly, in both cases, the organisations changed the economic 'rules' that govern property and employment rights. At Grameen, consumer ownership of the bank led to a different relationship between lenders and borrowers (because members were making decisions on both lending and borrowing at the same time at both group and branch level). In Argentina, employment rights were superseded by member ownership, transforming the relationship between workers and the machinery needed to sustain production. Property was *subordinated* to labour (and public) interest, rather than the reverse. Lastly, in both cases the 'local struggles are a direct result of national and international policies and of the global context' (Ranis, 2005: 115). In Grameen, the struggle was against the poverty created by globalisation in rural communities. In Argentina, the struggle was against urban unemployment created by 'liberalisation'. From this, we can draw some conclusions.

Conclusions

In this chapter, we initially considered the development of a global economy and the concept of globalisation. We highlighted the critiques of Gray and Polanyi, and drew attention to the problems of treating people (labour), money and the environment (land) as if they are commodities to be traded in global markets. We explored two examples of global social entrepreneurship rooted in US perspectives on participatory democracy. Each enterprise attempts to individualise power through the use of global internet technologies with the goal of enfranchising people in the production of knowledge (Wikipedia) and international trade (eBay).

We then adopted a more collectivist view, rooted in an EU perspective on social enterprise, to discuss alternative approaches. Using examples from Africa (fair trade), Asia (community micro-finance) and South America (recovered companies) we discussed how social enterprise offers a robust *response* to globalisation that *relocalises* enterprise activity and grounds it in local needs. In each case, the role of people (labour), land (environment) and money were modified, and the enterprises created used *organisational* innovations to extend ownership and control to producers, consumers and workers. Unlike the US cases, where social entrepreneurship has a market focus (Martin and Osberg, 2007), the collectivist solutions have an organisational focus based on member ownership and participatory economics (Albert, 2003). While both, arguably, attempt to advance participatory democracy, collectivist approaches emphasise *social and economic participation in the enterprise itself*, while the US perspective emphasises *participation in global markets*.

SUMMARY OF LEARNING

In this chapter, we have argued that:

- Globalisation is a concept linked to the creation of global markets and removal of barriers to global trade using an Anglo-American model of capitalism.
- Critics of globalisation draw attention to the unsustainability of free markets that treat land, labour and money as commodities.
- A US-style social entrepreneurial perspective supports globalisation by creating transnational enterprises based on values that underpin liberal democracy (e.g. eBay, Wikipedia).
- Non-US-style social enterprises adopt a more collectivist response to local economic problems created by global financial institutions. In cases such as fair trade in Africa, the Grameen Bank in Asia, and the recovered companies of South America, more collective forms of ownership and control assist in re-establishing local control of city factories and rural economies.
- Polanyi's concept of 'fictitious goods' is helpful in explaining the changed approach to land management, labour relations and financial investment in social enterprises.

QUESTIONS AND POSSIBLE ESSAY ASSIGNMENTS

1 Using international examples (from outside the US and EU), critically assess the relevance of Polanyi's concept of 'fictitious goods', and the contribution of social enterprise to countering the commodification of land, labour and money.
2 Using examples from the 'recovered companies' movement in South America, critically assess the role of social enterprises in responding to the effects of globalisation.
3 Critically assess the opportunities and threats posed by global 'free markets' to the development of social enterprise.

FURTHER READING

Excellent primers for globalisation include *Global Sociology* by Cohen and Kennedy (2000) and Giddens' (1982) highly readable critical introduction to sociology. The international spread of social enterprise is covered in *The Social Economy: International Perspectives on Economic Solidarity* by Amin (2009a). This publication uses cases in Australasia, Europe, North America and Latin America to explore the social economy and its contribution to an alternative future. The position of the social entrepreneur, and the nature of individual agency in a global economy, is discussed in Grenier's (2006) chapter from Nicholls' (2006a) book *Social Entrepreneurship: New Models of Sustainable Social Change*.

The papers referenced in this chapter on the Grameen Bank offer considerable insights into the development of micro-finance. Jain (1996) is particularly useful for the depth of study at all levels of the organisation. Dowla's (2006) paper focuses more on the institutional processes that have contributed to the development of social capital. Further insights into Asian social enterprise (in India) can be found in *Stories, Visions and Values in Voluntary Organisations* by Christina Schwabenland (2006).

For more information on the Argentine 'recovered companies', see the documentary *The Take* by Lewis and Klein (2004), filmed on location in Argentina. Howarth's (2007) academic review provides detailed insights from studies first published in Spanish, and includes a useful comparison between the Argentine movement and other movements in earlier periods of history.

Two sources offer good coverage of fair trade issues. Nicholls and Opal's (2004) book *Fair Trade* provides a comprehensive overview, while deeper insights on competitive advantage have been explored in an award-winning paper 'Resource advantage theory and fairtrade social enterprises' by Doherty et al. (2009a).

Further reading material is available on the companion website at www.sagepub.co.uk/ridleyduff.

USEFUL RESOURCES

The Corporation (documentary website), http://www.thecorporation.com/
The Globalisation Website, http://www.sociology.emory.edu/globalization/
Global Exchange, http://www.globalexchange.org
The International Labour Organization, http://www.ilo.org/
The International Cooperative Alliance, http://www.ica.coop/al-ica/
Cooperatives for Development, http://www.internationaldevelopment.coop/

International Social Enterprise Exchange, http://www.nesst.org

Skoll World Forum, http://www.skollfoundation.org/skollworldforum/

OneWorld, http://us.oneworld.net/

Fairtrade Foundation, http://www.fairtrade.org. uk/

China–UK Social Innovation Project, http://dsi.britishcouncil.org.cn/Projects/20070828/136.jsp

Africa Social Enterprise Forum, http://asef2009.weebly.com/

The Take (documentary website), http://www.thetake.org/

Upside Down World (Latin America), http://upsidedownworld.org/main/

NOTES

1 The definition of 'rural poor' used by Muhammad Yunus was a person with assets to the value of less than half an acre of land.

The Practice of Social Enterprise

PART II

Management Debates

6

Learning Objectives

In this chapter, we consider key practical debates that influence management practice in social enterprises. By the end of this chapter you will be able to:

- critically assess the ambiguity surrounding management as a concept in social enterprises

- critically evaluate attitudes to democratic management, ownership and governance

- compare and contrast arguments about social enterprise as a process and an organisational form

- identify and compare perspectives on the key issues facing social enterprise managers

- evaluate the impact of different philosophies on social enterprise management practice.

Seven key debates identified in this chapter:

Debate 1: Should social entrepreneurs accept private and public sector management theory?

Debate 2: How far should social entrepreneurs embrace democratic management theory?

Debate 3: What is 'social' about social enterprise?

Debate 4: Is social enterprise a form of organisation or an entrepreneurial process?

Debate 5: How is power understood, developed and deployed in social enterprises?

Debate 6: What approaches to learning are most helpful to social enterprise managers?

Debate 7: What are the key challenges in social enterprise management?

Introduction

In Part I, we considered the historical and ideological contexts in which social enterprise has developed as a concept. Chapters 1 to 3 covered the manner in which social enterprise thinking has emerged partly from charitable, cooperative and voluntary sector traditions, and partly from contemporary debates about direct democracy in the ownership and control of economic activity. An important dimension of this debate was a tension between neoliberal arguments that governments should not directly manage industry or social services, and 'local socialist' arguments that organisations should be democratically owned and controlled, supported by programmes of regional development in partnership with local government. In Chapters 4 and 5, we considered theoretical perspectives on the primary 'output' of social enterprise, in particular their capacity to distribute social and economic power by propagating alternative ethical arguments that lead to different business practices both locally and globally.

In Part II, we consider management debates that preoccupy those teaching, researching, commissioning and practising social enterprise focused on the United Kingdom. Before we explore this in further detail, it is worth considering one overarching question. Is it better to adopt a *managerial* or a *developmental* perspective in the chapters that follow? A managerial perspective typically involves an analysis of the functions of the organisation (see Doherty et al., 2009b), supported by discipline-specific discussions of the expertise needed to develop managerial competence. This is sometimes considered a **functionalist** approach to the study of organisations (Burrell and Morgan, 1979) that renders it as a series of 'systems' over which 'management' can exert 'control'. It ignores the question of how management itself develops, and the political and social contexts that influence the development of a management style. We have, therefore, avoided putting the cart before the horse by adopting a particular approach based on a cycle of issues faced in organisation development. Figure 6.1 outlines business development as a cyclical and recursive process, rather than a set of business functions (Cornforth, 1995). This makes more explicit the constructed and evolving nature of 'management' so that its role(s) and purpose(s) become visible and amenable to debate.

Outlining a Perspective on Social Enterprise Education

Chapters 7 and 8 consider pre-trading and developmental phases of organisation development. What purpose(s) and goal(s) do founders embed in a new organisation? Can organisations be structured in a way that supports the pursuit of both social and economic goals? In Chapter 8, we consider how social enterprises develop and choose to operationalise practice. Social enterprise activities may be set up by collegial groups of people as well as 'visionary' entrepreneurs (Seanor and Meaton, 2008). As a result, there is often a first phase of organisation development that is more dependent on mutual commitment and trust than formalised systems to select, monitor and control different groups of staff.

As organisations evolve, they are faced with a range of choices on how to develop the relationships that support their work. This increases the need to consider members' rights and responsibilities, including discussion of whether these should be the

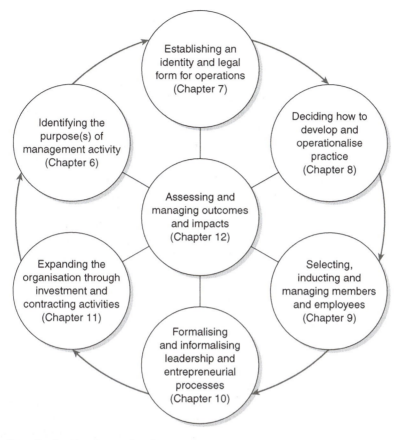

Figure 6.1 Cyclical business development

same or different for various stakeholder groups. External parties (funders, banks, investors, support organisations) may seek to impose (or find satisfactory evidence of) formal management and leadership responsibility as a condition of financial support or **organisational legitimacy** (Dart, 2004; Ridley-Duff, 2009a). This can increase tensions between different stakeholders who compete with each other over practical and ideological aspects of sustainable development. Often there is an increased need to manage the disjuncture between the informal and formal policies and values propagated by different stakeholder groups (Wallace, 2005). We consider these questions, ways of understanding them, and the processes to manage them, in Chapters 9 and 10.

Lastly, we consider the issues faced by growing organisations. Their development is supported by expansions in their base of customers and clients, or ever larger contracts with public and private bodies. This may involve the development of new processes to attract investment, or bid for larger contracts. It may bring members and employees into contact with stakeholders who possess more political power, and who make new (more complex) demands. In Chapters 11 and 12, we consider such issues alongside the need to scrutinise and evaluate the relationships that develop as managerial groups are asked to 'prove' the value of their work to various stakeholders.

In developing the text, we take the view that management philosophy is constructed and reconstructed through successive cycles of business development (Weick, 1995). The adoption of a business-cycle perspective, therefore, highlights not only the constructed nature of 'management', but also the constructed notion of a 'manager' (Watson, 1994). While Part II is squarely focused on *management practices*, we leave open the question of how social enterprise practitioners approach the employment of 'directors', 'managers' and 'administrators' (i.e. staff employed exclusively to assume responsibility for non-production tasks). As case studies will reveal, some social enterprises employ people in recognised management roles while others divide management functions up and distribute them amongst organisation members. In some well-documented cases, social enterprises have developed systems for involving far more people – perhaps three to five times as many people – in strategic decision-making. For example, Bradley and Gelb (1983: 54) surveyed both cooperative and conventional businesses and found that 33 per cent of Mondragón's owner-workers state that they participate in 'important decisions', with 60 per cent reporting some level of influence. This compared to a finding of 7 per cent and 21 per cent respectively in comparable private businesses.

Debate 1:   Should social entrepreneurs accept private and public sector management
theory?

Put simply, the first management debate is whether private and public sector notions of 'management' and 'manager' provide an appropriate starting point for social enterprise management practice. While Dart (2004) draws attention to the growing reliance of social enterprises on private sector models, Hudson (2002) outlines the recognition of efficiencies and high-level management skills and professionalism within the third sector. Cheney (1999) indicates that some of these practices are penetrating cooperative thought, with examples of cooperative and democratic management practice challenging private and public sector thinking (Johnson, 2006). Social enterprises, therefore, are active in reshaping and remoulding the notion of management itself, to suit a business environment where organisations aim to be profit making, but not immorally profit maximising.

The rest of this chapter is organised into two parts. In the first, we consider a debate between academics who are active in social enterprise education. This goes some way towards identifying contrasting perspectives on management that are central to social enterprise education. The second part uses key texts (Hudson, 2002; Paton, 2003; Doherty et al., 2009b) to stimulate further discussions, and to draw out different ways of learning about management issues and approaching the challenges that are identified.

Living the Management Debate

In the pages that follow we discuss Case 6.1, a series of exchanges between four people involved in developing programmes of social enterprise education. These debates tackle the overarching issues that affect smaller-scale discussions (such as management tasks and functions), and how they might be approached. In the first instance, we consider contrasting views on the application of democratic principles to management theory in social enterprises.

Case 6.1   A living management debate

The conversation in this section is based on a transcript of an e-mail exchange between Jon Griffith, Rory Ridley-Duff, Tim Curtis and Doug Foster between 12 and 20 March 2009. The material has been edited only to remove repetition and to select issues of interest for discussion: the wording of the original e-mails has been retained. A fuller transcript (and an exercise based on it) is available on the accompanying website at www.sagepub.co.uk/ridleyduff.

The problem with [the idea of mixed boards as a panacea for problems of governance] for me is that a social enterprise might be a voluntary organisation which has turned to trading, and has an unbreakable commitment to its double bottom line, but remains a company limited by guarantee with an unelected board of directors, or a registered charity with an unelected group of trustees, or an incorporated association with an unelected management committee, and no-one involved gives a flying +%@# about its democratic credentials, because that is not what they happen to be interested in, because they don't come from the world of cooperative politics and economics ... Now (as ever) please don't get me wrong: I like coops a lot, and I would dearly like to see them grow towards the dizzy heights of 10% of the economy, and then maybe eventually 20% or even 50% if the country really turns upside down. But that is me as a private citizen saying what I think ought to happen. This is a completely different thing from me as a professional observer needing to pay attention to what is actually happening. (Jon Griffith, e-mail, 12 March 2009)

The passion with which people debate the necessity of democratic management and governance in social enterprises goes back to a decision taken by the UK government during the consultation on the community interest company (DTI, 2003).

> *Debate 2:*   How far should social entrepreneurs embrace democratic management theory?

During the consultation, the government invited responses on whether there should be a statutory requirement for CICs to involve stakeholders, including (but not exclusively) paid and unpaid staff, in business development. As the report highlighted:

This proposal generated a much more mixed reaction than any other proposal in the consultation paper. This reflected the complexity of the arguments for and against a statutory requirement. (DTI, 2003: 25)

The report provides illustrative quotations from respondents arguing for and against multi-stakeholder democracy. There is a notable split between institutions linked to democratic and cooperative development (in favour of a statutory requirement) and institutions acting for public, voluntary and charitable interests (who either express reservations, or come out against the proposals). Even though 43 per cent of respondents to the consultation were in favour of statutory stakeholder participation, with 25 per cent non-committal and 32 per cent against, the government decided *against* the requirement (see DTI, 2003: 25–27, Proposal 9). Below are some of the illustrative quotations:

> Stakeholder involvement is central for successful social enterprises … all CICs should be required to involve stakeholders. (Social Enterprise Coalition)

> There should be no exceptions, with even the smallest CICs required to show some effort to involve stakeholders. We recognise, however, that the Government may wish to make the CIC form available to entrepreneurs who have little interest in stakeholder involvement. What is important, therefore, is transparency. (Cooperatives UK)

> [This requirement] would run contrary to the 'light touch' regulation that the Government intends for CICs, making them an unattractive option for social entrepreneurs. (Association of Chief Executives of Voluntary Organisations)

> WCVA has reservations about the proposal .. and does not feel that the small CIC exemption will necessarily overcome this. It is felt that statutory stakeholder requirements should only be applied on a sector specific basis by way of specific regulation. (Wales Council for Voluntary Action)

To some extent, these differences mirror divisions based on the historical legacies outlined in Chapter 1. Perhaps more significant is how this decision separates the UK from other EU countries who legislate for social enterprises under cooperative rather than company law (CECOP, 2006). As the response to Jon's contribution argues:

> This begs the question of how [voluntary organisations] ended up being regarded as social enterprises in the first place (i.e. how the definition was modified to include them). This is a prime topic for both critical management research (both inside and outside the Third Sector) and social enterprise research (inside the Third Sector). While the idea of social enterprise as 'trading for a social purpose' has currency now, it had little currency when, in 1997, Social Enterprise London triggered this bandwagon by writing its Memorandum & Articles of Association. Back then, democratic trading and social organisation was the assumption of all the founder organisations. It changed quite quickly in the run up, and particularly during, the 2002/2003 consultations on the Community Interest Company … This changed the definition of social enterprise itself (at least amongst those close to the consultation process). (Rory Ridley-Duff, e-mail, 13 March 2009)

Has the definition of social enterprise been subverted by a switch from a democratisation agenda to one restricted to the achievement of a social purpose? Indeed, what does 'democratisation' mean to different stakeholders? Further, has the issue of stakeholder engagement been fully understood, or been made sufficiently clear to different people, especially within the third sector and social economy? A focus on *social purpose* rather than *social organisation* relegates democracy from its status as a core characteristic to just one of many purposes a social enterprise might pursue.

Regarding people as the *means* of achieving an organisational 'mission' or 'task', rather than as the *ends* of the enterprise, goes some way to explaining the 'mixed reaction' in the CIC consultation, and the surfacing of this debate in academic articles (see Reid and Griffith, 2006; Ridley-Duff, 2007; Curtis, 2008). In short, can a theory of enterprise that maintains a functionalist outlook (Burrell and Morgan, 1979), and which regards people instrumentally as the means of achieving an organisational mission, ever be adequate as a theory of *social* enterprise? Or is it, perhaps, a defensive move to protect *anti*-social theories of enterprise?

For now, we need to note the influence that democratic commitments (or the lack of them) will have on *all* other aspects of management practice. As Tim Curtis added:

> I was struck by the BBC4 film the other night about Rough Trade records and how their espoused values shifted and morphed through democracy, a focus on the music, a focus on the customer and then a focus on the artists as the beneficiaries of the ethic. But, as well as having different motivations (perhaps informed by the generation in which we engage with SE as a movement) we may also be aware of the extent to which this is also an internal discourse – as we develop as individuals and make sense of the movement through different periods of our lives. When we all intersect these changing ethics with that of our colleagues, workers and beneficiaries, we can get a sense of how woefully under-theorised 'the social' is in social enterprise. (Tim Curtis, e-mail, 16 March 2009)

In this contribution, Tim Curtis raises a number of further issues. Firstly, he outlines a view expressed by Pateman (1970) that democratic participation has the capacity to influence our values and beliefs. As Pateman states, any argument against participatory democracy is weakened by evidence that most people want more input into workplace decision-making (particularly in their own sphere of work), and also that confidence and competence develop rapidly when people are able to participate in the decision-making activities that affect their lives. But, as Griffith comments earlier, there is also evidence that not all people want this kind of participation (compare Cornforth et al., 1988). Any perception that democracy is (or is not) effective is tied up with the broader question of how those engaged in social enterprise view the issue of social inclusion.

EXERCISE John Bird and *The Big Issue*

The founder of *The Big Issue*, John Bird, is renowned in the UK for his contributions to debates about social enterprise through the development of a newspaper sold by people who are homeless. Vendors buy the newspapers from *The Big Issue* then keep the profits from selling them. In the following video clip, Bird connects social entrepreneurship and participatory democracy. Watch and consider the questions below:

Video: http://www.youtube.com/watch?v=KAtVcL2qFjw&feature=related

Questions:

1 Critically assess John Bird's view that you can change the world through entrepreneurial (and consumer) action rather than parliamentary democracy.
2 How does John Bird describe 'participatory democracy'?
3 How does this compare to 'representative democracy'?

Debate 3:   What is 'social' about social enterprise?

Tim Curtis also points out how the stage at which we engage with social enterprise (and the institutions through which this engagement is mediated) affects the way that we understand it. Part of this, as he points out, is our own personal development and the way we each struggle to frame the debate. When we share these struggles, we learn how 'woefully under-theorised' are the *social* aspects of 'social enterprise'. One impact of this under-theorisation is a rampant, and largely unchecked, discourse on 'enterprise' as a way of developing the third and public sectors (see Hood, 1995; Dart, 2004; Arthur et al., 2006). Previous studies have identified a number of areas where the under-theorisation of the 'social' has substantially impacted on practice: the advice social enterprises receive from business and legal services (Hines, 2005; Knell, 2008); the way that enterprise development tools are designed and developed (Bull and Compton, 2006; Bull, 2007); the role of business in relation to community and family development (Aldrich and Cliff, 2003; Ridley-Duff, 2008a); and the language and concepts that are used to characterise social enterprise purposes and practices (Seanor et al., 2007; Seanor and Meaton, 2008; Curtis, 2008).

Picking up the issue of sense-making and language, the e-mail conversation then turned to the issue of organisational forms:

> There might indeed be a great plurality of organisational forms, but social enterprise may 'prove' to be a mere passing aberration, and in ten years we go back to talking about cooperatives and ethical businesses – or we find there is yet another groovy sort of organisation that seems to have a new name (but of course has a long history of previously unrecognised examples of this in the past). Yet such a 'discovery' might only come about through us challenging our own and others' experience of social enterprises, rather than prizing it like the received grace of God. (Doug Foster, e-mail, 18 March 2009)

Is there substance to the concept of social enterprise or is it simply a passing management fad? In raising this question, Doug Foster takes us into the realm of 'language games' whereby social movements adopt new expressions of language that simultaneously enable 'old' and 'new' communities to discuss and contest emergent forms of social action (Wittgenstein, 2001; Biletzki, 2009). The rhetoric that accompanies the concept of social enterprise is not unimportant (see Case 6.2 on the companion website).

Debate 4:   Is social enterprise a form of organisation or an entrepreneurial process?

By way of a further example, the exchanges that follow show how social enterprise is variously understood as a form of organisation, or as a process of social entrepreneurship:

> My argument isn't about organisational forms: it's about the hugely varied characteristics of the whole population of things called social enterprises – what they

do, why they do it, how they do it, where they came from, how they are structured, who is in them, who they serve, etc. (and yes, this includes what people think they should be doing, as well as what they are actually doing, the debates which are taking place within them, between them, and about them, and the ones that aren't). (Jon Griffith, e-mail, 19 March 2009)

This focus on entrepreneurial people and processes prompted the following response:

Interesting. But if social enterprises are anything, then they are an organisational form or forms. And who decides 'they' are a 'social enterprise'? The government (55,000 apparently)? Those who set 'one' up (one what?)? Academic experts? Practitioner experts/consultants? Anybody else who wants to jump on the bandwagon? Or perhaps we might start by claiming that 'social enterprise' is a fiction? (Doug Foster, e-mail, 19 March 2009)

The issue under discussion here is the boundary between conceptions of social enterprise (see Chapter 3) and other forms of enterprise activity (private enterprise, public enterprise, voluntary action etc.). To manage social enterprise, we must first think about what it is. Only then, perhaps, can we turn to the issue of 'what they do, why they do it, how they do it, where they came from, how they are structured, who is in them, who they serve'. These are all highly relevant questions, but equally true of public, private and voluntary sector organisations. These are not, as Peattie and Morley (2008) claim, *distinguishing characteristics*. Once we start to think about what social enterprise is, it becomes problematic. As Tim Curtis responds:

This is a little like the debate that raged for 25 years in urban sociology – what is urban and how is it different from rural? Eventually, we ended up researching urban processes (rather than entities in their own right) and took for granted the urban. Social enterprises are socially enterprising through processes and people, not institutions. We needn't fret about identifying one, as that is a positivistic view of the organisational form. What we should be interested in is the social processes of power (Foucauldian, not Marxist conception) that comprise social enterprising. (Tim Curtis, e-mail, 20 March 2009)

The reference to **Foucault** here emphasises the power of language and talk in determining who is included and excluded, and who is silenced or rendered invisible in the way that social enterprise is constructed in discourse. In terms of management debate, discourse renders visible or invisible any one or more of the following in various management discussions: 'member', 'employee', 'trustee', 'volunteer', 'director', 'manager', 'customer', 'volunteer', 'supplier', 'client', 'governor'. Discourses construct them, influence their status, and shape how they are regarded in relation to each other. They determine the rights that each will acquire, and the responsibilities that they will be expected to uphold. Discourse, as Curtis argues, influences how people are defined and accepted into social entrepreneurial processes, and the power they have within them to shape other people's lives. While this linguistic approach may be considered a 'soft' perspective, it is experienced as 'hard' when encountered during enterprise development:

I'm sympathetic to Foucauldian views, and process views, but there is no fudging that those wishing to become socially enterprising have to navigate and establish institutional forms for their activities. I think a rounded understanding of the subject needs engagement on all these levels otherwise those who have identified the people and processes will continually find their plans rejected because they have:

* *No 'company' or incorporated legal entity*
* *No 'bank account' or 'financial control'*
* *No 'governance'*
* *No ... anything that anyone else insists they 'have' before they will support their socially enterprising activity*

Of course, innovative individuals might find ways around all the obstacles that others put in their way, but we need to study the obstacles as well as the ways they navigate around or through them. And once they have navigated, we need to study if, how and whether they institutionalise new forms of organisation, and the impact of such institutionalising (in terms of processes and impacts on people). (Rory Ridley-Duff, e-mail, 20 March 2009)

As Curtis later adds, the power of one party or group to prevent social and economic activity on the basis that another person or group has not conformed to their social conventions reveals the power of discourse. It also illustrates how dominant groups impose their world view on others, and make support conditional on acceptance of their own **discursive reasoning**. One role of social enterprise education, therefore, is to make this explicit so that it is visible, amenable to debate and open to challenge.

Debate 5:   How is power understood, developed and deployed in social enterprises?

In debating management, the argument is not only which people and processes are involved, but how institutional obstacles and enablers of social enterprise come in many forms, ranging from 'soft' issues regarding philosophy, culture and engagement (of staff, customers, suppliers, investors) to 'hard' issues such as access to technology, buildings, infrastructure and space for development. Whether soft or hard, they are mediated by the political interests of those who can control or influence the resources needed to facilitate enterprise development (Doherty et al., 2009a).

In the case of fair trade organisations, alternative networks were developed to sustain and grow a market by prioritising public over private sector customers (e.g. universities), and using extensive networks of informal contacts to generate customer awareness and increase demand for products. Curtis argues that 'power' is embedded in linguistic resources as well as tangible resources. For example, Divine Chocolate and Café Direct go beyond terms like 'return on investment', 'financial management', 'supply chains', 'human resources' and 'management competence', to create additional terms that make up the concept of 'fair trade' itself. Control over the meaning, interpretation and operationalisation of the fair trade discourse gives fair trade companies ownership of what it means to do 'ethical trading'. Part of the approach is to guarantee 'minimum prices' to producers (even when market prices drop below this) in order to ensure that a 'social premium' can be paid to the democratically controlled fund that makes community investments (Lacey, 2009). By defining these standards (i.e. developing a discourse that constructs and justifies the new concepts), fair trade companies create a new business environment in which trading activities do not conform to the norms of a neoliberal market economy (Nicholls and Opal, 2004).

The same process is occurring in the field of social enterprise itself. By defining what is meant by terms such as 'social purpose', 'social ownership' and **'social return on investment (SROI)'**, so power is acquired over the legitimacy of social enterprise itself. Control of the terms provides control of the tacit rules that underpin this new approach to enterprise development. Moreover, if these definitions are accepted and spread, power shifts to the people who control access to, and use of, the new terms.

Exercise   The Social Enterprise Mark

In the UK, the Social Enterprise Coalition has added its support to a regional project aimed at establishing a national kitemark for social enterprises (http://www.socialenterprisemark.co.uk/). The provisions of any quality mark, however, privilege some definitions over others (see Chapter 3) and reveal the political character of an emergent standard. Examine these six criteria for the Social Enterprise Mark and then consider the questions that follow:

1   Social and environmental objects can be evidenced in constitutional documents.
2   Must be an 'independent business', legally constituted, with autonomous governance.
3   Must earn 50 per cent or more from trading, evidenced using 'standard accounting practices'.
4   Devote 50 per cent of more of the organisation's profits to 'social/environmental purposes'.
5   Ensure that all residual assets are distributed for 'social/environmental purposes' (if dissolved).
6   Can demonstrate that social/environmental objects are being achieved.

The questions are:

- Would a democratically owned and controlled enterprise in which the workforce decides for itself how to distribute its own surpluses (on a one-person, one-vote basis) be eligible for the Social Enterprise Mark?
- Would a trading charity with a range of social and environmental projects, but in which no member of the workforce is permitted to participate in the governing body or strategic decisions about charitable objectives, be eligible for the Social Enterprise Mark?
- Would a sole trader making their living entirely from providing advice and guidance to social enterprises at below market rates be eligible for recognition?

Full details on the criteria are available at http://www.socialenterprisemark.org.uk/apply/criteria.

Further materials for seminars are available on the accompanying website (www.sagepub.co.uk/ridleyduff).

In the case of the Social Enterprise Mark, a paradox exists that the development of democratic ownership and management practices is not, in itself, considered to be a social purpose or to constitute a social benefit (unless the people who benefit from the arrangement are 'disadvantaged' in some way). The image of the Rochdale Pioneers in 1844 as a disadvantaged group is somewhat different to the image of cooperatives today. Nor is it likely that a person who opts for self-employment and devotes 100 per cent of their energies to social purpose trading activities will achieve recognition. This raises some provocative questions for debate about the politics behind the proposed standard.

Should *private* enterprise concepts such as 'market trading', 'incorporation' and 'accounting' be at the heart of the definition of *social* enterprise? Surely a *social* enterprise award should contain reference to the *quality of stakeholder relationships* using concepts such as 'participative democracy', 'social inclusion' and 'stakeholder engagement'? So, we have come full circle back to the debate outlined earlier in the chapter!

It appears that trading, incorporation and profitability, previously the *means* rather than primary purposes of social economy activity, have succumbed to the power of a 'business' discourse and become the *ends* (Dart, 2004). The Social Enterprise Mark, however, contains few of the 'ends' that appeared in the 1997 **Memorandum and Articles of Association** of Social Enterprise London. These ends (specified as 'company objects') included 'participative democracy', 'equal opportunity', 'social justice' and 'cooperative economic development'. Why do they not appear amongst the characteristics needed to achieve recognition as a 'quality' social enterprise?

Comparing Key Texts on Social Enterprise Management

Another way to generate debates about management in social enterprises is to compare various sector-specific books on management practice. For the purposes of this chapter, we consider *Managing Without Profit: The Art of Managing Third Sector Organisations* (Hudson, 2002), *Managing and Measuring Social Enterprises* (Paton, 2003), and *Management for Social Enterprise* (Doherty et al., 2009b).

Debate 6:   What approaches to learning are most helpful to social enterprise managers?

The selected books each have a different approach. Hudson's book includes many abstract models on the nature of 'third sector' organizations, focusing mainly on charities and voluntary agencies. Good reading lists are provided, but the models and theories are mostly unsourced. As a result, the impression is one of *distilled experience* generated by activities as a practitioner. Inside the front cover we find that Hudson is part of a management consultancy and graduated with an MBA from the London Business School.

Paton's (2003) book, on the other hand, developed out of the writer's research activities on organisational performance. After examining public and private sector performance management systems, the author examines how these are taken up and used by social enterprise managers. The author examines benchmarking, the use of **kitemarks** and quality models before theorising how different philosophies of management are enacted in social enterprises (see Table 6.1). The perspective, therefore, is on *theorising others' experience*. On the back cover of the book we learn that the author is Professor of Social Enterprise at the Open University.

Doherty et al. (2009b) explore the recent development of social enterprise as both an idea and a set of organisational practices. They break up the functions of management in a fairly conventional way with separate chapters on strategy, people, finance, marketing, ethics and **governance**. In this case, the book is an aid to teaching and covers the principal theories and sources of knowledge that enable a student to develop a research-informed perspective on the subject. If we turn to the inside pages, we find that the authors are all lecturers at Liverpool John Moores University engaged in the delivery of a social enterprise masters programme.

Some Conclusions

The three texts create a debate about ways of acquiring knowledge about social enterprise management. Should knowledge be acquired through reflective practice and theorisation of one's own experience? Alternatively, should it be a product of carefully designed research activities into specific issues or problems? Lastly, can be it acquired by doing searches of available articles and books? How might these strategies be combined to deepen insight?

> *Debate 7:* What are the key challenges in social enterprise management?

In the conclusions to Paton's book, he considers the various approaches deployed by managers to meet the challenges they face. In doing so, he distinguishes between three board philosophies that influence attitudes to management activities (see Table 6.1).

Table 6.1 Attitudes to social enterprise management

	The committed approach	The cynical approach	The reflective approach
Philosophical position	Positivist/ rationalist	Sceptic	Constructivist
Attitude to measuring	Generally positive	Generally negative	Interested but cautious
Where measures come from	Goals	Someone's agenda	Problems and issues

(Continued)

Table 6.1   *(Continued)*

	The committed approach	The cynical approach	The reflective approach
Expected use of measures	For learning and accountability	For control	Various – for dialogue, clarity, challenge, check and conformity
What matters in performance reporting	The facts	Creative accounting	A grounded narrative, analysis tailored to stakeholder needs
Relationship between professional, managerial and institutional interests	Close alignment	Close alignment with own view – or decoupling	Loose coupling (to accommodate differences, change and performance concepts)
Attitude to new methods	Useful tools	Fads, waste of time	Depends on use and context
Ways of applying methods	Follow the rules, do it properly	Tactically, perhaps collusively, with a view to appearances	Open-minded, willing to improvise, adapt and collude
Internal/external orientation	Internal (for integration or emulation)	External (bearing or badging)	If possible, dual integration (creating integration)
Benefits sought	Improved performance	Maintain confidence of external bodies; preserve autonomy	Develop relationships with external bodies and make some improvements

Source: adapted from Paton, 2003: 166

In a *committed approach*, managers accept the **rationality** of management theory and have confidence that target setting and adherence to quality systems will yield performance improvements. Goals are developed, and management systems are designed to pursue and monitor progress. Such a commitment, leading to confidence in the professionalism of management, often relies on studies that deploy a positivist research philosophy (that tests propositions by collecting quantitative data and comparing findings to theoretical understandings). Paton contrasts this with a *cynical approach* whereby staff members regard management as a system of control created to satisfy an elite or fulfil a political agenda. Attitudes are machiavellian – positive or negative depending on the political context and the current need to curry favour with external parties or avoid scrutiny by giving the impression of being in control. Lastly, there is a *reflective approach* that recognises the constructed nature of knowledge linked to political or ideological interests, but also the capacity of carefully adapted systems to clarify specific issues, provide opportunities to build productive relationships with other stakeholders, or to solve pressing problems.

Across the three books, the authors identify key characteristics and challenges facing managers in social enterprises (see Table 6.2). These are helpful in mapping additional issues and identifying specific challenges. As Hudson comments, many

Table 6.2   Key management challenges and characteristics

Managing Without Profit (Hudson, 1995: 18–20)	*Managing and Measuring Social Enterprises* (Paton, 2003: 33)	*Management for Social Enterprise* (Doherty et al., 2009b: 47–8)
• Difficulties working with 'vague' (non-economic) objectives • Difficulties assessing social and environmental impacts • Difficulties accounting to multiple stakeholders • The complexity and intricacy of management structures that develop in enterprises pursuing social objectives • The influence and expectation of voluntarism on paid and unpaid staff/governors • The influence of 'purpose' on management style and practice • The impact of 'profit' being a subordinate objective, or viewed as a means to an end, rather than an end in itself	• The ambiguities and conflicts that arise when social outcomes are sought for individuals, groups and communities simultaneously • The integration and conflicts created by combining professional values and managerial 'rationality' • The involvement of lay people and non-executive directors in multi-stakeholder governance • Mixed funding regimes drawing on voluntary, public and commercial sources, including quasi-markets in the public sector • Public scrutiny and the concurrent threat of interventions by regulators, funders, and an active membership • Partnership working for financial or statutory reasons, involving partners from different sectors of the economy	• Developing a supportive regulatory regime for social enterprises • Improving the quality of products and services • Upgrading skills and jobs • Securing management expertise • Securing finance • Establishing networks and cooperatives • Establishing adequate governance structures

social organisations have tales to tell of the inability of experienced private and public sector managers to adapt to a management context that is more ambiguous (financially) and demanding (socially). The table above indicates some of the reasons. Whilst Doherty et al. (2009b) remind us that social enterprises have to address similar issues to private sector companies, Hudson (2002) and Paton (2003) focus on issues that constitute unique or unusual challenges.

Having identified key debates and major challenges, we now summarise the contribution of this chapter. The conclusion to this chapter is purposely open-ended.

SUMMARY OF LEARNING

In this chapter, we have outlined:

- Ambiguities that surround the concept and acceptance of 'management' and 'managers' in social enterprises, and the extent to which private and public sector models should be accepted.
- A perspective on management that values enabling and reflecting upon a cycle of business development activities, rather than acquiring a set of competencies in management control.
- A debate about democracy in social enterprise, and its contested status as a central or peripheral aspect of social enterprise definition and management practice.
- A debate over social enterprise as a process or form of organisation.
- An argument about the power of 'discourse' to define and acquire control over ideas, business concepts and market opportunities.
- The contribution of key authors to the identification of management styles in social and third sector organisations, and the unique challenges faced by social enterprise managers.

QUESTIONS AND POSSIBLE ESSAY ASSIGNMENTS

1 'Managers in social enterprises need not be concerned about advancing democracy either inside or outside the workplace so long as they fulfil the organisation's social purpose.' Using case studies, or personal examples, discuss the viability of this philosophy for social enterprise.
2 'Social enterprise is best conceived as a process rather than a form of organisation.' Using examples, discuss situations in which this view might provide a political or business advantage.
3 'Management is best served by a constructivist rather than a rationalist philosophy of management.' Using examples, discuss the impact of taken-for-granted assumptions on management practices in social enterprise.

FURTHER READING

A useful insight into viewing social enterprises as trading entities is provided in Bob Allan's article 'Social enterprise through the eyes of the consumer' (2005). This provides three perspectives on social enterprise, each with implications for management style: as 'ethical businesses'; and as enterprises 'trading for a social purpose'; and as 'socially owned' businesses. The final chapter of Paton's (2003) book *Managing and Measuring Social Enterprises* contains a fascinating discussion of the way managers engage with the issue of performance, and adapt management systems to their organisational context.

For enterprises in the voluntary and charity sector, Chapters 6–13 of Hudson's *Managing Without Profit* (1995) provide helpful discussions of most aspects of management in formalised environments. For those less sympathetic to Hudson's claim that 'there is always a boss', *The Cooperative Workplace* by Rothschild and Allen-Whitt (1986) provides a range of case studies and insights into the challenges of self-management.

For a fascinating discussion of macro- and micro-economic issues facing the development of a social-enterprise-based economy, the final chapter of Alec Nove's *The Economics of Feasible Socialism* (1983) identifies key questions on the scale and limitations of democratic accountability in business, and the contexts in which social enterprises are likely to thrive.

Further reading material is available on the companion website at www.sagepub.co.uk/ridleyduff.

Identities and Legalities   7

Learning Objectives

In this chapter we consider how legal forms are designed to meet the needs of social enterprises. By the end of this chapter you will be able to:

- critically evaluate how the legal membership of an organisation is established

- articulate how issues of social identity affect the choice of legal form and management practice

- compare and contrast model rules for social enterprises

- develop and critique the concept of a democratic multi-stakeholder social enterprise.

The key arguments that will be developed in this chapter are:

- Social identity and business purpose influence the choice of legal form.
- Different legal forms influence the power and benefits allocated to each stakeholder.
- Social enterprises are developing legal forms that enfranchise more than one stakeholder.
- In the last 15 years, new models for democratising business have been established.
- Multi-stakeholder social enterprise can be regarded as a 'paradigmatic' shift in the constitutional underpinning of business, or a naïve form of liberalism.

Introduction

In the previous chapter, we considered a number of debates that affect the choices made in the management of social enterprises. In this chapter, we turn our attention to one of the first tasks facing a person or group who wishes to create a social enterprise: the identity that they will adopt and how to express this through a legal form. We will argue that the decision to choose a particular legal form is often an afterthought, or something decided by business advisers on the basis of the forms they are familiar supporting. Alternatively, the legal form may imposed by a funder to protect their own investment.

As Davies points out:

> It is the initial shareholders of a company who bring it into existence ... and who become the first members of the organization thus created. Subsequent shareholders also become members of the company. The point is of theoretical, even ideological, significance, because the train of thought which makes the shareholders the members of the company leads naturally to making the shareholders' interests predominant within company law. (2002: 7)

Davies questions why directors, employees and creditors are not recognised as legal members of the company and why they have no voting rights in key meetings that decide future policy and strategy. The question is not an idle one because virtually all forms of social enterprise seek to constrain or reverse the legal arrangement that privileges financial investors in company law.

In the first part of the chapter, we consider the issue of social identity and the way this can influence the choice of legal form. We explore how different legal forms are designed to privilege one or other stakeholder and ensure they can acquire or retain control over intellectual property, **physical assets**, trading surpluses and decision-making bodies. To illustrate these points, we examine how popular legal forms for establishing companies, charities, societies and cooperatives distribute rights within the organisation. In the second half of the chapter, we consider the emergence of model rules for social enterprises that seek to reconcile divergent interests by **enfranchising** stakeholders typically excluded from membership in private or state enterprises. By comparing four examples, and considering the history of their development, we can observe two things: firstly, social enterprises develop legal forms that seek to reconcile divergent economic and social interests; and secondly, these interests still influence the way power is distributed to different stakeholders. In the conclusions, we review whether the attempt to enfranchise groups typically excluded from membership is a paradigm shift in business thinking (Kuhn, 1970), or a form of naïve liberalism that continues to privilege an elite.

Values, Identities and Social Practices

Many writers on the left of the political spectrum have alluded to the tendency of people in a society to become imbued with particular ways of thinking, and for the ideas of a dominant class to become pervasive in educational, governmental and economic institutions. In Marxian thought, it is argued there has been a transition from primitive to **feudal society,** then feudal to **capitalist society** (Cornforth, 1995). The question that preoccupied later generations became the manner in which capitalism would give way to socialism, and then how socialism would give way to communism. Marx wrote little about the next stage of transition: how the *relations of production* would have to be changed to produce both socialism and communism. He was, however, explicit that revolutions occur when a class of people in society who were subordinated under the previous socio-economic system establish a way to become dominant. For example, in the case of feudal society, Marx tracked how a class of privately financed merchants increased their control of economic and political thought until their way of thinking became dominant in government (see Gray, 1998). Kalmi (2007) highlights how this dominant mode of thought gradually colonised educational texts to exclude various alternatives.

In the case of capitalism, Marx and Engels are uncompromising in their criticisms of the changes that took place:

> The bourgeoisie, wherever it has got the upper hand, has put an end to all feudal, patriarchal, idyllic relations. It has pitilessly torn asunder the motley feudal ties that bound man to his 'natural superiors', and has left remaining no other nexus between man and man than naked self-interest, than callous 'cash payment'. It has drowned the most heavenly ecstasies of religious fervour, of chivalrous enthusiasm, of philistine sentimentalism, in the icy water of egotistical calculation. It has resolved personal worth into exchange value ... veiled by religious and political illusions, it has substituted naked, shameless, direct, brutal exploitation. (1998 [1848]: 37–8)

A contemporary analysis that reaches similar conclusions is *The Corporation*, a documentary that draws attention to the way financial capital is continually moved out of societies and companies where workplace democracy and trade union organisation are increasingly effective, and reinvested in regional economies where those movements are either unsupported by the state or actively suppressed (Achbar et al., 2004). As Klein (2007) goes on to argue, corporations did not stop at the level of the nation, but proceeded to dominate policy and practice in the International Monetary Fund (IMF) and World Bank until the banking crises of 1997 (in the Far East) and 2008 (globally) undermined confidence in globalisation (see Chapter 5).

There is another perspective, however. Liberal democracy, however imperfectly it succeeds in its goals, has successfully advanced the principle of equality before the law, equality of voice in political deliberations and decision-making, and equality of opportunity to participate fully in work and society (see Friedman, 1962; Rawls, 1999). Friedman (1962) argues in *Capitalism and Freedom* that distributing political power is much harder to achieve than the distribution of economic power. For this reason, he argues for the widest possible distribution of economic power in order to balance political power in governmental institutions. Rawls (1999) goes even further, arguing that social rights are also needed to limit the power of the state. Taken together, economic and social liberalism still provide one of the intellectual bedrocks on which arguments are built for a strong **civil society**, employee and community ownership, and alternative economic and educational systems (see Ellerman, 2005).

Frequently, the division between those with 'progressive' **communitarian** and liberal sentiments is not that they differ in their desire for democracy or a fairer society, but that they have a different understanding of the way individuals can work together to effect change in society (Cladis, 1992). These different assumptions produce different organisational solutions, each believed to increase social inclusion and workplace democracy and to produce a civil society.

Table 7.1 The Camp Nou way

	Barcelona	Arsenal
Shareholders	142,000 members ('socios') One person one vote	Four major shareholders own 87% of voting shares[a]
Leadership	President elected by members for four-year term (maximum two terms)	No meaningful elections. Chair of the board decided by major shareholders
Cheapest adult season ticket	£69	£885
Most expensive adult season ticket	£579	£1825

[a] Wikipedia, on 8 December 2009, states that in November 2009 86.9 per cent of shares were held by four shareholders: Stan Kroenke (29.9%), Danny Fiszman (16.1%), Nina Bracewell-Smith (15.9%) and Red & White Securities (25%). Red & White Securities is a company owned by Russian billionaire Alisher Usmanov and London-based financier Farhad Moshiri.

The question arises, therefore, how individuals shape the institutional forms that produce particular social and economic outcomes. The scale of the differences should not be underestimated, as the following examples will illustrate. The first example (Table 7.1) involves a comparison between Barcelona and Arsenal football clubs based on an article about football supporter trusts (Conn, 2006).

The body of law under which Barcelona is constituted is similar to the Mondragón cooperatives (see Case 2.3). The key difference, however, is that the dominant group are consumers (football fans) rather than members of the workforce. At Barcelona, while the fans benefit from reduced prices, the disparities in the pay of the workforce are extremely wide: the wage of an administrator remains a tiny fraction of a Barcelona footballer's wage.

This can be contrasted to the Mondragón industrial enterprises where the focus is on the workforce rather than consumers. The long-term outcomes are dramatically different to the norm for Anglo-American businesses. A ratio of 6:1 is the norm between the *highest* and *lowest* paid in almost all Mondragón companies because the ratio is itself decided by a vote of all worker members (Whyte and Whyte, 1991; Ridley-Duff, 2005). By way of contrast, the gap between CEO pay and the *average* manual worker in US corporations increased from 85:1 to 419:1 throughout the 1990s (Aslam, 1999: claim based on data from US Bureau of Labor Statitics). The Mondragón outcome is a product of the values that underpin the worker cooperative model (Figure 7.1) and the body of law under which cooperative enterprises are regulated.

These examples illustrate the vastly different *long-term* outcomes (both internal and external) that can result when organisational forms are designed to benefit a particular social group. In the case of Arsenal (a privately owned football club), the pricing strategy is set to maximise profit for the major shareholders. Shares are not publicly available and are traded in secret amongst a select group of people. Season ticket prices for fans are high. In the case of Barcelona (a socially owned football club), the adoption of a different organisational form (a consumer-owned enterprise) offers membership to football fans rather than financial investors. This

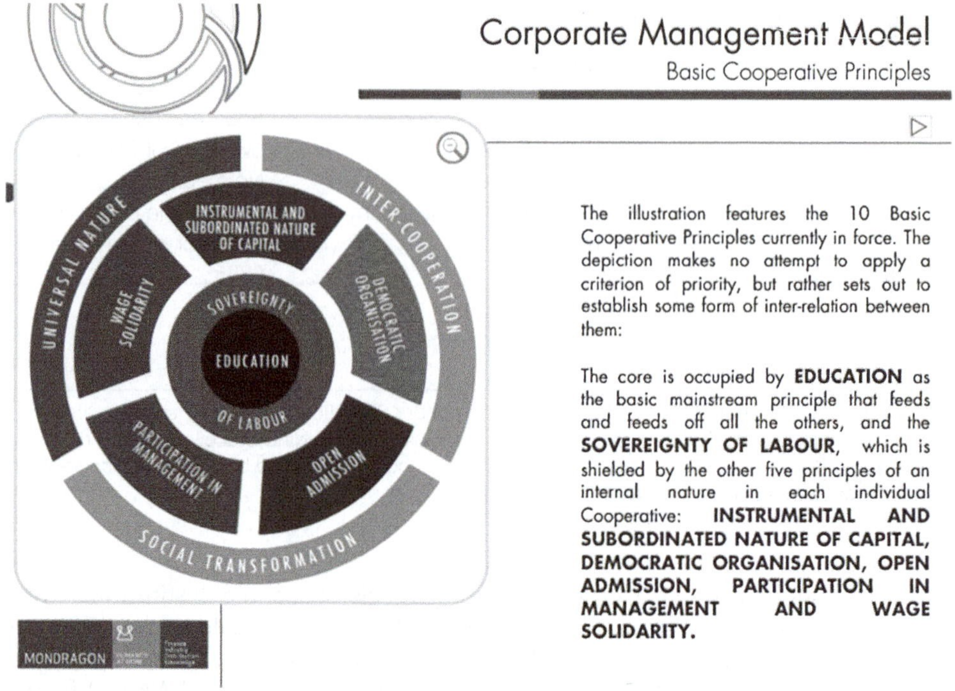

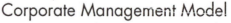

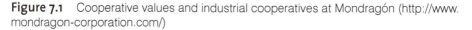

Corporate Management Model
Basic Cooperative Principles
INSTRUMENTAL AND SUBORDINATED NATURE OF CAPITAL
INTER-COOPERATION
DEMOCRATIC ORGANISATION
UNIVERSAL NATURE
WAGE SOLIDARITY
SOVEREIGNTY
EDUCATION
OF LABOUR
PARTICIPATION IN MANAGEMENT
OPEN ADMISSION
SOCIAL TRANSFORMATION
MONDRAGON
The illustration features the 10 Basic Cooperative Principles currently in force. The depiction makes no attempt to apply a criterion of priority, but rather sets out to establish some form of inter-relation between them:
The core is occupied by EDUCATION as the basic mainstream principle that feeds and feeds off all the others, and the SOVEREIGNTY OF LABOUR, which is shielded by the other five principles of an internal nature in each individual Cooperative: INSTRUMENTAL AND SUBORDINATED NATURE OF CAPITAL, DEMOCRATIC ORGANISATION, OPEN ADMISSION, PARTICIPATION IN MANAGEMENT AND WAGE SOLIDARITY.

Figure 7.1 Cooperative values and industrial cooperatives at Mondragón (http://www.mondragon-corporation.com/)

not only extends ownership into the community, it dramatically reduces the cost of a season ticket because a leadership group elected by fans, and not by financial investors, sets the prices. In the Mondragón industrial enterprises, although a cooperative form is still used, the workforce is the primary beneficiary: neither external investors nor customers are permitted to become members. Ownership is still extended into the community on the basis of a work rather than a consumer role.

Coule summarises a key point about identity and membership when she states:

> *Resources have the potential to steer organisations and how they raise the resources they need has a strong influence on what an organisation is and what it can be. From a sustainability perspective, reducing resource vulnerability through the diversification of funding sources is recognised as an important task … [Organisations] are vulnerable in another way as well. Strategic choices in terms of resources have implications beyond their reliability, they affect what the organisation stands for. (2008: 2)*

In each of these cases, the social identity of the owners (investors, consumers and employees) radically transforms the way the organisation is run, and the way the benefits of ownership and trading are distributed. The scale of the differences that can accrue are often only visible when studied after many years of trading (Ridley-Duff, 2009a).

It is important, therefore, to understand the intersection between legal form and social control. It would, for example, be easy to compare the wages of the footballers at Barcelona and Arsenal and conclude that the clubs are not so different. This would miss the social and economic outcomes for the 'consumers' of football rather than those who work to produce it. Similarly, we could compare the prices charged by the Mondragón cooperatives for the domestic appliances they manufacture and conclude that they are not so different from the prices charged by Anglo-American corporations. This would ignore the social and economic outcomes for the 'producers' of these domestic appliances, and how these differ from other producers.

Put simply, legal forms evolve to suit the needs of key stakeholder groups in both market and non-market contexts. They are retained to the extent that they are successful (i.e. produce the outcomes that are sought) and can develop and protect the educational, political and economic environments needed to sustain them. In the context of a discussion about social enterprise, the question is whether legal forms that privilege a particular group over others are a barrier to, or an enabler of, social enterprise itself. Figure 7.2 summarises the different stakeholders (social identities)

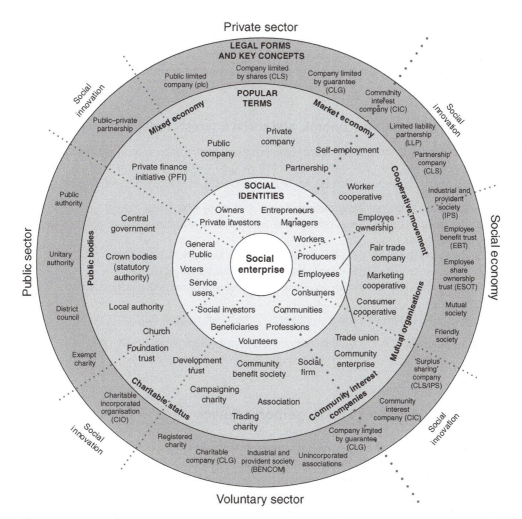

Figure 7.2   Identities and legalities in the development of social enterprise

that are associated with particular legal forms. Some of these are well established (such as a company limited by shares and a company limited by guarantee) while others are less well known, even though they have been popular (or dominant) during other historical periods (e.g. charitable companies, friendly and mutual societies, and cooperatives).

It is beyond the scope of this chapter to discuss each legal form (see 'Useful resources' at the end of the chapter for more on this). It is, however, relevant to ask how previously dominant models for private companies, charities and cooperatives compare to new forms of organisation that have emerged in the last two decades. With the growth of social enterprise as a concept, there has been a conscious attempt to structure organisations so that *multiple* stakeholders are involved in both governance and wealth sharing arrangements.

In Figure 7.2, the perspective outlined towards the end of Chapter 3 is echoed. Social enterprise is framed as a way of brokering and balancing the interests of stakeholders by including them in the membership of the enterprise (legally and/or culturally). In Figure 7.2, the 'third system' identified by Pearce (2003) is elaborated to identify legal forms and concepts, and the porous boundaries between sectors where innovations in legal forms are taking place. Underpinning their differences is a consideration of who the organisation operates *for* (for the benefit of the public, the community, private individuals or a particular group of members).

EXERCISE   Linking economic and social interests to legal forms

Using Figure 7.2, make a list of the legal forms you have encountered in your studies and working life, then sort them into the following six groups. Based on what you know about each organisation's criteria for *legal membership*, enquire which legal forms are:

1 designed to benefit the *economic* interests of those who invest money
2 designed to benefit the *economic* interests of those who buy/sell particular goods and services
3 designed to benefit the *economic* interests of those who supply labour
4 designed to benefit the *social* interests of those who invest money
5 designed to benefit the *social* interests of those who use particular goods and services
6 designed to benefit the *social* interests of those who supply labour.

Materials to support this exercise can be found at www.sagepub.co.uk/ridleyduff.

Old Legal Identities and Hegemonic Power

To develop a sense of the issues facing those starting up or developing social enterprises, it is worth highlighting how popular forms of organisation (see Table 7.2) are frequently designed (consciously or unconsciously) to produce *hegemonic power* (Lukes, 1974). Hegemonic power occurs where staff members and supporters have been 'schooled' in particular discourse (i.e. to use particular language, concepts and

Table 7.2 Popular legal forms for social enterprise

Community benefit society (BENCOM)[a]	Registered as a friendly society: one person, one vote.
Community interest company (CIC)	Adapted business form (can be CLG or CLS), limited profit distribution, board dominated, asset locked. Cannot be a charity.
Company limited by guarantee (CLG)[a]	Typically a £1 guarantee, no dividends, may be board rather than member controlled. Can register as a charitable company if objectives are charitable and there is an appropriate dissolution clause.
Company limited by shares (CLS)	Adapted business form to encourage consumer, charity, community and/or employee ownership. In law a CLS can be a charity, but in practice this form is rarely accepted by the Charity Commission.
Industrial and provident society (IPS)[a]	Friendly society form for industrial undertakings (typically use £1 shares, or equity holdings capped at £20k); one-person, one-vote control.
Voluntary organisation[a]	Usually constituted, with commitments to one-person, one-vote control. Can register as a charity if the organisation has a written constitution and charitable objectives.

[a]Legal forms that can (or commonly) register as charities.

ideas) and find it difficult to conceptualise alternative ways of thinking and talking. The language may have a **'unitary'** feel to it (see also Chapter 9), claiming that all parties to an enterprise have 'shared interests', that all parties can have 'shared values' or that all parties are 'equal before the law'.

In private companies, the norm is for membership to be extended to shareholders in accordance with their financial investment (Davies, 2002). People employed by a private company are required by law to act in the financial interests of the owner (i.e. financial investors). In charities, membership may be extended differently, together with the expectation that everyone included will support the charitable objects set by the board of trustees. **Trustees** themselves, and those employed by trustees, are assessed (in law) against the pursuit and achievement of the organisation's charitable objectives (Charity Commission, 2008). Similarly, in worker cooperatives, membership is extended to the workforce, and those employed by them are obliged to act in their interests. In consumer cooperatives, the obligation is to act in consumer interests.

The act of including or excluding particular groups from membership (and thereby limiting their voice in making decisions about the future of the organisation) is one of the processes affecting the distribution of power. In different bodies of academic theory, the behaviour of 'other' stakeholders is framed as problematic. For example, in private companies, the behaviour of directors and managers is framed as the 'problem' of corporate governance by shareholders (Joerg et al., 2004; Slapnicar et al., 2004). In both management and economic theory, the 'problem' of staff motivation receives considerable attention (Watson, 1996; Sloman and Sutcliffe, 2001). In cooperative theory, the behaviour of *external* investors is framed as a 'problem', so much so that they are frequently excluded from legal membership (Oakeshott, 1990).

In all these unadapted forms of organisation, the rights of the dominant group are regarded as paramount and taken for granted. Legal and governance theory, in relation to each form, develops to address the perceived 'problems' created by the exclusion of other groups, and their attempts to compete for power and wealth. For example, the concept of **hard HRM** in traditional management theory regards labour as a cost to be minimised by paying a fixed wage that is the minimum the labour market will bear (Truss, 1999). This may apply equally in private companies (to maximise investor returns) and charities (to maximise the funds available for charitable projects). As Kalmi (2007) argues, the same logic can also apply in consumer cooperatives (to maximise dividends for consumer members). Theories about how to treat 'labour' may vary, but they are all taken within a **paradigm** of thought leading to the exclusion of labour from membership (or governance) of the organisation. Alternatively, they are accepted into membership only if they abandon institutions designed to protect labour interests (e.g. trade unions).

Similar injunctions exist in charity and cooperative practice with regard to financial investors. In this case, external investors are not permitted to buy equity in the charity or cooperative (although such rights are preserved when the charity or cooperative wishes to buy equity in other enterprises). If external investment is permitted, the rights of investors are reduced either by barring them from membership, or by adjusting their membership rights so that they do not acquire decision-making rights accorded to full members.

As we will see below, however, social enterprise **model rules** are now openly challenging these assumptions by recognising multiple interest groups and forms of relationship in their constitutions, and are seeking to institute democratic forums to manage the competition and conflicts that arise. It is worth recalling the comment of Michels that:

> Democracy in large measure rests on the fact that no one group is able to secure a basis of power and command over the majority so that it can effectively suppress or deny the claims of the groups it opposes. (1961: 36)

While some liberal theorists – most notably Friedman and his followers – abhor attempts to advance social democracy within a business, the views of Pateman (1970), Ellerman (1982) and Turnbull (1994) put democracy at the core of a 'socialised' form of enterprise where rights are attached to corporate citizenship rather than property (see Chapter 2). Attempts to institutionalise arrangements in business so that 'no one group is able to secure a basis of power and command over the majority so that it can effectively suppress or deny the claims of the groups it opposes' represent an evolution in business practice. It takes the argument beyond 'single-loop' arguments that social enterprises are a more efficient solution for state or market failures, to a 'double-loop' argument that social enterprises trade more effectively in any

Table 7.3 Model 1 and model 2 enterprise design

Model 1	Model 2
Governing values	
• Achieve the purpose as the actor defines it • Win, do not lose • Suppress negative feelings • Emphasise rationality	• Valid information • Free and informed choice • Internal commitment
Primary strategies	
• Control environment and task unilaterally • Protect self and others unilaterally	• Sharing control • Participation in design and implementation of choices
Usually operationalised by	
• Unillustrated attributions and evaluations • Advocating courses of action that discourage inquiry • Treating one's own views as obviously correct • Making covert attributions and evaluations • Face-saving moves that leave potentially embarrassing facts unstated	• Attribution and evaluation illustrated with observable examples • Surfacing conflicting views • Encouraging public testing of evaluations
Consequences include	
• Defensive relationships • Low freedom of choice • Reduced production of valid information • Little public testing of ideas	• Minimally defensive relationships • High freedom of choice • Increasing likelihood of double-loop learning

Source: Argyris et al., 1985: 89

context by developing different business objectives, values and organisational norms. As Smith (2001 [online]) comments:

> Single-loop learning seems to be present when goals, values, frameworks and, to a significant extent, strategies are taken for granted. The emphasis is on 'techniques and making techniques more efficient' (Usher and Bryant, 1989: 87). Any reflection is directed toward making the strategy more effective. Double-loop learning, in contrast, 'involves questioning the role of the framing and learning systems which underlie actual goals and strategies' (op. cit.).

Argyris et al. (1985) summarised the characteristics and management strategies of 'model 1' and 'model 2' organisations (see Table 7.3). In as much as interest groups seek to perfect the use of existing legal forms (e.g. the private company, the charity, the cooperative etc.), they represent examples of single-loop learning within a framework of model 1 behaviours. Where groups are collaborating to reformulate the norms and objectives of business, embracing both *value* commitments and links to evidence-based reasoning, they are orienting themselves towards model 2 thinking, opening up the possibility of double-loop learning.

Social enterprise, in its emergent legal forms, can be viewed as attempts to address business problems using model 2 thinking in the *constitution* of the business, rather than through supplying goods and services to a disenfranchised section of the population, or deploying sophisticated HRM practices designed to induce high commitment from the workforce (Purcell, 1987). To explore this further, we discuss four sets of social enterprise model rules and discuss the implications for practice. Later we will critique these forms and discuss possible limitations.

New Legal Identities and Social Power

In this section, we examine four sets of model rules that have evolved from practice. Each illustrates how social entrepreneurs are attempting to recognise and legitimise the interests of multiple stakeholders. We will firstly explore the key characteristics of each set of rules by discussing how they change the relative balance of power. Subsequently, we will explore the extent to which different rules *still* privilege one group over others and shape the levels of involvement in decision-making. The sets of rules are illustrative, and have been selected for their education value and influence on practice (see Table 7.4).

At first glance, each set of model rules enfranchises both internal and external stakeholders. *Stakeholder Model Ltd* (Case 7.1) offers shares to three groups: stewardship

Table 7.4 Multi-stakeholder model rules for social enterprises: Cases 7.1–7.4

Stakeholder Model Ltd (Case 7.1)
The rules were designed by Geof Cox Associates, a specialist in the development
and support of social firms, and were published by the Common Cause Foundation.
Underpinned by a company limited by shares, the model rules define the power of an active
board, elected by each shareholder group. Three share types are defined:

- stewardship shares
- partnership/customer shares
- investment shares

Cooperative CIC Model (Case 7.2)
Designed and published by Cooperatives UK in response to the introduction of community
interest company legislation. Underpinned by a company limited by guarantee, the model
rules are framed to encourage active service user and workforce membership on the basis
of one person, one vote, with a commitment to consult:

- employees
- funders
- suppliers
- customers
- community representatives

(Continued)

Table 7.4   *(Continued)*

NewCo Model (Case 7.3)
Designed by Morgan Killick and Bill Barker in 2002, with support from the Sheffield Community Economic Development Unit. Underpinned by a company limited by shares, a 2004 version developed rules giving control and decision-making power to three classes of shareholder, and investment rights to a fourth:

- class A shares (for social entrepreneurs)
- class B shares (for charities and social enterprises)
- class C shares (for employees)
- class D shares (for supporting organisations)

Surplus Sharing Model (Case 7.4)
With a heritage stretching back to the work of Guy Major and Gavin Body in the mid 1990s, the surplus sharing rules developed by Rory Ridley-Duff, at Sheffield Business School, embrace cooperative principles across the labour/capital divide. The rules provide for active membership control on the basis of one person, one vote, with special provisions for issuing:

- founder shares
- labour shares
- investor shares

The case studies are on the website at www.sagepub.co.uk/ridleyduff.

shares provide for a role similar to trustees in a charity who safeguard the objectives and values of the organisation; *partnership shares* are provided for staff, customers and suppliers who have long-term contracts with the enterprise; *investment shares* influence the distribution of profits and are offered to both staff and external funders. Each group controls one-third of the votes in general meetings.

The *Cooperative CIC Model* (Case 7.2) provides membership options for both service users (consumers) and workers (employees), but has no specific provision for external investors. The decision to use a company limited by guarantee, rather than one limited by shares, provides for membership that confers voting rights, but no rights to profits and assets. As a CIC, the rules include an **asset lock**: a clause is included naming a registered charity or social enterprise to which any residual assets will be transferred upon dissolution.

The *NewCo Model* (Case 7.3) has superficial similarities to Stakeholder Model Ltd. It provides for three groups to receive ordinary shares: founding social entrepreneur(s) and investors; social enterprises and charities; and employees. Unlike Stakeholder Model Ltd, however, the balance between the shareholdings in the three groups is not fixed. Furthermore, in addition to ordinary shares, additional 'social equity' preference shares enable supporting organisations to invest in the enterprise and received a fixed dividend.

The final *Surplus Sharing Model* (Case 7.4) provides for shares to be held by founders (*founder shares*), suppliers of labour (*labour shares*), and suppliers of capital (*investor shares*). Labour shares entitle holders to a share of surpluses (typically split 50/50 with investor shareholders). As in the case of Stakeholder Model Ltd, founder shares recognise the value of a trustee role oriented towards protecting the democratic ethos and social objectives of the enterprise.

What is striking about all these models is that they seek to change the nature of company membership so that both internal and external stakeholders have voting rights, and, in three of the four models, rights to a share of profits and assets. Of the four, only the Cooperative CIC Model (Case 7.2) fully observes the principle of common ownership (i.e. that monies invested are fully locked into the development of commonly owned assets held in trust for community benefit). Are the other models, therefore, a degradation (or reformulation) of the idea of social ownership?

Consideration of this question is assisted by a review of the histories of the various models. The Cooperative CIC Model (Case 7.2) is rooted in a historical connection to both the cooperative movement and the industrial common ownership movement (ICOM), so it is unsurprising that there is no provision for equity investment. It was developed in response to enquiries requesting a cooperative model that integrated the provisions of the CIC regulations. As described in Chapter 6, part of this demand was created by the removal of stakeholder governance during the government consultation in 2003. The Cooperative CIC Model filled this gap in provision.

The other models all have a more mixed heritage. Stakeholder Model Ltd (Case 7.1) was developed in response to the needs of wholefood companies that depended on both a workforce and a loyal customer base, and to the needs of social firms.[1] Ideological sympathy with principles of cooperative management are combined with charitable objects and **equity investment instruments**. In place of a charity and a wholly owned subsidiary is a single enterprise that accommodates divergent voices. The Surplus Sharing Model (Case 7.4) was initially a product of a cooperative encountering problems raising finance from *both* members and external parties. The first iteration of the rules was developed when it was found that government funding for cooperatives could not be accessed without the ability to convert loan finance into equity (Ridley-Duff, 2002). The rules were then developed after collaborations with employers seeking to extend employee ownership, with the goal of facilitating trust and community ownership alongside cooperative management. Of interest here is a mechanism to facilitate a gradual 'succession' in ownership (to the workforce) that does not involve a trade or private sale to outside interests. The NewCo Model (Case 7.3), on the other hand, was conceived during an attempt to establish an ICT organisation servicing third sector clients. The model aimed not only to provide services, but also to share profits with recipients of the services provided. Interestingly, this allows customers to share the costs of establishing the enterprise, and shape the way that services are provided to meet their needs. Help was provided by a community enterprise development unit which recognised the need to provide rewards for founding entrepreneurs and investors as well as employees and customers. In this case, the CIC was rejected in favour of a model that allowed those taking entrepreneurial risks to achieve capital gains through the issue of shares that accrue in value (which are not permitted in the CIC model). Under the CIC model, directors (and others) can financially benefit from dividend payments, but cannot sell shares at a profit.

In each of the models (and company law), various rights are allocated to different classes of shareholder. Gates (1998: Appendix B) describes the rights that can be defined in articles of association. These are summarised, with reference to social enterprise practice, in Table 7.5.

Shares distribute voting rights at general meetings and board meetings, and define what can take place outside those meetings. They can also be used to distribute rights to a proportion of annual trading surpluses or profits (however this is expressed) and

Table 7.5   Rights in a modern corporation

Liquidation rights

Mostly associated with property rights, liquidation rights enable shareholders or creditors to force a company into liquidation if it becomes apparent that it is insolvent, likely to go insolvent, or unable to pay its creditors. In social enterprises, particular attention is paid to the dissolution clause in order to *prevent* (or limit) liquidation for private benefit. As Jensen (2006) argues, liquidation rights also give investors the ability to force a profitable company providing value to the community into liquidation (either to remove competition or to cash in on the value of its assets). Social enterprises include clauses that take away (or limit) the incentive to liquidate the company except in cases of genuine insolvency.

Appreciation rights

This right defines how the value of an organisation is reflected in its share price. Some social enterprises define shares as having a 'par value' that does not appreciate. In other cases, shares do appreciate in value and reflect a valuation of the company's assets or future profit stream. If appreciation rights are defined, each share is based on the value of the company divided by the shares issued. A CLG (or CIC constituted as a CLG) has no shares, and therefore does not grant appreciation rights.

Transfer rights

Articles of association often contain clauses controlling the transfer of assets and shares. In social enterprises, both rights may be limited. In the case of assets, restrictions may apply to who can receive them. Shares may not be transferable to prevent their acquisition by interests unsympathetic to the social aims of the organisation, or to prevent transfer to private interests (including members as individuals), or to ensure that voting and income rights are retained by all stakeholders.

Income rights

Clauses may be added to define how income can be derived from membership (via dividend payments), or from loans to the company. In social enterprises, there may be a cap on loan interest, and a cap on, or the elimination of, dividend payments. Alternatively, social enterprises may attach dividend rights to shares distributed to employees, customers and suppliers to ensure they have the rights normally reserved for external investors.

Voting rights

These rights influence who can participate in decisions on mergers, acquisitions, winding up the organisation, changing its rules, approving large contracts, and the election of directors and/or company officers. In some cases, the rights are extended to business plans and decisions on surplus sharing. In social enterprises, voting rights are often distributed on a one-person, one-vote basis, rather than one vote per share: this promotes corporate citizenship and democratic control.

Information rights

Clauses can be included to define who can access information held by company officers and staff, and what information is covered. Rights may be extended only to directors, or to all members. Where a social enterprise is not independent from the state, it may have to comply with the Freedom of Information Act and provide information to the public. These rights can

(Continued)

Table 7.5   *(Continued)*

also be defined in the company rules to promote transparency. In the case of a public limited company (plc), the public have some statutory rights.

Public rights

Where an organisation has 'spun out' from the public sector, a 'golden share' may be retained by government to protect the public interest. Similarly, in charities and CICs, public rights are expressed in terms of charitable or social objects that satisfy the standards set by the Charity Commission or the Community Interest Company Regulator (who may intervene if the public or the community interest is not satisfied). Public rights are problematic, however, when an organisation is active in multiple counties. In this case, public authorities may compete to protect their (divergent) interests.

a proportion of the organisation's assets. Charitable associations, and companies limited by guarantee, may declare in their rules that they have 'no share capital'. Even if this is the case, the articles of association will still define who can be a member, the rights and responsibilities that members acquire, and the powers that members have to elect and control their executive.

The Stakeholder Model Ltd and NewCo Model allocate most rights to either founders or directors. The board, in both cases, is free to exercise its powers largely unchecked by the wider membership who are cast mainly as beneficiaries. The Cooperative CIC Model and Surplus Sharing Model build in greater powers for the wider membership. They contain clauses on the operation of general meetings as well as board meetings. Importantly, both sets of rules require executives to maintain open management systems accessible to all members during normal working hours.[2] In the Stakeholder Model Ltd, only board members have access to management information.

The implications for practice should be noted in each case. Of the four examples, only the Cooperative CIC Model – constituted as a company limited by guarantee – is likely to be a good vehicle for traditional fundraising activities. While this is not the priority of social enterprises trading in commercial markets, it is a concern for social enterprises contracting with public authorities and local government bodies, particularly where contracts do not meet the full cost of providing a particular service. These social enterprises benefit from an asset lock to secure further public and charitable funding on which they depend for survival. The choice, however, is not always voluntary. It can be the case that public and charitable funders instruct recipients of grants (or contracts) that their enterprises need to be constituted in a particular way to be eligible for funding.

The CLG is not a good vehicle for raising money from staff, suppliers, customers and other investors as it fails to provide security or a return commensurate with the risks associated with an unsecured investment. Faced with investing in one's own business or an established savings scheme, a social enterprise has to compete with other saving schemes. In the cases reviewed, the enterprises are structured to increase voice and control (governance), and/or to increase participation in the rewards of trading (i.e. through surplus or profit sharing). The underlying philosophy of the legal forms, therefore, is to spread the risks and benefits across multiple internal and external stakeholders.

Critique and Conclusions

Close examination of each multi-stakeholder model reveals that they are not free of potential conflicts between stakeholders, and that the relative power of one stakeholder over others still remains an issue. As such, they are vulnerable to the criticism that they constitute a naïve form of liberalism that ignores or glosses over disparities in power, and fail – on their own – to address the capacity and confidence of those socialised to accept subordination in decision-making (Heaney, 1995). The *recognition* of 'other' stakeholders does not necessarily mean they participate equally, nor does it guarantee that collaboration will occur.

Nevertheless, the model rules differ in that they reopen the question raised by Davies (2002) regarding who can be a company member, and the rights they acquire through membership. Each acts as a template in reframing business norms so that corporate citizenship either limits or replaces **property rights** as the basis of company membership. How this is operationalised becomes a matter of management practice. Devising a set of rules does not guarantee that the rules are followed; this rests on the understandings, ability and commitment of those currently involved in an enterprise, and their capacity and willingness to devise appropriate management systems (Ridley-Duff, 2009a). Each emergent model approaches this challenge in a different way (informed by the social contexts in which they developed). Each shifts business thinking towards the representative governance models favoured by Schumpeter (1942), or the participative democratic model of Pateman (1970).

The model rules discussed in this chapter provide some templates for how people have sought to achieve these changes. Importantly, the goal is not achieved by superimposing employee and stakeholder consultation on top of existing charity or company structures. Instead, there is an attempt to rewrite the legal principles and social norms on which business activity is based (Argyris et al., 1985; Gates, 1998; Turnbull, 2002). Consequently, they represent early attempts at model 2 thinking regarding the nature of (and possibilities inherent in) business itself (see Table 7.3). New configurations for company membership allocate rights in different ways, and lead to organisations with social identities more aligned to the complexities of the societies in which they are embedded.

CLASS EXERCISE   Comparing social enterprise model rules

Materials to support this exercise can be found at www.sagepub.co.uk/ridleyduff.

Allow approximately 1 hour for this exercise.

- Divide the class into groups of three or five and ask each group to elect a chairperson. With the exception of the chairperson, allocate cases 7.1, 7.2, 7.3 and 7.4 (Table 7.4) to the group members. You can, optionally, issue copies of the model rules as well.
- Ask the chairs to take responsibility for recording the comparisons made by group members.

(Continued)

(Continued)

- Give group members 10 minutes to read and make notes on their case (or ask them to do this in advance of the seminar). The chair should read Table 7.5 and familiarise themselves with the different rights that can be defined in Articles of Association.
- Using the theoretical framework in Table 7.5, give the groups 30 minutes to identify who the members of each company are, and which rights have been accorded to each class of member.
- Ask the chair of each group to present the results, and (where applicable) express the preference of group members.

SUMMARY OF LEARNING

In this chapter, we have argued the following:

- An organisation's rules influences how members are selected and included in decision-making.
- Unlike private enterprises, social enterprise rules aim to balance the needs and rights of founders, service users, consumers and staff, rather than private (financial) investors.
- The long-term impacts of choosing a constitution are evident only after many years of trading.
- Social problems can be addressed through innovative approaches to business formation.
- Model 1 (single-loop learning) seeks to *improve upon existing models*.
- Model 2 (double-loop learning) seeks to *reformulate the norms of enterprise activity*.
- Emerging norms for social enterprise model rules aim to engage multiple stake-holders in governance and surplus sharing.

QUESTIONS AND POSSIBLE ESSAY ASSIGNMENTS

1 'A company's social and commercial performance will be compromised if it allows both staff and customers to become company members.' Critically assess the evidence for and against this claim.
2 Critically discuss the extent to which company rules can be written to ensure that 'no one group is able to secure a basis of power and command over the majority so that it can effectively suppress or deny the claims of the groups it opposes' (Michels, 1961: 36).
3 'Social identity is a matter of management practice, not company rules.' Critically discuss this statement, and the way that company rules and management practice affect an organisation's social identity.

FURTHER READING

In the UK, a number of practitioner guides are available. One widely publicised guide is *Keeping It Legal*, available from the Social Enterprise Coalition and co-authored with Bates, Wells and Braithwaite (SEC, 2009b). One weakness of this publication is the relatively poor coverage on cooperative and employee ownership structures. Stronger guidance on this is available in *Simply Legal*, updated in 2009 with support from the Big Lottery (downloadable from Cooperatives UK, http://www.cooperatives-uk.coop/SimplyLegal). Information on the use of trusts and share incentive schemes can be obtained from the Employee Ownership Association (UK) and the National Center for Employee Ownership (US) (see links in the 'Useful resources' section). Charity-specific information on the link between governance and the Charities Act 2006 has been commissioned by NCVO (downloadable from http://www.ncvo-vol.org.uk/node/30096).

Academic discussion of the link between social identity and legal forms is relatively rare. Nevertheless, a readable introduction to general issues in company law that considers both historical and theoretical issues can be found in Davies' *Introduction to Company Law* (2002). A highly watchable (and critical analysis) of the modern corporation is *The Corporation,* available on both DVD and YouTube (Achbar et al., 2004).

A sophisticated argument for worker ownership, based on a critique of economic theory, can be found in *The Democratic Corporation* by David Ellerman (1997) (available for download from http://www.ellerman.org). Similar arguments for a fundamental rethink of firm structures are developed in Gates' book *The Ownership Solution* (1998). A critical response to Ellerman's underlying argument has been published by Zundel (2002) in the *Journal of Business Ethics*, while a study exploring the practical impact of company rules on (financial) management practices can be found in 'Cooperative social enterprises: company rules, access to finance and management practice' in the *Social Enterprise Journal* (Ridley-Duff, 2009a).

Further reading material is available on the companion website at www.sagepub.co.uk/ridleyduff.

USEFUL RESOURCES

Charity Commission Model Rules, http://www.charity-commission.gov.uk/registration/mgds.asp

Common Cause Foundation Model Rules, http://www.commoncausefoundation.org/?q=node/4

Cooperatives UK Model Rules, http://www.cooperatives-uk.coop/live/welcome.asp?id=2705

Employee Ownership Association (UK), http://www.employeeownership.co.uk/publications.asp

National Center for Employee Ownership (US), http://www.nceo.org/main/publist.php/

NewCo Model Rules for Social Enterprise, http://newco.org.uk/

Somerset Cooperative Services CIC – Somerset Rules, http://www.somerset.coop/node/17 (offers an interesting set of IPS multi-stakeholder model rules)

Surplus Sharing Model Rules, http://www.scribd.com/doc/11545936/Social-Enterprise-Model-Rules

NOTES

1   Social firms in the UK equates to a subset of the social economy that focuses on people who are disadvantaged in the labour market. In the US and Europe we find that people use the term slightly differently.

2   This is also true of a NewCo implementation developed in 2004.

Strategic Management and Planning

8

Learning Objectives

In this chapter, we consider the nature, role and process of strategic management. By the end of this chapter you will be able to:

- describe the principal themes and challenges of strategic management in social enterprises

- distinguish between prescriptive and descriptive theories of strategic management

- critically appraise the role and purpose of a business plan, and business planning

- analyse different approaches to strategic management using a theoretical framework

- make an informed choice on how to assess strategic management practices.

The key arguments that will be developed in this chapter are:

- Strategic management aims to elicit the medium- and long-term goals of organisational stakeholders, and then devise a strategy to fulfil them.
- Both *intended* and *emergent* strategies affect what can be realised in practice.
- Strategic management involves planning, but does not necessarily involve written plans.
- Approaches to strategic management can be radically affected by social philosophy, legal form and economic conditions.
- When assessing the benefits of strategy, both 'soft' and 'hard' data help determine social value.

Introduction

Organizations that succeed, organizations that thrive, organizations that are going to be the providers of services in the next century all know where they are going. (Brinckerhoff, 1994: 130)

This comment from *Mission-Based Management* goes to the core of this chapter. Do 'successful' organisations know where they are going? Mintzberg et al. (1998), in their entertaining book *Strategy Safari*, argue that this view may be misleading. Using the story of the 'The Blind Men and the Elephant', Mintzberg argues that managers are mostly like 'blind men' and strategy is an 'elephant' that no-one can see without carefully listening to, and cooperating with, others. As the poem concludes:

So oft in theologic wars,
The disputants, I ween,
Rail on in utter ignorance
Of what each other mean,
And prate about an Elephant
Not one of them has seen!

Jon Saxe, 1816–87

In this chapter we discuss the challenge of conceptualising the 'elephant', and the processes by which stakeholders can reduce their blindness and contribute to sense-making and future planning. In doing so, we draw attention to two groups of theories (*prescriptive theories* and *descriptive theories*) that capture *intended* and *emergent* aspects of strategic management (Mintzberg et al., 1998). To this, we add views from *critical management studies* that strategic management primarily serves the interests of owners (and their agents) and maintains their control over economic, social and human capital (Alvesson and Willmott, 2003).

Developing strategies (planning) is a key aspect of management. In social enterprises it can involve challenges that are more diverse than in private or public organisations. As we have found working with local practitioners, there are points of departure between social economy and private sector management that lead practitioners to question whether the product of strategic management in the social economy should be labelled a 'business plan'.

With this in mind, we explore the conceptual side of strategic management and planning, and why it is believed to be important. We also take a critical look at the process of strategic planning using three case studies. These focus on how the strategic goals of individuals and collegial groups can be elicited and constructed into workable planning documents (artefacts). Lastly, we introduce the reader to a diagnostic tool called Balance that provides a self-help approach to analysing strategic management performance.

CLASSROOM DISCUSSION   Planning challenges

The following extract appears in teaching materials available from Social Enterprise Europe.

Setting up a social enterprise calls for a different type of business planning. The key characteristics of social enterprises can differentiate them from private businesses in the following ways:

(Continued)

(Continued)

- governed by social objectives, not financial
- driven by values and ethics
- financed through mixed receipts
- democratically managed
- cooperation and networking rather than competition
- profits reinvested rather than distributed to shareholders
- committed to creating social wealth not private capital
- rooted in a community of disadvantage
- committed to solving social problems
- seek to empower members
- part of public policy.

The plan can therefore look very different and may be called a *social enterprise plan* rather than a 'business plan'.

Discussion questions:

1 Is the phrase 'business plan' or 'social enterprise plan' more meaningful to you?
2 What would you expect to see (or not see) in a 'social enterprise plan' compared to the 'business plan' of a private, third or public sector organisation?

As we argued in Part I of this book, social enterprises mix social, environmental and economic objectives. In doing so, they eclectically draw on techniques from private, cooperative and voluntary organisations in an attempt to establish practices that work for members and beneficiaries. With no dominant framework for social enterprise, the variety of strategic choices presents a significant challenge. The diversity of organisational forms (linked, in many cases, to different strategic goals) represents an additional challenge. What will happen in a large (or small) social enterprise when the owners are members of staff and/or users of the organisation's services? What happens when beneficiaries and/or staff are prevented from involvement in strategic decisions? The *concept* of strategic management spans all types of organisation, but *practice* is neither predictable nor uniform.

There are many books on the subject of strategic management, mostly written from the perspectives of the private sector. New public management theory in recent years has also, if somewhat resisted in practice, attempted to advance business-like techniques in the public sector (see Chapter 2). Third sector organisations have also embraced strategic management and planning techniques. According to Hudson (2002) this has been a relatively recent phenomenon, becoming popular from the 1980s onward and accelerating with the rise of 'corporate governance' throughout the 1990s (see NCVO, 2005). In social enterprises (established as a subject discipline only in the mid to late 1990s) strategic management and planning is still poorly understood. As a result, this chapter explores the thin end of a thick wedge. What we offer here falls short of an overview, and represents early reflections on how strategic management theory can be used to understand social enterprises, and how strategic management practices might be adapted by them.

The context for strategic management and planning

Before we start, let us consider a case that highlights the challenges faced by social enterprises. Seedley and Langworthy Trust (SALT) is in the city of Salford, in the north-west of England. It runs a busy drop-in centre for the community, providing services that support local residents; help with domestic issues; settle neighbourhood disputes; and aim to increase community cohesion. This organisation is typical of many striving to become social enterprises delivering a wide range of services with limited (financial) resources (Case 8.1).

Case 8.1   Seedley and Langworthy Trust (SALT)

Seedley and Langworthy Trust was established in 1997. It was set up to develop effective links between people who live and work in Seedley and Langworthy and partners from the public, private and voluntary sectors. Seedley and Langworthy are neighbouring areas within the City of Salford, near Manchester in the north of England. Both are labelled 'deprived wards', suffering a decline in manufacturing and high unemployment, and coping with the knock-on effects to the social, economic and cultural fabric of their communities.

You may find it helpful to read the short history of SALT at www.sagepub.co.uk/ridleyduff.

With single regeneration budget (SRB) funding at an end, SALT needs to develop a social enterprise plan to secure new sources of income.

1   If you were tasked with helping SALT think about their future, what would you do?
2   How would you help SALT?
3   Where would you start?

Conceptualising Strategic Management

Strategic management involves reflective thinking within an organisation about its place within its environment (political, economic, socio-cultural, technological, legal and environmental) and according to a marketplace (business) or non-marketplace (not-for-profit) world view. Mintzberg et al. (1998) describe how a 5Ps approach can assist in:

- adopting various *perspectives* ...
- ... to identifying *patterns* ...
- ... so you can determine your *position* ...
- ... and develop a *plan* ...
- ... or a *ploy*.

We argue that strategic management is (potentially, but not necessarily) a unifying and motivationally important process because it helps frame (analyse need), shape (devise frameworks and systems), articulate (set objectives) and communicate the ideas, decisions and rules that build '**social capital**' (see Chapter 4). Strategic management brings people together for planning, making decisions or undertaking activities. At the same time strategic management is also 'socially constructed', by which we mean that the processes and outcomes are (subjective) agreements between people – managers, board, staff and stakeholders – represented through artefacts that communicate their authors' understanding of structures, systems and plans. The aim is to translate concepts (ideas) into both pragmatic theories ('theories in use') that produce tangible outcomes ('actions').

A level of scepticism, however, regarding the complexity of strategic management is worth retaining, Hudson adds:

> Strategic planning has had a very chequered history. It migrated to the third sector in the 1980s and, more often than not, promised more than it could deliver. Massive effort was put into preparing plans, involving endless meetings and lengthy documents . . . and within a year or two the plan either would have been forgotten or would be so out of date as to render it irrelevant. (2002: 112)

After the takeover of the Zanon factory in Argentina (see Chapter 5), one of the new worker-owners commented that:

> We pay ourselves a fair salary. We discuss how much money we have, how much to save, and how much to take. For us as workers, accounting is easy. I don't know why it is so hard for the bosses to pay salaries, buy materials, and pay the bills. For me it is easy, you add and subtract.

Similar sentiments were expressed by Muhammad Yunus (see Chapter 5, Grameen Bank) about the elimination of poverty. Poverty is frequently *represented* as a complex intractable problem, but straightforward solutions were established once assumptions about banking and people had been challenged.

The above points are worth bearing in mind because Alvesson and Willmott (2003) argue that strategic management can obscure and mystify management processes in order to marginalise and disempower strategic stakeholders (the workforce, customers or service users and suppliers). As such, strategic management may not be organised to simplify and clarify the choices facing an organisation, or to promote effective discussion. It may be an opportunity to devise new rhetorics and arguments that alter the distribution of power and wealth between owners, managers, workers, customers, service users and suppliers. In this case, strategic management processes may deliberately use complex arguments to make it harder for a lay person to argue against proposals.

EXERCISE   Legal forms and strategic management

You can explore the extent to which you agree or disagree with Alvesson and Willmott (2003) by attempting Exercise 8.1, available at www.sagepub.co.uk/ridleyduff[1].

In this exercise, participants are divided into groups of four people (named John, Belinda, Helen and Kevin) to discuss reward management. After undergoing the discussion, the

(Continued)

> *(Continued)*
>
> groups reorganise into Johns, Belindas, Helens and Kevins to discuss how the different organisation structures and constitutions under which they conducted their meetings affected the strategic management process.
>
> Experience of using this exercise in a teaching context suggests that some legal forms create the need for complex (and perhaps deceptive or coercive) arguments because they are intended to exclude or limit the influence of some stakeholders. Once this occurs, complex arguments become necessary to persuade parties to continue cooperating with each other.

Table 8.1 Three groups of theories about strategic management

Group	School	Primary characteristic
Prescriptive theory Concerned with how strategies *should* be developed	Design school	Strategising is a *conceptualising* process
	Planning school	Strategising is a *formal* process
	Positioning school	Strategising is an *analytical* process
Descriptive theory Concerned with *actual* descriptions of strategic management	Entrepreneurial school	Strategising is a *visioning* process
	Cognitive school	Strategising is a *mental* process
	Learning school	Strategising is an *emergent* process
	Power school	Strategising is a *negotiating* process
	Cultural school	Strategising is a *collective* process
	Environmental school	Strategising is a *reactive* process
Critical theory Concerned with the *social and political objectives* of management and managers	Critical management school	Strategising is a *mystifying*, *marginalising* and *obfuscating* process that enables managers to *colonise* power to achieve hegemonic control over other social groups
	Configuration school	Strategising is an *integrating* process that selectively applies any of the above approaches and combines them in the pragmatic pursuit of social and economic objectives

Source: based on Mintzberg et al., 1998; Alvesson and Willmott, 2003

Table 8.1 summarises approaches identified by Mintzberg et al. (1998) and Alvesson and Willmott (2003). In each case, 'strategising' is given a different emphasis. While there is insufficient space to consider each in detail (see 'Further reading'), it is worth drawing out the key differences.

Firstly, there are *prescriptive* theories – formalised processes of conceptualising and analysing the issues faced by an organisation. These are aimed at facilitating discussion in management events, awaydays and planning activities, and are guided by handbooks, guidance, policy documents and quality management processes. While recognising the contribution of consultants and business schools to the dissemination of 'prescriptive' theories, Mintzberg et al. (1998: 6) identify six additional schools that 'have been concerned less with prescribing ideal strategic behavior than with *describing* how strategies do, in fact, get made'. These are 'configured' through:

- entrepreneurial 'visioning'
- cognitive 'mental processing'
- negotiation of power
- collectively evolving a culture
- adapting to the environment.

These processes are *emergent* and not as open to formalisation or facilitation at preplanned events. They may be embedded in social practices rather than written down (see DiMaggio and Powell, 1983), and may be realised by accident or design, manifesting themselves in a 'community of practice' that arises in a particular context (see Wenger, 1998).

For the purpose of this chapter, strategic management is characterised as a way of managing organisational complexities and uncertainties. It is a way of rationalising abstract or perceived realities so that a (sometimes shared) set of artefacts (systems and documents) can be formulated, communicated, implemented and evaluated. The purpose of strategic planning, whatever 'school' embarks on the task, is the working out of a set of guiding principles for an organisation, perhaps including a set of (written) objectives, and/or a 'vision' and 'values'. These may be stated formally or learned informally, passed on in manuals and seminars, or learnt by trial and error.

In its formal guise, strategic planning is a framework for guiding an organisation to: organise; provide vision and objectives; give people purpose and motivation; give direction; provide a route map for followers; provide clear boundaries; enable decisions and judgements to be taken within defined risk contexts; and create written plans. Hudson (2002: 96) provides an account of the benefits of formalised strategic management and planning:

- Everyone becomes clearer about his/her objectives and how they fit into the organisation as a whole.
- It leads to more effective use of resources.
- It is an ideal way of building commitment and motivation.
- Diverse constituencies can be brought together around a common purpose.

Empirical research to confirm the above, however, is not easy to find. **Ethnographies**, in particular, question the extent to which the above can be achieved. In Ridley-Duff (2005), for example, it was found that management trainees in several social enterprises were not clear about their organisation's vision and objectives, even (in one case) at the *end* of a management course during which participants had to recite the organisation's 'vision' during each session. Staff would not be swayed by statements from managers or owners once they had accumulated the working experience necessary to form their own view.

Formalised strategic planning, however, holds out the possibility of encapsulating an organisation's vision for the future using formal statements of the organisation's values and mission, and linking this to other organisational plans and management practices. There are some contexts in which written plans are purposeful: applying to financial institutions, seeking grants, undertaking social marketing, gaining legitimacy and credibility in social networks. But if we continue producing formal plans outside such contexts, what purpose do they serve? Is it habit, or part of an attempt to gain *internal* legitimacy (or power) over other internal groups? Can the production of 'plans' decrease efficiency too?

Operationalising Strategic Management and Planning

This section discusses ways in which social enterprises have approached strategic management. A formal (or written) strategic plan is one way that organisations present an analysis of their organisation's future development. However, a lot of strategising also takes place in small steps. Collins (2001) reports that 'great' companies rarely undertake 'launches' of new strategies devised by senior managers; instead, their performance 'takes off' when multiple strategic choices at all levels of organisation fit together in a way that provides a competitive (or collaborative) edge.

Prescriptive theories typically focus on *organisational* questions and the pursuit of 'best practice'. Descriptive and critical approaches may involve processes to find the 'best fit' between individual skills and aspirations, and organisational goals on which people can reach agreement (Storey, 2001). Table 8.2 highlights some of the questions that might arise in either case.

Table 8.2 Questions that help with strategic planning

Organisational/group focus	Individual focus
• Where are we now?	• Where am I now?
• What do we stand for?	• What do I (want to) stand for?
• What are we trying to achieve?	• What am I trying to achieve?
• How are we going to do it?	• What can I contribute?
• What are our capabilities?	• What abilities do I have?
• What are the critical issues we must address along the way?	• What will keep me committed?
• What are the short-, medium- and long-term objectives?	• What are my short-, medium- and long-term objectives?
• Are we best placed to get where we want to be?	• Am I on a 'journey' I want to continue?
• Who are our customers?	• Who currently wants to work with me?
• Who do we want to be our customers?	• Who do I want to work for?
• How will we know we are getting there – and how will we know we are there? (review)	• How will I assess my own progress?

Table 8.3   Strategic management case studies: Cases 8.1–8.3

SALT (Case 8.1)

Seedley and Langworthy Trust (SALT) was established in 1997. It was set up to develop effective links between people who live and work in Seedley and Langworthy (areas within the City of Salford, near Manchester in the north of England) and partners from the public, private and voluntary sectors.

Broomby CIC (Case 8.2)

Broomby CIC was established by Mark Powell – a specialist in the development of social firms – after his previous employer (IMBY, a registered charity) changed its policy on social firm development. As Mark was committed to employing disabled people in social firms, he set up Broomby CIC in 2006 to take over projects started by IMBY.

SoftContact (Case 8.3)

SoftContact was founded in 1979 by six friends who met at college. The founders wanted to create an egalitarian place to work where they were free from management supervision. The company grew to 15 staff in the 1980s by fulfilling the social objective of providing IT training, advice and support services to third sector organisations.

The case studies are on the website at www.sagepub.co.uk/ridleyduff.

Having set out what strategic management aims to achieve, we now discuss three cases to explore the extent to which they are achievable (Table 8.3). We have already met SALT (Case 8.1).

SALT (Case 8.1) illustrates how a strategic awayday can support the development of a written business plan that fulfils the marketing needs of an organisation. This took place at a venue (and with the equipment needed) to create a 'space' where the participants had time to reflect on, and develop, a sense of direction. The issues for discussion were decided beforehand (after interviewing people at all levels in the organisation) and formulated into a workshop. The awayday agenda for SALT was organised to develop:

- *Purpose*: vision, mission and values.
- *Position*: where is the organisation compared to others working in this field?
- *Plan*: where does the organisation want to be?
- *Performance*: milestones, achievements, monitoring, management and evaluation.

Alongside these four key Ps, teams were encouraged to follow a formula to guide the preparation of the business plan:

1 Review current status.
2 Identify goals.
3 Agree initiatives.
4 Set targets/objectives.
5 Agree assessment and evaluation.
6 Reflect and continuously improve.

While the agenda set for SALT focused almost wholly on the needs of their organisation, the other two cases (8.2 and 8.3) adopted an approach that focused on the intersection between individual and organisational aspirations. In Broomby CIC

(Case 8.2), participants were initially provided with a questionnaire that gave them 24 'scenarios' and asked them to assess which of five choices most closely reflected their organisation. The questionnaire was a **'heuristic'**, designed to introduce people to the *diversity* of choices, and multiple relationships, that are managed through a strategic management process. Following this, the framework was used to conduct one-to-one (coaching-style) interviews. These were written up and provided to each participant: they brought questionnaire responses and the interview transcript to a workshop in which they analysed and planned actions with other members of their organisation.

The process sought to identify 'issues' (that needed resolution) and 'actions' (that people wanted to undertake together). While the process was designed to aid people in understanding their own and others' values, the process did not involve *establishing* shared values. Nor was the 'output' a formal business plan: it was a one-page document that sought to summarise the issues/actions that future management and/ or board meetings should seek to address, plus a one-page document for each individual that summarised their own issues/actions.

At SoftContact (Case 8.3), an 'annual review' took place each year at self-catering accommodation rented by the company. In this case, the annual review was organised to reflect the strategic goal of the founders to generate and reinforce an egalitarian culture:

> members were expected to share responsibilities for cooking and washing up, coffee making, house cleaning, minute taking, chairing sessions, preparing and presenting papers, and writing up minutes. These policies promoted member interaction and supported equality policies and objectives ... Saturday night usually involved a meal out, followed by drinks and various games at the self-catering accommodation. Watching TV was discouraged but not prohibited. Members usually played card games (poker, bridge), or other games that involved a lot of interaction. Alcoholic drinks were always available. Opportunities to chat informally were highly valued and viewed as an integral and vital part of the induction of new members.

As with Case 8.2, there was a strong focus on identifying *individual* goals and reflecting on these during discussion of business proposals and organisational goals. On the Friday evening, several hours were devoted to *personal reports*, a process by which all members (based on previously undertaken peer appraisals) made others aware of their career aspirations. The whole of Saturday was devoted to business proposals which were introduced, discussed and voted upon by all members (on a one-person, one-vote basis). On Sunday, annual budgets were discussed and revised in light of the decisions taken the previous day.

EXERCISE   Appraising different approaches to strategy making

Additional materials to support this exercise are available at www.sagepub.co.uk/ridleyduff.

In groups of three or six:

1 Allocate Cases 8.1, 8.2 and 8.3 to group members.
2 Read and carefully consider the case you have been given (10 minutes).

(Continued)

(Continued)

3 Using Table 8.1, find examples of each school of strategic management in the cases you have read (20 minutes).

4 Discuss the merits of 'configuring' approaches based on these schools of strategic management (15 minutes).

5 In what contexts might one configuration be preferable to another? (15 minutes).

In the case of SALT (Case 8.1), the consultation was guided by a management/consultant-led approach in which the content (i.e. section headings) of the business plan was *designed* in advance. The awayday was *planned* so that it would create statements on the vision, mission and shared values of the organisation (so that they could be added to marketing materials and business plans). Next, there was a focus on socio-economic *analysis* (using a PESTLE),[2] market *analysis* (using a SWOT), the identification of sources of income, and the *design* of services.

The Broomby CIC case (Case 8.2) was also management/consultant led, but there is no evidence that the goal of the development process was the production of a formal business plan. Instead, there was a focus on *emergent learning* and *analysis*. This was supported by a diagnostic questionnaire to generate questions for face-to-face discussions; participants developed their *cognitive* skills through *reflection* on questionnaire responses and interview summaries. The content of a plan was developed through *analysis*, but no cultural 'normalising' (vision, mission or value statements) was attempted. Instead, there was an attempt to establish 'critical success factors' (a form of *visioning*).

Lastly, the SoftContact case (Case 8.3) represents an *informalised* and institutionalised strategic management process devised over many years (DiMaggio and Powell, 1983), without any external support and not driven by the need to write a formal business plan. There is evidence of *collectivisation* through the proactive establishment of behavioural norms (playing games, self-catering etc.) that are intended to reinforce *cultural values* (e.g. an egalitarian culture, workplace democracy). It is, perhaps ironically, a highly structured process (with months of advance planning, peer appraisals, minute taking, voting). It is *critical* in the sense that it is *designed* to increase individual participation and minimise dominance by powerful groups.

Doherty et al. (2009b) suggest that 'strategic workshops' (such as 'awaydays') can be detached, singular events that may fail to embed changes in day-to-day practice. They can fail to penetrate the consciousness of people, and once they return to their everyday worlds very little changes. They also express concerns that, unless everyone in the organisation is on the awayday, the resentment and suspicion of those who did not attend creates barriers to implementation.

Strategic planning, therefore, can be viewed both as an expression of management philosophy and as a process of inquiry. Beinhocker, in his book *The Origin of Wealth* (2007: 323–8), suggests that strategising is less concerned with outlining a course of action and more concerned with *negotiating understanding of uncertainty*. Even if this is so, that is not to say that the effort is wasted: it becomes a learning process that supports the development of both individual and group strategies. The words on the pages of a business plan, however, may matter less than the process through which it is produced (see Berry et al., 2005). Weick regards this as a 'sense-making' process.

I consistently argue that the likelihood of survival goes up when variation increases, when possibilities multiply, when trial and error becomes more diverse and less stylized, when people become less repetitious, and when creativity becomes supported. (2001: 351)

These arguments favour emergent approaches and cast doubt over formalising strategy in written plans. Strategic management enacted through analysis, planning and evaluation is replaced by organic, flexible and adaptable practices that create a culture of strategising. This orients the process toward preparing and flexing the mind, developing an adaptive culture where strategies, scenarios and alternatives can be meaningfully compared and evaluated. It becomes more of a process of gazing for options than gazing for a set of answers (Beinhocker, 2007).

Mintzberg et al. (1998) would probably characterise this as the *configuration school* (see Table 8.1), in which different approaches to 'strategising' are used to draw out strands of thinking to establish preferences. As Weick implies, this comes close to 'thriving on chaos' (Peters, 1989), deploying the management equivalent of freestyle jazz or improvised theatre as a way of generating ideas. Once generated, they can be selected, honed and crafted until they produce the results desired (Weick, 2001: 351). With this in mind we now turn our attention to ways in which strategic management performance might itself by assessed.

Assessing Strategic Management Performance

Strategic management performance analysis tools for the private sector are commonplace. There are business 'excellence models' (EFQM), **Balanced Scorecard (BSC)** adaptations, centres for total quality management (TQM); or you can choose between strategies based on **management by objective (MBO)** and business process re-engineering (BPR). Adapting these for the social (enterprise) sector is one option open to social enterprises (as well as public and voluntary sector organisations). Given vehement criticism of business schools after the financial crisis of 2008 (see James, 2009), it is appropriate to consider the implications of adapting private sector theory.

Anheier (2000) claims that 'business' focused strategic analysis tools are not readily translated for use in social enterprise contexts because the latter have *multiple* bottom lines. Paton conducted extensive research into performance management and concluded that:

the very reasons why activities are undertaken in the non-profit sector are also the reasons why performance measurement will be deeply problematic. (2003: 49)

In stating this, he draws attention to the social costs of private (and public) sector management. It makes no sense (businesswise, or otherwise) for the social economy to uncritically accept practices they have identified as root causes of problems they seek to resolve. So, at the very least, the drive towards 'contracts' and adopting 'business-like' behaviour requires social performance indicators (and forms of social organisation) that do not reproduce the social costs of private and public sector organisations.

Strategic management tools designed and created from the perspectives of profit-based businesses need to be carefully critiqued to establish their value for social enterprises (Speckbacher, 2003; Alter, 2007). Several authors also draw attention to the issue of differences between large and small businesses (Storey, 1994; Scase and Goffee, 1980; Jennings and Beaver, 1997). Small businesses are less driven by formality, and lack the resources to implement systems designed for large organisations. Indeed, both Dandridge (1979) and Wynarczyk et al. (1993) have suggested that small-business people have *less tolerance for inefficiency* than larger organisations. As a result, they adopt different business ideologies, ethics and organisational structures. The implication of this comment (and bearing in mind the **critical management school** identified earlier in the chapter) is that strategic management 'tools' are sometimes established by large consultancy companies as revenue opportunities within multinational companies (MNCs). Logically, this market exists only because large organisations can tolerate inefficiencies that smaller organisations cannot sustain, or – seen in Marxian terms – the 'tools' find a market because they increase the 'rate of exploitation' of either labour or consumers. If this is the case, it is an inauspicious starting point for their use in social enterprises.

An unavoidable difference is that performance measurement and quantification in social enterprises extend to evidencing *social* value. Social returns may be related to levels of trust, or similar unexpressed, unquantifiable or hard-to-measure 'returns' (Paton, 2003). As Thomas (2004) notes, this is likely to be expensive, both in terms of generating data, and also in terms of staff time and investments in information technology. There are, therefore, human resource and financial issues in instigating, analysing and implementing strategic performance analysis. A final caveat raised by Holloway (1999) is how little empirical evidence confirms that performance analysis tools have an impact on the practices of organisations.

One of the issues here is the objective/subjective standpoint in conducting business analysis. Thomas highlights the problem of perception and interpretation:

> the performance captured by a particular set of measures will always be partial and contextual, reflecting the fact that the measures have been selected, analyzed and interpreted through the lenses of the organizations and individuals involved with the process. (2004: 11)

Add to this the multifaceted nature of performance, and its fluid, ambiguous and contested nature (Pestoff, 1998), and it is unsurprising that tools for assessing the effectiveness of strategic management and planning are seldom adopted in the social enterprise sector.

One exception to this is the Balanced Scorecard (BSC) as this adopts a holistic approach to performance measurement that steers thinking away from economic indicators (Kaplan and Norton, 1992). As Bennett et al. claim:

> The concept of the BSC is based on the assumption that the efficient use of investment capital is no longer the sole determinant for competitive advantages, but increasingly soft factors such as intellectual capital, knowledge creation or excellent customer orientation become more important. (2003: 19)

Kaplan and Norton (1992) suggested that the BSC is appropriate for transfer to non-profit organisations, and two sector-specific projects have provided some early progress towards this goal. Firstly, Social Firms UK constructed an online 'Dashboard' intended as an integrated management performance tool based on the principles of the BSC. Secondly, the **New Economic Foundation** (NEF) worked with the Social Enterprise Partnership (SEP) to pilot the BSC in social enterprises. Their research highlighted that the BSC needed to be adapted to incorporate the commercial practices of social enterprises by including: multiple bottom lines; multi-stakeholder and social objectives; social goals; a broader financial perspective focused on sustainability; and a broader 'relationship' perspective that goes beyond the customer to capture a larger group of stakeholder perspectives (Somers, 2005). Case 8.4 describes a further project funded by the European Social Fund (ESF) to create a practical tool for use in social enterprises.

Case 8.4   Balance: developing a strategic management tool for social enterprises

Balance is a strategic management diagnostic tool for social enterprises and other third sector organisations (Bull, 2006). It was developed in 2005 by Mike Bull during a research project that involved Dilani Jayawarna, Helen Crompton, Alison Wilson and Robin Holt at the Centre for Enterprise, Manchester Metropolitan University. The tool was the outcome of three years' research (between 2004 and 2007) on the management practices of social enterprises and was funded by a regional European Social Fund (ESF) grant. It identified language and concepts appropriate for use in social enterprises. The basis of Balance is shown in Figure 8.1.

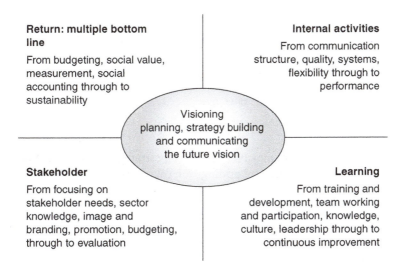

Return: multiple bottom line

From budgeting, social value, measurement, social accounting through to sustainability

Internal activities

From communication structure, quality, systems, flexibility through to performance

Visioning planning, strategy building and communicating the future vision

Stakeholder

From focusing on stakeholder needs, sector knowledge, image and branding, promotion, budgeting, through to evaluation

Learning

From training and development, team working and participation, knowledge, culture, leadership through to continuous improvement

Figure 8.1   Balance

A teaching case with questions, and an academic article on the reformulation of the Balanced Scorecard into Balance, is available at www.sagepub.co.uk/ridleyduff.

One of the early advocates and users of Balance was Unlimited Potential in Salford. They have used the tool annually since 2004 to monitor their progress. Case 8.5 provides a summary of the outputs from Balance to illustrate how progress can be monitored. Results can be compared not just against the organisation's own previous results, but also against the average for all organisations that have used the Balance tool.

Case 8.5   Unlimited Potential

At the launch of the Charlestown and Lower Kersal New Deal for Communities (NDC) in March 2000, local people who wanted to be involved in planning the new health services started identifying themselves. Six months later, they were meeting on a regular basis, analysing data, shaping the plan and forming themselves into the Community Health Action Partnership and subsequently Unlimited Potential. In 2007 they undertook a further self-assessment using Balance and compared it to their findings from 2006. The results were:

- stakeholder perspective: good progress (was 60%, now up to 73.4%); above average
- internal activities: excellent progress (was 70%, now up to 86.6%); well above average
- multiple bottom line: good maintenance (was 80%, now up to 86.6%); well above average
- learning: excellent progress (was 63.4%, now up to 86.6%); significantly above average
- visioning: excellent progress (was 75%, now up to 95%); well above average.

Read the full case at www.sagepub.co.uk/ridleyduff and then answer the following questions:

1 Using Table 8.1, critically evaluate whether Balance is a *prescriptive*, *descriptive* or *critical* management tool.
2 Critically assess the language deployed in the Balance tool. To what extent is the language (and its implicit assumptions) appropriate for the organisation(s) in which (or for which) you have studied or worked?

Having identified that there may be value in using strategic management performance tools, we conclude the chapter by adding our own thoughts on the distribution of power and responsibility between employees, members, managers or a governing body (board of trustees or directors).

Critical Reflections

Our experience as researchers, lecturers and practitioners suggests that theory is both useful and limited. Devising strategy is much more messy than theory would suggest. It also varies across the social economy depending on the philosophical assumptions that are dominant amongst organisation members (see Ridley-Duff, 2007).

In the case of voluntary organisations and charities that trade, boards are (by law) required to be voluntary and *external* (in the sense that they comprise people who are not paid employees). This may also be the case in consumer cooperatives, as the members are primarily customers rather than members of the workforce. In both cases, employees either cannot be board members, or are elected to represent consumer or charitable interests rather than labour interests. The *reverse* is true in staff-controlled companies (employee owned and worker cooperatives). In this case, members of the workforce may be the *only* people permitted to serve on the board (although external directors are possible in *co-owned* companies).[3] In well-evidenced cases, directors in staff-controlled companies were also found to be 'voluntary' in the sense that no additional payment was made for services as a director (see Ridley-Duff, 2003; 2009a), reflecting a cultural (rather than legal) norm within the social economy. As for the new legal form of the community interest company (CIC), insufficient research has been conducted to establish norms regarding the payment of **directors**. Legally, however, there is no obstacle to making payments.

The size of organisation matters. In cooperative organisations, even though they are notionally democratic, members may only be involved in a few decisions and have limited opportunities to exercise control (Kasmir, 1996). Appointed executives can still gain power over both the process and the outcomes of strategic management (Whyte and Whyte, 1991). In CICs, the legal form has been designed (as is the case with US non-profits) so that there can be a managing director who is a full member of the **governing body** (see Low, 2006). This follows organisational norms established by the private sector promoting the possibility that the founding entrepreneur(s) will maintain control of the organisations they create.

With this variety of possible relationships between members, managers and directors, the crucial question arises: who is involved in strategic management? Is it the paid management staff? Or is it the responsibility of the board or management committee? Legally, strategising is the responsibility of the board (or management committee). Research suggests that there is a negotiating space between paid managers and board members (and *worker-owners* in cooperatives). As Coule (2008; Chadwick-Coule, 2010) found, this negotiating space is itself a stabilising influence. She found that organisations become *more vulnerable* if they rely on the advice dispensed by umbrella bodies who have been influenced by private sector reviews of governance (see NCVO, 2005). In three of four cases, the organisations most at risk were over-reliant on the relationship between the chair and the CEO. This resulted in the marginalisation of members, managers, trustees and directors in decision-making, through the non-disclosure of the information they needed to make strategic choices.

Figures 8.2 and 8.3 highlight two ideals of strategic control that reflect 'private' (Anthony, 1965) and 'cooperative' thinking (Turnbull, 2002). Norms in the private sector can be traced back to a study by Berle and Means (1932). They produced a theory that organisational growth results in a gradual separation of ownership (by shareholders) and control (by professional managers). The powers given to shareholders (and board members) to control executives, therefore, stem from the assumption that they are *agents* of the owners, employed to follow the wishes of the owners. Secondly, the Nobel prize-winning paper by Coase (1937) argued that entrepreneurial control of decision-making leads to the development of firms only

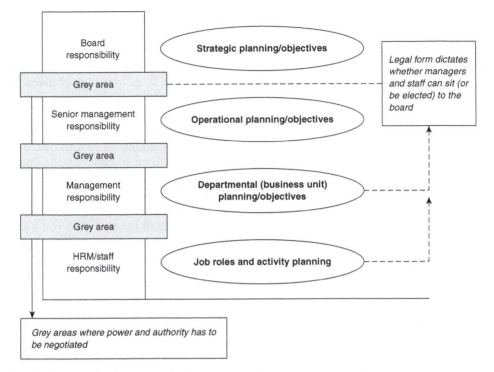

Figure 8.2   Strategic, operational, departmental and job responsibilities

where market transactions are more costly (to the entrepreneur) than employment contracts. Figure 8.2 reflects this 'rationalist' perspective, and hints at the link between *prescriptive* theories of strategic management and control and the way the founders wish their organisations to be run (see Carver, 1990; Hudson, 2002).

Charities, however, operate on the basis of **trust law** (rather than company law). This leads to a justification that trustees must be empowered to ensure that donated monies are used in accordance with the donors' wishes (or for charitable objects). While the rationale for top-down control is different, the management control system is still designed to separate the governing body (responsible for strategic management) and executive management (responsible for operations). Executive managers are still, in law, subordinate to the board.

In recent times, the 'rationalist' argument for top-down (line management) control has weakened. Beer (1966) shifted the argument by pointing out how often cybernetics and robotics rely on control *loops* and *localised feedback mechanisms* for effective governance in a complex system. This has, over time, strengthened the argument for cooperative governance based on an **ecological perspective** that networks are more effective because they allow parties to learn about (and influence) each other's behaviour. Figure 8.3 is an interpretation of Cornforth's (1995) study of Suma Wholefoods, in which members divided their organisation into 'sectors' rather than departments. Each sector was free to formulate management systems that met their local needs (e.g. each could exercise autonomy during staff recruitment and production). At the same time, sector members were elected to a **'hub'** to coordinate with other sectors.

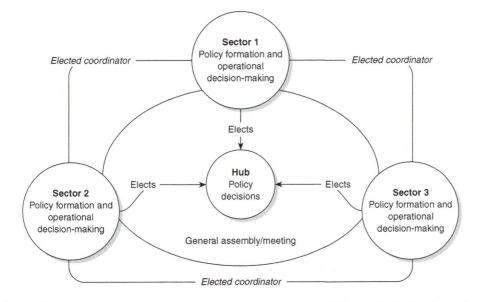

Figure 8.3   Strategic management and network governance (Ridley-Duff, 2009a: Figure 3, Suma Wholefoods)

Gates (1998) and Turnbull (2001; 2002) claim this approach can remove the communication barriers that hierarchies *create*, and replace them with a system of network governance that reduces exploitation and increases collaboration. Applied to organisations, the workforce, service users (customers) and suppliers become *strategic stakeholders* without which the organisation cannot operate. From this perspective, investors (and funders) are recast as an optional extra that can accelerate development, but not an absolute necessity. Ecological perspectives, not least because of their link to evolutionary thinking, are more strongly linked to *emergent* theories of strategic management.

Strategic management in organisations based on the thinking shown in Figure 8.2 may be viewed positively as a partnership between the board (governing body) and the management team, with the grey areas indicating areas of interaction to negotiate authority and control. Unlike the assumptions in Figure 8.3, authority is conceptualised as being at the 'top' of the organisation, exercised *downwards* in various 'controls' and to ensure **(legal) 'compliance'**. In Figure 8.3, authority is deliberately dispersed and the governing body is more like the 'heart' of the organisation, ensuring that resources and information are 'pumped' around the organisation so that both sector meetings and the general assembly or meeting can make strategic decisions.

Conclusions

In this chapter, we have introduced the concept of strategic management, and explored different approaches that reflect different contexts and outlooks on management itself. In the absence of established management practices, it is not surprising that *prescriptive* theories may be sought to provide a starting point from which to develop practice. When these prescriptions fail, however, it is necessarily to consider *descriptive* theories that focus on sense-making and critical reflection that uses accumulated experience. These theories – which avoid the fallacy of the 'quick fix' – enhance cognitive and learning skills, enabling managers to progressively engage with *critical perspectives* on management. A critical perspective can help with the devising of strategies to mitigate the effects of centralised power, and promote the 'configuration' of strategies so that they meet needs in particular situations. Over the long term, managers will gradually equip themselves with the cognitive awareness to assess which 'tools' are designed to increase economic or social opportunities for their designers, and which are likely to contribute to organisational learning and the well-being of organisation members.

SUMMARY OF LEARNING

In this chapter, we have explained:

- Ways of reducing our 'blindness' to the way strategic management is developed and enacted in social enterprises.
- How the starting point for strategic management in social enterprises has both similarities to and differences from the starting point for private, public and third sector enterprises.
- Different theories of strategic management, and how they are grouped into *prescriptive*, *descriptive* and *critical theories.*
- The problems of assessing the effectiveness of strategic management (in a social enterprise context), and the use of a sector-specific adaptation of the Balanced Scorecard called Balance.
- How the application of strategic management techniques and reflection can change practice.
- How the ideals of strategic management that arise out of 'rational' and 'ecological' thinking can lead to centralised and decentralised strategic planning.

QUESTIONS AND POSSIBLE ESSAY ASSIGNMENTS

1 'Private sector theories of strategic management are of limited use in social enterprises.' Using examples, critically assess the case for and against this statement.
2 Drawing on *prescriptive*, *descriptive* and *critical* theories of strategic management, assess strategic management practice in an organisation in which (or for which) you have worked or studied.
3 Using Figures 8.2 and 8.3, critically compare the scope and role of the governing body in the strategic management of a community interest company (CIC) and an industrial and provident society (IPS).

Note: for question 3, you can substitute legal forms that are appropriate to your regional or national context.

FURTHER READING

If you have insufficient time to read the whole of Mintzberg et al.'s *Strategy Safari* (1998), we heartily recommend the first chapter which provides an overview of *intended* and *emergent* strategic management, and the contribution of different schools of thought. Another excellent introduction that considers a wide range of perspectives on studying organisations as organisations is Christopher Grey's *A Very Short, Fairly Interesting and Reasonably Cheap Book about Studying Organizations* (2005). We have also found Ralph Stacey's book *Strategic Management and Organizational Dynamics: The Challenge of Complexity to Ways of Thinking about Organisations* (2007) a good resource.

Doherty et al.'s *Management for Social Enterprise* (2009b) also has a chapter entitled 'Strategic Management for Social Enterprises' that takes a different approach to the topic. For broader third sector discussions, Hudson's *Managing Without Profit* (2002) provides useful chapters on managing strategy and the concepts of vision, mission and values. For more critical coverage, we recommend Chadwick-Coule's article 'Social dynamics and the strategy process' (in press, 2010), due to appear in *Nonprofit and Voluntary Sector Quarterly*.

In addition to Mike Bull's published reports on the ESF Balance project (downloadable from http://www.socialenterprisebalance.org/Publications.aspx) we commend his 2007 article on its development in the *Social Enterprise Journal*. In the same journal, we also recommend Clifford Conway's (2008) article on business planning training in social enterprises .

Further reading material is available on the companion website at www.sagepub.co.uk/ridleyduff.

USEFUL RESOURCES

Balance, http://www.socialenterprisebalance.org

Balanced Scorecard Institute, http://www.balancedscorecard.org/

Forth Sector's Business Planning Guide, http://www.forthsector.org.uk/docs/New_BusPlanGuide.pdf

Free Management Library, http://managementhelp.org/plan_dec/str_plan/str_plan.htm

New Economics Foundation (Democracy and Participation), http://www.neweconomics.org/programmes/democracy-and-participation

Social Firms Dashboard, http://www.prove-andimprove.org/new/tools/socialfirm.php

USDA, Business and Cooperative Programs, http://www.rurdev.usda.gov/rbs/coops/crmd.htm

Venture Navigator, http://www.venturenavigator.co.uk/socialenterprise

NOTES

1 This is easily illustrated by using only the private and cooperative organisations in Exercise 8.1 on the companion website. In class exercises, the entrepreneur of the privately owned company is rarely able to reach agreement with their staff, while the worker cooperative members typically reach agreement quickly and easily (unless they seek a complex grading system).

2 A PESTLE analysis is similar to a PEST analysis (political, economic, socio-cultural and technical), but adds legal and environmental impact analyses.

3 For more on co-ownership see the website of the Employee Ownership Association (UK) in the 'useful resources' section for Chapter 7.

Governance, HRM and Employee Relations

9

Rory Ridley-Duff and Tracey Chadwick-Coule

Learning Objectives

In this chapter, we consider the practical application of different approaches to recruitment, selection, retention and control of people involved in running a social enterprise. By the end of this chapter you will be able to:

- outline system and relational views of governance

- explain hard and soft approaches to human resource management

- explain unitary, pluralist and radical perspectives on employee relations

- critically evaluate the impact of theoretical perspectives on the treatment of each stakeholder

- describe the source and impact of written and psychological contracts

- critically assess the impact of legal forms on the management of people.

The key arguments that will be developed in this chapter are:

- The concept of 'best practice' changes depending on the stakeholder perspective adopted.
- Multiple bodies of knowledge compete to shape thinking on governance and HRM.
- Board members and HR professionals concurrently comply with and resist the influence of law.
- Social enterprises are diverse in the way they interpret and enact their legal responsibilities.
- Governance and HRM styles are strongly influenced by personal philosophy.

Introduction

In this chapter, attention is focused on management practices that seek to control and develop people. Frequently, the development and control of people at work is studied as 'human resource development' when the focus is on learning (see Harrison, 2005), and 'human resource management' when the focus is on social control and employment law (Storey, 1987). In this chapter, we resist the temptation to approach the subject from the perspective of 'human resources'. We also resist what we believe to be an unnatural separation between the study of 'human resources' and 'governance'. The justification for this is based on a rejection of the idea that 'control' necessarily emanates from the 'top' of the organisation (see Grey, 2005; Jackson and Parry, 2008). Whilst there may be periodic attempts to run organisations in this way (or present this as the model of control to various stakeholders for political advantage), we argue that the development of people, and attempts to control them, can be usefully studied by seeking to understand the way they interact and shape each other's activities (Watson, 1994; Darwin et al., 2002). In social enterprises, this is particularly important because there may be deliberate attempts to subvert traditional management practices through the introduction of participative democracy. This requires a more holistic perspective to contextualise and contrast the rationale for different management practices (see Ellerman, 1990; Johnson, 2006).

Our own research supports Stewart's (1983) view that close study of management, and attempts to proactively manage people, produces a picture quite different from that propagated by the founding texts of scientific management (see Fayol, 1916; Taylor, 1917). In these texts, organisations are dissected and managers learn how to plan, organise, command, coordinate and control their financial, human and physical resources (Clegg et al., 2008). In contrast, ethnographic studies of management reveal something different:

> The picture that emerges ... is of someone who lives in a whirl of activity, in which attention must be switched every few minutes from one subject, problem, and person to another; of an uncertain world where relevant information includes gossip and speculation. It is a picture, too, not of a manager who sits quietly controlling but who is dependent upon many people, other than subordinates, with whom reciprocating relationships should be created; who needs to learn how to trade, bargain, and compromise. (Stewart, 1983: 96, cited in Watson, 1994: 36)

Watson's study of managers' lived experience – of **reciprocal** and interdependent relationships – needs reconciling with the aims of law and regulation. Frequently, the desire to treat people with dignity, as capable of reflecting on and learning from complex and difficult situations, comes into conflict with a much 'harder' world of authority, embedded in company rules and employment laws. This chapter is important for developing a fuller understanding of the way that entrepreneurs, managers and staff can approach the implicit conflict between 'soft' approaches that emphasise understanding, reflection and emotional intelligence, and 'harder' approaches that rely on the enforcement of rules and deference to authority.

Coule (2008) identifies a number of interrelated organisational and environmental systems that trigger the production of operating rules and norms (Figure 9.1). These include:

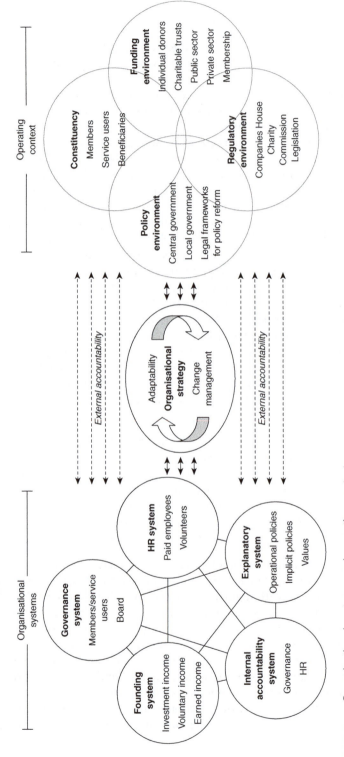

Figure 9.1 Organisational systems and operating contexts

With permission from the author. Coule, T. (2008) *Sustainability in Voluntary Organisations: Exploring the Dynamics of Organisational Strategy.*

- a governance system
- a funding system
- an HR system
- an explanatory system
- an internal accountability system.

This chapter is focused on the development of *organisational systems*, rather than the operating context (see Chapter 8). The process of developing rules – whether implicit in cultural norms or expressed in written form – rests on an assumption that a nominated or elected executive is capable of discovering, defining and then enforcing the general will of a population (Younkins, 2005). This **managerialist** mindset (Dart, 2004; Johnson, 2006) potentially obscures how frequently governing bodies, management groups and individuals establish structures and practices that minimise the power of other organisational stakeholders (Turnbull, 2002; Alvesson and Willmott, 2003). As a result, an alternative perspective on governance is to consider power asymmetries in relationships between different stakeholders, and to work to improve the quality of the interactions between them in order to trigger collaborative work (see Figure 9.2).

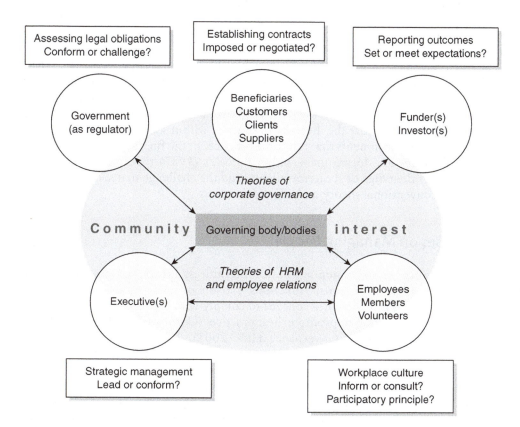

Figure 9.2 Relational view of governance, HRM and employee relations
Adapted from Ridley-Duff, 2008b.

As suggested in Figure 9.2, there are different bodies of theory depending on your perspective of the organisation. Firstly, *governance* theory focuses on relationships between regulators, external stakeholders, funders and governing bodies (and the systems that sustain them). Secondly, there is *human resource management* (HRM) that studies the relationships and interactions between executives and the productive workforce. While *HRM theory* generally adopts a management perspective, there is a third body of theory (**employee relations**) that studies the role of trade unions and employees in negotiating and resisting changes to HRM practice. This third body of theory is much more open to the possibility that organisations can be controlled 'from below', by collective action on the part of the workforce.

All bodies of theory have an interest in the processes by which the 'rules' of organisational life are decided, and the way governments, employers and employees react to their introduction (Salamon, 2000). This three-pronged theoretical approach encourages a more holistic view of organisational life, and provides a framework for rethinking HRM policies within social enterprises. It does not, however, go far enough because it omits the issue of how to involve customers and suppliers in governance. To achieve this, we have to turn to the concept of **network governance** that underpins the approach of successful cooperatives and employee-owned enterprises, as well as innovative private and public sector enterprises (Turnbull, 2002). This holistic view not only makes visible the way strategic stakeholders (employees, customers, suppliers and community institutions) influence each other, but also makes visible the *bodies of knowledge* that compete to influence our understanding of human interaction.

In the following section, we delve further into the discourses of governance, HRM and employee relations and then set out some useful concepts: soft/hard management practices; written and psychological contracts; and **unitary, pluralist** and radical perspectives on the relationship between the employer and workforce. This is followed by case studies that explore the diversity of practice within social enterprises, and the social and legal environments that reinforce practice. In the final section, we critically evaluate the cases and locate them within Purcell's (1987) theory of management styles to clarify the range of choices available, and the challenge that social enterprise presents to conventional theory and practice.

Discourses on Managing People

In both mainstream and voluntary sector literatures, HRM and governance are portrayed as benign management 'functions' capable of selecting and implementing 'best practice'. This is fuelled by a concern to comply with legislation, or government attempts to use legislation to promote 'best practice' (Cornforth and Edwards, 1998; Monks and Minow, 2004; Governance Hub, 2005). The idea of 'best practice', however, *narrows* the choices presented to practising managers, and draws 'theory' mainly from untested prescriptions devised by consultants, regulators, organisation founders, board members and senior managers (Storey, 2001).

In staff-controlled cooperative social enterprises, the norms governing interaction between the workforce and 'management' are fundamentally different to those adopted by public, private and charity sector managers. Governance is also more broadly defined because conventional advice on the separation of governance and management collapses when either there is a 'closed-loop' form of control, as happens when a workforce elects its own management (see Chapter 2), or multiple (compound) boards replace a single (unitary) board (Turnbull, 2001; 2002). Compound boards, because they are dispersed and endorse a separation of powers, are more accepting of stakeholder relationships within and across organisational boundaries. They are also of interest because they invite study of the way (staff) members control *executive power* through elections and **participative democracy** (see Cornforth, 2004).

While the ideological perspectives of **corporate governance theory** and employee relations theory tend to mirror each other, the advent of social enterprise encourages study of the common ground between them where both study the effects of employee directors, employee and community ownership, and forms of 'voice' that allow multiple stakeholders a more direct role in defining strategic goals (Dundon et al., 2004; Vinten, 2001; Brown, 2006). The focus of more-than-profit social enterprises has typically been oriented towards employees (staff) and consumers (service users), rather than funders and founders who dominate non-profits. In non-profits, democratic participation is generally limited to *external* stakeholders as charity law bars employees from voting on governing bodies.[1] Any 'democratic' claims, therefore, are limited to the involvement of external, rather than internal, stakeholders (see Governance Hub, 2005; Low, 2006). The logic of charity law reinforces the view that employees are subordinate to board authority, and adopt the role of 'servant' in the master–servant relationships that underpin employment law (see Chapter 7).

In Doherty et al.'s (2009b) consideration of governance in social enterprise, the legal forms typically deployed (CLGs, CICs, IPSs and CLSs) are marginalised in favour of a discussion about the role and purpose of trustees (none of the above legal forms have 'trustees' *per se* unless fulfilling a dual role in a registered charitable company). Such language (and thinking) is more characteristic of charity and trust law, and shifts the emphasis away from laws framing cooperatives, community interest companies, and other company forms driving the growth of the social enterprise sector. As set out in Chapters 1, 2, 6 and 7, the enfranchisement of internal and external stakeholders through more balanced management practices (Bull, 2006; 2007) and more equitable systems of ownership and control (Brown, 2006; Ridley-Duff, 2007) constitutes an important alternative to traditional private and charity sector practices.

Theories of governance spotlight the processes of selection, development, retention and replacement of board members, as well as the decision-making processes that affect the relationship between regulators, investors (funders), creditors, executives and governing bodies. In law, their activities are regulated through the **Companies Acts** 1985 and 2006, the **Industrial and Provident Society Act** 2002, the **Community Interest Company Regulations** 2005 and the **Charities Act** 2006, depending on the legal form adopted at registration.

HRM theory, on the other hand, has been developed by management researchers to clarify the selection, retention, development, reward and control of productive staff. In an excellent overview, Clegg et al. (2008) point out that the language of HRM betrays its managerialist origins. Firstly, it is applied to productive staff, not board or company members. Secondly, humans are constructed as 'resources' that appear as 'costs' on the profit and loss account, and 'liabilities' on a balance sheet.

This presents the workforce as work objects contributing *labour* to be deployed instrumentally alongside other 'inputs' such as finance, equipment and technology (see Ellerman, 1990).

HRM policies focus on regulating the relationship between the organisation as a legal entity and people engaged in *productive* work, and are subject to employment law. This is only applied when particular relations of power and control are satisfied in law: a multiple test is needed in employment tribunal cases to determine whether a person is an employee or not. These tests seek to establish whether a person is controlling, or is controlled by, the enterprise to which they belong (Gennard and Judge, 2002).

In recent years, HRM theory has adapted to EU employment laws linked to the 'social chapter' of the 1992 Maastricht Treaty. These advance the following principles:

- freedom to travel and work anywhere within the EU (Directive 2004/38/EC)
- equitable remuneration (National Minimum Wage Act)
- maximum working hours each week (Directive 93/104/EC)
- freedom to associate in trade unions (Human Rights Act)
- rights to collective bargaining (Employment Relations Act)
- training and development
- freedom from various forms of discrimination (Single Equality Act)
- minimum health and safety provisions (Health and Safety at Work Act)
- employer–employee consultation and participation forums (ICE Regulations)
- minimum working age of 16
- minimum pension rights.

Social enterprises are frequently established to advance these principles and help to embed them in society. Despite these changes, UK laws do not change the premise and assumptions that spring from Master and Servant Acts dating from 1823. A 'servant' (employee) has a duty to obey the lawful command of their 'master' (employer) and can only reasonably refuse on the grounds that a course of action would be unlawful or dangerous. Common law retains the injunction that an employee must 'obey his or her employer's instructions' and 'be loyal' (Kendall, 2002: 1).

Employment relations law, however, does provide ways for employees (both individually and collectively) to mitigate their employers' power. The Employment Relations Acts 1999, 2000 and 2004 all support co-determination on terms and conditions at work, and require consultations when changes in the social and economic environment affect the future prospects of a workforce. In the past, such 'rights' were only won through industrial action. A proposal to extend consultation rights to wider stakeholders was rejected both in the Company Law Review 2000 (Coad and Cullen, 2001), and again in the community interest company consultations (DTI, 2003). As a result, the Companies Act 2006 limits itself to the concept of 'enlightened shareholder interest'. A board must consider the interests of employees, customers, suppliers and the community, but does not have to be bound by their interests or incorporate their representatives into company governance. Despite this, the fiduciary duty of directors to put the company before the interests of stakeholders has been removed from UK company law and has been replaced by a series of directors' duties (Wainwright, 2009). In future, directors' duties rather than fiduciary duties will be used as the benchmark for standards without involving them directly in service development, strategic management and governance (see Chapter 8).

Shared Governance and HRM Concepts

Usefully, some concepts are shared across all bodies of knowledge. Clegg et al. (2008) summarise the concepts of **'hard'** and **'soft'** HRM (Table 9.1). They trace 'hard' approaches to the Michigan school and contrast these with 'soft' approaches advocated at Harvard. In recent years, soft HRM has become the orthodoxy in Anglo-American and Japanese corporations. Doherty et al. (2009b) argue that soft HRM, with its focus on a suite of 'high-commitment' HRM practices, provides a model for social enterprises. This argument is based on empirical studies showing that soft HRM benefits both employees and employers, and that it is linked to good performance outcomes (Huselid, 1995; Purcell, 1999). Soft HRM – on the surface – appears to be well suited to workplace cultures seeking to actively develop shared missions and social goals.

Table 9.1 Hard (theory X) and soft (theory Y) HRM

	Hard	Soft
Assumptions about people	Staff will work to rule if not managed correctly. Emphasis is on individualising management and maximising control. People are regarded as a 'resource', and should be managed as such. Emphasis is on matching people with particular traits to defined tasks.	Staff are looking for self-fulfilment and meaning, or social relationships at work. Emphasis is on teamwork, collaboration and participation. Managers should focus on creating fulfilling work that supports autonomous decision-making and self-management. People are assets.
Selection	Is focused on finding the best person for the job.	Is focused on finding the best person for the organisation, with regard to knowledge and expertise beyond immediate job tasks.
Retention	Is less important than maintaining productivity and efficiency. Low-level jobs are relatively easy to fill so staff turnover is not regarded as a problem.	Is important so that social networks can develop and encourage affiliation and a sense of commitment to the organisation.
Learning and development	Is tailored to specific jobs, and used to develop task-specific skills that improve efficiency. The best training should be provided to the best people.	Is geared towards personal and organisational development, to harness the full intellectual potential of each individual. If people are not right for the task, redesign the tasks, or find the right job for the individual.

(Continued)

Table 9.1 *(Continued)*

	Hard	Soft
Performance	Is set by managers, measured at an individual level against job-specific outcomes. Poor performance is rationalised as a product of poor management control.	Is set within teams; is assessed against task requirements and also in terms of a person's contribution to team effectiveness. Performance is measured in a holistic way, taking account of non-job-specific skills and contributions (e.g. community work).
Motivation	Grounded in a theory X orientation (McGregor, 1960), based on extrinsic rewards such as money, benefits, and performing well against targets.	Grounded in a theory Y orientation (McGregor, 1960), where intrinsic rewards such as promotion, recognition, autonomy and social opportunities are prioritised.
HR model	Michigan.	Harvard.

Source: adapted from Clegg et al., 2008: 175–6

Legge (2001), however, offers a powerful critique of 'high-commitment' practices and the research assumptions that underpin them. She points out the paucity and inconsistency of the evidence on which claims are based, and the management bias built into measures of performance. Moreover, high-commitment HRM practices are often selectively employed to benefit 'core' staff (i.e. those already favoured within the organisation) rather than the larger ranks of low-paid, temporary, voluntary or contract staff. As such, the practices not only exacerbate social exclusion, they actually tighten rather than loosen managerial control over the thoughts and choices of core staff, increasing the frequency of 'burnout' after periods of work intensification (see Kunda, 1992; Willmott, 1993).

Another suite of concepts located in the study of industrial relations (Fox, 1966; Salamon, 2000) has been imported into studies of social enterprise and voluntary sector governance (Ridley-Duff, 2005; 2007; Coule, 2008; Chadwick-Coule, 2010). Fox (1966) defined three perspectives on employer–employee relationships within the workplace. Firstly, he set out a **unitarist** view that reflects the outlook of those who have acquired (or who defer to) executive power. This is supported by rhetorical strategies that justify increased management control to produce harmony in working towards common goals. Implicit in this view is managers' 'right to manage' and the suppression of challenges to managerial authority.

Secondly, Fox identified a **pluralist** perspective in which organisations comprise competing groups that have different values, interests and objectives. In employee relations and governance, this surfaces in the establishment of negotiating and debating forums through which collective bargaining can take place (i.e. agreements reached between *groups* of people based on their collective, rather than individualised, interests). From a pluralist perspective, conflict is inevitable, requiring employer and employee representatives to devise and utilise conflict resolution processes. In considering the social enterprise sector, pluralist perspectives are typically extended to volunteers, beneficiaries and the community in which the enterprise is located, manifest in governance arrangements that involve these stakeholders.

Lastly, Fox (1966) outlined a radical perspective in which conflict is viewed not simply as inevitable, but as a product and driver of *social transformation*. As Hunt (1981: 90) argues, conflict is 'desirable and constructive in any social system' as it can open up different solutions to a problem, encourage creativity, and surface emotive arguments. Approached in such a way, positive conflict is a means of challenging organisations' norms and empowering people. Fox's radical perspective, therefore, has been linked to arguments for participative democracy at work (Pateman, 1970; Willmott, 1993; Johnson, 2006).

The question is: which of these perspectives (and therefore which associated practices for managing people) are best geared towards the socialisation of business ownership and management and/or the organisation's social purpose? Table 9.2 outlines

Table 9.2   Applying Fox's perspectives to social enterprise practice

Unitarist	Pluralist	Radical
Management prerogative		
Absolute right	*Curbed*	*Challenged*
Board/CEO is sole source of authority and meaning	Shared decision-making on limited issues	No automatic right of managers to manage
Board and senior managers establish values, policies and practices	Some co-determination on 'employee' and 'stakeholder' issues	Authority delegated to managers by workers' assembly or elected governing body
		Values and attitudes are emergent, based on informally accepted social practices
Attitude to conflict		
Not valid	*Accepted*	*Endemic*
Pathological, irrational	Within limits. Rejected if managers' right to manage is challenged	Provides opportunity for creative discussions on how to transform working arrangements. Based on the goal of embedded member ownership principles
Managed through disciplinary and grievance procedures to reassert management prerogative	Managed mostly through disciplinary and grievance procedures using 'natural justice' principles to ensure fairness. Openness to alternative dispute resolution (ADR) in the form of arbitration, conciliation and mediation where it may help	Managed primarily through debate in democratic forums (group) and mediation (one-to-one), with disciplinary and grievance procedures (or arbitration) used only where mediation fails

(Continued)

Table 9.2 *(Continued)*

Unitarist	Pluralist	Radical
Debating forums and collective bargaining		
No or limited role	*Accepted / tolerated*	*Embedded in culture*
If used, managed by board members or executives, or limited only to strategic decision-making at board/ management level	Limited scope within agreed 'boundaries'. Managers seek to limit to 'business' matters, rather than matters of management control	Continuous and active learning in cooperative management bodies and/ or trade union meetings. Joint councils and/or sub-boards are embedded in the organisation culture and constitution
No collective bargaining on terms and conditions of employment, or strategic management	Avoids joint decision-making on business and strategic management decisions	Agreements reached through collective bargaining and mediation processes

the practical impacts of adopting different perspectives on management practice, conflict resolution and democratic debate.

The value of outlining the impact of different perspectives is that it makes visible how they are expressed in written and psychological contracts (Rousseau, 1995; Guest, 1998). The concept of a psychological contract – based on the unstated and unwritten expectations that organisation stakeholders have of each other – has become useful for understanding the volatile and evolving nature of contractual relationships. In Table 9.3, some sources of written and psychological contracts are suggested. Taken together, they offer strategic choices for managing people in social enterprises, and the 'spaces' that can define how internal and external stakeholders are integrated into the organisation.

Table 9.3 The foundations of written and psychological contracts

Written contracts embedded in:	Psychological contracts embedded in:
Governance perspective	
• Articles of association (members) • Governing document (trustees) • Shareholder agreements (investors) • Board minutes (directors/trustees) • Trading contracts (suppliers of goods) • Service-level agreements • Company law (company regulator) • Charity law (charity regulator) • IPS law (industrial society regulator)	• Previous personal and working relationships • Family/friendship commitments • Experiences during recruitment to the board/executive • Social interaction in tender processes • Social interaction in contract negotiations • Social interaction in board meetings • Knowledge of interpersonal goals and aspirations

(Continued)

Table 9.3 *(Continued)*

Written contracts embedded in:	Psychological contracts embedded in:
Human resource management perspective	
• Offer letters (to new staff) • Contracts of employment (and related company policies) • Disciplinary and grievance procedures • Contract for services (self-employed staff) • Employment law • Appraisal recommendations and outcomes (non-binding)	• Experience of recruitment, selection, induction, development and promotion • Impact of HRM policy and practice on work friends and family members • Attitudes observed in appraisal and disciplinary meetings • Willingness to mediate/negotiate resolution to disputes • Interpretation of organisational goals and policies
Employee relations perspective	
• Union recognition agreements • Collective bargaining agreements • Employment relations law • ACAS codes of conduct (non-binding) • Employment tribunal procedures • Articles of association (employee owned companies only)	• The scope and quality of participation in managerial decision-making • Evaluation of the integrity of staff consultation exercises • Interpretation of collective bargaining processes • Experience of employment tribunal proceedings

As Cornforth (2004) outlines, different theories of governance each emphasise a different aspect of contractual relations (biased toward one or other philosophical perspective). Taken together, however, they serve to emphasise the multifaceted nature and paradoxical experience of governing an enterprise. When we consider the multitude of written and psychological contracts (Table 9.3) and how these can be framed and interpreted from unitary, pluralist and radical perspectives, the ambiguity of managing people becomes more understandable (and bearable).

In the next section, therefore, we explore the application of these concepts. Two cases are drawn from a study of sustainability in the voluntary sector (Coule, 2008), and two cases are drawn from private businesses adopting a social enterprise outlook (Ridley-Duff, 2005). The cases are summarised in Table 9.4.

Table 9.4   Case studies: Cases 9.1 – 9.4

Custom Products (Case 9.1)
Founded in 1990 by a school teacher and one of his pupils, the company provides goods and services to schools. In 2004, the founders and 130 employees voted (separately) to convert to a trading company (CLS) owned by an employee trust. 100% of income comes from trade.

(Continued)

Table 9.4 *(Continued)*

Trading Trust (Case 9.2)

Founded in 1930, and registered as a charity in 1960. The organisation has a strong faith-based ethos and over a third of the organisation's income is earned through sales: vocational courses that satisfy charitable objectives. In 2007, there were 80–100 volunteers and 40–45 staff.

Rights Now! (Case 9.3)

Founded in 1998 as a charitable company (CLG), the organisation fights for the rights of people with learning disabilities, including those who have a sensory impairment, and generates a third of its income through sales. The organisation has 20 staff and 10 volunteers.

SoftContact (Case 9.4)

Founded in 1979 by six friends, the company grew to 15 staff in the 1980s providing training, advice and support services to third sector organisations, then shrank after the GLC was closed. The company, an industrial and provident society (IPS), helped found Social Enterprise London.

The case studies and additional teaching materials are all available on the website at www.sagepub.co.uk/ridleyduff.

 CLASS EXERCISE   Locating people management cultures

Materials to support this exercise can be found at www.sagepub.co.uk/ridleyduff.

- Divide the class into groups of four and distribute Cases 9.1, 9.2, 9.3 and 9.4 to group members (Table 9.4).
- Give the students 10 minutes to read and make notes about their case.
- Each student can take 5 minutes to explain key aspects of their case to the other members of their group.
- Locate each case on a handout of the ideological map shown in Figure 9.3.

1 What management style would you advocate for social enterprise?
2 Is it possible to have a culture that both is radical and uses 'soft HRM' practices?

Recruitment, Selection and Induction

Differences are apparent in the way each organisation recruits board members. At Custom Products, all directors had connections through family or friends. The conversion to an employee-owned company has changed this. Any permanent employee (with over two years' service) is now eligible for election to the board, subject to conditions set out by executive managers. This contrasts with Trading Trust where a separation of governors from staff was preserved to satisfy charity law. Recruitment at Trading Trust was based on professional expertise and commitment to a faith-based ethos. Rights Now! took a different approach, combining trustees with a disability and others possessing specialist management skills. Of the four organisations, however, only SoftContact has an identical recruitment process for both staff and directors. This was a product of its legal form (a cooperative registered as an IPS) whereby all members passing their probationary period became full members (and directors).

In the other three organisations, only Custom Products was evolving in a similar direction (a by-product of its conversion to a CLS owned by an employee trust). Nevertheless, the executive group imposed its own criteria to limit candidates who could stand for board membership, and required them to go through 'culture management' training as a *precondition* of eligibility. This potentially enables executives to control which employees can be elected governors. At Rights Now! and Trading Trust, the separation of trustees and staff under charity law meant there was no progression path to the board unless staff gave up their employment.

Rotation practices for board members differed. At Custom Products, elected members of a governing council would serve four years (two will change every two years). A similar situation existed at Rights Now! with policies ensuring a turnover of board members. While Trading Trust and SoftContact did not rotate directors, the rationale was different. At Trading Trust, there were no formal mechanisms for the re-election of trustees and some had served over 10 years. At SoftContact, rotation was not needed because all members acquired voting rights at general meetings after completing their probation period (no separate board meetings took place).[2]

In employment, Custom Products had a two-stage interview process that assessed behavioural characteristics (values and philosophy) before invitation to an interview to assess job skills. Applicants were required to fill in an application form (CVs were not accepted). This was similar to SoftContact where formal applications were processed in accordance with a carefully designed equal opportunity process, including interviews that assessed both job skills and suitability for co-operative management. These formal approaches were less in evidence at Trading Trust where paid staff were selected, at least in part, on the basis of their faith. From a staff perspective, however, this was regarded as a key benefit of working there. Rights Now! also had relatively informal processes that sought to employ and develop people with learning disabilities. Recruitment aimed to pair able-bodied and disabled persons, with the disabled person leading (in accordance with charity objects).

Dispute Resolution

Rights Now! and SoftContact were both characterised by vibrant debate, with social norms that facilitated dialogue between staff. Despite the 'official' separation of trustees and employees at Rights Now!, a CEO who withheld information triggered a transformation in the culture when their actions threatened organisational survival. In the wake of this, trustees and staff started taking lunch together. As one staff member reports:

I think that relationship makes the board less detached from the workers on the ground, because they're not sat up in this hierarchy. I don't feel like it's all going on and I'm not contributing ... and decisions are just being made. I feel that if it came to it, I could walk in there [the board meeting] and say 'this isn't ok', not that I've ever needed to, but I wouldn't feel frightened to do that or intimidated. (see Case 9.3)

Similar sentiments existed at SoftContact, and members reported strong exchanges in general meetings. However, in this case, all members had a constitutionally defined role in shared decision-making, leading to different reflections:

> The practicalities of exercising [democratic] 'choice' … led to heated arguments that made SoftContact – in the words of one founder – 'a hell of place to work'. Solutions to conflict, however, were inventive. Disputes over product choice were resolved by allocating each member free time to devote to his [sic] own projects … Counter-intuitive management practices arose (voluntary self-suspension, voluntary termination of contract) that challenge strongly held beliefs that 'management' is necessary to enforce discipline. In one case, a member left voluntarily after severe criticism by a client. Far from needing to discipline him, workers 'felt guilty about not "supporting" their colleague'. (see Case 9.4)

The absence of formal 'management' did not result in indiscipline: it tended to produce extraordinary levels of self-discipline (see also Jackson and Parry, 2008). During downturns in trade, members would defer making expense claims, defer taking wages, take unpaid leave, take out loans to support either their families or the organisation, take temporary jobs in order to work fewer hours – anything that ensured organisational survival and prevented the need for redundancies. As trade improved, staff would return and claim the monies owed to them.

In contrast, at Trading Trust there was a deep-seated and underlying expectation that management, and their instructions, must always be respected. Because management-led change was constructed as a technical necessity – for the 'common good' – any conflict, disobedience or resistance to change programmes was portrayed as irrational behaviour, ignorance or stupidity, and an illegitimate challenge to managerial authority. Trading Trust's chair comments:

> I think the main challenge I've had is … bad relationships with staff. Occasionally you get someone who's not quite fitting and it causes unhappiness. I think that's been the main challenge because the difficulty is … it's hard to sack people so you might think someone's the source of a problem but you can't just say, right, you're out mate. You've got a procedure to go through. (see Case 9.1)

Those who did not comply left the organisation, or were ostracised until they did. Similar processes of ostracism were noted in findings at Custom Products, although this was managed through a 'softer' approach to dispute resolution with HR staff following **CIPD** recommended practices. After 2003, HR staff at Custom Products decided not to enact formal disciplinary proceedings against staff. Instead they provided support for unhappy staff to leave the company. Staff reports of Custom Product's HRM practices, however, do not suggest that managers always sought solutions based on compromise.

Discussion of Case Studies

The above cases can be usefully located within Purcell's (1987) theory of management styles in order to clarify the range of choices made by social enterprise practitioners and to critically evaluate their approach (see Figure 9.3). It could be argued that the

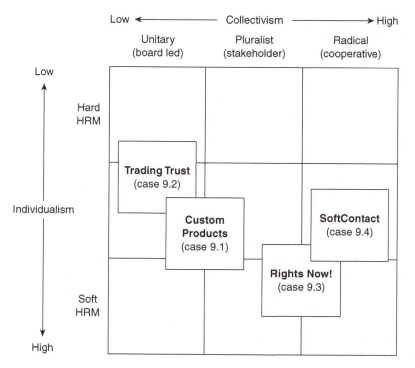

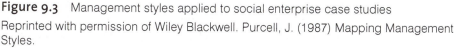

Figure 9.3 Management styles applied to social enterprise case studies

Reprinted with permission of Wiley Blackwell. Purcell, J. (1987) Mapping Management Styles.

legal form of organisation that members choose, and the organisational structures subsequently adopted, steer it towards a particular approach. However, the cases presented suggest a level of **pragmatism** and ambiguity.

We argued earlier that the logic of charity law reinforces the view that employees are subordinate to board authority, taking on the role of 'servant' in the master–servant relationship. Codes of good practice recommend a clear separation of governance and management functions (Governance Hub, 2005) so it follows that a charitable social enterprise would be encouraged (through law and codes of practice) to adopt a unitary approach to governance and management. Case evidence suggests that this only has a limited impact. Trading Trust and SoftContact show a high degree of consistency between legal form and ideology, while Rights Now! and Custom Products have an ambiguous relationship to the discourse encouraged by their legal form.

Trading Trust is characterised by a unitary structure and ideology. Staff assume everyone in the organisation will benefit from decisions made at a senior level and tend to ignore or hide conflicts of interest. Its charity model and history are entrenched in operations and mechanisms for legitimising the authority of a select group of leaders (the trustees and chief officer) over a group of subordinate followers (staff and volunteers). While Custom Products has adopted a legal form that will more easily allow for democratic governance and management practices, it is taking time to change its culture. Proposals for a social council, and direct democracy in all executive appointments and business planning, were rejected before they could be put to staff.

At Trading Trust, this orientation produces a 'hard' approach to HRM: practices focus on maximising control; jobs are considered to be relatively easy to fill and high turnover is not regarded as a problem; learning and development tend to focus on vocational courses of direct relevance or benefit to the organisation; and supervision is primarily a mechanism for holding staff to account for implementing board and management plans. Though Custom Products takes a softer approach, close scrutiny of the recruitment, induction and socialisation processes revealed deliberate use of psychological techniques to reinforce desired behaviours and beliefs. This screens out those who will not subscribe (or conform) to the company's stated social values. The appearance on the outside is 'soft', but internalised values have a distinctly 'hard' edge.

Moreover, within Trading Trust, board members were strongly motivated to meet legal obligations through the development of formal operational policies. The unitary approach to governance and management is thus manifest in a heavy bias towards written contracts, with the foundations of psychological contracts receiving little explicit attention. Again, although framed within a 'softer' approach to HRM and a stronger focus on psychological contracts, Custom Products created policies, procedures and practices that actively reinforced particular values through the exclusion of those who would not conform.

Our research suggests that acceptance and legitimisation of certain approaches are associated with the coherence between governance and management practices and the social values expressed in the organisation's ideology. It is, therefore, incoherent for an organisation espousing egalitarian social values to employ a **totalitarian style** of governance and management. Nevertheless, it appears in the case of Trading Trust that such an approach is adopted. Unfortunately, for employees in Trading Trust and Custom Products who can envisage an alternative to the status quo, the result is subversive conflict and treatment of employees at odds with rhetorical claims about social values. In relation to conflict and dispute resolution, both organisations lean towards a unitary (authority-driven) approach, which ultimately promotes **hegemony**, though the means by which this is achieved varies (see Figure 9.4).

In contrast to Trading Trust, the organisational members of Rights Now! have made a deliberate decision to challenge the dominant norms suggested by the charity form. Whilst there was no indication that board members or managers in Rights Now! would knowingly flout legal requirements, they created practices that transcended the boundaries of a traditional charity model and share similarities with SoftContact. Unlike SoftContact, whose legal form is arguably more amenable to radical ideology and practice, Rights Now!, as a charitable company, is – by necessity – characterised by a unitary structure. Nevertheless, it has created and sustained a radical ethos as a pragmatic response to a former chief officer withholding vital information.

Organisational members in Rights Now! and SoftContact see organisations as being constituted by diverse groups 'whose pursuit of disparate sectional interests inevitably produces manifestations of conflict' (Darwin et al., 2002: 97). Even though SoftContact had no CEO, it evolved a highly formalised recruitment and induction process, giving its culture a slightly harder edge than Rights Now!. Within this, there was constitutional support for conflict between various organisational stakeholders, including employees, rendering conflict itself as 'normal', and producing regular creative transformations in practice.[3] Power is thus a central

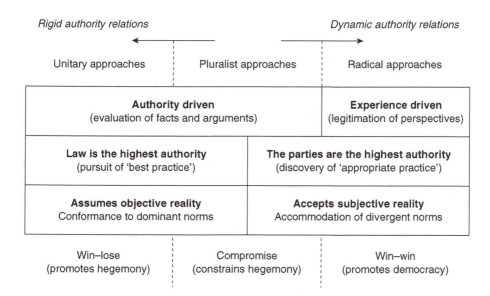

Figure 9.4 Theorising dispute resolution in social enterprises

With permission from the author. Ridley-Duff, R.J. and Bennett, A. (2009) *Mediation-Developing a Theoretical Framework for Understanding Alternative Dispute Resolution.*

concept within these organisations, as it is used to explain relationships between people (Foucault, 1977).

The complex decisions made by trustees and managers occur within a moral framework where 'managers have to judge their actions not only in terms of their efficiency but also by whether or not they are morally correct' (Garvey and Williamson, 2002: 7). The moral and social values of Rights Now! and SoftContact are thus embedded in practices throughout the organisations, and they are explicit about how there is an environment conducive to sharing ideas and helping each other to solve problems. A critical factor appears to be recognition that the workplace, and involvement in decision-making, is potentially a rich learning opportunity. Clawson (1996: 8) describes this as a shift away from a 'bureaucratic way' where 'the boss knows best' to a 'process way' where 'the process owner knows best'.

Such an approach is characteristic of soft HRM that *also* promotes the possibility of alternative modes of practice located in **democratic discourse**. Here, the importance of the psychological contract surpasses that of written contracts and procedures. This undermines and displaces **technocratic**, top-down management through asking ethical questions about collective priorities (Forrester, 1989). Its purpose is to 'open up radically new understandings of organisational life that have a potential to promote new modes of work that give voice to, and promote, critical reflection and autonomy' (Alvesson and Willmott, 1996: 114).

Conclusions

In this chapter, it is worth noting that the relationships between stakeholders, and their interdependencies, present strategic choices to board members and managers

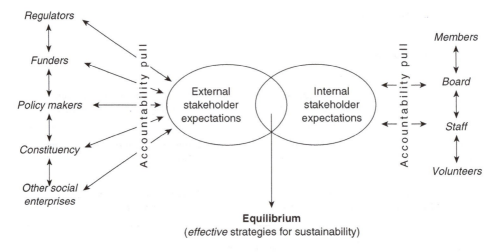

Figure 9.5 Developing effective strategies for sustainability
With permission from the author. Coule T. (2008) *Sustainability in Voluntary Organisations: Exploring the Dynamics of Organisational Strategy.*

of social enterprises. In making choices, they also respond to external and internal accountability 'pulls' (see Figure 9.5).

We have highlighted that accountability relationships are multiple, diverse, conflicting and fluid. They are also central to organisational sustainability, as many stakeholders have the potential to affect survival. This challenges the idea that 'control' emanates from the top of an organisation. The core theoretical issue is that when different stakeholders' expectations are aligned, there are fewer difficulties. However, when they are not, organisational members must decide whose expectations should be prioritised (or live with their differences). Despite the acknowledgement by many that board and staff members within social enterprises are stakeholders in terms of accountability, there is little research that explicitly considers the way in which accountability pressures can influence the interpretation of governance and staff roles, and the implication this has for board–staff interactions. Our research suggests that a central issue here is the way in which organisational members apply (often implicit and taken-for-granted) social values and theories about the nature of people and organisations to the governance and management of social enterprises.

To study, govern and manage social enterprise involves thinking about economics, philosophy, politics and ethics. Accepting the argument presented above – that effective strategies for sustainability involve devising a system of relations that can manage competing stakeholder expectations – consideration must be given to who says what the job is and how it should be done, and how people are affected by doing it one way rather than another (see Grey, 2005). Two cases presented a challenge to the commonly held view that management structures in not-for-profit organisations are, by virtue of a strong sense of altruism, more democratic than their private and public sector counterparts (see Markham et al., 2001; Alatrista and Arrowsmith, 2004). Ultimately, the strategic management style is more likely to be a result of the social values held by those involved in governance and management than of the sector in which it resides, or the legal form it takes. It cannot be taken for granted that a social enterprise will attract people who are committed to participatory governance and management styles. It may (to fulfil its mission) employ people who are in need of a job and who (at least at the time of joining) do not subscribe to the political goals of the founders or governing body (Amin, 2009b). We exit these debates by raising an important question: to whom are 'governors' and 'managers' accountable?

SUMMARY OF LEARNING

In this chapter, we have developed the arguments that:

- The rationale for managing people need not be grounded in theories of human resource management (HRM).
- Three 'discourses' on managing people derive from bodies of knowledge that theorise owner, manager and employee perspectives on social organisation.
- Theories of *corporate governance*, *HRM* and *employee relations* compete to provide explanations of how the 'rules' of organisational life are (and should be) established.
- Contrasting perspectives on human beings are expressed in theories of 'hard' and 'soft' human resource management.
- Written and psychological contracts contain unitary, pluralist and radical perspectives on managing people, and each is socially constructed.
- Management practices regarding recruitment, induction and dispute resolution can be analysed using an adaptation of Purcell's theory of management styles.
- Those practices derive from personal and organisational learning, and tend to override the dictates of legal form.
- The 'accountability pulls' can influence the interpretation of the roles of staff and governors.

QUESTIONS AND POSSIBLE ESSAY ASSIGNMENTS

1 Do radical approaches to governance and management strengthen psychological contracts at the expense of written contracts? Using examples, critically assess the potential impact of a radical approach to the management of people.
2 Can a 'systems' view of governance ever fully meet the needs of a social enterprise? Using examples, outline the benefits and limitations of a 'systems' view of governance.
3 'A unitary culture is a product of internal dynamics more than the external regulatory environment.' Using examples, discuss the extent to which you agree with this statement.

FURTHER READING

A vital read for students is the NEF pocket book *A New Way to Govern* (Turnbull, 2002) which describes the concept of network governance, and how *strategic stakeholders* (employees, customers, suppliers, community representatives) can be incorporated into company management. We also recommend Chapter 4 of *Managing and Organizations* (Clegg et al., 2008). This readable text covers both HRM and employee relations, asking key questions about the nature and purpose of HRM.

For more detailed coverage of governance issues, a popular textbook is *Corporate Governance* by Monks and Minow (2004). This has a useful and surprisingly detailed section on governance practices in the Mondragón cooperatives. For social-enterprise-specific discussions, see Low (2006) for an overview of the tensions arising out of non-profit and for-profit orientations, and Cornforth (2004) and Ridley-Duff (2007) for recent development in cooperative governance and the implications of the CIC. Doherty et al. (2009b) provide useful guidance on social enterprises relying on trustee governance in the voluntary/charity sector, while Ridley-Duff's (2010) ethnographic study of two social economy organisations provides 'insider' insights.

For critical coverage of HRM, David Storey's edited volume *Human Resource Management: A Critical Text* (2001) provides insightful coverage of the tension between managerial and non-managerial interests. Social-enterprise-specific discussions are rare, but useful insights have been contributed by Royce (2007) in relation to volunteering, and on soft HRM practices by Doherty et al. (2009b). For an overview of cooperative self-management, it is still hard to improve on Rothschild and Allen-Whitt (1986).

Further reading material is available on the companion website at www.sagepub.co.uk/ridleyduff.

USEFUL RESOURCES

ACAS, http://www.acas.org.uk/index.aspx?articleid =1461

Charity Governance, http://www.charity-commission.gov.uk/enhancingcharities/default.asp
Charity Trustee Network, http://www.trusteenet. org.uk/
CIPD, http://www.cipd.co.uk/default.cipd
Cooperantics, http://www.cooperantics.co.uk/
DIY Committee, http://www.diycommittee-guide. org/
Department for Business, Innovation and Skills, http://www.berr.gov.uk/whatwedo/employment/
Governance Hub, http://www.ncvo-vol. org.uk/governanceandleadership/?id=9164
Governance Diagnostic Questionnaire, http://www.scribd.com/doc/14295317/
Open Space Technology, http://www.openspaceworld.org
Workforce Hub, http://www.ukworkforce-hub.org.uk/

NOTES

1 In the UK, charity law permits employee representatives at board meetings only with the consent of the Charity Commission, and this itself is contingent on the charity's articles permitting staff attendance at board meetings.
2 While it might be thought that this practice would be limited to small cooperatives, it can be scaled. At Suma Wholefoods, where there are 80 members, all are invited to monthly general meetings, and votes are taken on resolutions prepared in advance. At Mondragón, where membership runs to hundreds in each business unit, general meetings of all members are held quarterly and elected governors meet monthly or fortnightly with appointed managers.
3 Members of SoftContact talked of rejecting 'sacred cows' (i.e. culturally embedded ways of thinking) following decisions at their annual review. This was viewed as a product of their democratic decision-making and cooperative management practice.

Leadership and Social Entrepreneurship

10

Rory Ridley-Duff and Pam Seanor

Learning Objectives

In this chapter, we consider leaders and the concept of leadership, and social entrepreneurs and the concept of social entrepreneurship. By the end of this chapter you will be able to:

- describe and evaluate different theories of leadership

- distinguish between leaders and leadership

- apply leadership theory to social entrepreneurs and social entrepreneurship

- compare and contrast individual and collective approaches to social entrepreneurship

- critically discuss the drivers and barriers to the practice of social entrepreneurship.

The key arguments that will be developed in this chapter are:

- Leader-centric and follower-centric theories of leadership emphasise individual and collective processes that produce recognised 'leaders'.
- Leadership can be centralised, co-produced or distributed amongst a group of people.
- Social entrepreneurship theory focuses on attributes and skills that facilitate opportunity recognition, (social) innovation, and the creation of social and economic value.
- Divergent theories of social entrepreneurship are related to divergent theories of leadership.
- Social entrepreneurship can be understood as both an individual and a collective process.

Introduction

In the previous three chapters on legal forms, strategic management and the management of people, we have emphasised how the different values and assumptions that people bring to the process of social enterprise formation, planning and governance lead to many diverse practices. These assumptions also impact on leadership style and the choice of leader. They may even lead to questioning whether leaders (in the formal appointed sense) are needed at all. It is, therefore, helpful to understand theories of leadership to make informed choices about an organisation's context and approach to leadership.

Moreover, the assumptions we make about leadership will, in turn, influence the level of support we give to different approaches to social entrepreneurship. Social entrepreneurs are seen as people committed to radically changing their society, and who benefit their communities. As Bill Drayton, the founder of Ashoka, comments:

> Social entrepreneurs are not content just to give a fish, or teach how to fish. They will not rest until they have revolutionized the fishing industry. (http://philippines.ashoka.org/node/3829, accessed 21 May 2010)

What approaches to leadership and entrepreneurship make socially enterprising activities sustainable? Might the style of leadership vary in different ventures?

So, this chapter explores and discusses both leaders and leadership. As Hosking and Morley (1991) ask: Who are they? What do they do? With whom do they do it? The chapter starts by looking at these questions through the lens of leadership theory, and then moves on to consider the effect that this has on both the theory and the practice of social entrepreneurship.

Why Leadership Matters

Hosking and Morley (1991: 240) describe leadership as 'a more or less skilful process of organizing, achieved through negotiation, to achieve acceptable influence over the description and handling of issues within and between groups'. The systematic study of leadership offers the prospect of being able to develop an understanding of two things. Firstly, it helps to understand the character attributes and skills that leaders acquire, and which both they and others believe are necessary to improve the quality of leadership in an organisation. This is helpful not only to those responsible for leadership, but also to those who have to recruit leaders (and entrepreneurs) or who want to know how to work effectively with them. Secondly, it helps to understand the contexts in which different approaches to leadership are effective. Social enterprises are varied: small, large, rural, urban, in highly regulated and unregulated industries, growing rapidly, or not at all. Add to these variables the many histories that have shaped their development (Spear et al., 2007) and the need for a theoretical understanding becomes more urgent.

In the case of social enterprise, how can users of a service lead its development? How can managers, staff and volunteers combine their efforts in projects to tackle entrenched problems in their communities? One common assumption is that stakeholders in a social enterprise share a common goal or vision that enables them to work together effectively (Pearce, 2003). Making this assumption leads to an emphasis on '**unitary**' control, with leadership controlled by a board and/or social entrepreneur. What if the assumption about shared values is mistaken (see Willmott, 1993)? Or that shared values are 'manufactured' to promote passivity and compliance amongst the organisation's shareholders, membership and workforce (Alvesson and Deetz, 2000)? How is this type of leadership theorised, and what entrepreneurial approaches might prevent it occurring?

A key challenge for those working in and with social enterprises is how to help others to be aware of the diverse range of abilities and cultural assumptions that influence the leadership process. All those working in organisations (not just leaders themselves) can benefit from understanding how leadership processes affect their organisation. For this reason, this chapter is aimed not just at 'leaders', but also at 'followers', and considers not only the question of how people lead, but also how leaders are guided and controlled by their followers.

Lastly, those who acquire leadership roles are charged with developing, controlling and excluding people, with nurturing an environment where conversations can take place as well as curtailing conversations that put organisational survival at risk. They are variously expected to be inspiring, to prioritise, to decide on and give meaning to situations, and to direct the organisation towards its (social) objectives (see Smircich and Morgan, 1982).

Theories of Leadership

The dominant approach to studying and writing about leadership is to focus on the leader. Prior to the 1940s, most leadership studies explored the *qualities* of the leader and their leadership style, and assessed their effectiveness by researching the views of their followers. A good example of this is the study by Lewin et al. (1939) who created environments and trained leaders to apply '**authoritarian**', '**democratic**' and '**laissez-faire**' principles, then studied the behaviours and feelings of those they led. Authoritarian leaders gave instructions and did not permit any challenge to their authority. Democratic leaders adopted a participative style of management, while laissez-faire leaders encouraged group members to make decisions for themselves. The experiments were repeated many times (see White and Lippett, 1960) and findings from them suggested that:

1 Laissez-faire climates are not the same as democracy:

- less work is done and it is of poorer quality
- there is more play in 'laissez-faire' groups
- 95 per cent of group members prefer a 'democratic leader' to a 'laissez-faire' leader.

2 Democracy can be efficient:

- although the quantity of work can be greater under an autocracy ...
- ... work motivation is stronger, particularly when the leader is not present
- originality is greater in democracy.

3 Autocracy leads to:

- hostility, aggression and submissive behaviour
- rebellion or people dropping out of the group
- more discontent than in democracy
- loss of individuality.

Some substantive criticism can be made of these studies. Firstly, 'democratic' leaders were not elected (and could not be sacked by group members), so issues of legitimacy and trust created by a democratic process are not reproduced in the design of the research. Secondly, questions can be raised over the training of the leaders charged with 'laissez-faire' leadership. Their approach to encouraging collective decision-making and individual participation (Pateman, 1970) was not informed by the knowledge underpinning high-performing companies today (see Whyte and Whyte, 1991; Owen, 2008).[1] Lastly, no comparison was made with self-managing groups. As a result, the studies do not compare the performance of groups with *emergent leadership* to those who have *appointed leaders*. They only compare leadership styles within a paradigm that accepts the dominance of leader-centric theories.[2] Nevertheless, the findings are consistent with the research of Coch and French (1948) who found that change projects were more successful if command and control approaches were replaced by participative approaches.

More recently, writers studying leadership in the private and third sectors (Hubbard, 2005; Jackson and Parry, 2008) have been more sensitive to the distinction between *leaders* (as people) and *leadership* (as a process). Part of this shift is a backlash against leader-centric approaches, fuelled by an improved understanding of corporate scandals in the 1980s and 1990s. As Guthey and Jackson (2005) argue, there is now greater receptivity towards alternative theories of leadership (as a process) that may be 'co-produced' (shared by two people), 'distributed' (shared by more than two people) or 'collective' (driven by a 'grassroots' action). Table 10.1 summarises the broadening of leadership studies and the implications of alternative perspectives.

Table 10.1 Theories of leadership

Theory type	Key assumption	Research approaches and implications	Grounded in
Leader-centred theories	Leadership is a product of personal qualities and character traits	We can understand leadership by focusing on who the leader is (leader identity) and what they do (leader behaviour). If we understand their character traits and behaviours, we can screen for people with particular personalities and provide training to mould their behaviour	Liberal philosophy, rationalism
Higher-purpose theories of leadership	Leadership is the product of pursuing a higher purpose, such	We can better understand leadership if we investigate the moral frameworks that underpin leaders' actions, and how this influences the actions of followers. If we can do this, we can discover the	Virtue ethics, servant leadership

(Continued)

Table 10.1   *(Continued)*

Theory type	Key assumption	Research approaches and implications	Grounded in
	as support for the intellectual and moral transformation of followers	transformative power of leadership, and increase our capacity for ethically informed leadership behaviour	
Follower-centred theories	Leadership is a product of followers socialising their leaders, and constructing stories about their leadership	We can understand leadership by focusing on the way followers value particular qualities, create stories, and exercise political control over leaders in their community. If we can understand this, we can evaluate the qualities that will enhance a person's leadership potential within a particular community	Communitarian philosophy, interpretivism
Cultural perspectives on leadership	Leadership is a product of culturally defined activities, norms and rituals that reproduce the legitimacy of leaders and the leadership function	We can understand leadership by focusing on the ways leaders socialise (and are socialised) through rituals and stories in order to legitimise the institution of leadership. If we can understand this, we can evaluate the process by which people become leaders, and the ways in which they reproduce the institution of leadership	Institutional theory
Critical perspectives on leadership	Shared forms of leadership that are co-authored, distributed and collective in character have been mystified and obscured by leader-centric theory	We can better understanding leadership by deconstructing dominant leadership discourses and re-evaluating how they reflect political interests and power. In doing so, we can re-evaluate 'lost' or 'hidden' discourses, and consider the evidence for co-leadership, distributed leadership and leadership through collective action	Critical theory

Source: an interpretation of Jackson and Parry, 2008

In this consideration of (social) entrepreneurship, it is worth pausing to evaluate the implications of different perspectives on leadership. The contrast between leader- and follower-centric views of leadership rests on the relative importance attached to the internal qualities of the leader (and their leadership behaviours) and the group processes that shape (and limit the effects of) their leadership. Leader-centric approaches have tended to emphasise the characteristics, traits and competencies of the entrepreneur (see London and Morfopoulos, 2010). Within this tradition, there is a drift towards organisation charts and hierarchies of power as a way of understanding how entrepreneurs practise leadership: the top of the organisational chart shows the CEO, then senior managers, then middle managers, and then the staff they supervise (Hosking and Morley, 1991). From this perspective, organisations are designed to support an *authority-driven model* of leadership, whereby leaders instruct 'subordinates' on the achievement of organisational goals. This model propagates control *downward* through the organisation based on an assumption that 'superiors' are equipped to lead their 'subordinates'.

During the 1940s, leader-centric theories underwent a period of intense research. Prior to 1948, it was assumed that character *traits* differentiated leaders from followers (see Stogdill, 1974). Despite popular assumptions about the qualities of 'great' people, systematic study revealed no consistent correlation between character traits and success as a leader. Jackson and Parry (2008) regard these research programmes as historically important for *discrediting* trait theories of leadership. However, the surge of interest in (social) entrepreneurship has reignited interest in trait theories, often under the guise of *competencies*. For example, in one of the most recent additions to the social entrepreneurship literature, London and Morfopoulos instruct us to:

> Be grateful for social entrepreneurs. They are driven by an overarching desire to improve society ... They are movers and shakers – people who are not satisfied with the status quo and are always trying to make things better. They care, and they are action-oriented. (2010: 2)

This characterisation of the social entrepreneur as a visionary leader is propagated by umbrella organisations in the United Kingdom, including the Social Enterprise Coalition (SEC), the Community Action Network (CAN) and academic institutions. For example, heroic social entrepreneurs are described by Jeff Skoll, who funded the Skoll Centre for Social Entrepreneurship at Oxford University, as people who:

> have a vision of the future and will stop at nothing to see that future come true. It is up to us to help them succeed in order to ensure that the failures of the past do not become the failures of the future, and to build a world where all people, regardless of geography, background, or economic status, enjoy and employ the full range of their talents and abilities. (Nicholls, 2006a: vi)

The policy implications of these beliefs are that agencies should assist dynamic individuals who are catalysts for social change (compare Martin and Osberg, 2007) and pay less attention to established sociological knowledge about community organising, group processes and organisation development. There is also an implication that institutional forms do not matter (see Black and Nicholls, 2004) because social entrepreneurs will check out 'the market' in legal forms and choose the one that suits their needs.

Chell (2007) points out that the popular image of 'economic entrepreneurs' differs from that of 'social entrepreneurs' only in respect of the mission or goal they pursue. The above description acts to reinforce the stereotype that entrepreneurs (of whatever type) are energetic and 'driven' people. Such an image is problematic not only because empirical research does not support such a simplistic statement, but also because *it may be an effect of followership rather than a reflection on the leader.* Moreover, Paton (1989) reports that half of all entrepreneurial activity is a response to personal or community hardship, and that people become entrepreneurial because it is their only survival option at that time (Case 10.1). This gives a new meaning to the notion of a 'driven' entrepreneur: they are driven by circumstances as well as innate character traits (see Lewis and Klein, 2004).

Case 10.1   Social entrepreneurship: a regeneration agency view

I mean if you think about the people that have started business up, if you think about the Denzils of this world, if you think about the Pats of this world, if you expand that out to, you know ... Dave ... they are all charismatic, dogged. I mean you talked about a dog-eared business plan, they are dogged people. But it does take that individual to drive it, and I can't think of [pause] ... a successful social enterprise that I've come across that hasn't been driven by somebody who hasn't got a little bit more, there's a spark, there's something about them, there's a doggedness, there's a determination to succeed, there's a determination not to let the bureaucrats of this world stand in their way. (Regeneration agency manager)

Despite this, the resurgence of interest in trait theories of leadership has continued to grow. It takes an interesting turn in *Good to Great* (Collins, 2001; 2006). Despite personal scepticism, Collins explains at some length how his research team insisted that there were personal qualities that contributed to long-term sustainability in the enterprises they studied. The research team eventually differentiated between 'level 4 leadership' based on a 'visionary' approach, extrovert personality and *individual* leadership, and 'level 5 leadership' that was rooted in 'humility' combined with a 'professional will' dedicated to *participative* leadership. It is worth, at this point, highlighting the difference between 'leader-centric' and 'higher-purpose' leadership, and the way this rests on an assumption that ethical values can be promoted through entrepreneurial action (see also Chapter 4).

Collins argues that 'level 4 leaders' make a difference while they are in post, but also that performance deteriorates rapidly after their departure. Level 5 leaders, on the other hand, focus on the 'higher purpose' of developing leadership capabilities throughout their organisation (or social network) and performance does not decline after their departure. Similar findings are reported in the non-profit sector (Hubbard, 2005; Crutchfield and McLeod-Grant, 2007). Hubbard found that qualities of calmness and emotional security amongst non-profit leaders are more strongly correlated with sustainability than extroversion and charisma.

The concept of level 5 leadership – while leader focused – places more emphasis on the quality of the interactions between 'leaders' and 'followers', and the *behaviours* that influence these interactions (Case 10.2). They can be studied not just from

Table 10.2 Follower-centric theories of leadership

Followers accept leadership influence	Leaders can only be leaders if accepted by followers. As leadership is legitimised when it is acted upon by followers, leadership is 'in the eye of the follower' rather than the leader
Followers moderate leadership impact	Followers have to interpret the desires of leaders, and can moderate the impact of the leader when they operationalise their instructions
Followers can find substitutes for leaders	If followers lose confidence in a leader, they can avoid them and seek advice from leader substitutes (i.e. other followers). High performance may be a product of leader substitutes, rather than the leader
Followers construct leaders and leadership	Leaders are 'constructed' through the stories of their followers, based more in myth than fact, and they sustain these constructions for their own well-being by reproducing particular outcomes, then attributing them to the leader
Followers are leaders	There is no justifiable distinction between leaders and followers: leadership is a 'shared' process that is distributed throughout a group of people. All stakeholder groups affect organisation sustainability, not just formally appointed leaders

a leader-centric perspective, but also by considering their effects on followers (follower-centric theory) or the impact of culture and discourse on their legitimacy (e.g. a cultural and critical perspective). In follower-centric studies (see Meindl, 1993; 1995), five aspects of the leader–follower relationship are highlighted (Table 10.2).

Case 10.2   The soft side of leadership

Individuals are important and leaders or leadership is important. The trouble is I think it's just more complicated than that … leadership can be that, you know, thrusting, setting the direction and you know punching the air ahead of the staff following you, and all that sort of thing. That is sometimes appropriate, but so is the sort of peer support, putting yourself in the position of supporting your managers as their peer; so, a kind of equal relationship and a supportive relationship. (Social enterprise manager)

The essence of the follower-centric argument is that:

leaders keep on winning [or losing] largely because their followers perceive them to be winners [or losers]. They, therefore, do everything they can to ensure this continues to be the case; for example, Manchester United players would do everything they could to keep Sir Alex Ferguson in his winning ways. (Jackson and Parry, 2008: 41)

As Smircich and Morgan (1982) also argue, leaders have an impact on followers not only in terms of devising strategies for action, and issuing instructions, but also through the meanings that they ascribe to events that are taking place in their organisation(s). Leadership, more than any other role, is based on 'attempting to frame and define the reality of others' (1982: 258). For example, the cultural and critical perspectives explored in the previous three chapters (the choice of legal form, the approach to strategic management, the deployment of a management style) are all attempts to create a 'shared reality' and shape the organisational choices open to different stakeholders.

EXERCISE   Individual and collective models of leadership

Bill Drayton established Ashoka to advance *social entrepreneurship*. It now operates internationally and involves young people in creating change. Watch the video linked below and critically analyse:

1 The theory or theories of leadership that inform Ashoka's approach.
2 The theory or theories of leadership that Ashoka fellows apply in their enterprises.

Video: http://www.youtube.com/watch?v=yu5DhOHLJ-s

Now compare your analysis of Ashoka fellows to leadership in the Venezuelan cooperatives. Watch the video linked below and consider the following questions:

Video: http://www.youtube.com/watch?v=DttTSJEO47g&feature=channel

1 How does leadership function in the Venezuelan cooperatives?
2 What theory or theories of leadership best explain their approach?

Critical perspectives on leadership

A focus on followers, culture and discourse is the starting point for developing a critical perspective on leadership. While there are calls for skilled leaders to plug gaps in leadership training and development (NCVO, 2007), the question still arises, 'What kind of leadership skills should be developed?' Hubbard (2005) argues that leadership in the private sector offers little insight into the development needs of the social enterprise sector. She makes this claim on the basis that leadership development in the private sector is based on the needs of (and findings from) multinational corporations seeking to maximise profit.

Grenier (2006: 137) finds that 'it appears that social entrepreneurship is seeking its learning and legitimacy from business, as well as seeking to make connection into the business world where **civil society** organisations have generally struggled and often failed'. She continues by suggesting that 'some care therefore needs to be taken as to what extent social entrepreneurship offers an alternative to existing forms of social change, or to what extent it is simply the extension and intrusion of 'business' into the 'social' and political arenas' (2006: 138). Amin et al. (2002: 125) make the point that social enterprise challenges the assumptions of globalisation (see Chapter 5): 'the key move is to ... challenge the dominant conception of the mainstream, rather than to cast the social economy in the image of the mainstream and in the interstices that the mainstream has abandoned'. Amin's argument, therefore, is that the notion of social enterprise leadership should emanate from practices that are effective *in the* **social economy**, rather than through the adoption of private economy models. With this in mind, we turn our attention to social entrepreneurship as a product of group process, rather than the enactment of an individual's vision.

Perspectives on Entrepreneurship

Whereas the study of leadership is strongly focused on understanding the relationship between leaders and followers, entrepreneurship has a different focus. Chell (2007) charts three separate strands in entrepreneurship studies. Firstly, there is entrepreneurship as a field of study that focuses on different forms of entrepreneurial behaviour. In this sense, it is a professional discipline that seeks to define and apply knowledge that supports the endeavours of enterprising individuals. Secondly, she draws an analogy between the musician and their musician*ship* (a term which refers to increased skill levels that are acquired through their practical applications) and the entrepreneur and entrepreneur*ship*. In this sense, entrepreneurship refers to the way entrepreneurs hone and craft their skills and apply their knowledge to practice.

The third focus, around which she argues there is the most significant level of convergence, is the symbiotic relationship between opportunity recognition and innovation. It is here that Chell argues there is a 'convergent theory' that recognises the common ground between the 'economic entrepreneur' (focused on wealth creation) and the 'social entrepreneur' (who seeks a social outcome). Both seek out opportunities. Both innovate. This convergent theory, however, assumes that the social entrepreneur has little (or no) interest in wealth creation. This flies in the face of empirical research that social entrepreneurs are deeply committed to (and interested in) wealth creation (Bornstein, 2007). The difference is in the way they influence the distribution and investment of any wealth generated through their efforts.

Another way to distinguish between economic and social entrepreneurship is not to look for convergence, but to look for divergence in the way that 'means' and 'ends' in the entrepreneurial process are socially constructed. In doing this, material in the previous chapter is helpful. Economic entrepreneurship treats labour as instrumental, and also maintains that the product of entrepreneurship is the utility value of its goods and services (or the financial capital realised). So, 'economic entrepreneurship' tends to adopt a theory X view of both labour and the consumer (McGregor, 1960), to treat them as costs to be minimised or income streams to be maximised. The workforce and customer base (consumers) are not developed as human beings unless such development makes them 'better' labourers or consumers. Secondly, the product of economic entrepreneurship is the utility value of the goods and services that can be exchanged (for other goods and services or money), with the measure of success expressed as economic capital (i.e. profits, GDP, share price, value added). Economic entrepreneurship therefore regards the workforce and customer base as 'means', and entrepreneurial outputs (goods, services and money) as 'ends'. In short, people have an *instrumental* role in this paradigm of entrepreneurial thought.

If we apply a *relational* view to enterprise (see Figure 9.2), the nature of the entrepreneurial process changes. Now the workforce and customers (who are regarded as instrumental in 'economic entrepreneurship') suddenly become *ends*. Social entrepreneurship, therefore, can be defined as a 'socially rational' form of entrepreneurship (Ridley-Duff, 2008a), in which the 'capital' developed is 'social' (in the form of cohesive and vibrant social networks), 'human' (in the form of intellectual development) and 'ethical' (in the form of behaviour informed by moral reasoning). Moreover, social, human and ethical capital are developed *for their own sake*, not in an instrumental (and contingent) way to generate economic capital. Of course, economic capital is still required (and produced) by social entrepreneurship, and many studies justify social entrepreneurship on the basis that more economic capital is created by *social* entrepreneurship than economic entrepreneurship (see Harding and Cowling, 2004; Forcadell, 2005; Erdal, 2008). This, however, is to miss the point that the two forms of entrepreneurship switch the priority of – and therefore the value placed upon – the inputs and outputs that shape the entrepreneurial process. People can be the 'ends' as well as the 'means' of production (compare Collins, 2001; 2006) (see Case 10.3).

Case 10.3   The community company model

In 1989, Peter Beeby – helped by his former teacher – invested £5000 in the creation of Sportasia Ltd. Fifteen years later, Peter stood before the workforce and shareholders of School Trends Ltd (one of the companies created by Sportasia Ltd) and asked the question, 'Who rightly owns this company?' The round of applause told its own story. Two months later, the shareholders (on a one-share, one-vote basis) and the workforce (on a one-person, one-vote basis) voted to convert their company to employee ownership.

Read the remainder of Case 10.3 (www.sagepub.co.uk/ridleyduff) and then consider the following questions:

1 Using Table 10.1, analysis the forms of leadership that are in evidence throughout this case.
2 To what extent is the organisation led by Peter Beeby?
3 To what extent is the organisation led by the staff?
4 Is Peter Beeby an economic or a social entrepreneur?

Alternative perspectives on social entrepreneurship, therefore, are based on developing individuals in ways that enable them to contribute to the creation and distribution of 'social goods'. Leadership is viewed as the outcome of many people organising for a mutually beneficial purpose, using a social enterprise as the means of achieving this. Visions and decisions are based upon the values of the members who comprise a social network, underpinned by a 'democratic ethos' (Spear, 2006). This view of leadership can be extended to those working in organisations governed by a voluntary or elected board of directors, or to the 'partners' of a firm that comprise the workforce (e.g. John Lewis).

This can have a dramatic impact on the notion of entrepreneurship itself, even to the extent that structural and mechanical metaphors are replaced with biological analogies. One of these is offered by Ellerman (1982) who described Mondragón's example as the 'socialisation of entrepreneurship'. Over the years, Ellerman has updated the metaphor and now portrays social entrepreneurship as a process that produces organisational 'offspring'.

> *The workers in each part of a company have their own standing as members of the company. This does not mean that the workers in cooperatives are automatically oriented to taking entrepreneurial risks with spinoff cooperatives. The most common attitude in most businesses, cooperative or conventional, is to try to stabilize, improve, and perpetuate one's position with the company. The point is that with a cooperative, there is no structural constraint against … the biological principle of plenitude, growth through offspring. (Ellerman, 2006: 13)*

Turnbull (2002) also uses the ecological metaphor of 'DNA' to explain how the banking system that supports the Mondragón cooperative network reproduces social entrepreneurship by institutionalising network governance. A 'contract of association' with the bank sets out the role of governing bodies in reproducing a culture of participative democracy, embedding entrepreneurial DNA in the 'offspring' enterprises. Both Ellerman and Turnbull argue that this is fundamentally different to the private sector (and, by implication, economic entrepreneurship). It *discourages* growth through predatory and competitive behaviour (acquisitions, takeovers, capital accumulation and the creation of wholly owned subsidiaries). Instead there is an incubation period, after which a cooperative enterprise is born and treated as a living organism (and composed of living people) entitled to a life of its own.[3] It is not to be regarded as a machine (or 'project') to be switched on and off as needed, or property to be bought and sold at the whim of its owner(s).

This approach has been characterised as 'cooperative entrepreneurship' by Morrison (1991). Its claim to be 'social' is based on two arguments. Firstly, enterprises cooperate, rather than compete, to create new enterprises. Secondly, the result is an enterprise that conforms to social economy norms regarding the democratic control of capital, and key decisions based on one member, one vote. Spear (2006), therefore, advances a straightforward proposition. Social entrepreneurship is the process of creating social enterprises within a social economy. There is no need to bolt it onto, or to adapt, 'mainstream' definitions in order to describe it. Indeed, doing so can be highly misleading (not to mention subversive). Its paradigmatic assumptions (Kuhn, 1970), particularly regarding the nature and purposes of enterprise, are different. It cannot be adequately explained using public administration or private sector concepts because these concepts reproduce public and private sector notions of enterprise.

An insight into this comes from Scott-Cato et al. (2008). While they take a similar view to Spear (2006), they acknowledge the dominance of US-style social entrepreneurship in linking 'social entrepreneurship' to liberalism and the pursuit of a social purpose, rather than transformations in social organisation. While social economy organisations do engage in social entrepreneurship that meet the US definition (entrepreneurship for a social purpose), they do this in a fundamentally different way. Scott-Cato et al. use the term 'associative entrepreneurship' (entrepreneurship driven by collective action) to capture this additional dimension. This distinction can be helpful in distinguishing Anglo-American constructions of the *entrepreneur* (driven by a personal vision) from European constructions of *coopérateurs* (driven by their desire – or need – to collaborate). The latter term, rarely used in English, comes from the French word for 'collaborators', and is used to describe the members of a cooperative enterprise.

Collective and cultural perspectives on entrepreneurship, therefore, place much more emphasis on networking and action-oriented social dialogue. As Hosking and Morley (1991: 253) argue, networking activity 'is about creating ... particular relationships, understandings, and actions'. This is something Austin et al. frame as follows:

> *Networking across organizational boundaries to create social value is a powerful strategy for social entrepreneurs because the objective of creating social value does not require that value be captured within organizational boundaries. (2006: 18)*

This fits with Ridley-Duff's (2008a) argument that social entrepreneurial actions have a 'distributive' logic that reorganises social relations and wealth distribution both internally and externally (compare Spreckley, 2008). Similarly, Crutchfield and McLeod-Grant (2007) use the metaphor of the starfish to illustrate the importance of 'decentralised' network structures in achieving wider social impact. They state that starfish, like successful social enterprises, are:

> *highly decentralised, relying on peer-to-peer relationships, widely distributed leadership and collaborative communities united by shared values ... with a headless starfish, if you cut off an arm, the old starfish will simply regenerate a new arm, and the other arm will grow into a new starfish. (2007: 125)*

So, social enterprises can enhance their chances of survival through the adoption of a 'network mindset', working collaboratively with allies, engaging in collective forms of social entrepreneurship, seeking to achieve wider social impact rather than fostering dependence on 'visionary' individuals (Case 10.4).

Case 10.4   Transforming the social entrepreneur

Graham Duncan, the manager at St Mary's Church, assisted by two colleagues (Aroose and Saffiena), undertook an action research project in 2007. They set out to establish an employee-owned social enterprise called the Food Factory involving Pakistani women in the Sharrow region of Sheffield. His first encounter with writers on social entrepreneurship offered encouragement:

> *I was attracted to this discourse and loved the promise of certainty and control implied by the objective language and economic terminology – it offered the clarity which I yearned for – in contrast to the muddle and confusion of my everyday working life.*

He found that the work of Somers (2005), Nicholls (2006a), Collins (2006) and Todres et al. (2006) talked 'confidently of value propositions, social impact metrics, robust mechanisms, double bottom lines and social capital'. Six months later, he and his colleagues were on the point of giving up their project. It had not worked out as expected. All blamed the women's attitude and believed that 'they do not want to change'.

Read the rest of case 10.4 (www.sagepub.co.uk/ridleyduff) and consider the following questions:

1   What theory of leadership informs Graham's approach to social entrepreneurship at the outset of the project? Have you ever *presumed* that this approach to leadership is most effective?
2   Assess the extent to which 'follower-centric' views of leadership provide an explanation for Graham's changing view of social entrepreneurship. What insights do follower-centric views provide into your own experiences?
3   In what circumstances might leader-centric theories maintain their applicability?

Conclusions

Table 10.3 summarises the discussions in this chapter and the implications for practice. The treatment of different approaches to leadership is not intended to obscure that leader-centric theories may still be applicable to situations where:

- followers are familiar with the discourse used by their leaders
- followers understand the stories and cultural references used by the leader to develop and explain plans
- followers are prepared to accept (or conform to) the discursive and behavioural norms of the leader.

Table 10.3 Applying leadership theory to social entrepreneurship

Leadership theory	Social entrepreneurial assumptions	Implications for practice
Leader-centred theories	Social entrepreneurship occurs when individually 'driven' people pursue a social mission or purpose	Support for social entrepreneurship can be provided by selecting and developing individuals with the greatest ability to catalyse change
Higher-purpose theories of leadership	Social entrepreneurship is a morally driven variant of traditional entrepreneurship, rooted in the pursuit and propagation of a religious, charitable or transformational lifestyle	Support for social entrepreneurship depends on the capacity of moral leaders to steer organisational members towards 'higher' ethical behaviours, social aims and transformative outcomes
Follower-centred theories	Social entrepreneurship is a socially constructed concept that arises out of the collective actions of followers who benefit from sustaining particular views of the leadership process	Support for social entrepreneurship will be achieved when a sufficient number of followers 'tell a better story' or 'support a more compelling vision' and start to propagate a new (social) entrepreneurial discourse

(Continued)

Table 10.3 *(Continued)*

Leadership theory	Social entrepreneurial assumptions	Implications for practice
Cultural perspectives on leadership	Social entrepreneurship is a culturally defined variant of (or antithesis to) economic entrepreneurship	Support for social entrepreneurship depends on the value propositions of social entrepreneurs and the extent to which they are accepted and adopted in a given cultural setting
Critical perspectives on leadership	Social entrepreneurship is a *social* (collective) not individual phenomenon: it describes collective processes that lead to the creation of social enterprises	Support for social entrepreneurship depends on developing institutions capable of supporting collective action, and maintaining discursive democratic debate about the use of economic, social and human capital

However, if one or more of the above does not hold, other theories of leadership provide insights into alternative leadership strategies. For example, in the case of the Food Factory (Case 10.4), follower-centric theory provides an insight into how effective leadership was re-established. If 'support for social entrepreneurship will be achieved when a sufficient number of followers "tell a better story" or "support a more compelling vision"', then the role of the leader might need to change to one that helps *followers* establish and propagate a story, a vision and a **discourse** that inspire them to follow a new course of action. Viewed another way, the leader has to (temporarily) become the follower until sufficiently knowledgeable to perform the leadership function effectively.

Social transformation occurs when large populations of people accept and institutionalise new norms of behaviour (i.e. rooted in changed ethical values). Leader- and follower-centric theories alert us to the dual nature of this transformation. It will be achieved not only by the (social) entrepreneur changing others and encouraging them to accept their vision, but also by the (social) entrepreneur leaving themselves open to change by adopting a reflexive attitude when others challenge their assumptions about the entrepreneurial process.

SUMMARY OF LEARNING

In this chapter, we have argued that:

- Leadership matters because it assists in maintaining an organisation of people, and clarifies and communicates individual and collective intentions.
- Leadership theory was initially leader centric, and focused on the traits, qualities and behaviours of individual leaders.
- As the field has matured, leadership theory has taken more account of follower, culture and critical approaches that emphasise context and social processes that legitimise different approaches to leadership.

- Social entrepreneurship (and entrepreneurship studies generally) has generated renewed interest in leader-centric views of organisation.
- Collective forms of social entrepreneurship have been characterised as 'cooperative entrepreneurship' and 'associative entrepreneurship' to reflect their focus on collective action.
- Social and economic entrepreneurship can be regarded as 'convergent' in their shared interest in innovation and opportunity recognition.
- Social and economic entrepreneurship can be regarded as 'divergent' on the nature and purpose of entrepreneurship, and the end product of the entrepreneurial process.
- Economic entrepreneurship adopts an instrumental view of strategic stakeholders (workforce, customers, suppliers, community institutions) and treats them as a 'means' of accumulating financial capital and producing goods and services that have utility value.
- Social entrepreneurship adopts a relational view of strategic stakeholders and regards them as the 'ends' of entrepreneurship: they are the recipients of financial, social, human and ethical capital in which social enterprise is the 'means'.

QUESTIONS AND POSSIBLE ESSAY ASSIGNMENTS

1 'Leadership [is] thrusting, setting the direction and ... punching the air ahead of the staff following you.' Critically assess the limitations of this statement with specific reference to follower-centric theories of leadership.
2 'Social entrepreneurship is a process of encouraging collective action and community solidarity.' With reference to US theory on social entrepreneurship, critically assess this statement and consider the impact of Ashoka on the development of social entrepreneurship.
3 'We need to study *coopérateurs* as well as entrepreneurs.' Explain the term *coopérateur* and critically assess its contribution to your understanding of social entrepreneurship.

FURTHER READING

An excellent text to consider perspectives on leadership (and how they might inform leadership education in social enterprise) is *A* *Very Short, Fairly Interesting and Reasonably Cheap Book about Studying Leadership* (Jackson and Parry, 2008). Do not be fooled by its title. This is an accessible, well-researched introduction to perspectives on leadership that fit well with social enterprise practitioners' needs. While they are not discussed in this chapter, we also recommend a close reading of Clutterbuck and Megginson on *Creating a Coaching Culture* (2005) and Garvey et al.'s (2009) contribution to *Coaching and Mentoring*. These describe leadership development programmes based on peer groups and coaching, rather than instructional approaches developed by 'inspirational' celebrity leaders.

Introductory books on social entrepreneurship tend to address one or other strand of thought set out in this chapter, but rarely all of them. A well established text is Alex Nicholls' edited book *Social Entrepreneurship: New Models of Sustainable Social Change* (2006a). This brings together the views of a number of leading social entrepreneurs. For a tightly argued paper on how social entrepreneurship can be defined in relation to the broader field of enterprise and entrepreneurship studies, see Chell's (2007) paper on the companion website. She moves towards, but stops slight short of, the critical perspective in Curtis's (2008) paper 'Finding that grit makes a pearl' (2008).

For more on social entrepreneurship as a collective approach, Spear's (2006) paper argues for a straightforward relationship between social entrepreneurship, social enterprise and the social economy. Scott-Cato et al.'s (2008) study of the renewal energy sector in Wales makes a similar argument to advance a theory of 'associative entrepreneurship'. Lastly, the concept of 'cooperative entrepreneurship' in Morrison's *We Build the Road as We Travel* (1991) challenges Schumpeter's assumption regarding the superiority of representative democracy.

Further reading material is available on the companion website at www.sagepub.co.uk/ridleyduff.

USEFUL RESOURCES

Cooperantics, http://www.cooperantics.co.uk
Cooperative Business Consultants, http://www.cbc.coop
Cooperative College, http://www.co-op.ac.uk
Harvard Business School, http://www.hbs.edu/socialenterprise/resources/entrepreneurship.html
School for Social Entrepreneurs, http://www.sse.org.uk
Skoll Centre for Social Entrepreneurship, http://www.sbs.ox.ac.uk/centres/skoll/
UnLtd, http://www.unltd.org.uk/

NOTES

1 An emerging field of practice is the use of Open Space Technology (Owen, 2008) which builds on the 'law of two feet' to achieve high levels of participation by creating an environment in which each person can take responsibility for their own learning.
2 In fairness to the researchers, they undertook much of their research on after-school clubs and these had to be supervised because the participants were not adults.
3 Charities such as NCVO have a history of incubating new organisations before proactively spinning them off. For example, the *Directory of Social Change* was previously a project within NCVO.

Income Streams and Social Investment

11

Learning Objectives

In this chapter we discuss the management of income streams and social investment. By the end of this chapter you will be able to:

- distinguish between income, revenue, cost recovery, fundraising and social investment

- explain restricted, unrestricted and designated funds

- critically appraise how combinations of income influence sustainability

- critically assess the arguments for diversification and trading to sustain an enterprise

- assess the strengths and weaknesses of social enterprise financial management strategies.

The key arguments that will be developed in this chapter are:

- In property-based societies, there is a need for incorporated enterprises to generate assets that exceed liabilities.
- There is an ideological difference between profit-making (for the purpose of making social investments) and profit-maximising (to accumulate private capital).
- Social economy organisations vary their accounting practice to track donor and member funds.
- Income management may be based on a 'whole economy' or a 'mixed receipts' strategy.
- The legal form of a social enterprise influences the accessibility of loan and equity funding.
- Social investment initiatives are not yet uniform, but can provide funds for different stages of social enterprise development.

Introduction

In previous chapters we have focused on: legal forms and identities (Chapter 7); strategic management (Chapter 8); governance, HRM and employee relations (Chapter 9); and leadership (Chapter 10). Each has implications for and is implicated by the income generation activities of a social enterprise. In this chapter, we consider strategies for generating sustainable sources of income and development capital. Income generation is the lifeblood of any organisation; social enterprises are no different.

Increasing income provides more opportunities to increase **social investments**, which in turn provide the means to build the capacity of an enterprise. Brinckerhoff (2000) argues 'no profit – no mission' and we think there is a grain of truth in this statement. At the same time, we need to be mindful that 'profit' and 'mission' are socially constructed concepts that are interpreted differently in various cultural settings. Moreover, social entrepreneurs may accept or reject business norms, prompting Emerson (2000: 23–4) to comment that '[economic rules are] the constructs of social perception ... fully imbedded within our social systems [that] act upon each other in an endless interplay'. As we discussed in Chapters 5 and 7, social enterprises are capable of 'rewriting' economic rules. The same can be true in the area of income generation.

In property-based economies (of which the UK is currently one), an incorporated organisation needs to acquire or generate assets that exceed liabilities. Given this requirement, the more a social enterprise relies on trading to generate its development capital, the more profitability matters. Placing profitability above all other considerations, however, creates an economy that 'exacerbates poverty, disease, pollution, corruption, crime and inequality' (Yunus, 2007: 5). For this reason, we need to clarify the difference between profit-*maximising* (in private enterprises) and profit-*making* (in social enterprises). Secondly, we clarify that *cost recovery* (seeking grants and donations to offset costs) is different from *social investment* (tracking the social impacts of financial investments). There is a subtle, yet crucial, difference here between for-profit organisations and social enterprises: private businesses are profit centres for shareholders and social enterprises are profit centres for stakeholders. Hence, the analogy that you can do more good with more income in a stakeholder organisation holds that more people benefit (in lots of different ways).

As Price (2008) argues, these investments include:

- employing marginalised people (minority groups, people with disabilities or health problems)
- regenerating the economy (in post-industrial, rural and deprived areas)
- creating 'low-profit' businesses to increase the availability of much needed goods and services
- creating businesses that pursue ideological or political goals (recycling, renewable energy, fair trade)
- creating goods and services for a specific community (geographically based or interest-based groups).

We deal firstly with the generation of profits through trading activities, then grants and donations. Later, we discuss **debt finance** (loans) and social investment (including

Table 11.1 Income streams, cost recovery and social investment

Classification	Accounting norm	Description	Regulated by
Trading	Revenue	Revenues and profits from the sale of goods and services, and contracts for service	Contract law (employment law)
Fees	Income	Member dues and subscriptions	Contract law Society law
Donations	Income	Individual and corporate giving	Trust law Charity law
Grants	Cost recovery	Monies received or paid to achieve a specific (charitable) aim	Trust law Charity law
Loans	(Social) investment (debt finance)	Loan finance, overdraft facilities, debentures, (fixed interest) bonds	Contract law (Financial Services Act)
Shares	(Social) investment (equity finance)	Preference shares, member equity, social investments, community share issues	Company law Society law Cooperative law [a]

[a]May be covered by cooperative law outside the UK. Inside the UK, it is covered by the Industrial and Provident Societies Act and, in the case of credit unions, the Financial Services Authority.

equity capital). By the end of the chapter, you will be able to explain and critique income generation and investment raising strategies that maximise 'blended value' (Emerson, 2000).

Theorising Income and Investment Activities

There are many terms used to describe the financial sources on which social enterprises rely. Some are income while others are payments to (re)cover costs. Table 11.1 sets out the order in which we will consider them.

At present, the primary discourse for social enterprises is to emphasise their *trading*. For example, the *Strategy for Success* (DTI, 2002) claims that social enterprises will strive for 100 per cent trading income, yet in the same document it is recognised that 50 per cent trading income is an important threshold. Empirical research suggests that 100 per cent traded income is an unrealisable goal for those social enterprises working with severely disadvantaged groups (see Pearce, 2003; Wallace, 2005). In one way, the line drawn in the sand provides people with a defining characteristic. On closer inspection (Seanor et al., 2007), we see that income is more fluid. Smallbone and Lyon (2005) apply a 25 per cent rule for those working towards social enterprise, but there are also times when organisations fluctuate between grants and contracts, and between debt and equity. So, we are interested in the mix of income streams and the way they fluctuate from one period to the next. Consequently, it is helpful to make a distinction between 'whole economy' social enterprises (trading in markets) and 'mixed receipts' social enterprises that combine a number of income streams (Coulson, 2009: 21).

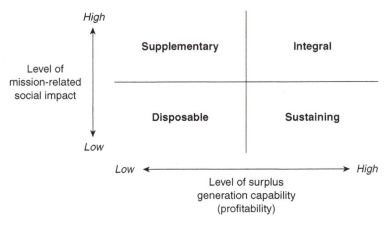

Figure 11.1   Classifying activities

With permission from SAGE Publications Inc. Wei-Skillern et al. (2007) *Entrepreneurship in the Social Sector*, Figure 4.1 and Table 4.1.

Bev Meldrum (formerly a member of the Tool Factory in London) explained to us that delivering contracts is different to selling goods and services. She believes, like Wallace (2005), that long-term sustainability is built through a strategy of diversification. Part of this debate (in the charity/voluntary sector) involves a move from grants to contracts. There is a rhetoric that grants are bad because they encourage dependency, while contracts are good because they encourage a more business-like organisation (Price, 2008). The other side of the debate involves cooperative finance. Unlike charities that are over-reliant on grants, cooperatives can be *over*-reliant on trading to generate capital (Cornforth et al., 1988), and can resist the creation of capital structures that encourage both member and social investments (Ridley-Duff, 2009a).

Wei-Skillern et al. (2007) offer a useful starting point for assessing trading opportunities. Figure 11.1 shows *disposable* activities as those that inhibit the achievement of both social impacts and trading surpluses. *Supplementary* activities may achieve social impact, but do not generate surpluses. Nevertheless, *supplementary* activities may be desirable, so an enterprise may engage in *sustaining* activities to provide the surpluses needed to fund them, even if these do not contribute to social impact. This approach to income generation can encourage '**mission drift**' that risks demotivating staff (Seanor and Meaton, 2008) and damaging the reputation of the enterprise (Coule, 2007). A strategic goal, therefore, is to find trading opportunities that are *integral* to the achievement of both social impact and **surplus** generation. Emerson (2000) describes this as seeking 'blended value' (the generation of both social and economic value simultaneously).

All activities, as Wei-Skillern et al. (2007: 138) warn, 'are initially, and on an ongoing basis, capital absorbing'. For example, selling goods and services to service users requires investments in marketing, not just in terms of devising and implementing strategies, but also in terms of the staff time to make them happen. Similarly, bidding for contracts takes time and commitment. If successful, the contract also needs servicing by monitoring outputs, outcomes and impacts and reporting them back to commissioning bodies. Consequently, experience and know-how are needed to identify ancillary and project management costs (including rents, building maintenance, office services and management time) so that bids are based on the principle of **full-cost recovery.**

Funds, profits and accounting

Before we consider trading, let us clarify the subtle differences between 'income', 'receipts', 'surplus', 'profit', 'revenues', 'costs' and 'investments' in accounting practice. Income is not the same as 'profit', nor is it necessarily helpful to regard it as 'revenue'. While income, revenues and receipts *may* be the same, the variation in language reflects different institutional and accounting environments. In the US, 'non-profit' organisations use Form 990 or Form 990-EZ to declare 'total receipts', while 'for-profit' companies report their income as 'sales revenue' (total turnover from the sale of goods and services). In the UK, smaller charities use cash accounting based on 'receipts' and 'expenses', while larger ones have to produce a 'profit and loss' statement.

Perhaps for this reason, there is ambiguity in accounting for grant income. While grant payments are 'receipts', they usually cover expenses that have already been incurred. For this reason, it is problematic to regard grant income as 'revenue'. In audited accounts, grants should be allocated as a (negative) cost against items for which a claim has been made. Grant income is also subject to trust law, not contract or company law. When money is 'granted', a 'trust' is formed between the donor and the recipient regarding the purposes for which the money can be used (Morgan, 2008).[1] If none are specified, the monies can be used for any purpose defined in the 'objects' of the recipient's organisation. Grants are allocated to *funds* so that any donor can inquire how their money has been used. Figure 11.2 is taken from the **SORP Regulations** (Charity Commission, 2005).

The presence of **'restricted' funds** (of any kind) indicates that the organisation is managing charitable funds under trust law. The scale of this activity affects its status as a social enterprise. The **Social Enterprise Mark** (see Chapter 6) expresses award criteria in terms of how the applicant uses 'profits', *not* how it manages 'funds'. The

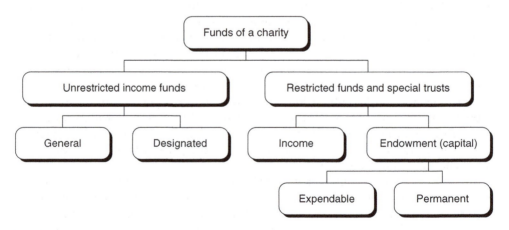

Figure 11.2   Fund management in a charity context

'Accounting and Reporting by Charities: Statement of Recommended Practice' (2005), p. 11, Figure 1, reproduced under the terms of Crown Copyright Policy Guidance issued by HMSO © Crown Copyright 2005.

assumption is that 'profits' (in the generally accepted sense of the word) are used to make social investments. This encourages the *investment* mindset favoured by Emerson:

> To move from charity to investing in change requires those who 'own' that future ...
> have the ability to track its performance over time – and tie that transformation back to
> the capital support and community resources that made it possible. (2000: 18)

Emerson's view is that the generation of profits, and then the tracking of their reinvestment, increase learning and understanding of 'blended value' (i.e. deeper knowledge of the relationship between social investments and economic and social impacts). The Social Enterprise Mark, therefore, is not making a 'mistake' using this language: it is tied to the new discourse that prioritises the generation of 'profits' to make 'investments', and which de-emphasises the raising of 'funds' to recover 'costs'. There is, inevitably, an overlap – and potential for greater 'blended value' – when an organisation pursues its social objectives through trading activities (as happens in primary purpose charitable trading and cooperative enterprises).

It is also worth commenting on the way cooperatives and mutual societies adapt their accounting practices. They deviate from norms by maintaining detailed records of member transactions for reasons other than market intelligence or legal require-ment. This is most apparent in retail chains where members' financial transactions are tracked *for the purpose of calculating their share of profits.* This applies in the provision of financial services as well as in retail cooperatives (based on the value of purchases). It may also be standard practice in worker cooperatives: wages paid and hours worked are not tracked simply to calculate tax payments to the Inland Revenue, but also for the purposes of calculating an employee's share of profits.

In summary, income (receipts) may come from trading, subscription income, dona-tions, grants, loan finance and equity capital: all or some (at different times) may have a role in developing the enterprise.

Income from Trading and Membership

In this section we discuss the differences between mission-related and mission-unrelated trading. As Price states:

> social enterprise is about making money rather than spending it – and that means
> trading the products and services or the value created with the enterprise for
> remuneration that generates the income to survive. (2008: 40)

Pearce concurs when he comments:

> it is a sine qua non *that social enterprises engage to some degree in trade by providing
> goods and services for which customers pay. Engaging in such economic activity is
> how social enterprises achieve their social purpose. (2003: 34)

The alternative, as Price (2008) states, is grant (or contract) dependency character-ised by periods of secure income followed by financial famines that dash hopes of sustaining innovations in service delivery. Social enterprise (allegedly) offers more stable financial resources that are less reliant on the whims of grant holders. For charities, it also constitutes a source of **unrestricted income**. A strategy that is *over*-reliant on trading, however, can also weaken the enterprise. Pharoah et al. (2004) suggest that a failure to secure trading income may *not* reflect a lack of entrepreneurial effort but may arise out of the diverse and difficult challenges that social enterprises take on. These challenges include: establishing local resources; navigating highly complex contracting arrangements; plugging gaps in service provision; and slowly *creating* markets that make further trading possible.

The association between trading and 'for-profit' businesses carries some rhetorical baggage. For-profit trading is labelled 'opportunistic', 'entrepreneurial', 'market focused,' 'creative', 'customer driven' and 'risky' (Bull and Crompton, 2005). Social enterprises and other third sector organisations have now created their own language to describe trading in a social economy (Bull, 2006; 2007). In doing so, it is clearer that income generation is not the preserve of the private sector. Wei-Skillern et al. (2007: 135) draw on the Johns Hopkins Comparative Non-profit Sector Project to show that over half the income of the social economy globally is 'earned' (53% fees, 35% government, mostly contracts, and 12% philanthropic giving). In some countries trading income is even higher: Kenya (81%), Mexico (85%), Philippines (92%).

Table 11.2 Streams of income by source (%)

	Fees (trading)	Government	Philanthropy
Latin America	75	15	10
Scandinavia	59	33	7
USA	57	31	13
Asia	56	22	12
Africa	55	25	19
Eastern Europe	49	31	19
Europe	38	56	6

Source: Wei-Skillern et al., 2007: 136

Table 11.2 provides insight into political and cultural influences on the propensity of social enterprises to trade. In some countries, income is more accessible from philanthropic sources (compare Africa at 19% to Europe at 6%). In other cases, government contracts offer more opportunities (compare Europe at 56% to Latin America at 15%). Hence, the income streams influence both the number and the nature of social enterprises.

In the UK, over half the income of voluntary and community sector organisations comes from trading (NCVO, 2008), outstripping all income from grants, gifts and donations. As Jim Brown confirms in reports to the Finance Hub, earned income from open market trading is the most valuable source of income, and contributes most to unrestricted funds. It is increasingly seen as a route to independence and growth potential. Pharoah et al. (2004) add that large voluntary sector organisations have been generating trading income for some time, but maintain a clear separation between mission-related activity and 'business' activity. For example, sales of Christmas cards and items from gift catalogues are examples of business activity that support mission-related investment. It is possible to base an income strategy on *primary purpose trading*, *ancillary trading*, *beneficiary trading* and *mixed trading* linked to an organisation's charitable objects (see box).

Charities and trading

In the UK, a charity can engage in trade, and not be subject to tax on its earnings, if:

- It is *integrated with the primary purpose*, specified by the charity's objects. Currently, there are 12 categories of charitable objects (see Charities Act 2006, Section 1, Clause 2(2)).
- It is *ancillary to the primary purpose*, but linked. For instance, an educational charity might sell books.
- It is *beneficiary trading*. For example, a charity teaching disabled people horticultural skills can then sell the horticultural products made by the beneficiaries.
- It involves the *sale of donated goods*, given for that purpose.
- It is *mixed trading* involving a single trading activity which has both primary purpose and non-primary purpose, but where the non-primary element is under £50,000 and less than 10 per cent of the total trading income.
- It is *occasional trading* (for any purpose) and is only a small part of the annual total income, defined by the Charity Commission as:

  up to £5000 if total income is less than £20,000
  up to 25 per cent of total income between £20,000 and £200,000
  maximum of £50,000 if total income is over £200,000.

- It *qualifies as an extra-statutory concession* which applies to fundraising events such as barbeques, auctions, festivals and concerts. The events are supposed to be one-off, but up to 15 such events at the same venue within one year can be exempt.

Source: Finance Hub Reports (2007), series edited by Deborah Turton, NCVO, http://www.financehub.org.uk/research/default.aspa

Associations and societies can raise considerable amounts of income from members. Quite apart from the example of trade unions, campaigning charities can also create significant income streams by developing an integrated strategy. The National Council for Voluntary Organisations (NCVO) increased its membership from around 300 to 4500 between 1996 and 2006, with fee income from members exceeding half a million pounds from 2003 onwards. Moreover, the membership base became a key market for courses and conferences, with course bookings up nearly tenfold between 1998 and 2002. A similar strategy was used at the Careers Research and Advisory Centre (CRAC) where the acquisition of membership organisations increased the take-up of course places on their Insight Programme. From 2004, course bookings exceeded 10,000 a year. In short, linking membership development to (primary purpose) trading opportunities can constitute an integrated strategy for income generation.[2]

If an activity is likely to attract corporation tax, it may be cost-efficient to set up a **trading arm** and gift the profits back to a parent charity (to reclaim the tax). Trading arms can also take on contracts that fall outside the charitable objects of the parent charity, and so protect against undermining its autonomy or ethos. By developing trading arms, charities can obtain the benefits of both charitable and commercial trading. However, there is a question over whether the trading arm constitutes a social enterprise. The rationale for creating a trading arm is to gift profits back to the parent organisation, but there is more than one way of doing this.

Typically, a charity trading arm is a company limited by shares (CLS), with 100 per cent ownership of share capital by the charity. However, it is not uncommon for the trading arm to be constituted as a company limited by guarantee (CLG) with an independent board. The use of a CLS trading arm raises the question of whether the subsidiary satisfies the criteria for the 'social' aspects of 'enterprise'. Is the trading arm 'social' in the sense of being subject to democratic control? Is it 'social' in the sense of being able to exercise autonomy? Whilst a trading arm has autonomy from the state, the parent charity can impose management controls that remove its autonomy and internal democracy. This being the case, it can simultaneously satisfy 'social purpose' criteria but fall well short of 'socialisation' criteria that depend on the democratisation of production methods and wealth distribution.

To illustrate this point, it is worth comparing the 'trading arm' perspective to arrangements in the Mondragón Cooperative Corporation (see Cases 2.3 and 11.4). Member cooperatives are free to vote themselves in and out of the cooperative network, and internal democracy ensures they take their own decisions on profit distribution (Ridley-Duff, 2005). Aside from cooperative laws that require 10 per cent of profits to be invested in social and educational projects, members can exercise democratic control. The theorisation of 'social', therefore, matters. Prioritising 'social purpose' can undermine autonomy and democracy (i.e. the 'socialisation' of the entrepreneurial process). The reverse is also true: democratisation can subvert the 'social purposes' of the organisation's founders if not regulated by an external body.

The case of Ealing Community Transport (ECT) further clarifies this. Established in 1979, it provides transport for people with disabilities and the elderly in the Ealing borough of London. ECT became a flagship, award-winning social enterprise, and its former CEO (Stephen Sears) was a key contributor to the development of community interest company (CIC) legislation.[3] We pick up the story 30 years on in Case 11.1.

Case 11.1   Anna Whitty, current ECT Chief Executive

Ealing Community Transport started life as an industrial and provident society (exempt charity) providing community transport to local organisations using grant funding from its local authority. Over the years a variety of other grant opportunities allowed the organisation to grow. A grant to develop furniture reuse and later paint exchange was integral to ECT's development of its environmental services. The drying up of these grants with changing political priorities led ECT to use its enterprising spirit to develop innovational recycling opportunities which its local council contracted as part of a pilot scheme. This also roughly coincided with the award of a handful of home-to-school contracts to the core transport business.

Read the full case at www.sagepub.co.uk/ridleyduff and consider the following questions:

1 How did ECT go about raising funds to develop different community services?
2 What role did contracts play in the development of ECT?
3 How would you characterise the mix of income streams at ECT?

Ealing Community Transport created the ECT Group as a wholly owned subsidiary and converted it to a CIC in 2005 (for history see SEC, 2005: 37). The case provides an outline of the ravelling and unravelling of income sources and opportunities for social enterprise through their 30-year history (from 1979 to 2009). Its first six years was dominated by grant funding (as a charitable project) before it was established as a legal entity that was 'both commercial and charitable' (2005: 37). It engaged in a period of diversification, using opportunities to blend social enterprise activities with income from gifts (grants), trading (contracts) and finance (debt). By 2009, it had 24 separate companies. Many had been converted to CICs to 'reinforce the social mission of each company' (2005: 37). As Case 11.1 highlights, ECT moved from traditional sources of grant income to trading opportunities, using contracts with the public sector.

In the ECT case, its reliance on debt finance meant it was hit hard by the economic downturn of 2009. By selling its recycling subsidiaries, it was able to inject £15 million into its community transport services. As Bridge et al. (2009) outline, social enterprises need to accept that borrowing and financial risks need to be taken in order to build capacity. The developments at ECT indicate the challenge of accepting these risks and how they can compromise community ownership.

The sale of various trading arms within ECT Group attracted controversy both for the valuation placed on one £47 million turnover business generating about £2 million profits a year, and also because the sales seemed to confirm that the asset lock in the CIC regulations was not secure (Schwartz, 2008). While the CEO Stephen Sears viewed this as an 'opportunity' that demonstrated the 'flexibility' of the CIC, others raised substantive questions about the integrity of the asset lock, and the likely backlash from funding bodies which may now avoid awarding contracts to CICs because they fear them being sold to private sector companies (Gosling, 2008).

In ECT's case, the regulator confirmed that ECT operated within its own rules (Gosling, 2008) and that the money raised from the sale of subsidiaries enabled ECT to service debts in its parent businesses. The events surrounding ECT, however, highlight two things about CICs and income streams: firstly, income can be generated *for* social enterprises by selling CIC assets to the private sector; secondly, the 'asset lock' does not effectively prevent CICs from transferring their income streams to organisations outside the social economy.

To conclude our discussion of trading activity, we summarise the options open to social enterprises in Table 11.3.

Table 11.3   Trading choices of social enterprises

Direct sales (charging customers for products and services that are core activities)	If a social enterprise can earn income from direct sales linked to their mission, this is the 'holy grail'. Direct sales opportunities tend to be most available to organisations that can operate in viable markets by satisfying unmet needs, forging new market opportunities, or working in established markets
Indirect sales (charging customers for products and services that are non-core activities)	This approach involves selling products and services made by the organisation (such as training or consultancy) to offset the cost of providing other (core) services that deliver the social objects of the enterprise
Contracts for services	This involves entering into contracts to provide specific services, goods, or support for specified activities. The caveat here is that the contract may be written by the funder to support *their* social agenda (which may or may not be compatible with the objects of the social enterprise)
Retailing (selling products or services *not* made by the organisation)	This may involve selling products/services, some of which are mission related. As Hudson (2002) points out, environmentally friendly washing machines and fridges can be bought from Friends of the Earth, Oxfam can supply furniture, Amnesty provides ethical investment plans. The UK's largest charities for blind and deaf people (RNIB and RNID respectively) have multi-million-pound trading arms selling products from catalogues geared to the needs of blind and deaf people
Running a charity shop	Retailing can be further supported by establishing dedicated retail outlets. Shop income is counted as *earned* income rather than *gift* income, and can contribute to unrestricted funds

Gifts and Donations

Gifts have been a successful source of income for charities and voluntary organisations for centuries. At the same time, grants can be less flexible than trading income, particularly if they do not meet the full cost of an activity, or are tied to a restricted fund. A culture of grant dependency increases the pressure *for* social enterprise (see Case 8.1, Seedley and Langworthy Trust). For example, a grant to work with homeless people may cover the costs of short-term accommodation, but not food or other support. Unless other income streams are put in place, then sustainability is at risk because support is delivered without fully recovering the cost. As a result, the concept of 'full-cost recovery' is gaining ground as an accounting practice in not-for-profit organisations (see Doherty et al., 2009b: 114).

In an organisation dependent on restricted funds, the organisation could have money in the bank, but be unable to use it (even as collateral for raising loans). There is always a risk that funds may have to be paid back to the grant giver if not used for the specific purpose of the award. The holding of funds, therefore, may create a balance sheet that shows a positive amount which obscures issues of sustainability. Seeking sustainability through grant funding involves careful financial management that may (possibly) be seen as more of a burden than an opportunity. Kenton Mann of Music Unlimited – a social enterprise based in Greater Manchester in the UK – states:

> I think for us, as soon as the grant stopped I said, 'We're not going to do that again' – because spending other people's money is really hard. (Bull and Crompton, 2005: 23)

This said, unspent funds can be carried over from one financial year to the next with the agreement of the funder, and may be transferable to other projects.

Social enterprises can gain considerable benefits from acquiring charitable status. As Price (2008) points out, there are approximately 2500 grant giving trusts in England and Wales, and acquiring charitable status increases access to them. Charities get 80 per cent relief on business rates and exemptions from corporation tax on primary purpose trading. One area for caution, however, is the nature of services that might be provided with grant funding. Grants may be tax free, but there may be **VAT** to pay (on supplies or on the provision of services that attract VAT). For example, while education services do not attract VAT, consultancy services do. A social enterprise needs to be clear that funds are being used to further their mission (primary purpose trading) and not for other services (secondary trading). If the organisation delivers VATable services to a value above the VAT threshold (£70,000 in 2010), it will have to register for VAT and face a bill that cannot be recovered from a funder.

Whatever the benefits and pitfalls, Pharoah et al. (2004) point out that grants remain a major source of funding for both charitable and non-charitable social enterprises, and continue to benefit a 'mixed receipts' strategy in support of social and charitable objects. Moreover, Pearce (2003) contends that the problems created by grant dependency cannot be solved by the recipient organisations. Funders *create* a culture of dependency through the way they attach conditions to their grants. Ellerman (2005) believes they must share responsibility for the effects of the way they make social investments.

An alternative to grants is *donations* from private individuals or organisations. One advantage is that they are received in advance of expenses, improving cash flows and providing opportunities for investment income. There are different types of donations: time, skills and personal resources. While non-financial donations do not add to income, they can reduce the cost of providing services. Case 11.2 highlights a particularly innovative development for increasing donations to non-profit and charitable organisations.

Case 11.2   MissionFish

MissionFish is a technology that adds value to eBay auctions. eBay is a global community undertaking a large number of auctions all around the world. Sellers can use MissionFish to donate part of their sales revenue directly to a recognised charity or non-profit organisation. eBay calls this the Giving Works program. It also allows non-profits to sell their goods on eBay and raise funds. In addition to facilities that are attached to sale items, a 'Donate Now' button can be added to allow direct donations from a PayPal account without affecting an auction.

A fuller teaching case can be found on the accompanying website at www.sagepub. co.uk/ridleyduff.

Questions:

1 What governs the way the income passing through MissionFish can be used by the non-profit or charity that receives it?
2 If a non-profit or charity sells goods on eBay and uses MissionFish to allocate all the income, are the funds raised 'earned income' or 'gifts'?
3 If people use the 'Donate Now' button, what type of income is this?

Donations made through MissionFish are a source of unrestricted funds (if not given in response to a charity appeal). The money can be used for any expenditure or held as a reserve and can be used to make *social investments*. While schemes like these are welcome, donations are often insufficient to generate the funding required for capital expenditure (in buildings or machinery), or the development of new products, services and viable markets. As Cadbury comments:

> The third sector ... will need access to finance to expand its activities and to adapt to ... ever changing demands of communities it serves. At the same time, the people managing these organisations will have to accept that borrowing and a certain degree of financial risk will enable them to achieve far more than if they take more restricted views of their capacities. (Cadbury, 2000, cited in Bridge et al., 2009: 148)

In the next section, we consider financial instruments that make this possible.

Loan and Equity Finance

Social investment in the form of loans and equity holdings has received more attention in recent years (see Brown, 2004; 2006; Ridley-Duff, 2009a). New financial instruments are being designed that meet the needs of social enterprises, and which have the potential to support (rather than inhibit) radical social change. Emerson (2000) clarifies the ownership implications of different forms of investment. Grants have no ownership rights attached to them, while social investments (in the form of equity) do. The emergence of multi-stakeholder ownership models (see Chapter 7) provides a capital structure for equity holdings and makes possible a 'social capital market':

> It is no doubt true there are social costs and economic costs, and that each should be tracked. However, it must also be understood that the interaction and trade-off between the two do not take place in a smooth line, one operating in directly inverse relationship to the other. The issue isn't wealth creation or social change – it is the creation of value, applying resources to the creation of the greatest value possible and the simultaneous pursuit of both economic and social good for investors and investees, as well as the greater community and global Integrated Social Capital Marketplace. (Emerson, 2000: 30)

As Emerson (2000: 16) points out, twentieth-century thinking has been plagued by the 'schizophrenia of capitalism'. Even charitable trusts separate their economic and social investment activities. They generate funds for social investment through economic investment portfolios, and 75 per cent give little consideration to the *social* impact of their *economic* investing. Blended value, as a concept, seeks to end this dichotomy by encouraging investors to learn about the generation of social and economic returns through investments in social enterprises.

There are, however, some barriers to overcome before this is possible. Doherty et al. (2009b: 43) state that in 1998, when Divine Chocolate set up, they struggled to attract start-up finance. Only a loan guarantee agreement helped them to secure a loan. The reasons for these difficulties can be partly explained by understanding the concept of **gearing** (the ratio of total capital to debt finance), demonstrated in Figure 11.3.

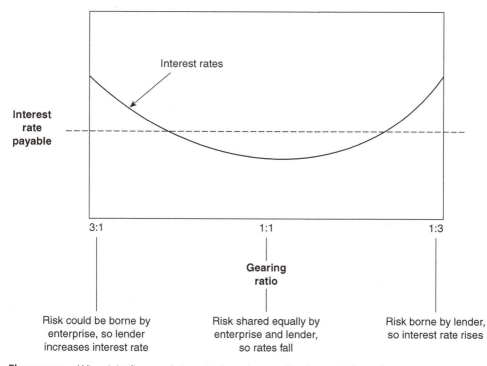

Figure 11.3 Why debt finance interest rates change: the impact of gearing on access to debt finance

The reason that many social enterprises pay higher interest rates or struggle to obtain finance is not, as is commonly supposed, that they focus on non-profit activities; it is because their capital structure is unattractive to lenders.[4] As Ridley-Duff (2009a) reports, lenders may want the facility to convert loans to shares as a condition of lending (i.e. turn 'low-risk' debt finance into 'high-risk' equity finance *in order to lower their own risks*). Non-profits constituted as a CLG cut themselves off from some sources of debt finance, and *encourage dependence on grants and donations* whether conscious of this or not.

This information is helpful when negotiating with banks. Faced with questions like 'So you are not primarily interested in profit?', 'What are your assets?', 'Who are your guarantors?', 'So no-one owns the enterprise as such?', what response can a social enterprise make? If the organisation is a CLG, one response is to develop a plan for trading that will generate regular surpluses, then return to the bank with evidence that surpluses are being made. This 'chicken and egg' situation, however, will be uninviting for those ideologically opposed to profit-making. However, such activities do not imply profit-maximisation, only the making of profits to service a debt (effectively keeping the finances of the enterprise 'in balance'). If opposition to profit-making cannot be overcome, the best income strategy remains one based on fundraising in order to acquire assets. Debt finance, however, will remain inaccessible while the organisation has no assets or trading surpluses.

In 1999, the UK Treasury published the *Enterprise and Social Exclusion* report that brought these issues to the fore. As a result, the DTI established the Phoenix Fund, which ran from 1999 to 2006. This was the forerunner to community development finance initiatives (**CDFIs**) providing loans to disadvantaged communities. Doherty et al. (2009b: 15) state that by 2003 there were 23 CDFIs in existence supporting social enterprises in communities across the UK.

Concurrently, there has also been a resurgence of interest in **credit unions**: membership in the UK has doubled from 343,155 to 704,535 over the last six years (ABCUL, 2009: 6). In 2010, the legislative framework will change to allow credit unions to open business accounts and lend to social enterprises (making possible lending similar to that practised by the Grameen Bank, discussed in Chapter 5). In the UK alone, this will open up more than half a billion pounds of additional capital that can be lent to cooperatives and social enterprises.

Social Investment Funds

In the last two decades, banks more sympathetic to social enterprise have emerged or rebranded themselves. Significant amongst these are Charity Bank, Cooperative Bank, Triodos Bank and Unity Trust Bank. While they support social returns, they do not necessarily assess risk in ways that are fundamentally different to mainstream banking institutions, and are not necessarily a cheaper source of debt finance. They are, however, more likely to offer expertise and networks of investors who are ideologically sympathetic.

Alongside these banking institutions are new social enterprise investment funds. Examples include The Social Enterprise Loan Fund, Key Fund Yorkshire, Big Issue Invest, SOVEC and Bridges Community Ventures (see Case 11.3). There is currently no consistency in the way they offer investment support and advice. Of the five, Key Fund Yorkshire is notable for offering a mix of grant, loan and equity finance in the form of **patient capital** (repayable over longer periods at competitive rates of interest).

Price (2008) comments that the trend towards social investment is supported by **venture philanthropy**. The contentious aspect of this development is the extent to which external investors will acquire voting rights and be able to control the social enterprises in which they invest. One strategy for limiting influence is to grant only one vote to each *shareholder* rather than one to each *share* (see Table 7.5). The upside of granting shares, according to Emerson (2000), is that it promotes a *learning culture* *amongst social investors* by encouraging them to track the social and economic value they create. This learning will, in cases of investor satisfaction, increase the funds available for social investment. This consideration applies equally to *internal (staff) investors* as robust and attractive arrangements can encourage employee owners to move their savings out of mainstream banks and 'economic investments' into their own **credit unions,** social enterprises or ethical and social investment funds (Brown, 2006; Erdal, 2008).

As Brown highlights, equity offers can raise larger amounts of capital to support social enterprise development. In 2002, Triodos Bank helped the Ethical Property Company raise £4.2 million. In 2004, it helped Café Direct raise £5 million. In both cases the interest from investors was sizable and both launches were heavily over-subscribed. Brown further highlights the social emphasis of some investors:

> in 1990 the Centre for Alternative Technology (CAT) raised £1 million by selling shares to investors who have no voting rights, have never received a dividend and who cannot easily sell their shares. Traidcraft has raised nearly £5 million through four successive share issues over the last twenty years, but up to 2004 had never paid a dividend to shareholders. Until the most recent share issue in 2002, Traidcraft shareholders had no voting rights, and even now voting rights are restricted. (2006: 74)

He also states:

> the amount of capital raised by social enterprises and ethical businesses through the issue of share capital is small ... less than 1% of the total amount invested in ethical investment funds in the UK, which according to EIRIS stood at £4.3 billion in December 2003 (EIRIS, 2005). Ethical investment is only a tiny part of overall UK institutional investment, which was valued at £1,652 billion in 2002. (2006: 74)

Brown (2006: 75) estimates that growth of 10 per cent per annum in ethical investment markets and an increased share of the market for social enterprises could provide a £1.2 billion investment boost.

SEMINAR EXERCISE   Comparing approaches to social investment

Cases 11.3 and 11.4 are available on the companion website at www.sagepub.co.uk/ridleyduff.

Part 1 (approx. 40 minutes)

1   Divide the seminar participants into two equal groups (5 minutes).
2   Ask the members of group 1 to read Case 11.3, and members of group 2 to read Case 11.4 (10 minutes).
3   Ask all group 1 members to convene and outline the problems they would like to resolve in their 'social capital market' (25 minutes).
4   Ask all group 2 members to convene and clarify the innovations of the Mondragón banking system, and how this differs from financial institutions in the UK (25 minutes).

(Continued)

(Continued)

Part 2 (approx. 40 minutes)

5 Get the participants from each group to form pairs: each pair should comprise one person from group 1 and one from group 2 (5 minutes).
6 Ask each pair to critically assess what the financial institutions in Case 11.3 and Case 11.4 can learn from each other (25 minutes).
7 Report your findings to the other members of the seminar group and discuss them with your tutor (10 minutes).

Conclusions

We have discussed the opportunities for income generation and investment within social enterprises. While UK policies on social enterprise emphasise trading levels, we have also discussed the ongoing relevance of grants and donations, as well as the emergent social investment industry. The income streams for voluntary and charity organisations based on gifts (grants and donations) are being replaced by a growing reliance on trading (sometimes unrelated to mission). There are two questions to ask about this move to contracting. Firstly, can social enterprises delivering services under contract radically reshape society? Secondly, will contracts provide sufficiently robust resources for long-term capacity building, growth and sustainability when commissioning bodies tend to use them as a way of reducing their own costs? Cooperatives, on the other hand, have the challenge of ending their *over*-dependence on trading, and developing capital structures that can attract the support of members and social investors.

The social enterprise movement has encouraged a more 'business-like' approach to income generation, increasing the focus on market trading, entering into contracts for outsourced public services, and developing institutions to increase social investment. Alongside these efforts is the continuation of fundraising to generate funds that increase social impact. In the final parts of the chapter, we discussed social investment options and the increasing supply of loans and equity targeted at social entrepreneurs and enterprises. We used case studies to clarify the ebb and flow of practice, and the shifting sands of the social economy, as organisations move from grants to contracts, and CICs, cooperatives and employee-owned companies evolve models that are more attractive to private investors. We highlight, therefore, the diversity of practice and the benefits of retaining an open mind on the future mix of income streams in social and economic development.

SEMINAR EXERCISE   Analysing income streams and investments

Materials to support this exercise are available on the accompanying website at www. sagepub.co.uk/ridleyduff.

This exercise involves using Table 11.1 and Figure 11.2 to analyse three further cases (Cases 11.5, 11.6 and 11.7 available on the companion website).

(Continued)

(Continued)

1 Organise seminar participants into groups of three, and provide them with the three cases.
2 Use Table 11.1 and Figure 11.2 to analyse each case.
3 Identify the income streams and investment activity.
4 Identify the types of funds that each organisation uses and/or creates.
5 Report your findings and compare them to the rest of the group.

SUMMARY OF LEARNING

In this chapter, we have argued the following:

- Social enterprises (ideally) operate on a profit-making basis for the purpose of making social investments.
- A social investment mindset is different to a fundraising mindset. It involves tracking and learning from the investments made in order to increase both economic and social value.
- The concept of 'blended value' embodies the notion of creating enterprises that add economic and social value to their stakeholder communities.
- Social enterprises have a wide range of trading options open to them (direct sales, indirect sales, contracts for services and retailing).
- Some social enterprises continue to rely on grants and donations as part of a 'mixed receipts' strategy that contributes to sustainability.
- Social enterprises may need to carefully consider the impact of their constitution and income generating strategy when seeking to raise debt finance (loans).
- The availability of equity finance is limited to organisations capable of devising a capital structure that allows social investment while retaining political control over social aims, outcomes and impacts.

QUESTIONS AND POSSIBLE ESSAY ASSIGNMENTS

1 Using examples, describe and critically assess the contribution of *integrated*, *supplementary* and *sustaining* income generation strategies to the development of a social enterprise.
2 'Social enterprises should not issue shares or accept equity finance.' Critically assess the limitations of this statement and the strategies that can be used to raise equity finance without compromising the social and economic integrity of the enterprise.
3 What factors make it hard for a social enterprise to obtain loan finance? Critically assess the strategies that can be adopted to make an organisation more 'investment ready'.

FURTHER READING

Two useful primers, one practical and one theoretical, will help you to grasp the range and complexity of arguments initiated by this chapter. The first are the *Introductory Packs* available from the UK's Finance Hub (http://www.financehub.org.uk/introductory_guides.aspa). These are aimed primarily at voluntary and charity organisations, although some of the guides in the series do discuss equity finance. The second primer is Emerson's 'The nature of returns' (2000), provided on the companion website. While sometimes polemical, the paper grapples with the nature of social and economic returns, and articulates the case for 'blended value' as a strategy for investment.

Perhaps the best current example of 'blended value' is the social investment system at Mondragón. Chapter 8 of Whyte and Whyte's *Making Mondragón* (1991) describes the history of the cooperative banking system, and the contract of association that underpins the relationship between the member cooperatives and the bank. Chapter 16 examines the 'changing role' of the bank as it finds ways to defend and rescue organisations facing trading difficulties.

Further coverage is provided by two contributions from Jim Brown. The first is a practical 'toolkit' (Brown, 2007) written for the Finance Hub that helps voluntary sector organisations to prepare for funding applications. The second is 'Designing equity finance for social enterprises' (2006) . This will be of particular interest to cooperative social enterprises and mutual societies. Empirical research on the link between structure, management practices and finance can be found in Ridley-Duff's paper 'Cooperative social enterprises: company rules, access to finance and management practice' (2009a).

Further reading material is available on the companion website at www.sagepub.co.uk/ridleyduff.

USEFUL RESOURCES

Baxi Partnership, http://www.baxipartnership.co.uk/

Big Issue Invest, http://www.bigissueinvest.com/

Blendedvalue.org, http://www.blendedvalue.org

Bridges Community Ventures, http://www.bridgesventures.com/

CapacityBuilders, http://capacitybuilders.org.uk/

Charity Bank, http//www.charitybank.org/

ClearlySo, http://www.clearlyso.com/resource-library.jsf

Cooperative Bank, http://www.co-operativebank.co.uk

Cooperative Capital Fund, http://cooperativefund.org/coopcapital

Cooperative Enterprise Hub, http://www.co-operative.coop/enterprisehub/

FutureBuilders (England), http://www.futurebuilders-england.org.uk/

Key Fund Yorkshire, http://www.keyfundyorks.org.uk/

KnowHow NonProfit, http://www.knowhownonprofit.org/

New Economics Foundation, http://www.proveandimprove.org/new/

SOVEC, http://www.sovec.nl/

The Acid Test, http://www.seyh.org.uk/acidtest/

The Association of British Credit Unions, www.abcul.coop

The Social Enterprise Academy, http://www.theacademy-ssea.org.uk

The Social Enterprise Investment Fund, http://www.partnershipsuk.org.uk/View-News.aspx?id=100

The Social Enterprise Loan Fund, http://www.tself.org.uk/

The Social Investment Business, http://www.socialinvestmentbusiness.org/

Triodos Bank, http://www.triodos.co.uk/uk/business_banking/

UK Social Investment Forum, http://www.uksif.org/

Unity Trust Bank, http://www.unity.uk.com/

UnLtd Advantage, http://unltd.org.uk/template.php?ID=177&PageName=unltd advantage

NOTES

1 This is why the word 'trustee' to used to describe the member of a charity board.
2 This information was provided by Rory Ridley-Duff in his capacity as ICT consultant to both NCVO and CRAC. The claims are backed by information available from each organisation's ICT systems.
3 One author attended the launch of the CIC at Social Enterprise London, at which Stephen Sears spoke about his own role in the development of the legislation.
4 This said, scepticism that social economy organisations can repay loans plays a part (see Knell, 2008). One student, a banker turned social enterprise adviser, commented that there was a further substantive reason. The reputation of a bank could be severely damaged if it withdrew overdraft or loan facilities from a charity. This created a culture that led bank managers to be cautious in their lending to non-profits.

Measuring Social Outcomes and Impacts **12**

Rory Ridley-Duff, Pam Seanor and Mike Bull

Learning Objectives

In this chapter, we explore 'blended value' in accounting practice, and consider how social enterprises aim to concurrently assess and report their social and economic outcomes. By the end of this chapter you will be able to:

- critically assess 'performance' as a concept

- compare and contrast social accounting and audit (SAA) and social return on investment (SROI)

- explain the differences between outputs, outcomes and impacts

- critically evaluate how the criteria for assessing impact affect management practice

- evaluate the contribution of social auditing and SROI to understanding performance.

The key arguments that will be developed in this chapter are:

- Social performance and social impact are under-theorised concepts.
- Social enterprises that measure their social impact focus on outcomes and impacts, not outputs.
- Two dominant approaches to measuring social impact in the UK have emerged: one based on 'bottom-up' social auditing; the other based on 'top-down' social return on investment.
- Assumptions about social impact measurement affect management practice.
- Developing an understanding of systems theory helps to understand and conceptualise SROI.
- Social accounting emphasises inter-disciplinary skills in collecting, interpreting and reporting qualitative and quantitative data.

Introduction

So far in the second half of the book we have considered a wide range of issues that enable the formation and development of a viable enterprise. However, as discussed in previous chapters, *social* enterprises aim to achieve more than viability. This chapter asks a more challenging question. How can people assess if their organisation is *socially* sustainable? How can they assess their impact on the communities in which they are embedded, and the impact of their organisation on the environment? Indeed, how can 'social performance' be theorised?

This chapter tackles these questions. We will argue that different assumptions about the quality and quantity of evidence needed to assess 'social impact' affect *what* gets measured, and *how* it gets measured. Each approach makes assumptions about the role that stakeholders play in contributing to, and receiving information about, social impact. In line with previous chapters, we adopt a constructivist approach to emphasise the link between ideology and management practice. While recognising the political value attached to advocates' claims that social audit and social return on investment are 'objective', we do not regard either qualitative or quantitative measures as objective in an absolute sense. Instead, we regard them as aspects of an interpretive framework that stakeholders deploy in arguments for (or against) the allocation of resources. The reporting of social outcomes cannot sit outside this.

We continue to encourage a critical approach to the conceptualisation of performance and social impact. Firstly, we discuss the ambiguities of performance as a concept in order to create a framework for assessing social impact measurement itself. We apply this to an exploration of two approaches that have emerged in the UK: **social accounting and audit (SAA)** and social return on investment (SROI). The former is advocated by members of the Social Audit Network, while the latter, based on work in the mid 1990s by Jed Emerson (at the Roberts Enterprise Development Fund in the US), has been adapted by the New Economics Foundation in the UK (see Pearce and Kay, 2008; Nicholls, 2009a). Towards the end of the chapter, we critically discuss the implications for practice.

Performance as a Concept

Consider the statements in the accompanying exercise 'What is performance?' All the interviewees (from website Exercise 12.1), having lived under a target-driven regime for over a decade, were aware of the limitations of quantitative performance measures. To navigate the ambiguity in their statements, a multi-dimensional model of social and economic rationality was used (Ridley-Duff, 2005; 2008a). The model (Table 12.1) clarifies different constructions of 'performance', and how they link to each other and contribute to social impact.

EXERCISE   What is performance?

Exercise 12.1 on the companion website contains further materials to undertake this as a seminar activity.

Example 1

Performance can be shown as hard evidence, but you would surely want some qualitative change? If people are performing their job correctly, they are showing some change in their ethics ... their broad values and approaches which aren't open, or only with great difficulty, to hard facts.

(Continued)

(Continued)

Example 2

It's not about efficiency, not about tasks, it is about being effective ... and personal happiness and goals and things. If people aren't happy, they don't perform ... Happiness is the key to it all for me. Sounds a bit on the hippy side, but there you are.

Example 3

I get frustrated ... while I like the debate ... I like to move forward to action and achievement as a result. That will be different for different people ... The other thing that comes into it ... this is the bit where I hesitate because it is so difficult to measure ... it is someone who achieves what they've got to do, but also achieves growth and has a good attitude. Now how do you measure a good attitude?

Example 4

It's keeping that cycle of learning and ongoing movement ... not stagnating ... when you talk in all those [competency] terms that are the 'in' terms ... it switches people off ... it's good stuff, it is, but people think of all these manuals, and forms they have to fill in. I like to keep the free flow, something that you don't feel strangled by. That helps you to get through the competency framework.

(health sector manager interviews, February/March 2009)

Questions:

1 Can social dimensions of performance (ethics, attitude, happiness and learning) be measured?
2 What proxies might indicate 'good' social performance?
3 What impact does social performance have on the development of social, ethical and human capital?

Table 12.1   Theorising performance and social impact

Type	Characteristics	Performance and social impact
Social performance (supported by social rationality): 'developing a community of interest' Skills in getting and giving *attention* in order to form, develop, maintain and end relationships		
Emotion	Giving and getting access or information that clarifies emotional commitments Giving and getting access or information that stimulates emotion, and communicates emotional attitudes and intentions	Performance as the ability to interpret social network dynamics and clarify emotional commitments in order to help people process emotions and make decisions about their relationships

(Continued)

Table 12.1 *(Continued)*

Type	Characteristics	Performance and social impact
Information	Giving and getting information about people, ideas and tasks so that access to people can be organised or direct assistance offered Giving and getting attention through sharing knowledge, story-telling and joking	Performance as the ability to obtain, organise, analyse and use information to develop human relationships for their own sake (rather than in pursuit of a task)
Access	Giving and getting access to people, ideas and resources Giving and getting attention (verbal and non-verbal) that conveys personal interest Presenting oneself in ways that induce others to communicate and commit to ongoing relationships	Performance as the ability to create, use or shape tasks in such a way that they contribute to the formation and development of satisfying relationships

Economic performance (supported by economic rationality): 'getting the job done'
Skills in getting and giving *assistance* in order to complete tasks

Physical	Giving and getting commitments to meet face-to-face, travel and relocate. Facilitating meetings and providing direct assistance with physical tasks Physical behaviour that fuels commitments to care for (and economically support) colleagues and dependants	Performance as the capacity to motivate oneself to arrange and attend meetings with others, and adopt or model behaviours that support the effective and efficient completion of tasks
Intellectual	Giving and getting (sharing) conceptual ideas that provide alternative ways of understanding how to go about tasks Knowledge of how to give and get assistance in ways that induce and maintain mutual commitment	Performance as the capacity to develop and disseminate expertise, and apply it in ways that bring about the effective and/ or efficient performance of tasks
Material	Giving and getting non-physical and non-intellectual support (e.g. money, time, contracts) that lead to material gains in pay, cost-effectiveness and service or trading opportunities	Performance as the capacity to manage money and time effectively in the acquisition, delivery and completion of tasks and contracts

Source: adapted from Ridley-Duff, 2009b: 42, Table 5

The framework was developed during a three-year study of social enterprise governance to highlight competing rationales for enterprise that recursively shape each other (Ridley-Duff, 2005). It was revised further during a 12-month study of 'performance coaching' (Ridley-Duff, 2009b). The model outlines a *relational* perspective on organisations in which people – usually outside the management group – are viewed as the *primary* source of satisfaction (and dissatisfaction) at work. Relationships constitute the 'ends' of enterprise, rather than the 'means', and are valued for their own sake. This view competes with a task-based view in which people – more often managers or entrepreneurs – pursue goals (status, income, recognition) and organisational objectives (missions, targets). From this view, relationships are 'means' and not 'ends', subordinated to the pursuit of individual or collectively determined 'goals'. Exercise 12.1 (on the companion website) highlights that people as well as process matter, and that performance can be viewed through many lenses. Different people have different views on what they perceive is important (to themselves and to others).

Emerson (2000) frames this as a difference between 'interactive social capital' (social value created through the interactions of people with each other) and 'transactive social capital' (social and economic value deriving from the transactions that social interaction makes possible). The relational view of organisation is shaped by **social rationality,** a decision-making model that supports the formation, development, management and maintenance of relationships. Hunt (1928) frames this perspective as *social intelligence*. Gates' (1998) critique of Anglo-American societies suggests that this intelligence is being lost while technical competence develops. Competing with this perspective is the task-based view that organisations (and therefore the people in them) serve a mission, goal or 'higher purpose'. In this case, economic rationality dominates by elevating the pursuit of a 'task' or 'goal' above the individual members of the organisation (and even the organisation itself) so that they are regarded as subservient to it. This world view has been strengthening in western corporations, reshaping business practice (Miller and Rice, 1967), influencing public administration (Hood, 1995) and – despite resistance – affecting notions of management in the social economy (Dart, 2004).

As Turnbull (1994; 1995; 2001; 2002) claims, social interaction necessarily *precedes* any economic transaction, and therefore provides more scope for economy (in the broadest sense). This being the case, economy depends *primarily* on understanding efficient and effective 'social interaction' in which financial management is just one of many elements. This reverses the dominant logic of economics based on income–expenditure analysis, and has profound implications for accounting practice in social enterprises. Social intelligence not only acquires equivalent status to economic competence, it reframes economic competence as just one of many forms of social intelligence that captures only a small part of performance in the organisation (and therefore only a small part of its 'impact').

Ridley-Duff's model (2005; 2009b) makes clearer how the greatest potential for impact occurs when all aspects of social and economic performance can be 'blended'. Anything that decreases the ability of people to assist each other inhibits social performance (i.e. limits their capacity to develop sustainable satisfying relationships). Similarly, anything that inhibits relationship development potentially decreases economic performance (i.e. limits their capacity to collaborate to achieve goals or 'missions'). Consequently, the need for a holistic approach that interprets, analyses and reports 'blended value' continues to grow (see Nicholls, 2009b).

Social Accounting Practices

Early approaches to auditing and reporting social accounts in the UK (see box) can be traced back to work by the Industrial Common Ownership Movement and models for workers' cooperatives in the north of England. This is evidenced by *Social Audit: A Management Tool for Cooperative Working* (Spreckley, 1981).

Principles underpinning early social auditing in the UK

1   It must be multi-perspective, i.e. include views from key stakeholders, staff, customers, beneficiaries, funders and investors etc.
2   It should be comprehensive, i.e. cover all activities of the social enterprise.
3   The organisation should learn from the exercise by comparing performance over time with other, similar, organisations.
4   Social audit should be undertaken regularly and become embedded in the running of the social enterprise.
5   The social accounts prepared should be checked by an independent panel or assessor.
6   The findings of the verified (i.e. audited) social accounts should be circulated and discussed.
7   The process should underpin a philosophy of continuous improvement.

A social audit, therefore, starts with two interrelated questions:

- What questions do you need to ask to evaluate the organisation's social impact?
- How will you know if you are 'successful'?

The first question can be enlightened by examining a clause from Geof Cox's Stakeholder Model Ltd (Case 7.1). One clause (shown here) sets out the perceived purpose of social audit by providing a way to assess governance processes and their internal and external impacts. A social audit, therefore, delves into deeper questions of what and why the enterprise does what it does, and who it is done to (or for). For example, Balance (Case 8.4) analyses the former, stimulating SEs to critically reflect on 'How you do what you do – not what you do'. Clause 28 of Case 7.1 mentions 'employees', 'customers', 'suppliers', 'people living in areas where the Company operates' and the 'natural environment' as stakeholders for the purposes of social audit.

Case 7.1   Stakeholder Model Ltd, Articles of Association, Clause 28

28.2   A social audit of the Company's activities may, by resolution of the Directors, be undertaken annually in addition to the financial audit required by law.

    28.2.1   The role of the social audit shall be to identify the social costs and benefits of the Company's work, and to enable an assessment to be made of the Company's overall performance in relation to its objects more easily than may be made from financial accounts alone.

    28.2.2   Such a social audit may be drawn up by an independent assessor appointed by the Directors, or by the Directors, who may submit their report for verification or comments to any independent assessor.

    28.2.3   A social audit may include an assessment of the internal democracy and decision making of the Company; the wages, health and safety, skill sharing and education opportunities of its employees, or other matters concerning the overall personal or job satisfaction of employees; and an assessment of the Company's activities externally, including its effects on customers and suppliers, on people living in areas where the Company operates, and on the natural environment.

The second question (How will you know if you are 'successful'?) extends into the domain of research philosophy. 'Success' is itself a socially constructed concept, and the issue is whether the quality of the evidence and the interpretation by an 'independent assessor' meet the criteria of 'success' established by the members of the enterprise being audited, or the lens that the assessor has been trained to use during auditing. The stakeholder model relies on an independent assessor to prepare the social audit, or to verify one created by an enterprise's directors.

Paton (2003) observes that the current trend toward social auditing is part of an 'audit explosion' (see Powell and DiMaggio, 1991). Organisations use audit to demonstrate their efficiency and effectiveness. Paton emphasises a number of differences between social audits and regular 'institutionalised' financial audits: they are undertaken voluntarily; they involve certification by a third party; they apply to governance and management *systems* (not just outcomes); and they offer scope for interviews and observation alongside documentary evidence. As Mook et al. (2007a) point out, 'reporting and auditing' is the preferred lexicon of non-profit and social organisations, and the term 'accounting' may be avoided. The rationale for this 'alternative' language is explained by Pearce:

> *Social audit is best understood as a reaction against conventional accounting principles and practices. These centre on the financial viability and profitability of the individual economic enterprise. By contrast, social audit proposes a broader financial and economic perspective, reaching far beyond the individual enterprise ... which may not be amenable to quantification in monetary terms. (2003: 124)*

Part of this reaction is linked to a different philosophical outlook. Mook et al. (2007a) contrast the way the accounting profession is viewed by social auditors and 'rationalist' accountants. In mainstream accounting, 'concepts such as profit and loss are viewed as a reality rather than a particular way of constructing reality' (2007a: 3). In contrast:

> Social organizations can be understood more fully if they are studied contextually as organisms that affect and are affected by their communities. Within this context, accountants are active participants in shaping reality, a point of view that runs counter to the widely held perception of accountants as passive recorders of information. (2007a: 7)

Having set out the history and terrain that social accounting aims to cover, we now consider two approaches. The first (SAA) is becoming the method of choice in cooperative and community enterprises seeking to use accounting practice to engage stakeholders. The second (SROI) is becoming the method of choice for social and public sector investors seeking to understand the impact of their philanthropy and contracting.

A qualitative approach: social accounting and audit (SAA)

Social accounting and audit (SAA) is a flexible framework for capturing (and affecting) social impact. The framework is predominantly *qualitative* in nature, and according to the Social Audit Network it enables organisations to:

- account fully for their *social, environmental* and *economic* impacts
- report on performance
- provide essential information for planning future action and improving performance.

The process (see Figure 12.1) involves social enterprises following a cycle to develop their understanding of the impact they have on their community of interest and

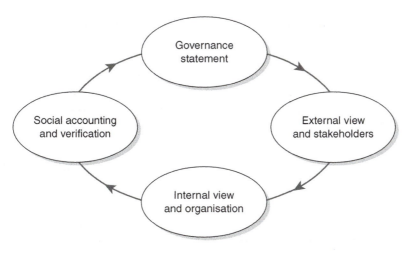

Figure 12.1   The process of social audit

The Social Audit was part of the initial development of social enterprise in 1978 at Beechwood College.

(where relevant) beneficiaries. Integral to the process is the opportunity to consult and account to stakeholders identified in the governance statement, and provide an honest assessment of the 'worth' of the enterprise.

Pearce and Kay state:

> *The first step is about organisations clarifying their mission, objectives and related activities, and the values and principles that underpin all their actions, as well as identifying their key stakeholders. The second step involves recognising the quantitative and qualitative indicators that enable the enterprise to report effectively on its performance and impact against its stated mission, objectives and values through data collection and consulting appropriately with its key stakeholders. The third step is about bringing all the collected information together into social accounts that are then verified by an independent panel that, once satisfied, issues a social audit statement. Most organisations keep social accounts for a period which usually runs concurrent with their financial year. (2008: 9)*

The SAA framework, available through the Social Audit Network, has a considerable following and is supported by a network of approved auditors. Gordon (2009) claims that the SAA framework is much cheaper to implement than SROI – with direct costs of £2000–3000 against £19k–£25k for SROI projects. External verification is a key selling feature that matches financial accounting practice, and the final report will have both marketing and management value.

Quantitative measures: social return on investment (SROI)

The SROI approach, originally developed by the Roberts Enterprise Development Fund, is adapted from more traditional economic tools of **cost–benefit analysis** (see Nicholls, 2009a). It aims to translate social impacts into financial values and is a predominantly (but not exclusively) *quantitative* approach. It is promoted in both the US and the UK, with the New Economics Foundation (NEF) adapting the model for use in the UK. The SROI Network outlines the approach as follows:

> *SROI is an approach to understanding and managing the impacts of a project, organisation or policy. It is based on stakeholders and puts financial value on the important impacts identified by stakeholders that do not have market values. SROI seeks to include the values of people that are often excluded from markets in the same terms as used in markets, that is money, in order to give people a voice in resource allocation decisions. SROI is a framework to structure thinking and understanding. It's a story not a number. The story should show how you understand the value created, manage it and can prove it.* (http://www.thesroinetwork.org/content/view/31/1/, accessed 20 May 2010)

NEF acknowledges that there are limitations if systems are not in place to collect data, and that the process is time consuming and demands a diverse range of 'soft' and 'hard' skills. Nicholls (2009a) also points out that SROI can rarely benchmark effectively and has to use proxies that can be directly linked to monetary values. Furthermore, in practice 'operating costs' are difficult to discern from 'core costs', and where organisations use goodwill, volunteer efforts and grant funding, these

Table 12.2 SROI impact analysis

Inputs	Activities	Outputs	Outcomes	Impacts
• Service contracts • Grants • Sales revenues • Volunteer time	• Training • Work placements • Jobs	• Number of people involved in training • Number and level of qualifications obtained	• Job skills learned • Soft skills learned • Well-being, social and personal development, • Life satisfaction • Increases in income • Reduced dependence on benefits • Reduction in reoffending and crime	• Subtract what would have happened anyway to estimate *impact* • Check that each column leads to accomplishing the mission

Source: based on NEF, 2006

may not be factored into the 'true cost' of a project. We add another consideration. The approach is based on an *a priori* model of change (inputs, activities, outputs, outcomes and impacts). While this enables comparisons to be made, and gives the process a structure, it inhibits an organisation from benchmarking against its own change model (as captured in a 'governance statement', for example).

The key innovation in the New Economics Foundation (NEF) approach is to move beyond 'outputs' and consider 'outcomes' and 'impacts'. While 'outputs' are amenable to quantitative measurement, 'outcomes' constitute *qualitative* changes in the lives of the people affected by the social enterprise's employment practices, products and/or services. 'Impacts', however, require further quantitative analysis. An assessment is made whether the 'outcomes' would have occurred anyway, or whether they are a result of contributions by the social enterprise (Table 12.2). If the latter, the monetary impact of the qualitative changes can be assessed and aggregated, then presented in such a way that the value of each £1 invested can be demonstrated to potential funders or investors.

SROI frames the issues it is going to address in terms of 'desired outcomes', and has sufficient flexibility to allow stakeholders to define these. While adopting a quantitative approach, it is justified on the basis that the social sector needs a method of financial accounting that can bridge into the world of public sector procurement and social investment. SROI, therefore, is designed primarily to meet the needs of social investors (just as statutory accounts are designed primarily to help financial investors). Also, just as management accounts are needed to supplement statutory accounts, an SAA report may be needed to supplement SROI to provide the 'internal' view needed for management activities.

Nevertheless, the attribution of financial values to 'outcomes' in order to calculate 'savings' to wider society *is* an accounting innovation. Where organisations need to demonstrate value to commissioning bodies, charitable trusts and social investors, SROI offers an advantage. Arguably, SROI is more than an accounting tool. It is also a way of thinking that enables a social enterprise to identify the benefits of their service to any other party (expressed in financial terms). As such it has value as a sales tool (in individual tender situations) and as a marketing tool (for sector-level promotion) by setting out how social value is created by social enterprises.

SAA and SROI: Similarities and Differences

The SAA and SROI approaches share the aim of benefiting people by clarifying and measuring social impacts. Nonetheless there are tensions between these two approaches. In our experience, support agencies appear to promote one, or the other, but rarely both approaches. SAA emphasises a bottom-up community development approach focused upon building capacity and resulting in a bespoke social auditing framework. The SAA approach emphasises social rationality by prioritising relationships with stakeholders, soliciting and reporting their views, and using the process to stimulate further discussion. While stakeholders play a role in SROI, their involvement is more instrumental. They provide 'data' on 'outcomes' to support econometric calculations.

A criticism of SAA's approach, however, is that it produces reports that are not (easily) comparable to those of other organisations (Nicholls, 2009a). Because SROI is focused on external relationships, it is driven by government and social policy agendas (mission is matched to the fundholder's objectives), and seeks to measure the effect of service delivery (tasks are matched to fundholder's objectives). This 'task-based' view encourages a level of standardisation in which individual organisations act as suppliers of data that commissioners and policy makers can use to decide their priorities. As Pearce and Kay write:

> SROI is attractive to investors, funders and contractors, especially in the public sector, because it speaks the language of business and gives them a number. However, a related concern is that such interest can tend to make the SROI process funder and investor led. (2008: 18)

Pearce (2009) comments that social return on investment is over-emphasised by government and warns of the danger that the UK and Scotland governments are expressing a 'worrying trend towards control' rather than acting as enablers of community-led enterprise.

Another difference is in the steps each approach requires: the Social Audit Network (SAN) has devised an infrastructure to support quality assurance, which is lacking in SROI. Pearce (2009) points out that the verification process for a social audit involves three to five persons, normally chaired by someone with experience, and drawn from a register of approved social auditors. The independence of the panel underpins a 'rigorous' and 'tough' day-long process of analysis that is concurrently 'creative and constructive'.

In practice, there is room for both frameworks, each serving different needs. Pearce and Kay (2008) report progress towards this by members of both networks (Table 12.3). Interestingly, practitioners in both networks also agreed how their approaches differ:

> One difference is that SROI is predicated on the notion that a financial indicator may be found for a change that is achieved (sometimes using a proxy if no actual indicator is available). While SROI argues that 'the number is not as important as the story' the reality is that most people (and SROI reports) tend to focus on the number and the basis on which it is calculated.

SAA by no means rejects the importance of numbers and indeed advocates the use of financial indicators when this is appropriate. However, SAA believes that there are some outcomes and impacts which can only be described and reported using the views and perceptions of stakeholders – in effect the 'story'. (Pearce and Kay, 2008: 15)

Table 12.3 Common principles underpinning SAA and SROI

Principle	Definition
Stakeholder engagement	Engaging with, and consulting, stakeholders is central to the process of social accounting in order to understand the impact of the organisation
Scope and materiality	Acknowledge and articulate the values and objectives of stakeholders before agreeing which aspects are to be included in the social accounting process, so that stakeholders can draw conclusions about performance and impact
Understanding change	Articulate clearly how activities work, and how they contribute to the social and charitable objectives of the organisation and its stakeholders. Evaluate these on the basis of the evidence gathered
Comparative	Make comparisons of performance and impact using appropriate benchmarks, annual targets and external standards
Transparency	Demonstrate the basis on which the findings may be considered accurate and honest; show they will be reported to and, where appropriate and feasible, discussed with stakeholders
Verification	Ensure appropriate independent verification of the social accounts
Embedded	Ensure that the process of social accounting and audit becomes embedded in the life cycle and management practices of the organisation

Source: based on Pearce and Kay, 2008

Pearce and Kay (2008) view the starting points for the two approaches as different. SAA is focused on the need for organisation members to be clear about their vision, mission, objectives and activities, and the identification of stakeholders who are either affected by, or can affect, the organisation. These stakeholders become partners in the process of social accounting and are consulted on how they view the organisation's performance and impact. While SROI starts from a similar point, it identifies the stakeholders' objectives in relation to their engagement with the organisation (as 'inputs', 'activities', 'outputs' etc.) and develops financial indicators to assess the value of their involvement.

The emphasis on and use of financial indicators places SROI within a positivist discourse linked to mainstream economics, without presenting any serious challenge to it. While the two frameworks appear to prescribe different paths for organisations – the SAA approach is presented as 'bottom-up' and 'grassroots', while the SROI community reflects a 'top-down' approach (Nicholls, 2009b) – both make claims to be 'objective' representations of 'reality'. However, those undertaking an SAA audit are advised to consult stakeholders on how performance should be evaluated: there is scope for stakeholders to *construct* criteria and shape their organisational reality. SROI advisers, on the other hand, seek to present performance in predefined ways (as outcomes and impacts) by deploying an *a priori* theory of social change. Measurements are presented in ways that meet the needs of public commissioners and social investors, rather than the organisation's stakeholders. This being the case, SAA emphasises the access, information and emotional needs of stakeholders and demonstrates commitment to a social rationality perspective. SROI requires access to information (in a one-way exchange), and then uses this to undertake an intellectual task that measures material value. It deploys social rationality instrumentally in order to pursue an economic rationality 'end'.

SEMINAR EXERCISE   Analysing approaches to social impact measurement

Further materials (and Cases 12.2 and 12.3) are available on the accompanying website at www.sagepub.co.uk/ridleyduff.

1 Organise the seminar participants into groups of three (members A, B and C).
2 Give Case 12.2 to group member A.
3 Give Case 12.3 to group member B.
4 Give an evaluation grid to group member C.
5 Ask group member A to explain the Icarus approach, while group member C analyses and records the types of performance that are stimulated and measured by it.
6 Ask group member B to explain the NEF approaches, while group member C analyses and records the types of performance that are stimulated and measured by it.
7 Ask group member C to show their analysis to members A and B. Discuss and, if necessary, amend the interpretation.
8 Join with another group and compare your analysis of the approaches to social accounting.

Critical Perspectives on Social Accounting

Nicholls (2009a) outlines the importance of evidencing social value as part of a search for sustainable solutions to social change. It is, however, more than this. It can also be seen as one of the principal marketing strategies for social enterprises (both individually and collectively), advancing 'balance' in enterprise management based on enterprise stakeholders' perceptions of performance (Bull, 2006; 2007). Paton (2003) hints at this motive when he reports that practitioners engage in performance measurement for many reasons. They may wish: to develop relationships with (different) stakeholders; to demonstrate competitive advantage; to improve performance; to satisfy funders' requirements. Each motive influences what is counted, how it is valued, and the level of willingness to change measures in the future. While it is assumed that social enterprise members will not be enthused in equal measure by these rationales, the disparity between the rhetoric and reality can sometimes be stark.

Coule (2008) suggests that these discrepancies can be partly explained by account-ability 'pulls' that influence stakeholder relationships and strategic priorities. This may explain why – in the wake of a decade consulting and promoting 'community interest companies' – there has been a 'pull' towards focusing on community benefit. The next decade, in light of recent events triggered by global banking institutions, and subsequent cuts in public services and jobs, may see the resurgence of arguments for the democ-ratisation of capital ownership and workplace management. Alternatively, the climate debate may move centre stage and increase the focus on environmental management. Whichever is the case, social accounting provides a means to explore (and critique) such questions as: who is setting the agenda? How much attention is paid to member, public and beneficiary interests? How much voice is given to funders and investors?

The proxies chosen to assess social impact *do* matter. The following items, for example, have already been used as proxies in discussing performance in this book:

- 50 per cent 'earned income' as a watershed for recognition as a social enterprise
- the volume of trading in different types of social enterprise
- the number of social enterprises reported in sector surveys
- the percentage of the workforce employed by social enterprises
- the number of jobs created (relative to investment levels) by social enterprises
- the number of people who benefit from the services of social enterprises.

Whilst we can acknowledge that the numbers superficially indicate significance and impact, these are quantitative, *income*- or *service*-related measures and *not* measure-ments of change or entrepreneurial innovation, or measures of well-being in society. In short, these are what NEF would call outputs, *not* outcomes. This, however, is not to suggest that qualitative measures are the most appropriate or without limita-tions, or that quantitative measures are irrelevant. Rather, we argue that there is a false dichotomy when qualitative and quantitative measures are separated from each other. They both need collection and interpretation to produce knowledge.

As Light (2008) comments, most measurement systems for social enterprise and entrepreneurship do not offer information on social change and impact. They offer a means for evaluating the effectiveness and efficiency of service delivery or the level and sophistication of internal organisational development (see Case 8.4, Balance).

Implications for Social Enterprises

In the drive to make social enterprise more 'efficient' and/or 'business-like', there is a comparison made by Stacey (2007: 39) that the systems have 'paid little attention … to ethics, ordinary human freedoms and the unknown nature of the final state towards which human action tends'. Though issues of ethics and human freedoms are talked about in social enterprise practices, both SAA and SROI are oriented towards the idea that organisations are systems of rational causality, with inputs leading to outputs, which can be 'objectively' assessed.

Grenier (2002) highlights that within this discourse, opportunity is presented as a 'fact' that the social enterprise needs to recognise or frame in order to take effective action. However, Maase and Dorst (2006) found that in practice the process does not begin by identifying a clear opportunity. Instead, there is a 'fuzzy' or 'trial-by-error-like' process guided by the desire to change something for the better. Goldstein et al. (2008) note that there is a decreasing tolerance for the emergent or unexpected outcomes that Mintzberg et al. (1998) see as a vital part of strategy development. There is less attention to the quality of network dynamics, and less discussion of the way structures and power relations are being changed by regimes of measurement and control. A potential problem is that organisation members may fail to question and challenge the thinking in which they become embedded, and be unable to relate this thinking to their own failure to achieve particular outcomes (Darwin et al., 2002).

One key assumption is the retention of a cause-and-effect model of change (Stacey, 2007) that has been rejected by an increasing number of social scientists as inadequate for understanding organisations and management practices (see Burrell and Morgan, 1979; Grey, 2005). Another key assumption is that, by considering input and output differences, feedback loops can be devised to sustain a balance, or an equilibrium, in a management system (Beer, 1966; 1972; Bateson, 2000). Examples of this in the social enterprise narrative include Meyskens (2008) who constructs social enterprise network relations based on a social and economic value continuum, using an inputs and outputs model. Martin and Osberg (2007) also describe the process of seeking equilibrium, while similar logic is embedded in strategic management development models such as Balance (Bull, 2006; 2007; see Case 8.4).

In practice, there is a gap between national policy and local interpretation with regards to outcomes, especially regarding the need to change systems and innovate. Commissioning bodies are still reluctant to risk what they perceive to be untried models. This being the case, not only do SAA and SROI still face an uphill struggle for legitimacy, but it may be a misplaced project. It might be more effective to focus on new **'communities of practice'** (Wenger, 1998) that utilise different economic logics to create new financial institutions and investment practices (see Brown, 2004; 2006). Though not yet discussed at length in the social enterprise literature, this sentiment echoes the emerging narratives in education and health care where concerns are being voiced over the continuing emphasis upon efficiency and national targets at the expense of local service quality (Drakeford, 2007; Darzi, 2008; Parker and Parker, 2007).

Conclusions

The private sector, as well as politicians on national and international stages, frequently talk of the need to seek a 'competitive advantage'. This chapter suggests that the marketing slogan used by cooperatives is equally apt for the social enterprise sector. There are also benefits from seeking a 'cooperative advantage' by modifying accounting practices and emphasising the value of collaboration in knowledge development, not just within the boundaries of a single organisation, but at the level of a social network that spans organisational boundaries. As Paton argues:

> Performance (particularly in social enterprises) is what … people more or less agree, implicitly or explicitly, to be performance. (2003: 5)

Where programme outcomes do not have a market, or a monetary value, but are valued within a community, it is difficult – perhaps impossible – to assess value using a commercial framework. The evidence in this chapter, and the book overall, suggests that these programmes can be valued through new forms of discursive democracy, and through research and audit processes that give a voice to stakeholders commensurate with their contribution to a cause.

Commercial frameworks marginalise social impact by emphasising discussions on what Emerson (2000) calls 'transactive social capital'. Social auditing has a different focus: 'interactive social capital'. As Pearce argues, social auditing can 'empower the many' rather than a few individuals. A second point in this chapter is the way social accounting involves stakeholders. In their deviation from traditional accounting practice, it becomes possible to envisage a business community where *any* group or individual who can affect or is affected by an organisation's business activity can decide how to influence the future direction of that business. They might be an employee, a volunteer, a customer, a client or a member of a geographic or interest-based community. Social audit and reporting provide an institution for capturing and acting on their feedback.

SUMMARY OF LEARNING

In this chapter, we have outlined issues in social audit, reporting and investment and the debates regarding the reporting of social performance. Principally, we have argued that:

- The concept and measurement of performance are hampered by an under-theorisation of the 'social' aspects of performance.
- Performance can be assessed from both a 'task' and a 'relationship' perspective.
- A constructionist approach is useful to understand the diversity of language and approaches in social accounting, and the role of the accountancy profession in shaping the 'reality' of social enterprise.
- Two approaches to assessing social performance have emerged, one based on auditing the views of stakeholders, the other based on monetising the 'impact' of the organisation's activities and assessing 'savings' to the public purse.
- The two approaches come together in the concepts of 'integrated accounting' and 'blended value accounting' that seek to report both economic and social outcomes together.
- SROI is grounded in a systems approach to assessing social impact, and in the econometric analysis of outputs, outcomes and impacts.
- Social accounting and audit (SAA) is grounded in assessing the perceptions of stakeholders in order to generate conversations, and stimulate changes in management action.
- Both approaches stress their 'objectivity', although SAA is more clearly oriented towards the development of a 'relational' approach to organisation development.

QUESTIONS AND POSSIBLE ESSAY ASSIGNMENTS

1 'Social accounting and audit (SAA) should be oriented towards the satisfaction of a social enterprise's internal stakeholders.' Critically assess the benefits and limitations of this view, and assess whether social auditing could also act as a marketing model for social enterprise.
2 Describe the analysis framework that underpins social return on investment (SROI). What advantages does this offer when tendering for public sector contracts or seeking social investment?
3 'Neither SAA nor SROI fully address the issue of social enterprise performance.' Critically assess the concept of performance, and the limitations in the way SAA and SROI assess it.

FURTHER READING

The debates surrounding the measurement of performance are well framed in Rob Paton's research into the topic in *Managing and Measuring Social Enterprises* (2003). The book is useful for its analysis of the way practitioners vary their engagement with performance measurement, and a constructivist perspective that 'gets inside' the different outlooks that inform practice. Further scholarly debate can be found in Mook et al.'s (2007b) paper in the journal *Voluntas* which advances the concept of 'integrated social accounting'. A useful examination and theorisation of 'blended value accounting' appears in Nicholls' 'We do good things, don't we?' (2009b), published in *Accounting, Organization and Society*.

There are several lengthy and accessible reports that refer to the development of practice. The first is a report from the Social Audit Network by Pearce and Kay (2008). Although somewhat partisan in its recommendations, it articulates findings from 70 participating organisations who have undertaken social accounting. Detailed practitioner guidance on social audit is available in the form of Spreckley's *Social Audit Toolkit* (4th edn, 2008) published by Local

Livelihoods, while guidance on SROI has been produced by the Cabinet Office (2009) in the form of *A Guide to Social Return on Investment*.

Further reading material is available on the companion website at www.sagepub.co.uk/ridleyduff.

USEFUL RESOURCES

Balance diagnostic tool, http://www.socialenterprisebalance.org/
Enhanced Analytics Initiative, http://www.enhanced-analytics.com
Local Livelihood (Social Audit), http://www.uk.locallivelihoods.com/Moduls/WebSite/Page/Default.aspx?Pag_Id=163
MaRS Social Metrics Report, http://www.marsdd.com/buzz/reports/socialmetrics
Prove and Improve, http://www.provean-dimprove.org
Social reporting blog, http://ifad-un.blogspot.com/
SROI Network, http://www.thesroinetwork.org
The Social Audit Network, http://socialauditnetwork.org.uk

Postscript – Social Enterprise in 2050

In this short postscript, each author gives their personal view on the possibilities for social enterprise in the decades ahead.

Rory Ridley-Duff

Naomi Klein (2007) attributes the following statement to Milton Friedman:

> When [a] crisis occurs, the actions that are taken depend on the ideas that are lying around. That, I believe, is our basic function: to develop alternatives to existing policies, to keep them alive and available until the politically impossible becomes politically inevitable.

While this statement was made to advance the case for free-market capitalism, it applies equally to cooperative and social enterprises. Developing 'alternatives to existing policies' for entrepreneurship, the formation and management of trading organisations, instruments for making investments in them, and mechanisms to distribute the wealth created by them, are among the benefits of publishing this book. With global financial institutions palpably failing the majority of people, it is also being published at a time of 'crisis'.

When Mike and I started writing, I was not convinced that social enterprise would break into the political and economic mainstream. As we finish the book, I am convinced that the conditions for it to do so have arrived. The question that remains, however, is whether social enterprise will have the radical edge that I (and others) expected it to adopt in 1998 when signing off documents to bring Social Enterprise London (SEL) into existence. Back then, we set out clear objects for the company we were creating (see box).

Memorandum of Association, Social Enterprise London, 26 January 1998

C. Objects

(1) The objects of the company are:

    (i) To promote the principles and values of the social enterprise economy in Greater London and its environs.

(Continued)

(Continued)

(ii) To promote co-operative solutions for economic and community development.
(iii) To promote social enterprises, in particular co-operatives and common ownerships, social firms, and other organisations and businesses which put into practice the principles of participatory democracy, equal opportunities and social justice.
(iv) To promote, develop and support local and regional economic resources and opportunities.
(v) To address social exclusion through economic regeneration.
(vi) To create a regional framework to support and resource development of the social enterprise sector.

Source: Companies House

By 2003, with the announcement of the government's intentions for community interest companies (CICs), it became clear the objects were not going to be quickly or easily realised, and that other social enterprise agencies were not supporting similar objectives. Despite this, I believe the argument for businesses that 'put into practice the principles of participatory democracy' continues to grow. My sense is that the more deeply the financial crisis grips the advanced economies of Europe, the stronger will become the argument for a business movement based on principles of mutuality and democratic control of capital. It will be the only way for people both to take back control of their economies and to enable themselves to act politically. It is possible (but not yet probable) that radical social enterprise movements developing in countries like Venezuela and Argentina may start to occur in (European) countries affected by austerity measures.

In the 2010 election campaign, the larger political parties professed commitment not only to social enterprise development, but specifically to mutual and cooperative forms of ownership and control. This is the first time in my life (of 48 years) that I can remember this happening. During conferences and network events I attended in the latter half of 2009, I was repeatedly surprised by the number (and diversity) of people engaging in conversations about social enterprises, cooperatives and employee ownership. At both national and regional conferences there was a vibrancy I have not experienced before. Furthermore, colleagues who have been travelling abroad continue to come back with stories from Eastern Europe and parts of Asia (including China) that they desire a European social economy model more than a US social entrepreneurial model. The battle of ideas, therefore, is set to continue.

So, my view is that for the next 10 years or so, we will continue to see steady growth in the number of social enterprises (particularly those that do not threaten state or private sector interests) and that there will be more examples of viable 'radical' social enterprises. The longer-term prospects for the sector depend, in my view, on the more ambitious enterprises as they will advance the legitimacy of alternatives to existing policies more quickly and completely. Consequently, I expect pressure will grow for three things.

Firstly, there will be increasing demand for an *educational infrastructure* in which ideas can be developed, legitimised and disseminated. This textbook is one of a number of contributions in recent years that seeks to address this broad need. So far as the authors can tell, however, this book is the first to approach the subject in a way that fully acknowledges the perspectives of SEL's founders. This is important because the CIC legislation still does not offer a corporate vehicle that is sufficiently robust to deliver democratic control of a social enterprise's economic, social and human capital.

As a result, I expect pressure will continue to grow for *cooperative law*, together with laws that allow 'expropriation' of idle private or state assets by cooperatives and social enterprises (using a public and/or community interest test defence). This will enable groups of people to take over the management (and ultimately ownership) of unproductive assets. Such a move, however, would meet strong opposition on the basis that it threatens the current system of private property.

So, the third and final pressure will be for an *independent political party* capable of representing social enterprise interests, and securing the legitimacy (and primacy) of cooperative and social property at places of work. If, for some reason, either the second and third pressures do not result in the changes set out, I expect the (UK) movement will lose any remaining radical edge and will fall into decline within a generation. Without popular and political support for legal reform, the radical wing of the social enterprise movement will (once again) be left biding their time until political conditions are conducive to the advancement of their ideas.

Mike Bull

While Rory and I come from very different disciplines and have our own life experiences, our journey in writing this book together has been illuminating on many levels. Drawing on Thomas Kuhn's notion of paradigm shifts, I see in both theory and practice a surfacing of ideas that will shape and redefine the models of social enterprise. I hope this book contributes to that debate and adds to wider debates about the reshaping of society in response to the many crisis points facing people, organisations and governments.

Today, social awareness is providing the groundswell for social change towards more ethical and democratically controlled business models. This has been provoked in response to numerous catastrophes within the capitalist system, for example the Enron debacle in the early 2000s, the bankers' bonuses in the UK negatively dominating the press in 2009, and the failures of public sector privatisations (creating monopolies, not free markets). People are rightly questioning the ethics and morals of mainstream business practices.

In this brief postscript I have chosen to consider three key examples of how social enterprise could become more widespread and embedded in society over the coming decades.

Renewable energy market-based solutions to the challenges of the environment

In 1950 Karl William Kapp wrote *The Social Costs of Private Enterprise*. He argued that:

conventional economic theory has a tendency to conceal rather than to elucidate the sequence of events in the actual world of affairs: its definition of and search for levels of equilibrium ... its measurement for growth ... do not constitute an adequate theoretical representation of the economy. Nor ... do they secure the maintenance of a reasonable relationship between economic growth and an environment compatible with requirements for human health, well-being and survival. (Kapp, 1971: vii)

It appears that Kapp's ideas are finally beginning to gain acceptance. By 2050, awareness of social enterprises should have continued to increase alongside public interest in the formation of new, socially owned, renewable energy organisations. These are likely to be predominantly community-based social enterprise solutions, developed along the lines of the Baywind Energy Co-operative in Cumbria and Stockport Hydro Limited (a BENCOM), where people will have a deeper awareness of the need to secure, as Kapp suggests, an environment compatible with requirements for human health, well-being and survival.

Alternative market-based solutions to the challenges of modern-day health care needs

In the coming decades, awareness of social enterprises should have increased alongside public interest and social ownership of health sector organisations. In 2010, in the UK, we are seeing the continuation of the devolution of the National Health Service and the creation of internal markets to allow the entry of alternative suppliers into the fold. Social enterprise responses should play a major part in reshaping the internal market, with alternative and entrepreneurial solutions to the ways in which end users of health and well-being services experience resolutions to their specific issues. Organisations such as Unlimited Potential (http://www.unlimitedpotential.org.uk/), which supports people to live healthier and happier lives in Salford, Greater Manchester, should thrive.

Commissioning services on behalf of the public sector are likely to more fully embrace entrepreneurialism and be a transparent activity, utilising local knowledge, with social outcomes and impact firmly acknowledged alongside economic figures within contracts for services. By the mid twenty-first century those interested in measuring social outcomes (as discussed in Chapter 12) should have advanced theoretical knowledge to the point that small local providers will be encouraged to join the supply chain.

Alternative solutions to the private ownership of football clubs

By 2050, awareness of social enterprises should have increased alongside public interest and ownership of football clubs. Here in the UK in 2010, the ownership structures of such great clubs as Liverpool, Manchester United, Notts County and Portsmouth have been called into question. There are many more that could also fall from grace – Chelsea, Manchester City, Aston Villa and Arsenal – as more and more clubs are becoming the commodities of billionaires from around the globe such as Randy Lerner at Aston Villa and Sheikh Mansour bin Zayed Al Nahyan at Manchester City.

There are growing fears for the future of football, with growing hostilities between owners and supporters. Some owners are bankrolling teams with millions of pounds, and this seems to keep most fans happy. Yet there are those owners that have (in the eyes of many supporters of football) financially destabilised clubs, removed a sense of belonging, and raised issues about their motives for ownership. Such questions are asked of Malcolm Glazer at Manchester United and Tom Hicks and George Gillett at Liverpool.

Disenfranchised football supporters are turning to social models, along similar lines to those of FC Barcelona and other supporter-owned clubs, as the future direction for their own clubs. In 2005, FC United of Manchester formed as a brand new football club. They wanted to create a member-owned, democratic, not-for-profit organisation. It has become a club accessible to all of the Greater Manchester community, dedicated to encouraging participation of youth – whether playing or supporting – and to providing affordable football for all (http://www.fc-utd.co.uk/history.php). This is something very different to how most football clubs have been run. By 2050 this should be the preferred model for most football clubs, as the value of the wider impacts of youth and community engagement and development are appreciated.

In ruminating on a future paradigm shift, I close with the vision of Andy Wynne, the network coordinator for Together Works, the social enterprise network for Greater Manchester:

> *My hope is that by 2050 social enterprise will be recognised as the movement that catalysed a new economic system. One based upon a shared understanding that our economic activity must operate within environmental limits and ensure a good quality of life for everyone. A system that acknowledges its dependency on the human community and the environment and that works to develop environmental and social capital rather than exploiting them for short term profit with long term negative consequences. Our current economic, environmental and social problems strongly suggest that there is no alternative!*

Glossary

Actors – a term used in some types of academic research to refer to the people being studied.

ARNOVA – an international membership organisation dedicated to fostering an understanding of the non-profit sector, philanthropy and volunteerism through research activities.

Articles of Association – see **Memorandum and Articles of Association**.

Ashoka – a global association of social entrepreneurs established by Bill Drayton in the USA.

Asset lock – a term used to refer to the permanent retention of assets which can only be used for the purposes set out in an organisation's constitution, and which must be transferred to another asset-locked organisation with similar objectives if it is wound up.

Authoritarian – the directive, dominant characteristic of an absolute ruler.

BENCOM – a cooperative organisation, registered under the Industrial and Provident Society Act, that acts as a society for the benefit of the community. Unlike other cooperatives, profit distributions are limited and may be ring-fenced for the benefit of the community. On dissolution, assets must pass to a similar organisation, or community organisation, rather than members.

Blended value – the pursuit of both economic and social value simultaneously, sometimes used interchangeably with the term 'double bottom line'.

British Empire – colonies established for the purposes of trade by the British Government between the late 16th century and mid 20th century.

British Gas – a public sector supplier of gas until its privatisation by the Conservative government during the 1980s.

British Telecom – a public telecommunications service until it was privatised in the late 1980s by the Conservative government.

BSC – Balanced Scorecard: a measurement-based strategic management analysis tool.

Capitalist society – a society in which the economic system is based on the principle of capital accumulation, and the private ownership of capital, land and the 'means of production' is considered preferable to cooperative and state ownership.

CDFIs – Community Development Finance Initiatives. The UK Social Investment Forum describes CDFIs as 'financial service providers whose mission specifically requires them to achieve social objectives'.

CECOP – the European Confederation of Workers' Co-operatives, Social Co-operatives and Social and Participative Enterprises.

Charity – a type of organisation that pursues public interest objectives defined in the Charities Act 2006. Historically, charities have prioritised the advancement of (religious) education, provided poverty relief, and sought to improve the lives of disadvantaged social groups.

Charities Act 2006 – an Act of parliament passed by the UK Government to update the regulation of charities in England and Wales.

Charity Commission – a statutory organisation operating in England and Wales that provides a range of services and guidance to charities, and with whom all charities must register and report their annual results.

Chicago School – school of economic thought associated with academics in the 1970s who had anti-state sentiments and an ideological commitment to free-market monetarist economics.

CIC – Community Interest Company – a new company form intended as a brand for social enterprise in the UK. Can be registered as a CLG or CLS, has limited profit distribution, board-level decision making power and an asset lock. They cannot register as charities.

CIO – Charitable Incorporated Organisation. Introduced in the Charities Act 2006 as a legal structure that was designed to alleviate the problems charities face in reporting to two governing bodies under the structure of a Company (Companies House) and a registered charity (Charity Commission). It is still awaiting final passage through parliament.

CIPD – the Chartered Institute of Personnel and Development is the United Kingdom's leading professional body for those involved in the management and development of people.

Civil society – forms of organisation that are not part of the public or private sectors that promote freedom of association and public debate about a 'good society'.

CLG – Company Limited by Guarantee: an alternative private form of incorporation that limits liability to members upon insolvency (usually to £1). CLGs have no share capital or shareholders. Members act as guarantors. This has been a popular company form for both charitable companies, non-profit and not-for-profit social enterprises.

CLS – Company Limited by Shares: a private form of incorporation that allows for shareholders. It limits the liability of shareholders upon insolvency to the sum of money invested. It is usually set up to allow people to buy share capital, but this cannot be offered to the general public without a due diligence report. This has been a popular company form for private businesses, more-than-profit and for-profit social enterprises.

Commissioning – an organised process through which a group of people scope the deliverables (products and services) into a contract for services, then seek a supplier to provide them on their behalf.

Communitarianism – a philosophy that emphasises how individuality evolves as a person reacts to developments in their community relationships and assimilates socio-cultural assumptions. It is often contrasted with liberalism, a philosophy that emphasises the autonomy of the individual and their capacity to make their own reasoned judgements.

Community of practice – a group of people who share a set of cultural assumptions and engage in taken-for-granted social practices.

Community Interest Company Regulations – regulatory rules laid down by the UK's Community Interest Companies Regulator based in Companies House.

Constructivist – a theory of knowledge (epistemology) that people generate knowledge and meaning by applying their learning from previous experiences to new situations. As no two people have the same previous experience, the learning processes developed by people are believed to be infinitely variable.

Consumer cooperative – a cooperative business owned by its customers for their mutual benefit. Examples include the Cooperative Group (retailing), housing cooperatives, mutual insurers and credit unions.

Corporate governance theory – a body of theory about the ways in which corporations can be controlled by different interest groups. Most theory focuses on the roles of directors within corporate boards and their relationships with government bodies, industry associations, shareholders and executive managers.

Cost benefit analysis – an analysis of a project proposal or enterprise that seeks to identify and report its anticipated costs and benefits.

Credit unions – a society form devoted to providing credit to members once they have established a track record of regular saving. Credit unions have a long history of providing credit to people in poorer communities.

Critical management school – a school of management thought that draws inspiration from the works of writers who have been influenced by Critical Theory. Critical theorists argue that organisations become exploitative and oppressive if they allow management control to be institutionalised. Critical management scholars are interested in organisation development techniques that limit management power in order to advance social and economic democracy.

CSR – Corporate Social Responsibility.

Debt finance – Loans and other forms of finance that appear as 'debts' in company accounts and which must eventually be repaid by the company. Debt finance differs from equity finance as the latter appears as an asset in company accounts.

Democratic – a system of governance in which people who govern are accountable to the people who are affected by their decisions.

Department of Trade and Industry – a department in the UK government from 1970–2007 responsible for trade, energy and other business related issues.

Development trusts – organisations that are community owned and led, and which pursue economic, social and environmental regeneration activities in a given area or region.

Directors – a legal and popular term for the people appointed by the members of an organisation to run their affairs.

Discourse – a set of inter-related, mutually supporting concepts, theories and stories that lead to a particular 'thought-style' or 'paradigm' of thought.

Discursive reasoning – knowledge development that depends on reasoned argument in dialogue with other people. It is often contrasted with decision-making based on intuition.

Dividends – payments made to the shareholders of an incorporated company, or the members of a cooperative, after a period of profitable trading.

Ecological perspective – a perspective based on the deployment of metaphors and arguments drawn from the study of animals in their natural environments.

EFQM – European Foundation for Quality Management.

EMES – a network comprising 11 research centres in different European universities who specialise in social economy research.

Employee relations – a field of study focused on examining the development of rules that govern the relationship between employers (the buyers of labour) and employees (the sellers of labour). Employee relations theory focuses on the social and economic impact of inequalities in the employment relationship.

Employee-owned organisations – organisations that are wholly or majority owned by employees who work in them.

Enfranchising – increasing opportunities for individual and group representation in a given social setting, such as granting them full citizenship, or providing social recognition by granting them voting and participation rights.

Equity capital – risk capital provided by the members of an organisation to support its development and to which are attached rights to information, speaking and voting during meetings, and a share of the wealth created by the organisation.

Equity investment instruments – legal and social norms that an organisation can adopt to enable existing and new members to purchase equity capital.

ESOC – Employee Share Ownership Centre – an organisation established in the UK in 1989 to promote US-style employee ownership.

Ethnography – a type of research based on anthropological techniques in which the researcher lives or works amongst the research participants in order to gain first-hand experience of their thoughts, feelings and cultural norms.

EU – European Union.

Fair trade – a system of (international) trade that guarantees minimum prices to producers and provides a premium for social investments under the control of a democratically run community organisation.

Feudal society – an agrarian society based on land-ownership and agricultural production. Legal and economic power is vested in a lord of the manor (or local elite) who derive their wealth from craftsmen and a peasant population who provide labour, or who give a proportion of their produce for the right to live and work on the land. Feudal societies are (have been) replaced by money-based market economies and/or state-owned industry after industrialisation.

Foucault, Michel – French philosopher best known for his studies of institutions and writings on power, knowledge, sexuality and discourse. His concept of discourse has been taken up by feminist, critical and postmodern writers to explain the power of language to shape (and limit) the way in which things can be known.

FTSE – the Financial Times Stock Exchange, an organisation that creates and manages company stocks, bonds and securities traded in the UK.

Full cost recovery – an approach to costing that takes into account indirect costs and overheads when bidding for contracts.

Functionalist – a term used in the work of Burrell and Morgan (1979) to describe research activity and management thought that regards people as if they are part of a machine with discrete parts, and who combine their labour to achieve organisational objectives. They compare functionalist thought with other perspectives emphasising the way humans assign meaning to objects and events, and can 'reframe' these meanings through learning and reflection to emancipate themselves from cultural and social constraints imposed by functionalist thought.

Gearing – the ratio of debt to equity finance in a company. Accounting theory hypotheses that risks are lowest when the ratio of debt and equity finance is 1:1 (i.e. that risks are shared equally by suppliers of equity capital and debt finance).

Governance – the institutional arrangements, powers and processes that enable individuals and groups working together in an organisation, and/or living together, to regulate their relationships.

Governing body – a legal term for the group of people who have been assigned responsibility to govern a particular organisation or community.

Greater London Council – a London-wide public authority abolished by the Conservative government during the 1980s, best known for the populist policies it pursued under the leadership of Ken Livingstone.

Hard HRM – an approach to human resource management that tends to treat labour as a cost rather than an asset and which should be managed as a resource that can be replaced if needed. It emphasises technical rather than social considerations in the management of people.

Hegemonic power – power based on the ability to shape others' thoughts and feelings by acquiring control over education curricula, the mass media and political institutions.

Hegemony – a pervasive form of social control based on **hegemonic power**.

Heuristic – something that provides a learning experience which accelerates the discovery of useful knowledge.

HRM – Human Resource Management.

Hub – a term derived from a metaphor of a wheel, spokes and hub. The hub exists to support and maintain relationships between different parts of a wheel for it to function to its full potential. In organisation studies it is helpful for describing organisations that emphasise the primacy of front-line production and marketing activities, but retain a 'hub' for the coordination of activities.

IMF – International Monetary Fund.

Industrial and Provident Societies Act – a body of UK law that supports the formation and development of industrial and welfare organisations using one-member, one-vote systems of governance.

ILM – Intermediate Labour Market: an organisation, or group of organisations, that work together to help people acquire the skills they need to obtain permanent employment. Organisations in an ILM employ people for relatively short periods to help them acquire technical, personal and 'employability' skills.

IPS – an organisation registered under the Industrial and Provident Societies Act.

Kitemark – an award, usually accompanied by a logo and brand that promotes the public profile of an industry (or industry standard practice).

Laissez faire – an approach to trade where transactions between people are not regulated by a higher authority. In economics, laissez faire refers to the doctrine of free markets that minimise state intervention and regulation. In management, it refers to a culture in which figures of authority are not accorded unlimited rights to impose their will and where formal systems of management are not accorded high social status.

Legal compliance – compliance with statutory laws and industry regulations.

Liberalism – a philosophy that emphasises individuality, and the human capacity for personal reflection and autonomous decision-making. In economics, liberalism is associated with freedom from state controls, private property rights and trade based on contracts between 'free' persons.

Local socialism – a description applied to local authorities where politicians committed themselves to the development of a social economy based on community ownership and democratic control of capital.

Managerialism – a body of thought that proceeds from the assumption that all organisations are essentially similar. Based on this assumption, management is regarded as a neutral technical activity capable of improving organisational efficiency through the application of generic management techniques. In critical writing, managerialism is regarded as a 'thought-style' that emphasises and prioritises management perspectives, or an organisational culture in which managers (and the staff they manage) have succumbed to a hegemonic discourse emphasising the right of managers to manage.

Marxian – a body of political, sociological and economic thought derived from the writings of Karl Marx and his followers.

Marx argued that political and economic thought changes in different historical periods based on the arrangements that prevail in the sphere of paid work (the 'relations of production'). New epochs begin when the relationships between people at work are transformed by technological, cultural and political changes.

MBO – Management by Objective: a performance management system based on the agreement and monitoring of objectives set by staff and managers during individual appraisals.

MCC – the Mondragón Cooperative Corporation: a network of cooperatives in the Basque region of Spain in which there are now approximately 100,000 worker-owners.

Memorandum and Articles of Association – documents that set out the purposes, powers and governance arrangements of an organisation. The UK Companies Act 2006 removed the need for a separate Memorandum.

Mission drift – the tendency of an organisation to deviate from their stated social objectives when they face political or economic obstacles to their fulfilment.

Mixed receipts – an approach to income generation based on a mixture of market trading, traditional fundraising and investment activity.

Model rules – a set of rules that provide a starting point for developing Articles of Association. The availability of model rules can speed up the process of incorporating a new company.

Mondragón – a town in the Basque region of Spain.

National Lottery – a lottery franchise created and supported by the UK government under a licence requiring 28p in every £1 to be allocated to good causes.

Network governance – a term used extensively by Shann Turnbull to describe approaches to corporate governance that do not depend on the dominance of a unitary board of directors (or trustees), or centralised control over decision-making.

New Economics Foundation (NEF) – an organisation founded in 1986 that describes itself as a 'think-and-do tank' promoting economics research and accounting practices that support human well-being.

New Labour – a term applied to the Labour Party in the UK to mark its break with old-style socialist politics, and the adoption of a 'social justice' agenda that appealed to a broader coalition of interests. New Labour won three consecutive victories between 1997–2010 before it was replaced by a coalition government of the Conservative and Liberal Democrat parties.

New Right – a term applied to the emergence of new political thinking in the 1970s and 80s that emphasised an economy based on private property, free markets and reductions in state welfare provision.

OECD – Organisation for Economic Co-operation and Development: an international organisation that brings together representatives of governments committed to liberal democracy to share knowledge and experience of market economics.

Organisational legitimacy – a term used in Institutional Theory to describe the ways in which legitimacy is accorded to organisations and affects their chances of survival.

Paradigm – a term used in philosophy to describe the relationship between a particular world view and the methods of inquiry that sustain and support it. Thomas Kuhn (1970) argued that scientific inquiry does not describe the world in which we live, but *sustains* particular world views through acceptance of underlying philosophical premises. He argued that 'paradigm shifts' occur when new methods of inquiring into the world, or a new theoretical perspective, provides a more plausible explanation for observed phenomena. Accepting a new theoretical perspective and the methods of inquiry that support them leads to a new world view.

Participative democracy – a form of democracy that seeks to increase direct participation in the formation and development of opinion, as well as final decision-making. It is often contrasted

with representative democracy based on the election of political/business elites from a small group of approved candidates.

Patient capital – equity or loan finance that is repaid over long periods, usually at lower rates of return. It is called 'patient' because of the length of time it takes to generate a return on investment.

Philanthropy – a way of life, or form of social action, based on systematic charitable giving and social investment.

Physical assets – buildings and other property that are tangible (i.e. can be seen and touched). It can be contrasted with 'intangible' assets such as goodwill and reputation.

Pluralist – a view of organisations that accepts the likelihood that individuals and groups use their agency to formulate and pursue different interests.

Positivism – a branch of philosophy derived from the writings of Auguste Comte that valid knowledge is based on systematic analysis of 'positively given' evidence collected through a scientific process.

Pragmatism – a branch of philosophy and decision-making theory that considers the consequences of accepting a proposition as true. Pragmatists argue that the true content of a proposition is not discovered until it is applied to practice. We accept as true any proposition that is practically adequate for a given purpose or task.

Property rights – legal rights attached to the ownership of property. Property rights are defined in Articles of Association and statutory laws that apply after incorporation.

Rationalism – a branch of philosophy that explores decision-making based on the application of reason and abstract reflection. It is often contrasted with empiricism, a branch of philosophy that emphasises the need to test theoretical claims after systematic collection and analysis of empirical evidence.

Reciprocity – positive or negative in-kind responses associated with the development of an equitable relationship (sometimes framed as 'give and take' within a relationship).

Restricted funds – funds donated under Trust Law which must be used for the purpose designated by the Trustor.

Secular associations – voluntary associations that are not affiliated to a religious tradition, are not influenced by religious authorities, or maintain neutrality in religious matters.

Social Accounting and Auditing (SAA) – an approach to establishing, verifying and reporting the social value created by an organisation.

Social capital – see Chapter 4.

Social economy – see Chapter 1.

Social Enterprise Coalition – the UK's national body that lobbies on behalf of social enterprises and which provides an infrastructure of regional and national networks to support development of the social economy.

Social Enterprise Mark – a trade mark created by RISE, a social enterprise agency in south west England, and later endorsed by the Social Enterprise Coalition. The mark is based on conformance to six criteria believed by RISE/SEC to define the characteristics of a social enterprise.

Social Firms – a type of social enterprise that actively seeks to employ people who are disadvantaged in the labour market and to provide them with career and personal development opportunities.

Social inclusion – attempts to enfranchise a greater number of people through radical management practices and social investment initiatives.

Social investment – a form of investment in which investors track both social and economic value creation to maximise their learning about the impact of investment activities.

Social rationality – a term applied to decision-making in which choices are guided by the projected impact on human relationships, rather than the likelihood of completing a task or mission.

SROI – Social Return on Investment: a methodology pioneered at the Roberts Enterprise Development Fund in the US and adapted by the UK's New Economics Foundation (NEF) to capture the non-market value created by investment activity.

Soft HRM – an approach to human resource management that treats labour as an asset, supported by personal development initiatives and opportunities to socialise at work. It emphasises social rather than technical considerations in the management of people.

Solidarity – intense loyalty between members of a community, social movement, workplace or trade union that inclines them to act together and protect each others' interests.

SORP Regulations – SORPs are 'statements of recommended practice' for organisations operating in a particular sector or industry. In the UK, SORP regulations were introduced in 1993 to improve the management (and reporting) of charitable funds. The regulations were updated in 2005.

Supply chain – the chain of suppliers that support a particular productive activity. The supply chain extends to all the people and organisations who extract and add value to materials in the course of producing a particular good or service.

Surplus – the net value assigned to all value-adding activities undertaken by an organisation in an accounting period minus all costs. Unlike profit, which usually refers to productive trading activities, surplus may include rents, investment interest and other gains in income or asset revaluations derived from non-productive activities.

Technocratic – a culture in which management is regarded as a technical activity to be undertaken by qualified professionals who provide impartial expert advice. It can be contrasted with a critical management perspective that emphasises how political and moral commitments are embedded in professional qualifications, undermining all claims to neutrality and impartiality.

Totalitarianism – a form of management and governance that seeks to maximise the power of a ruler (or ruling elite) to control the physical and psychological environments of those they govern.

TQM – Total Quality Management – a management philosophy based on the writings of Edward Deming that reconceptualises staff as 'customers' and 'suppliers' of each others' skills and expertise, and which advocates continuous improvements in control systems to reduce (or eliminate) production errors.

Trading arm – a subsidiary organisation, usually created by a non-profit or charitable company to make profits that can be gifted back to its parent company under Trust Law.

Triple bottom line – a system of accounting that seeks to measure the economic, social and environmental impact of trading activities.

Trust law – a body of law that covers the rights and obligations attached to gifts and donations intended to support a particular purpose, beneficiary or activity.

Trustees – the people to whom monies have been transferred under Trust law and who manage the money in accordance with the wishes of the Trustor. Charities are run by a Board of Trustees (to whom charitable funds have been given to pursue the objects of the charity).

Unincorporated – an organisation that has not registered Articles of Association in accordance with a body of law that regulates the formation of organisations. In an unincorporated organisation, individuals remain personally liable for any debts they incur.

Unitary – a view of organisations that emphasises the logic and benefits of a single loyalty structure and chain of command and which subsequently regards as illegitimate any organisation or outside interest that competes for the loyalty of its members.

Unrestricted funds – funds that are not subject to Trust Law that can be used for any purpose.

VAT – Value Added Tax.

Venture philanthropy – a form of investment that emphasises social rather than financial returns and which provides a board or organisational role for a philanthropist to monitor the social and economic return on their investment.

Voluntary sector – a sub-sector of the third-sector that depends on volunteer staff and/or trustees to help run organisations and provide services.

Whole economy – An approach to income generation based wholly on trading in commercial markets, without reliance on grants or fundraising activity.

Workers or producer cooperative – generally regarded as a trading organisation that provides goods and services to a market where a majority of the workforce own shares, and the majority of shares are owned by the workforce. In IPS law, there is a definition of a *bona fide* workers' cooperative wholly owned by those who work for it and governed using a system of one-person, one-vote.

World Bank – an international organisation that aims to bring about 'inclusive and sustainable globalisation' through two complementary institutions: The International Bank for Reconstruction and Development and The International Development Association. The bank offers loans and advice to around 100 developing countries.

References

ABCUL (2009) *ABCUL Annual Report 2008/2009*. Association of British Credit Unions. http://www.abcul.org/lib/liDownload/1229/ABCUL%20annual%20report%20(6).pdf, accessed 12 May 2010.

Achbar, M., Abbott, J. and Bakan, J. (2004) *The Corporation*. Big Picture Media Corporation. http://www.thecorporation.com/media/Transcript_finalpt1%20copy.pdf, accessed 8 December 2009.

Adler, P. and Kwon, S. (2002) 'Social capital: prospects for a new concept', *Academy of Management Review*, 27 (1): 17–40.

Aitken, M. (2006) 'Towards market or state? Tensions and opportunities in the evolutionary path of three UK social enterprises', in M. Nyssens (ed.), *Social Enterprise at the Crossroads of Market, Public and Civil Society*. London: Routledge.

Alatrista, J. and Arrowsmith, J. (2004) 'Managing employee commitment in the not-for-profit sector', *Personnel Review*, 33 (5): 536–48.

Albert, M. (2003) *ParEcon: Life after Capitalism*. New York: Verso. http://www.zmag.org/zparecon/pareconlac.htm.

Aldrich, H. and Cliff, J. (2003) 'The pervasive effects of family on entrepreneurship: toward a family embeddedness perspective', *Journal of Business Venturing*, 18: 573–96.

Allan, B. (2005) 'Social enterprise through the eyes of the consumer', *Social Enterprise Journal*, 1 (1): 57–77.

Alter, K. (2007) *Social Enterprise Typology*. www.virtueventures.com/typology, version 1.5, published 27 November 2007.

Alvesson, M. and Deetz, S. (2000) *Doing Critical Management Research*. London: Sage.

Alvesson, M. and Willmott, H. (1996) *Making Sense of Management: A Critical Introduction*. London: Sage.

Alvesson, M. and Willmott, H. (2003) *Studying Management Critically*. London: Sage.

Amin, A. (2009a) *The Social Economy: International Perspectives on Economic Solidarity*. London: Zed.

Amin, A. (2009b) 'Extraordinarily ordinary: working in the social economy', *Social Enterprise Journal*, 5 (1): 30–49.

Amin, A., Cameron, A. and Hudson, R. (2002) *Placing the Social Economy*. London: Routledge.

Anheier, H.K. (2000) 'Managing non-profit organisations: towards a new approach'. Civil Society Working Paper 1. http://www.lse.ac.uk/collections/CCS/pdf/cswp1.pdf, accessed 27 May 2010.

Anthony, R.N. (1965) *Planning and Control Systems: A Framework for Analysis*. Boston: Harvard University Press.

Argyris, C., Putnam, R. and McLain-Smith, D. (1985) *Action Science: Concepts, Methods, and Skills for Research and Intervention*. San Francisco: Jossey-Bass.

Aronson, E. (2003) *The Social Animal*, 9th edn. New York: Worth.

Arthur, L., Scott Cato, M., Smith, R. and Keenan, T. (2006) 'Where is the social in social enterprise?', paper to Social Enterprise Research Conference, London South Bank University, 22–23 June.

Aslam, A. (1999) 'U.S. wage gap widens', *Global Policy Forum*. http://www.globalpolicy.org/component/content/article/218-injustice-and-inequality/46639.html, accessed 14 December 2009.

Avila, R.C. and Campos, R.J.M. (2006) *The Social Economy in the European Union*. CIRIEC no. CESE/COMM/05/2005. The European Economic and Social Committee.

Banks, J. (1972) *The Sociology of Social Movements*. London: Macmillan.

Bateson, G. (2000) *Steps to an Ecology of Mind*, 2nd edn. Chicago: University of Chicago Press.

Beer, S. (1966) *Decision and Control: The Meaning of Operational Research and Management Cybernetics*. London: Wiley.

Beer, S. (1972) *Brain of the Firm: Managerial Cybernetics of Organization*. London: Wiley.

Beinhocker, E. (2007) *The Origin of Wealth*. London: Random House.

Bennett, M., Rikhardsson, P.M. and Schaltegger, S. (eds) (2003) *Environmental Management Accounting: Purpose and Progress*. Dordrecht: Kluwer.

Berle, A. and Means, G. (1932) *The Modern Corporation and Private Property*. New York: Commerce Clearing House Inc.

Berry, A., Broadbent, J. and Otley, D. (eds) (2005) *Management Control: Theories, Issues and Practices*, 2nd edn. Basingstoke: Palgrave.

Besiki, S., Twidale, M.B., Smith, L.C. and Gasser, L. (2008) 'Information quality work organization in Wikipedia', *Journal of the American Society for Information Science and Technology*, 59 (6): 983–1001.

Bibby, A. (undated) 'Case study: Greenwich Leisure'. http://www.andrewbibby.com/socialenterprise/greenwich-leisure.html, accessed 30 March 2010.

Biletzki, A. (2009) 'Ludwig Wittgenstein', *Stanford Encyclopedia of Philosophy*. http://plato.stanford.edu/entries/wittgenstein/, accessed 4 November 2009.

Billis, D. (1993) *Organizing Public and Voluntary Agencies*. London: Routledge.

Birch, K. and Whittam, G. (2008) 'The third sector and the regional development of social capital', *Regional Studies*, 42 (3): 437–50.

Black, L. and Nicholls, J. (2004) *There's No Business Like Social Business*. Liverpool: The Cat's Pyjamas.

Block, F. (2001) 'Introduction', in K. Polanyi, *The Great Transformation: The Political and Economic Origins of Our Time*. Boston: Beacon. pp. xviii–xxxviii.

Borch, O.J., Førde, A., Rønning, L., Vestrum, I.K. and Isos, G.A. (2007) 'Community entrepreneurship: the entrepreneurial process and resource acquisition', paper to Third International Social Entrepreneurship Research Conference (ISERC), August.

Bornstein, D. (1996) *The Price of a Dream: The Story of the Grameen Bank and the Idea That Is Helping the Poor to Change their Lives*. New York: Simon & Schuster.

Bornstein, D. (2007) *How to Change the World: Social Entrepreneurs and Power of New Ideas*. New York: Oxford University Press.

Borzaga, C. and Defourny, J. (2001) *The Emergence of Social Enterprise*. London: Routledge.

Bourdieu, P. (1986) 'The forms of capital', in J.E. Richardson (ed.), *Handbook of Theory of Research for the Sociology of Education*. New York: Greenwood. pp. 241–58.

Bradley, K. and Gleb, A. (1983) *Cooperation at Work: The Mondragón Experience*. Heinemann Educational Books.

Bridge, S., Murtagh, B. and O'Neill, K. (2009) *Understanding the Social Economy and the Third Sector*. Basingstoke: Palgrave.

Brinckerhoff, P. (1994) *Mission-Based Management*. Illinois: Alpine Guild, Inc.

Brinckerhoff, P. (2000) *Mission-based Management*, 2nd edn. New York: Wiley and Sons.

Brown, J. (2004) *Cooperative Capital: A New Approach to Investment in Cooperatives and Other Forms of Social Enterprise*. Manchester: Cooperative Action.

Brown, J. (2006) 'Designing equity finance for social enterprises', *Social Enterprise Journal*, 2 (1): 73–81.

Brown, J. (2007) *Tools for Loans and Other Forms of Finance*. London: Finance Hub.

Bull, M. (2006) *Balance: Unlocking Performance in Social Enterprise*. Manchester: Centre for Enterprise, Manchester Metropolitan University.

Bull, M. (2007) 'Balance: the development of a social enterprise business performance analysis tool', *Social Enterprise Journal*, 3 (1): 49–66.

Bull, M. (2008) 'Challenging tensions: critical, theoretical and empirical perspectives on social enterprise', *International Journal of Entrepreneurial Behaviour and Research*, 14 (5): 268–75.

Bull, M. and Crompton, H. (2005) *Business Practices in Social Enterprises*. ESF Project Report. Manchester Metropolitan University Business School.

Bull, M. and Crompton, H. (2006) 'Business practices in social enterprises', *Social Enterprise Journal*, 2 (1): 42–60.

Bull, M., Ridley-Duff, R.J., Foster, D. and Seanor, P. (2008) 'Seeing social enterprise through the theoretical conceptualisation of ethical capital', paper to 31st Institute for Small Business and Entrepreneurship Research Conference, Belfast, 5–7 November.

Burrell, G. and Morgan, G. (1979) *Sociological Paradigms and Organisational Analysis*. Farnham: Ashgate.

Cabinet Office (2002) *Social Capital: A Discussion Paper*. Performance and Innovation Unit. London: Cabinet Office.

Cabinet Office (2007) *The Future Role of the Third Sector in Social and Economic Regeneration*. Final Report. London: HM Treasury.

Cabinet Office (2009) *A Guide to Social Return on Investment*. London: Cabinet Office.

Cadbury, A. (2000) 'A vision of community finance', in INAISE *Up-scaling Social Investment: Fifty Case Studies*. Paris: INRISE. pp. 8–9.

Campbell, K. (1998) 'When even your accountant betrays you', in *CAUT Bulletin*, ACPPU, 45 (9): 28.

Carver, J. (1990) *Boards That Make a Difference*. San Francisco: Jossey-Bass.

CECOP (2006) 'Social enterprises and worker cooperatives: comparing models of corporate governance and social inclusion', paper to CECOP European Seminar, Manchester, 9 November.

Chadwick-Coule, T. (2010) 'Social dynamics and the strategy process: bridging or creating a divide between trustees and staff?', *Nonprofit and Voluntary Sector Quarterly*, in press.

Chandler, J. (2004) 'In re eBay, Inc. Shareholders Litigation', *Delaware Journal of Corporate Law*, 29 (3): 924–32.

Chandler, J. (2008) *Explaining Local Government: Local Government in Britain Since 1800*. Manchester: Manchester University Press.

Charity Commission (2005) *Accounting and Reporting by Charities: Statement of Recommended Practice*. http://www.charity-commission.gov.uk/Library/guidance/sorp05textcolour.pdf, accessed 11 May 2010.

Charity Commission (2008) *The Essential Trustee: What You Need to Know*. http://www.charity-commission.gov.uk/publications/cc3.asp#b2, accessed 27 January 2010.

Chell, E. (2007) 'Social enterprise and entrepreneurship: towards a convergent theory of the entrepreneurial process', *International Small Business Journal*, 25 (1): 5–26.

Cheney, G. (1999) *Values at Work*. ILR Press/Cornell University Press.

Cladis, M. (1992) *A Communitarian Defence of Liberalism*. Stanford University Press.

Clawson, J.G. (1996) 'Mentoring in the information age', *Leadership and Organisation*, 17 (3): 6–15.

Clegg, S., Kornberger, M. and Pitsis, T. (2008) *Managing and Organizations*. London: Sage.

CLG (2009) *Communities in Control: Real People, Real Power. Government Response to the Improving Local Accountability Consultation*. London: Department for Communities and Local Government.

Cliff, T. and Gluckstein, D. (1988) *The Labour Party: A Marxist History*. Bookmarks.

Clutterbuck, D. and Megginson, D. (2005) *Making Coaching Work: Creating a Coaching Culture*. London: CIPD.

Coad, A. and Cullen, J. (2001) 'The community company: towards a competencies model of corporate governance', paper to 5th International MCA Conference, London, 4–6 July.

Coase, R.H. (1937) 'The nature of the firm', *Economica IV*, 386–405.

Coch, L. and French, J. (1948) 'Overcoming resistance to change', *Human Relations*, 1: 512–32.

Cohen, D. and Prusak, L. (2001) *In Good Company: How Social Capital Makes Organizations Work*. Boston: Harvard Business School Press.

Cohen, R. and Kennedy, P. (2000) *Global Sociology*. Basingstoke: Macmillan.

Coleman, J.C. (1988) 'Social capital in the creation of human capital', *American Journal of Sociology*, 94: 95–120.

Collins, J. (2001) *Good to Great*. London: Random House.

Collins, J. (2006) *Good to Great and the Social Sectors*. London: Random House.

Collins, J. and Porras, J. (2000) *Built to Last: Successful Habits of Visionary Companies*. London: Random House.

Conn, D. (2006) 'Barcelona's model of integrity show rights is might', *The Guardian*, 17 May. http://www.guardian.co.uk/football/2006/may/17/championsleague.europeanfootball, accessed 20 January 2010.

Conway, C. (2008) 'Business planning training for social enterprise', *Social Enterprise Journal*, 4 (1): 57–73.

Cook, B., Dodds, M. and Mitchell, W. (2001) 'The false premises of social entrepreneurship', paper to Social Entrepreneurship: Whose Responsibility Is It Anyway?, Centre for Full Employment and Equity, University of Newcastle (Australia), 21 November.

Cook, J., Deakin, S. and Hughes, A. (2002) 'Mutuality and corporate governance: the evolution of building societies following deregulation', *Journal of Corporate Law Studies*, 2 (1): 110–38.

Cooperatives UK (2007) *Co-operative Review 2007*. http://www.cooperatives-uk.coop/live/images/cme_resources/Public/Co-operative%20Review%202007/Co-operative-Review-2007.pdf, accessed 13 December 2008.

Cooperatives UK (2008) *Worker Co-operative Code of Governance: The Guide to Running a Successful Co-operative Business*. Manchester: Cooperatives UK. http://www.workercode.coop, accessed 24 November 2008.

Cope, J., Jack, S. and Rose, M.B. (2007) 'Social capital and entrepreneurism: an Introduction', *International Small Business Journal*, 25 (3): 213–19.

Cornforth, C. (1995) 'Patterns of cooperative management', *Economic and Industrial Democracy*, 16: 487–523.

Cornforth, C. (2004) 'The governance of co-operatives and mutual associations: a paradox perspective', *Annals of Public and Co-operative Economics*, 75 (1): 11–32.

Cornforth, C. and Edwards, C. (1998) *Good Governance: Developing Effective Board–Management Relations in Public and Voluntary Organisations*. London: CIMA.

Cornforth, C.J., Thomas, A., Spear, R.G. and Lewis, J.M. (1988) *Developing Successful Worker Co-ops*. London: Sage.

Cornforth, M. (1959) *Philosophy for Socialists*. London: Lawrence and Wishart.

Coule, T. (2007) 'Developing strategies for sustainability: implications for governance and accountability', in NCVO/VSSN Researching the Voluntary Sector Conference, University of Warwick, 5–6 September.

Coule, T. (2008) 'Sustainability in voluntary organisations: exploring the dynamics of organisational strategy'. Unpublished PhD Thesis, Sheffield Hallam University.

Coulson, N. (2009) 'ILM Level 5 Award in Understanding Social Enterprise'. Course Materials, Segment 3. Barnsley: Northern College and the Academy for Community Leadership in conjunction with Neil Coulson Associates.

Crutchfield, L. and McLeod-Grant, H. (2007) *Forces for Good: The Six Practices of High Impact Nonprofits*. San Francisco: Jossey-Bass.

Curtis, T. (2008) 'Finding that grit makes a pearl: a critical re-reading of research into social enterprise', *International Journal of Entrepreneurial Behaviour and Research*, 14 (5): 276–90.

Dahlgren, J.J. (2007) 'Do cooperatives destroy or create value?', in Stoel Rives LLP (ed.), *The Law of Cooperatives*. Minneapolis: Stoel Rives Agribusiness and Coops Team. Chapter 2.

Dandridge, T.C. (1979) 'Small business needs its own organisational theory', *Journal of Small Business Management*, 17 (2): 53–7.

Dart, R. (2004) 'The legitimacy of social enterprise', *Non-Profit Management and Leadership*, 4 (4): 411–24.

Darwin, J., Johnson, P. and McAuley, J. (2002) *Developing Strategies for Change*. London: Prentice Hall.

Darzi, Lord (2008) *High Quality Care for All*. London: Department of Health.

Davies, P. (2002) *Introduction to Company Law*. Oxford: Oxford University Press.

Dees, G. (1998) 'Enterprising non-profits: what do you do when traditional sources of funding fall short?', *Harvard Business Review*, January–February: 54–67.

Defourny, J. (2001) 'Introduction: from third sector to social enterprise', in C. Borzaga and J. Defourny (eds), *The Emergence of Social Enterprise*. London: Routledge. pp. 1–28.

Defourny, J. and Nyssens, M. (2006) 'Defining social enterprise', in M. Nyssens (ed.), *Social Enterprise at the Crossroads of Market, Public and Civil Society*. London: Routledge. pp. 3–26.

Della Paolera, G. and Taylor, A.M. (eds) (2004) *A New Economic History of Argentina*. New York: Cambridge University Press.

Della Porta, D. and Diani, M. (2006) *Social Movements: An Introduction*. London: Wiley-Blackwell.

Dholakia, N. and Dholakia, R.R. (1975) 'Marketing planning in a social enterprise: a conceptual approach', *European Journal of Marketing*, 9 (3): 250–8.

Dickson, N. (1999) 'What is the Third Way?', *BBC News*, 27 September. http://news.bbc.

co.uk/1/hi/uk_politics/458626.stm, accessed 15 September 2008.

DiMaggio, P.J. and Powell, W.W. (1983) 'The iron cage revisited: institutional isomorphism and collective rationality in organizational fields', *American Sociological Review*, 48: 147–60.

Doherty, B., Bryde, D., Meehan, J. and Letza, S. (2009a) 'Resource advantage theory and fairtrade social enterprises', paper to the International Social Innovation and Research Conference 2009, Oxford Saïd Business School, 14–16 September.

Doherty, B., Foster, G., Mason, C., Meehan, J., Rotheroe, N. and Royce, M. (2009b) *Management for Social Enterprise*. London: Sage.

Domenico, M., Tracey, P. and Haugh, H. (2009) 'The dialectic of social exchange: theorizing corporate–social enterprise collaboration', *Organization Studies*, 30 (8): 887–907.

Dowla, A. (2006) 'In credit we trust: building social capital by Grameen Bank in Bangladesh', *Journal of Socio-Economics*, 35 (1): 202–22.

Drakeford, M. (2007) 'Private welfare', in M. Powell (ed.), *Understanding the Mixed Economy of Welfare*. Bristol: Policy. pp. 61–82.

Drayton, B. (2005) 'Where the real power lies', *Alliance*, 10 (1): 29–30.

DTI (2002) *Social Enterprise: A Strategy for Success*. London: HM Treasury.

DTI (2003) *Enterprise for Communities: Report on the Public Consultation and the Government's Intentions*. London: HM Treasury.

Dundon, T., Wilkinson, A., Marchington, M. and Ackers, P. (2004) 'The meaning and purpose of employee voice', *The International Journal of Human Resource Management*, 15 (6): 1149–70.

Edwards, E. (2004) *Civil Society*. Cambridge: Polity.

EIRIS (2005) http://www.eiris.org/Pages/TopMenu/FAQ.htm, accessed 7 February 2006.

Ellerman, D. (1982) *The Empresarial Division of the Caja Laboral Popular*. Somerville: Industrial Cooperative Association.

Ellerman, D. (1984) 'Entrepreneurship in the Mondragón Cooperatives', *Review of Social Economy*, 42 (3): 272–94.

Ellerman, D. (1990) *The Democratic Worker-Owned Firm: A New Model for East and West*. Boston: Unwin Hyman.

Ellerman, D. (1997) *The Democratic Corporation*. Beijing: Xinhua.

Ellerman, D. (2005) *Helping People Help Themselves: From the World Bank to an Alternative Philosophy of Development Assistance*. Ann Arbor, MI: University of Michigan Press.

Ellerman, D. (2006) 'Three themes about democratic enterprises: capital structure, education and spin-offs', paper to IAFEP Conference, Mondragón, 13–15 July.

Emerson, J. (2000) 'The nature of returns: a social capital markets inquiry into elements of investment and the blended value proposition'. Working Paper. Boston: Harvard Business School. http://www.blendedvalue.org/media/pdf-nature-of-returns.pdf, accessed 12 May 2010.

Erdal, D. (2000) 'The psychology of sharing: an evolutionary approach'. Unpublished PhD Thesis, University of St Andrews.

Erdal, D. (2008) *Local Heroes: How Loch Fyne Oysters Embraced Employee Ownership and Business Success*. London: Viking.

ESOC (2000) *About ESOPs in the United Kingdom*, www.mhcc.co.uk/esop/esop/abesops.htm, Employee Share Ownership Centre, accessed June 2000.

Etchart, N. and Davis, L. (1999) *Profits for Nonprofits*. NESsT.

Etherington, S. (2008) 'Does a strong and independent third sector mean a strong and healthy civil society?', keynote speech to the Centre for Voluntary Sector Research, Sheffield Hallam University, 23 October. http://www.shu.ac.uk/search.html?q=ncvo.

Etzioni, A. (1973) 'The third sector and domestic missions', *Public Administration Review*, 33: 314–23.

Evans, M. and Syrett, S. (2007) 'Generating social capital? The social economy and local economic development', *European Urban and Regional Studies*, 14 (1): 55–74.

Evers, A. (2001) 'The significance of social capital in the multiple goal and resource structure of social enterprises', in C. Borzaga and J. Defourny (eds), *The Emergence of Social Enterprise*. London: Routledge. pp. 298–311.

Fawcett, B. and Hanlon, M. (2009) 'The "return to community": challenges to human service professionals', *Journal of Sociology*, 45: 433–44.

Fayol, H. (1916) 'Administration industrielle et générale', *Bulletin de la Société de l'Industrie Minérale*, 10 (3): 5–162.

Fenton, N., Passey, A. and Hems, L. (1999) 'Trust, the voluntary sector and civil society', *International Journal of Sociology and Social Policy*, 19 (7/8): 21–42.

Ferlie, E., Ashburner, L., Fitzgerald, L. and Pettigrew, A. (1996) *The New Public Management in Action*. New York: Oxford University Press.

Forcadell, F. (2005) 'Democracy, cooperation and business success: the case of Mondragón Corporación Cooperativa', *Journal of Business Ethics*, 56 (3): 255–74.

Forrester, J. (1989) *Planning in the Face of Power*. Berkeley, CA: University of California Press.

Foucault, M. (1977) *Discipline and Punish: The Birth of the Prison*, trans. Alan Sheridan. London: Penguin.

Fox, A. (1966) 'Industrial sociology and industrial relations'. Research Paper 3. Royal Commission on Trade Unions and Employers Associations. London: HMSO.

Fox, A. (1974) *Man Mismanagement*. London: Hutchinson.

Frail, C. and Pedwell, C. (eds) (2003) *Keeping it Legal: Legal Forms for Social Enterprises*. London: Social Enterprise London.

FRC (2000) Brochure. Cited in Westall (2001).

Friedman, M. (1962) *Capitalism and Freedom*. Chicago: University of Chicago.

Friedman, M. (1968) 'The role of monetary policy', *American Economic Review*, 58: 1–17.

Friedman, M. (1970) The social responsibility of business is to increase its profits, *The New York Times Sunday Magazine*, September 13, 1970. Reprinted in Jennings, M.M. *Business Ethics*. 4th ed. Mason, OH: Thomson; 2003. p. 41–6.

Friedman, M. (2003) 'Social responsibility: a waste of money'. Contribution to *The Corporation*. http://www.thecorporation.com/media/Friedman.pdf.

Fukuyama, F. (1995) *The Social Virtues and the Creation of Prosperity*. London: Penguin.

Fukuyama, F. (2001) 'Social capital, civil society and development', *Third World Quarterly*, 22 (1): 7–20.

Fulda, J.S. (1999) 'In defense of charity and philanthropy', *Business and Society Review*, 104: 179–89. http://ssrn.com/abstract=213248 or doi:10.2139/ssrn.213248.

Garvey, R. and Williamson, B. (2002) *Beyond Knowledge Management: Dialogue, Creativity and the Corporate Curriculum*. Essex: Prentice Hall.

Garvey, R., Stokes, P. and Megginson, D. (2009) *Coaching and Mentoring: Theory and Practice*. London: Sage.

Gates, J. (1998) *The Ownership Solution*. London: Penguin.

Gennard, J. and Judge, J. (2002) *Employee Relations*. London: CIPD.

Giddens, A. (1982) *Sociology: A Brief but Critical Introduction*. London: Macmillan.

Giddens, A. (1998) *The Third Way*. Cambridge: Polity.

Glasby, J. (1999) *Poverty and Opportunity: 100 Years of the Birmingham Settlement*. Studley: Brewin.

Goerke, J. (2003) 'Taking the quantum leap: nonprofits are now in business. An Australian perspective', *International Journal of Nonprofit and Voluntary Sector Marketing*, 8 (4): 317–27.

Goldstein, J., Hazy, J. and Sibberstang, J. (2008) 'Complexity and social entrepreneurship: a fortuitous meeting', *Emergence: Complexity and Organization*, 10 (4): 9–24.

Gordon, M. (2009) 'Accounting for making a difference', *Social Enterprise Magazine*, 25 November. http://www.senscot.net/print_art.php?viewid=8932, accessed 20 May 2010.

Gosling, R. (2008) 'Has ECT failed the social enterprise sector?', *Cooperative News*, 18 July. http://www.thenews.coop/news/Social%20Enterprise/1384, accessed 12 May 2010.

Governance Hub (2005) *Good Governance: A Code for the Voluntary and Community Sector*. London: NCVO.

Granitz, N. and Loewy, D. (2007) 'Applying ethical theories: interpreting and responding to student plagiarism', *Journal of Business Ethics*, 72: 293–306.

Granovetter, M. (1983) 'The strength of weak tie: a network theory revisited', *Sociological Theory*, 1: 201–33.

Gray, J. (1998) *False Dawn: The Delusions of Global Capitalism*. London: Granta.

Gray, J. (2009) *False Dawn: The Delusions of Global Capitalism*, rev. edn. London: Granta.

Grenier, P. (2002) 'The function of social entrepreneurship in the UK'. http://www.istr.org/conferences/capetown/volume/grenier.pdf, accessed November 2009.

Grenier, P. (2006) 'Social entrepreneurship: agency in a globalizing world', in A. Nicholls (ed.), *Social Entrepreneurship: New Models of*

Sustainable Social Change. Oxford: Oxford University Press.

Grey, C. (2005) *A Very Short, Fairly Interesting and Reasonably Cheap Book about Studying Organizations*, 2nd edn. London: Sage.

Grey, C. and Mitev, N. (1995) 'Management education: a polemic', *Management Learning*, 26 (1): 73–90.

Guest, D. (1998) 'Is the psychological contract worth taking seriously?', *Journal of Organizational Behavior*, 19: 649–64.

Gupta, A.K., Sinha, R., Koradia, D. and Patel, R. (2003) 'Mobilizing grassroots' technological innovations and traditional knowledge, values and institutions: articulating social and ethical capital', *Futures*, 35 (9): 975–87.

Guthey, E. and Jackson, B. (2005) 'CEO portraits and the authenticity paradox', *Journal of Management Studies*, 42 (5): 1057–82.

Habermas, J. (1984) *The Theory of Communicative Action. Volume 1: Reason and the Rationalization of Society*. Cambridge: Polity.

Habermas, J. (1987) *The Theory of Communicative Action. Volume 2: Lifeworlds and System: A Critique of Functionalist Reason*. London: Heinemann.

Harding, R. and Cowling, M. (2004) *Social Entrepreneurship Monitor United Kingdom 2004*. London Business School. www.theworkfoundation.com/publications/index.jsp, accessed 26 March 2004.

Harrison, J. (1969) *Robert Owen and the Owenites in Britain and America*. London: Routledge and Kegan Paul.

Harrison, R. (2005) *Learning and Development*. London: Chartered Institute for Personnel and Development.

Haugh, H. (2005) 'A research agenda for social entrepreneurship', *Social Enterprise Journal*, 1 (1): 1–11.

Haugh, H. and Kitson, M. (2007) 'The Third Way and the third sector: New Labour's economy policy and the social economy', *Cambridge Journal of Economics*, 31 (6): 973–94.

Heaney, T. (1995) 'Issues in Freirean pedagogy'. National Louis University. http://www3.nl.edu/academics/cas/ace/resources/Documents/FreireIssues.cfm, accessed 4 January 2010.

Hebson, G., Grimshaw, D. and Marchington, M. (2003) 'PPPs and the changing public sector ethos: case-study evidence from the health and local authority sectors', *Work, Employment and Society*, 17 (3): 481–500.

Hines, F. (2005) 'Viable social enterprise: an evaluation of business support to social enterprises', *Social Enterprise Journal*, 1 (1): 13–28.

HM Treasury (2006) *The Future Role of the Third Sector in Social and Economic Regeneration*. Interim Report.

Holloway, J. (1999) 'A critical research agenda for organisational performance measurement', paper (draft) at First International Critical Management Studies Conference, Manchester, 14–16 July.

Holmstrom, M. (1993) *The Growth of the New Social Economy in Catalonia*. Oxford: Berg.

Home Office (2008) *Public Services and the Third Sector: Rhetoric and Reality*. 11th Report of Session, 2007–8, Vol. 1. London: Public Administration Select Committee.

Hood, C. (1995) 'The new public management in the 1980s: variations on a Theme', *Accounting, Organisation and Society*, 20 (2/3): 93–109.

Hosking, D.M. and Morley, I.E. (1991) *Social Psychology of Organizing: People, Processes and Contexts*. London: Harvester Wheatsheaf.

Howarth, M. (2007) *Worker Co-operatives and the Phenomenon of Empresas Recuperadas in Argentina: An Analysis of Their Potential for Replication*. Manchester: Cooperative College.

Hubbard, B. (2005) *Investing in Leadership. Volume 1: A Grantmaker's Framework for Understanding Nonprofit Leadership Development*. Washington, DC: Grantmakers for Effective Organizations.

Hudson, M. (1995) *Managing Without Profit: The Art of Managing Third Sector Organisations*. London: Penguin.

Hudson, M. (2002) *Managing Without Profit*, 2nd edn. London: Penguin.

Hunt, T. (1928) 'The measurement of social intelligence', *Journal of Applied Psychology*, 12 (3): 317–34. PsycINFO Database Record ©2009 APA.

Hunt, J. (1981) *Managing People at Work: A Manager's Guide to Behaviour In Organizations*. London: Pan.

Hunt, T. (2004) 'Robert Tressell: The Man and His Times', introduction to *The Ragged Trousered Philanthropists*. London: Penguin.

Huselid, M.A. (1995) 'The impact of human resource management practice on turnover, productivity, and corporate financial performance', *Academy of Management Journal*, 38: 635–72.

ICA (2005) *World Declaration on Worker Cooperatives*. Approved by the ICA General Assembly in Cartagena, Columbia, 23 September. www.cooperatives-uk.coop/live/images/cme_resources/Public/governance/Worker%20co-op%20governance/ICA.pdf, accessed 27 September 2008.

Jackson, B. and Parry, K. (2008) *A Very Short, Fairly Interesting and Reasonably Cheap Book about Studying Leadership*. London: Sage.

Jain, P.S. (1996) 'Managing credit for the rural poor: lessons from the Grameen Bank', *World Development*, 24 (1): 79–89.

James, A. (2009) 'Academies of the apolcalypse?', *The Guardian*, 7 April. http://www.guardian.co.uk/education/2009/apr/07/mba-business-schools-credit-crunch, accessed 10 March 2010.

Jennings, P. and Beaver, G. (1997) 'The performance and competitive advantage of small firms: a management perspective', *International Small Business Journal*, 15 (2): 63–75.

Jensen, A. (2006) *Insolvency, Employee Rights and Employee Buyouts: A Strategy for Restructuring*. Alnmouth: Common Cause Foundation (Parliamentary Report).

Joerg, P., Loderer, C. and Roth, L. (2004) 'Shareholder value maximization: what managers say and what they do', paper to the BSI Gamma Foundation Corporate Governance Conference, London, 4 June.

Johnson, P. (2003) 'Towards an epistemology for radical accounting: beyond objectivism and relativism', *Critical Perspectives on Accounting*, 6: 485–509.

Johnson, P. (2006) 'Whence democracy? A review and critique of the conceptual dimensions and implications of the business case for organizational democracy', *Organization*, 13 (2): 245–74.

Johnson, P. and Duberley, J. (2000) *Understanding Management Research*. London: Sage.

Jones, D.R. (2000) 'A cultural development strategy for sustainability', *GMI*, 31 (1): 71–85.

Kaiser, L.F. and Kaiser, M. (1999) *The Official eBay Guide to Buying, Selling, and Collecting Just About Anything*. New York: Fireside.

Kalmi, P. (2007) 'The disappearance of cooperatives from economics textbooks', *Cambridge Journal of Economics*, 31 (4): 625–47.

Kant, E. (1998) *The Critique of Pure Reason*. Cambridge: Cambridge University Press, translated by Paul Guyer and Allen Wood from the orginial published in 1781.

Kaplan, R.S. and Norton, D.P. (1992) 'The Balanced Scorecard: measures that drive performance', *Harvard Business Review*, January–February: 71–9.

Kapp, K.W. (1971) *The Social Costs of Private Enterprise*, 2nd edn. New York: Schocken.

Kasmir, S. (1996) *The Myth of Mondragón*. New York: State University of New York Press.

Kendall, T. (2002) *The Personnel Guide for the Busy Manager*. Barnsley: Personnel Solutions.

Kerlin, J. (2006) 'Social enterprise in the United States and Europe: understanding and learning from the differences', *Voluntas*, 17 (3): 246–62.

Klein, N. (2007) *The Shock Doctrine: The Rise of Disaster Capitalism*. Metropolitan.

Knell, J. (2008) *Share Value: How Employee Ownership Is Changing the Face of Business*. London: All Party Parliamentary Group on Employee Ownership.

Kotter, P. and Heskett, J. (1992) *Corporate Culture and Performance*. New York: Free.

Krueger, N., Kickul, J., Gundry, L., Verman, R. and Wilson, F. (2009) 'Discrete choices, trade-offs and advantages: modelling social venture opportunities and intentions', in J.A. Robinson, J. Mair and K. Hockerts (eds), *International Perspectives on Social Entrepreneurship*. Basingstoke: Palgrave. pp. 117–44.

Kuhn, T. (1970) *The Structure of Scientific Revolutions*. Chicago: University of Chicago.

Kunda, G. (1992) *Engineering Culture: Control and Commitment in a High-Tech Corporation*. Philadelphia: Temple University Press.

Lacey, S. (2009) *Beyond a Fair Price: The Cooperative Movement and Fair Trade*. Manchester: Cooperative College.

Latour, B. (2005) *Reassembling the Social: An Introduction to Actor-Network Theory*. Oxford: Oxford University Press.

Laville, J.L. and Nyssens, M. (2001) 'Towards a theoretical socio-economic approach', in C. Borzaga and J. Defourny (eds), *The*

Emergence of Social Enterprise. London: Routledge. pp. 312–32.

Law, A. and Mooney, G. (2006) 'The maladies of social capital II: resisting neo-liberal conforms', *Critique*, 34 (3): 253–68.

Leadbeater, C. (1997) *The Rise of the Social Entrepreneur*. London: Demos.

Legge, K. (2001) 'Silver bullet or spent round? Assessing the meaning of the "high commitment"/performance relationship', in J. Storey (ed.), *Human Resource Management: A Critical Text*. London: Thompson. pp. 21–36.

Lewin, K., Lippitt, R. and White, R.K. (1939) 'Patterns of aggressive behavior in experimentally created social climates', *Journal of Social Psychology*, 10: 271–301.

Lewis, A. and Klein, N. (2004) *The Take*. Barna-Alpa Productions and the National Film Board of Canada. http://www.thetake.org/.

Light, P. (2006) 'Searching for social entrepreneurs: who might they be, where might they be found, what they do', in R. Mosher-Williams (ed.), *Research on Social Entrepreneurship: Understanding and Contributing to an Emerging Field*, 1 (3). Indianapolis, IN: Arnova. pp. 13–37.

Light, P. (2008) *The Search for Social Entrepreneurship*. Washington, DC: Brookings Institute.

Lincoln, A. (2006) 'Welcome address'. DTI presentation to Third Annual UK Social Enterprise Research Conference, London South Bank University, 22 June.

Lindsay, G. and Hems, L. (2004) 'Sociétés coopératives d'intérêt collectif: the arrival of social enterprise within the French social economy', *Voluntas*, 15 (3): 265–86.

Livingstone, K. (1988) *If Voting Changed Anything: They'd Abolish It*. London: Fontana.

London, M. and Morfopoulos, R.G. (2010) *Social Entrepreneurship*. New York: Routledge.

Low, C. (2006) 'A framework for the governance of social enterprise', *International Journal of Social Economics*, 33 (5/6): 376–85.

Lukes, S. (1974) *Power: A Radical View*. Basingstoke: Macmillan.

Luxton, P. (2001) *The Law of Charities*. Oxford: Open University Press.

Luyt, B., Aaron, L., Thian, L.H. and Hong, C.H. (2008) 'Improving Wikipedia's accuracy', *Journal of the American Society for Information Science and Technology*, 59 (2): 318–30.

Lyon, F. and Sepulveda, L. (2009) 'Mapping social enterprises: past approaches, challenges and future directions', *Social Enterprise Journal*, 5 (1): 83–94.

Maase, S. and Dorst, I. (2006) 'Exploring the process of grassroots social entrepreneurship'. Accessed January 2010.

MacDonald, M. (2008) 'Social enterprise experiments in England: 1660–1908', paper to the 5th Social Entrepreneurship Conference, London Southbank University, 26–27 June.

MacGillivray, A., Conaty, P. and Wadhams, C. (2001) *Low Flying Heroes: Micro-Social Enterprise below the Radar*. London: New Economics Foundation.

Major, G. (1996) 'Solving the under-investment and degeneration problems of worker's co-ops', *Annals of Public and Co-operative Economics*, 67: 545–601.

Major, G. (1998) 'The need for NOVARS (non-voting value added sharing renewable shares)', *Journal of Co-operative Studies*, 31 (2): 57–72.

Markham, W.T., Walters, J. and Bonjean, C.M. (2001) 'Leadership in voluntary associations: the case of the International Association of Women', *Voluntas*, 12 (2): 103–30.

Martin, R. L. and Osberg, S. (2007) 'Social entrepreneurship: the case for definition', *Stanford Social Innovation Review*, Spring. pp. 29–39.

Marx, K. and Engels, F. (1998) *The Communist Manifesto: A Modern Edition*, 1848, based on trans. Samuel Moore, 1891. London: Verso.

Mawson, A. (2008) *The Social Entrepreneur*. Bodmin: MPG.

McGregor, D. (1960) *The Human Side of Enterprise*. New York: McGraw-Hill.

McIndoe, A. (2007) 'Small loans make a big difference to some Filipinos', *The Strait Times*, 8 May. http://business.asiaone.com, accessed 18 January 2010.

McNulty, T. and Ferlie, E. (2004) 'Process transformation: limitations to radical organizational change within public service organizations', *Organization Studies*, 25 (8): 1389–1412.

Meindl, J. (1993) 'Reinventing leadership: a radical social psychological approach', in J.D. Murningham (ed.), *Social Psychology in Organizations*. Englewood Cliffs, NJ: Prentice Hall. pp. 89–118.

Meindl, J. (1995) 'The romance of leadership as a follower-centric theory: a social constructionist approach', *Leadership Quarterly*, 6 (3): 329–41.

Melman, S. (2001) *After Capitalism: From Managerialism to Workplace Democracy*. New York: Knopf.

Mertens, S. (1999) 'Nonprofit organisations and social economy: two ways of understanding the third sector', *Annals of Public and Cooperative Economics*, 70 (3): 501–20.

Meyskens, M. (2008) 'The symbiosis of entities in the social engagement network: the role of social entrepreneurship organizations'. http://www.oikos_international.org/fileadmin/oikos_international/international/oikos_PhD_summer_academy/Papers_2008/meyskeys_paper, accessed December 2009.

Michels, R. (1961) *Political Parties: A Sociological Study of the Oligarchical Tendencies of Modern Democracy*. New York: Free.

Miller, E. and Rice, A. (1967) *Systems of Organization*. London: Tavistock.

Mintzberg, H., Ahlstrand, B. and Lampel, J. (1998) *Strategy Safari: A Guided Tour through the Wilds of Strategic Management*. New York: Free.

Monks, R. and Minow, N. (2004) *Corporate Governance*, 3rd edn. Malden, MA: Blackwell.

Monzon, J.L. and Chaves, R. (2008) 'The European social economy: concept and dimensions of the third sector', *Annals of Public and Cooperative Economics*, 79 (3/4): 549–77.

Mook, L., Quarter, J. and Richmond, B.J. (2007a) *What Counts: Social Accounting for Nonprofits and Cooperatives*, 2nd edn. London: Siegel.

Mook, L., Richmond, J. and Quarter, J. (2007b) 'Integrated social accounting for nonprofits: a case from Canada', *Voluntas*, 14 (3): 283–297.

Morgan, G.G. (2008) 'The spirit of charity', professorial lecture, Centre of Individual and Organisation Development, Sheffield Hallam University, 3 April.

Morrison, R. (1991) *We Build the Road as We Travel*. Gabriola Island, BC: New Society.

Mort, G., Weerawardena, J. and Carnegie, K. (2003) 'Social entrepreneurship: towards conceptualisation', *International Journal of Nonprofit and Voluntary Sector Marketing*, 8: 76–88.

Murdock, A. (2005) 'Social entrepreneurial ventures and the value of social networks', paper to Social Enterprise Research Conference, Milton Keynes, 1–2 July.

Murdock, A. (2007) 'No man's land or promised land? The lure of local public service delivery contracts for social enterprise', paper to Social Enterprise Research Conference, London South Bank University, 3–6 July.

Mutuo (2009) *Mutuals Yearbook 2009*. http://www.kellogg.ox.ac.uk/researchcentres/documents/Mutuals%20Yearbook%202009.pdf, accessed 29 March 2010.

NCVO (2005) *Good Governance: A Code for the Voluntary Sector*. London: NCVO.

NCVO (2007) 'DCLG: third sector strategy for communities and local government. NCVO briefing paper'. http://www.ncvo-vol.org.uk, accessed October 2007.

NCVO (2008) *The Civil Society Almanac*. London: NCVO.

NEF (2006) *Prove and Improve: A Quality and Impact Toolkit*. London: New Economics Foundation.

NEF/SAS (2004) *Unlocking the Potential*. London: Social Enterprise Coalition.

NHS (2008) *Social Enterprise – Making a Difference: A Guide to the Right to Request*. London: Department of Health.

Nicholls, A. (2006a) *Social Entrepreneurship: New Models of Sustainable Social Change*. Oxford: Oxford University Press.

Nicholls, A. (2006b) 'Playing the field: a new approach to the meaning of social entrepreneurship', *Social Enterprise Journal*, 2 (1): 1–5.

Nicholls, A. (2009a) 'Capturing the performance of the socially entrepreneurial organization: an organizational legitimacy approach', in J.A. Robinson, J. Mair and K. Hockerts (eds), *International Perspectives on Social Entrepreneurship*. Basingstoke: Palgrave. pp. 27–74.

Nicholls, A. (2009b) 'We do good things, don't we?', *Accounting, Organization and Society*, 34: 755–67.

Nicholls, A. and Opal, C. (2004) *Fair Trade*. London: Sage.

Nove, A. (1983) *The Economics of Feasible Socialism*. London: Allen and Unwin.

Nyssens, M. (2006) *Social Enterprise at the Crossroads of Market, Public and Civil Society*. London: Routledge.

Oakeshott, R. (1990) *The Case for Worker Co-ops*, 2nd edn. Basingstoke: Macmillan.

OTS (2008) *Review of Social Enterprise Networks* [online] Rocket Science Ltd for Cabinet Office, London: Office of the Third Sector, available from http://www.cabinetoffice.gov.uk/third-sector, accessed April 2008.

Owen, H. (2008) *Open Space Technology: A User's Guide*. San Francisco: Berrett-Koehler.

Owen, R. (1849) *The Revolution in the Mind and the Practice of the Human Race*. London: Wilson.

Parker, S. and Parker, S. (2007) *Unlocking Innovation: Why Citizens Hold the Key to Public Service Reform*. London: Demos.

Pateman, C. (1970) *Participation and Democratic Theory*. Cambridge: Cambridge University Press.

Paton, R. (1989) *Reluctant Entrepreneurs*. Milton Keynes: Open University Press.

Paton, R. (1991) 'The social economy: value-based organizations in wider society', in J. Batsleer, C. Cornforth and R. Paton (eds), *Issues in Voluntary and Non-Profit Management*. Wokingham: Addison-Wesley.

Paton, R. (2003) *Managing and Measuring Social Enterprises*. London: Sage.

Pearce J. (2003) *Social Enterprise in Anytown*. London: Calouste Gulbenkian Foundation.

Pearce, J. (2009) 'Social economy: engaging as a third system', in A. Amin (ed.), *The Social Economy: International Perspectives on Economic Solidarity*. London: Zed. pp. 3–21.

Pearce, J. and Kay, A. (2008) *Really Telling Accounts: Report on a Social Accounting and Audit Research Project*. Exeter: Social Audit Network.

Pearl, D. and Phillips, M.M. (2001) 'Grameen Bank, which pioneered loans for the poor, has hit a repayment snag', *Wall Street Journal*, 27 November. http://online.wsj.com/public/resources/documents/pearl112701.htm, accessed 18 January 2010.

Peattie, K. and Morley, A. (2008) *Social Enterprises: Diversity and Dynamics, Contexts and Contributions*. Cardiff: ESRC/Brass Research Centre.

Perrini, F. (2006) *The New Social Entrepreneurship: What Awaits Social Entrepreneurial Ventures?* Northampton, MA: Elgar.

Pestoff, V.A. (1998) *Beyond the Market and State: Social Enterprises and Civil Democracy in a Welfare State*. Aldershot: Ashgate.

Peters, T. (1989) *Thriving on Chaos*. New York: Harper Perennial.

Pharoah, C. (2007) *Sources of strength*, [online] from Baring Foundation. Available at: http://www.baringfoundation.org.uk/sources of strength.pdf.

Pharoah, C., Scott, D. and Fisher, A. (2004) *Social Enterprise in the Balance: Challenges for the Voluntary Sector*. West Malling: Charities Aid Foundation.

Polanyi, K. (2001) *The Great Transformation: The Political and Economic Origins of Our Time*. Boston: Beacon.

Portes, M. (1998) 'Social capital: its origins and application in modern sociology', *Annual Review of Sociology*, 24: 1–24.

Powell, W. and DiMaggio, P. (1991) *The New Institutionalism in Organizational Analysis*. Chicago: University of Chicago Press.

Preuss, L. (2004) 'Aristotle in your garage: enlarging social capital with an ethics test', in L.J. Spence, A. Habisch and R. Schmidpeter (eds), *Responsibility and Social Capital: The World of SMEs*. Basingstoke: Palgrave. pp. 154–64.

Price, M. (2008) *Social Enterprise: What It Is and Why It Matters*. Dinas Powys: Fflan.

Prochaska, F. (1990) 'Philanthrophy', in F. Thompson (ed.), *The Cambridge Social History of England, 1750–1950*, Vol. 3. Cambridge: Cambridge University Press.

Purcell, J. (1987) 'Mapping management style in employee relations', *Journal of Management Studies*, 24 (5): 533–48.

Purcell, J. (1999) 'Best practice and best fit: chimera or cul-de-sac', *Human Resource Management Journal*, 8: 311–31.

Putnam, R. (2001) *Bowling Alone: The Collapse and Revival of American Community*. New York: Simon and Schuster.

Ranis, P. (2005) 'Argentina's worker-occupied factories and enterprises', *Socialism and Democracy*, 19 (3): 93–115.

Ransom, D. (2004) 'Tales of the unexpected', *New Internationalist*, June: 9–12.

Rawls, J. (1999) *A Theory of Justice*, rev. edn. Oxford: Oxford University Press.

Reeves, R. (2007) *CoCo Companies: Work, Happiness and Employee Ownership*. London: Employee Ownership Association.

Reid, K. and Griffith, J. (2006) 'Social enterprise mythology: critiquing some assumptions', *Social Enterprise Journal*, 2 (1): 1–10.

Ridley-Duff, R.J. (2002) *Silent Revolution: Creating and Managing Social Enterprises.* Barnsley: First Contact Software Ltd. http://www.scribd.com/doc/2885922.

Ridley-Duff, R.J. (2003) 'Mondragón Cooperative Corporation', transcript of Seminar on Corporate Governance, Otalora Management School, Mondragón, 5 March. http://www.scribd.com/doc/21644627, accessed 21 November 2009.

Ridley-Duff, R.J. (2005) 'Communitarian perspectives on corporate governance'. PhD thesis, Sheffield Hallam University. http://www.scribd.com/doc/3271344/, accessed 21 November 2009.

Ridley-Duff, R.J. (2007) 'Communitarian perspectives on social enterprise', *Corporate Governance: An International Review*, 15 (2): 382–92.

Ridley-Duff, R.J. (2008a) 'Social enterprise as a socially rational business', *International Journal of Entrepreneurial Behaviour and Research*, 14 (5): 291–312.

Ridley-Duff, R.J. (2008b) 'Interpreting results: governance diagnostic questionnaire', paper to Bridging the Divide: Governance and Decision-Making in the Third Sector Conference, Sheffield Hallam University, 9–10 July.

Ridley-Duff, R.J. (2009a) 'Cooperative social enterprises: company rules, access to finance and management practice', *Social Enterprise Journal*, 5 (1), 50–68.

Ridley-Duff, R.J. (2009b) *Coaching for Performance: Evaluation Report for Nottinghamshire NHS County.* Sheffield: Sheffield Business School, Centre for Individual and Organisational Development.

Ridley-Duff, R.J. (2010) 'Communitarian governance in social enterprises: case evidence from the Mondragón Cooperative Corporation and School Trends Ltd', *Social Enterprise Journal*, 6 (2): 125–45.

Ridley-Duff, R.J. and Bennett, A. (2009) 'Mediation: developing a theoretical framework for understanding alternative dispute resolution'. Working Paper, Centre for Individual and Organisational Development, Sheffield Business School. http://www.roryridleyduff.com/18%20-%20Mediation%20-%20An%20Introduction.pdf, accessed 21 June 2009.

RISE (2008) 'The Social Enterprise Mark'. http://www.socialenterprisemark.co.uk/, accessed 11 October 2008.

Robinson, L. and Halle, D. (2002) 'Digitization, the internet, and the arts: eBay, Napster, SAG and e-Books', *Qualitative Sociology*, 25 (3): 359–83.

Rodrick, S.S. (2005) *Leveraged ESOPs and Employee Buyouts*, 5th edn. Oakland, CA: National Center for Employee Ownership.

Rothschild, J. (2009) 'Workers' cooperatives and social enterprise: a forgotten route to social equity and democracy', *American Behavioral Scientist*, 52 (7): 1023–41.

Rothschild, J. and Allen-Whitt, J. (1986) *The Cooperative Workplace.* New York: Cambridge University Press.

Rousseau, D. (1995) *Psychological Contracts in Organizations: Understanding Written and Unwritten Agreements.* Thousand Oaks, CA: Sage.

Royce, M. (2007) 'Using human resource management tools to support social enterprise: emerging themes from the sector', *Social Enterprise Journal*, 3 (1): 10–19.

Ruzicho, A.J. (2006) *Ebook Success: Complete Guide to Starting Your Ebook Business Now.* R&W.

Salamon, M. (2000) *Industrial Relations: Theory and Practice*, 4th edn. Englewood Cliffs, NJ: Prentice Hall.

Savio, M. and Righetti, A. (1993) 'Cooperatives as a social enterprise: a place for social integration and rehabilitation', *Acta Psychiatrica Scandanavica*, 88 (4): 238–42.

Scase, R. and Goffee, R. (1980) *The Real World of the Small Business Owner.* London: Croom Helm.

Schumpeter, J. (1942) *Capitalism, Socialism, and Democracy.* New York: Harper.

Schwabenland, C. (2006) *Stories, Visions and Values in Voluntary Organisations.* Ashgate: Hampshire.

Schwartz, R. (2008) 'The sale of ECT Recycling: a cause for celebration or a cause for concern?', *Social Business Blog.* http://www.clearlyso.com/sbblog/?p=62#comment-3001, accessed 12 May 2010.

Scott-Cato, M., Arthur, L., Keenoy, T. and Smith, J. (2008) 'Entrepreneurial energy: associative entrepreneurship in the renewable energy sector', *International Journal of Entrepreneurial Behaviour and Research*, 14 (5): 313–29.

Seanor, P. and Meaton, J. (2006) 'Learning from failure, ambiguity and trust in social enterprise', presentation to Critical Reflections on Social Enterprise Seminar, Manchester Metropolitan, November.

Seanor, P. and Meaton, J. (2008) 'Learning from failure: ambiguity and trust in social enterprise', *Social Enterprise Journal*, 4 (1): 24–40.

Seanor, P., Bull, M. and Ridley-Duff, R.J. (2007) 'Contradictions in social enterprise: do they draw in straight lines or circles?', paper to 31st Institute of Small Business and Entrepreneurship Conference, Glasgow, 5–7 November. http://shura.shu.ac.uk/732/.

SEC (undated) 'Margaret Elliot – Sunderland Care Home Associates'. http://www.socialenterprise. org.uk/pages/margaret-elliott-sunderland-home-care-associates.html, accessed 30 March 2010.

SEC (2005) *Keeping It Legal: A Guide to Legal Forms for Social Enterprises*. London: Social Enterprise Coalition.

SEC (2009a) *State of Social Enterprise Survey*. London: Social Enterprise Coalition. http:// www.socialenterprise.org.uk/data/files/ stateofsocialenterprise2009.pdf, accessed 24 May 2010.

SEC (2009b) *Keeping It Legal*, 2nd edn. London: Social Enterprise Coalition. http://www. enterprisingsolutions.org/pages/keeping-it-legal.html, accessed 26 January 2010.

Sen, A. (2000) *Social Exclusion: Concept, Application and Scrutiny*. Manila: Asian Development Bank.

Simmons, R. (2008) 'Harnessing social enterprise for local public services: the case of new leisure trusts', *Public Policy and Administration*, 23: 278–301.

Slapnicar, S., Gregoric, A. and Rejc, A. (2004) 'Managerial entrenchment and senior executives compensation', paper to 6th International MCA Conference, Edinburgh, 12–14 July.

Sloman, J. and Sutcliffe, M. (2001) *Economics for Business*. London: Prentice Hall.

Smallbone, D. and Lyon, F. (2005) *Social Enterprise Development in the UK: Some Contemporary Policy Issues*. http://www.sbaer. uca.edu/research/icsb/2005/177.pdf, accessed 15 October 2008.

Smircich, L. and Morgan, G. (1982) 'Leadership: the management of meaning', *Journal of Applied Behavioural Studies*, 18: 257–73.

Smith, M.K. (2001) 'Chris Argyris: theories of action, double-loop learning and

organizational learning', *The Encyclopedia of Informal Education*. www.infed.org/thinkers/ argyris.htm, accessed 5 January 2010.

Smith, S.S. and Kulynych, J. (2002) 'It may be social, but why is it capital? The social construction of social capital and the politics of language', *Politics and Society*, 30 (1): 149–86.

Somers, A. (2005) 'Shaping the Balanced Scorecard for use in UK social enterprise', *Social Enterprise Journal*, 1 (1): 1–12.

Somers, A. (2007) 'Blurring boundaries? New Labour, civil society, and the emergence of social enterprise', presentation to the 4th Social Entrepreneurship Research Conference, London Southbank University.

Spear, R. (1999) 'Employee-owned UK bus companies', *Economic and Industrial Democracy*, 20: 253–68.

Spear, R. (2006) 'Social entrepreneurship: a different model?', *International Journal of Social Economics*, 33 (5/6): 399–410.

Spear, R. (2008) Personal communication. Discussions at The Social Entrepreneurial Mindset, University of East London, 9 October.

Spear, R., Cornforth, C. and Aitken, M. (2007) *For Love and Money: Governance and Social Enterprise*. Milton Keynes: Open University Press.

Speckbacher, G. (2003) 'The economics of performance management in non-profit organisations', *Nonprofit Management and Leadership*, 13 (3): 267–281.

Spreckley, F. (1981) *Social Audit: A Management Tool for Cooperative Working*. Leeds: Beechwood College.

Spreckley, F. (2008) *Social Audit Toolkit*, 4th edn. Herefordshire: Local Livelihoods. http://www.locallivelihoods.com/documents/ socialaudittoolkit.pdf, accessed 10 August 2010.

Stacey, R. (2007) *Strategic Management and Organizational Dynamics: The Challenge of Complexity to Ways of Thinking about Organizations*. Harlow: Pearson.

Stewart, R. (1983) 'Managerial behaviour: how research has changed the traditional picture', in M. Earl (ed.), *Perspectives in Management*. Oxford: Oxford University Press. pp. 82–98.

Stogdill, R.M. (1974) *Handbook of Leadership: A Survey of the Literature*. New York: Free.

Stone, I., Robinson, F., Braidford, P. and Allinson, G. (2007) *Scoping Report for the Office of the Third Sector*. Durham: Durham University.

Storey, D. (1987) 'Developments in the management of human resources: an interim report'. Warwick Papers in Industrial Relations. Coventry: University of Warwick.

Storey, D. (1994) *Understanding the Small Business Sector.* London: Routledge.

Storey, D. (2001) *Human Resource Management: A Critical Text.* London: Thompson.

Subramanian, J. (1998) *Rural Women's Right to Property: A Bangladesh Case Study.* Madison, WI: Land Tenure Center, University of Wisconsin.

Sydow, J. (1998) 'Understanding the constitution of interorganizational trust', in C. Lane and R. Bachmann (eds), *Trust within and between Organisations: Conceptual Issues and Empirical Applications.* Oxford: Oxford University Press. pp. 31–63.

Tan, W., Williams, J. and Tan, T. (2005) 'Defining the social in social entrepreneurship: altruism and entrepreneurship', *International Entrepreneurship and Management Journal,* 1: 353–65.

Taylor, F. (1917) *Principles of Scientific Management.* New York: Harper and Brothers.

Tesfatsion, L. (2007) 'Notes on the Grameen Bank and the international microcredit movement'. Course materials. http://www.econ.iastate.edu/classes/econ353/tesfatsion/grameen.htm, accessed 18 January 2010.

Thomas, P. (2004) 'Performance measurement, reporting and accountability: recent trends and future directions'. Public Policy Paper Series 23. The Saskatchewan Institute of Public Policy.

Todres, M., Cornelius, N., Shaheena, J. and Woods, A. (2006) 'Developing emerging social capital through capacity building', *Social Enterprise Journal,* 2 (1): 61–72.

H M Treasury (1999) *Enterprise and Social Exclusion,* London: H M Treasury, authored by National Strategy for Neighbourhood Renewal, Policy Action Team3.

Tressell, R. (2004) *The Ragged Trousered Philanthropists.* London: Penguin.

Trigona, M. (2006) 'Recuperated factories in Argentina: reversing the logic of capitalism'. Citizen Action in the Americas no. 19. http://americas.irc-online.org/pdf/series/19.recoupent.pdf, accessed 9 April 2010.

Trigona, M. (2009) 'Argentine factory wins legal battle: FASINPAT Zanon belongs to the people', *Upside Down World,* 14 August.

http://upsidedownworld.org/main/content/view/2052/1/, accessed 9 April 2010.

Truss, C. (1999) 'Soft and hard models of human resource management', in L. Graton, V.H. Hailey, P. Stiles and C. Truss (eds), *Strategic Human Resource Management: Corporate Rhetoric and Human Reality.* Oxford: Oxford University Press. pp. 40–58.

Turnbull, S. (1994) 'Stakeholder democracy: redesigning the governance of firms and bureaucracies', *Journal of Socio-Economics,* 23 (3): 321–60.

Turnbull, S. (1995) 'Innovations in corporate governance: the Mondragón Experience', *Corporate Governance: An International Review,* 3 (3): 167–80.

Turnbull, S. (2001) 'The science of corporate governance', *Corporate Governance,* 10 (4): 261–77.

Turnbull, S. (2002) *A New Way to Govern: Organisations and Society after Enron.* London: New Economics Foundation. http://papers.ssrn.com/sol3/papers.cfm?abstract_id=319867.

Usher, R. and Bryant, I. (1989) *Adult Education as Theory, Practice and Research.* London: Routledge.

Vinten, G. (2001) 'Shareholder versus stakeholder: is there a governance dilemma?', *Corporate Governance: An International Review,* 9 (1): 36–47.

Wagner-Tsukamoto, S. (2007) 'Moral agency, profits and the firm: economic revisions to the Friedman theorem', *Journal of Business Ethics,* 70: 209–20.

Wainwright, T. (2009) 'The Companies Act 2006 for Cooperatives'. Cobbetts Solicitors. www.cooperatives-uk.coop, accessed 19 July 2009.

Wallace, B. (2005) 'Exploring the meaning(s) of sustainability for community-based social entrepreneurs', *Social Enterprise Journal,* 1 (1), 78–89.

Watson, T. (1994) *In Search of Management.* London: Routledge.

Watson, T. (1996) 'Motivation: that's Maslow isn't it?', *Management Learning,* 27 (4): 447–64.

Weick, K.E. (1995) *Sensemaking in Organizations.* London: Sage.

Weick, K.E. (2001) *Making Sense of the Organization.* Malden, MA: Blackwell.

Weinbren, D. (2008) *Families and Friendly Societies.* Friendly Society Research Group.

Weinbren, D. and James, B. (2005) 'Getting a grip: the roles of friendly societies in Australia and Britain reappraised', *Labour History*, 88. www.historycooperative.org/journals/lab/88/weinbren.html, accessed 16 December 2008.

Wei-Skillern, J., Austin, J., Leonard, H. and Stevenson, H. (2007) *Entrepreneurship in the Social Sector*. Thousand Oaks, CA: Sage.

Wenger, E. (1998) *Communities of Practice: Learning, Meaning and Identity*. Cambridge: Cambridge University Press.

Westall, A. (2001) *Value-Led, Market-Driven: Social Enterprise Solutions to Public Policy Goals*. London: IPPR.

Westall, A. and Chalkley, D. (2007) *Social Enterprise Futures*. London: Smith Institute. http://www.smith-institute.org.uk/pdfs/social_enterprise.pdf, accessed May 2007.

White, L. (2002) 'Connection matters: exploring the implication of social capital and social networks for social policy', *Systems Research and Behavioural Science*, 19: 255–69.

White, R.K. and Lippett, R. (1960) *Autocracy and Democracy: An Experimental Inquiry*. New York: Harper.

Whyte, W.F. and Whyte, K.K. (1991) *Making Mondragón*. New York: ILR Press/Itchaca.

Williams, C. (2007) 'De-linking Enterprise Culture from Capitalism and its Public Policy Implications', *Public Policy and Administration*, 22 (4): 461–74.

Williamson, O.E. (1989) 'Transaction cost economics', in R. Schmalensee and R. Willig (eds), *Handbook of Industrial Organization*. Amsterdam: Elsevier.

Willmott, H. (1993) 'Strength is ignorance; slavery is freedom: managing culture in modern organisations', *Journal of Management Studies*, 30 (4): 515–52.

Wilson, F. (2004) *Organizational Behaviour and Work*, 2nd edn. Oxford: Oxford University Press.

Wittgenstein, L. (2001) *Philosophical Investigations*. Malden, MA: Blackwell.

Woodin, T. (2007) *A Good Way to Do Business: Supporting Social Enterprises in Greater Manchester*. Manchester: Cooperative College.

Woolcock, M. (1998) 'Social theory, development policy and poverty alleviation: a comparative-historical analysis of group-based banking in developing economies'. Unpublished PhD thesis, Brown University.

World Bank (2007) 'Argentina: the power of self-management. Part 1'. New York: World Bank. http://www.youtube.com/watch?v=zApzKF45rnQ&feature=related, accessed 18 January 2010.

Wynarczyk, P., Watson, R., Storey, D., Short, H. and Keasey, K. (1993) *Managerial Labour Markets in SMEs*. London: Routledge.

Younkins, E.W. (2005) 'Rousseau's general will and the well-ordered society', *The Quebecois Libre*. http://www.quebecoislibre.org/05/050715-16.htm, accessed 21 June 2009.

Yunus, M. (1999) *Banker to the Poor: Micro-Lending and the Battle against World Poverty*. New York: Public Affairs.

Yunus, M. (2007) *Creating a World without Poverty: Social Business and the Future of Capitalism*. New York: Public Affairs.

Zundel, A.F. (2002) 'Ordinary jurisprudence and the democratic firm: a response to David Ellerman', *Journal of Business Ethics*, 35 (1): 51–6.

Index